FICTION'S OVERCOAT

�֎

FICTION'S OVERCOAT

Russian Literary Culture and the Question of Philosophy

EDITH W. CLOWES

Cornell University Press
Ithaca and London

First published 2004 by Cornell University Press
Printed in the United States of America

Library of Congress Cataloging-in-Publication Data

Clowes, Edith W.
Fiction's overcoat : Russian literary culture and the question of
philosophy / Edith W. Clowes.
p. cm.
Includes bibliographical references and index.
ISBN 0-8014-4192-7 (alk. paper)
1. Philosophy, Russian—19th century. 2. Philosophy, Russian—20th
century. I. Title.
B4231 .C57 2004
197—dc22
2003019026

Cornell University Press strives to use environmentally responsible suppliers and materials to the fullest extent possible in the publishing of its books. Such materials include vegetable-based, low-VOC inks and acid-free papers that are recycled, totally chlorine-free, or partly composed of nonwood fibers. For further information, visit our website at www.cornellpress.cornell.edu.

Cloth printing   10 9 8 7 6 5 4 3 2 1

We all came out from Gogol's "Overcoat."
—attributed to Dostoevsky

For Lidia Andreevna Kolobaeva

Contents

Preface

OVER THE LAST TWO HUNDRED YEARS Russian philosophers have played a crucial role on the edges of their national culture as dissidents, critics, and "inner exiles" from officially permitted cultural life. As a group they have been silenced, crushed, or murdered for their courage to speak their minds freely in the context of a strongly conformist society and state. Despite fairly consistent oppression, they have helped to shape Russian writing culture through their unique experiments in language and genre. One hundred years after the brilliant flowering of Russian philosophy before the Bolshevik Revolution, this book reanimates an idiosyncratic but nonetheless rich and vital heritage of speculative philosophy. It is an especially opportune moment; for after decades of enforced Soviet silence Russians themselves are embracing their own philosophical heritage.

A few words will help to explain the title of this book, which might seem to point the reader toward fiction rather than philosophy. According to a famous but still undocumented anecdote, Fedor Dostoevsky observed that Russian writers of his generation "came out from" Nikolai Gogol's famous story, "The Overcoat" (1842). Gogol's impact on the literary issues, themes, and styles of his day, Dostoevsky suggested, was inescapable. Invoking Dostoevsky's image of overwhelming formative influence, the present book tells how modern Russia began to philosophize, a process that happened largely through the institutions and discourses of verbal art. It relates the story of the birth of philosophy from the institutional, stylistic, and generic "overcoat" of literature in modern Russia, starting with Russian writers' disputes about contemporary modes of Western philosophizing and moving toward the emergence of particularly Russian philosophical forms and idioms.

Seen here as a distinct cultural discourse, Russian philosophy developed during the nineteenth century in competition with other emerging cultural languages—particularly prose fiction but also the languages of social commentary and theology—each making its own claim to truth. As the most disputed of all these discourses, philosophy became the touchstone for an array of issues concerning national dignity and national identity. In the twentieth century, even as Russian philosophy was suppressed by the new

Soviet state, some of its leading figures—for example, Lev Shestov and Nikolai Berdiaev—emigrated and became noted existentialists in Western Europe. In addition, the reconsideration offered here of the work of these and other philosophers—Vladimir Solovyov, Vasily Rozanov, and Aleksei Losev—shows that they anticipate deconstructionist themes in unexpected and fruitful ways.

This book tells the story of the emergence of philosophy as an authentic cultural discourse in Russian modernity. It probes how and why systematic, rationalist philosophical tracts brought from Germany in the early nineteenth century, although on the surface wildly popular, were resisted on a deeper level. My discussion focuses on the advent of a less classically rigorous but more authentic form of philosophizing that aroused widespread interest among educated readers both in Russia and abroad. I explore the process by which this new philosophical register was integrated into the modern Russian language, the development of genres appropriate for philosophizing in the Russian context, the pursuit of a readership, and the legitimization of philosophy as a gateway to credible truth.

Many people and organizations have supported this project. I first thank John Burt Foster Jr., Judith Kornblatt, Donna Orwin, Bernice Rosenthal, James Scanlan, and Jay West for hours of discussion and for reading versions of the manuscript. I am grateful to Maria Carlson, Caryl Emerson, Joan Grossman, George Kline, Jonathan Mayhew, Jay Rosellini, and Heinrich Stammler for their commentary and encouragement. My colleagues in the Faculty Seminar for Philosophy and Literature at the Hall Center for the Humanities at the University of Kansas, and particularly Daniel Breslauer and James Woelfel, provided a congenial atmosphere in which to discuss my work. Thanks go to Aza Alibekovna and Elena Takho-Godi for sharing information about Aleksei Losev. Julia Sineokaya helped with archival photography.

My thanks go to a number of organizations that supported my research. Deutscher Akademischer Austauschdienst (DAAD) made possible a semester of research at the Slavistisches Seminar at the University of Bonn. Fellowships from the National Endowment for the Humanities and the Hall Center for the Humanities at the University of Kansas allowed me to finish the main project. A summer grant from the General Research Fund of the University of Kansas provided me the time to research the late-Soviet and post-Soviet period and to write the conclusion. I am grateful to N. B. Volkova and G. Iu. Drezgunova of the Russian State Archive for Literature and Art and to E. D. Mikhailova and O. Neskorodova of the Literary Museum in Moscow for allowing me and Julia Sineokaya to work and photograph in their portrait collections. Thanks also go to Bette Luther and the staff at the Center for Russian and East European Studies at the University of Kansas for their support in so many of the nuts and bolts required in finishing a manuscript.

I am grateful to Rita Bernhard, Karen Hwa, and Susan Barnett of Cornell University Press for their careful editing and production of *Fiction's Overcoat*. Finally, I thank John G. Ackerman, whose enthusiasm bore this project through its final stages.

Some material from chapters 4, 6, 7, and 10 appeared, respectively, in the following publications: Solovyov in *Slavic Review* 55, no. 3 (1996): 552–566; Rozanov in *Slavic Almanach* 8, no. 2 (2003), 1–28; Berdiaev in *American Contributions to the XIII World Congress of Slavists* (2003): 1–10; and Pasternak in *New Zealand Slavonic Journal* 36 (2002): 39–48.

I am deeply indebted to my mentor at Moscow University, Lidia Andreevna Kolobaeva. She began reading the Russian speculative philosophers in the philosophical "underground" at Moscow University during the Brezhnev years. When it was still forbidden to do so, she sought opportunities to teach their philosophies in her own seminars, and later she published research on them. She has generously shared her enthusiasm with me over the twenty-five years of our acquaintance. To her I dedicate this book.

Note on Transliteration and Translation

THE SYSTEM OF TRANSLITERATION of Russian words used in this volume is generally the Library of Congress system but with some alterations to facilitate reading the text. Proper names ending in -ii have been shortened to -y, for example, Dostoevsky, Vasily, and Chernyshevsky. Diacritical marks have been omitted. To encourage correct pronunciation Solov'ev is spelled Solovyov. Some names have been changed from their Russian spelling to traditional English spelling: for example, Herzen for Gertsen, Empress Catherine for Empress Ekaterina, Tsar Nicholas for Tsar Nikolai.

Unless otherwise specified, all translations are my own.

Abbreviations

AB: Lev Shestov, "Apofeoz bespochvennosti," *Izbrannye sochineniia* (Moscow: Renessans, 1993), 327–475.

ASKh: Nikolai Berdiaev, *Aleksei Stepanovich Khomiakov* (1912; rpt. Westmead: Gregg International, 1971).

D19: Aleksei Losev, *Mne bylo 19: Dnevniki. Pis'ma Proza,* ed. A. A. Takho-Godi (Moscow: Russkie slovari, 1997).

DM: Aleksei Losev, *Dialektika mifa*, in *Filosofiia. Mifologiia. Kul'tura* (Moscow: Izdatel'stvo politicheskoi literatury, 1991), 22–186.

DN: Lev Shestov, "Dostoevskii i Nitsshe: Filosofiia tragedii," in *Izbrannye sochineniia* (Moscow: Renessans, 1993), 159–326.

EK: Aleksei Losev, "Teoriia mificheskogo myshleniia u E. Kassirera," *Simvol* (Paris) 30 (December 1993): 311–336.

EP: Aleksei Losev, "Eros u Platona," in *Filosofiia. Mifologiia. Kul'tura* (Moscow: Izdatel'stvo politicheskoi literatury, 1991), 187–208.

FI: Aleksei Losev, *Filosofiia imeni*, in *Samoe samo* (Moscow: Eksmo, 1999), 31–204.

FTK: Nikolai Berdiaev, *Filosofiia tvorchestva, kul'tury i iskusstva*, 2 vols. (Moscow: Iskusstvo, 1994).

K: Andrei Platonov, *Kotlovan*, in *Gosudarstvennyi zhitel'* (Moscow: Sovetskii pisatel', 1988).

Kniga: *Kniga o Vladimire Solov'eve*, ed. B. Averin, D. Bazanov, and E. Pavlova (Moscow: Sovetskii pisatel', 1991).

L: Vasilii Rozanov, *Legenda o velikom inkvizitore* (Munich: W. Fink, 1970).

M: Aleksei Losev, "Muzyka kak predmet logiki," in *Samoe samo* (Moscow: Eksmo, 1999), 635–822.

MD: Nikolai Berdiaev, "Mirovozzrenie Dostoevskogo," in *Filosofiia tvorchestva, kul'tury i iskusstva*, 2 vols. (Moscow: Iskusstvo, 1994), 2:7–150.

OEK: Vasilii Rozanov, *Oboniatel'noe i osiazatel'noe otnoshenie evreev k krovi* (St. Petersburg: Novoe vremia, 1914).

P: Vladimir Solov'ev, *Pis'ma*, 4 vols., ed. E. L. Radlov (St. Peters-
          burg: Obshchestvennaia pol'za, 1908).

PNVS: Aleksei Stankevich, ed., *Perepiska Nikolaia Vladimirovicha
          Stankevicha, 1830–1840* (Moscow: A. I. Mamontov, 1914).

PSS: Aleksandr Pushkin, *Polnoe sobranie sochinenii,* 17 vols.
          (Leningrad: ANSSSR, 1937–1959).

PSS2:   Ivan Kireevskii, *Polnoe sobranie sochinenii*, 2 vols. (Moscow: Ti-
          pografiia imperatorskogo Moskovskogo universiteta, 1911).

PSS8:   Aleksei Khomiakov, *Polnoe sobranie sochinenii*, 8 vols. (Moscow:
          Kushnerev, 1911).

PSS30:   Fedor Dostoevskii, *Polnoe sobranie sochinenii*, 30 vols.
          (Leningrad: Nauka, 1972–1990.

PSSP28:   Ivan Turgenev, *Polnoe sobranie sochinenii i pisem*, 28 vols.
          (Moscow: ANSSSR, 1960–1968).

RF: Aleksei Losev, "Russkaia filosofiia," in *Filosofiia. Mifologiia. Kul'-
          tura* (Moscow: Izdatel'stvo politicheskoi literatury, 1991),
          209–236.

RFK: Vasilii Rozanov, *Religiia. Filosofiia. Kul'tura* (Moscow: Respub-
          lika, 1992).

RSCh: Nikolai Berdiaev, *O rabstve i svobode cheloveka (Opyt personalis-
          ticheskoi filosofii)* (Paris: YMCA, 1939).

S: Vasilii Rozanov, *Solitaria* (Moscow: Izdatel'stvo politicheskoi lit-
          eratury, 1990).

S1:   Nikolai Berdiaev, *Samopoznanie* (Moscow: Kniga, 1991).

S2:   Nikolai Chernyshevskii, *Sochineniia*, 2 vols. (Moscow: ANSSSR,
          1986–1987).

Shore: Alexander Herzen, *From the Other Shore* (Oxford: Oxford Uni-
          versity Press, 1979).

SI: Nikolai Berdiaev, *Sub"ektivizm i individualizm v obshchestvennoi
          filosofii i kriticheskii etiud o N. K. Mikhailovskom* (St. Petersburg:
          Elektricheskaia tipografiia, 1901).

SMPZ: Nikolai Berdiaev, *Samopoznanie* (Paris: YMCA, 1983).

SS2:   P. Chaadaev, *Polnoe sobranie sochinenii i izbrannye pis'ma, 2 vols.*
          (Moscow: Izdatel'stvo "Nauka," 1991).

SS5:   Boris Pasternak, *Sobranie sochinenii*, 5 vols. (Moscow: Khudozh-
          estvennaia literatura, 1989–1992).

SS6:   Lev Shestov, *Sobranie sochinenii,* 6 vols. (St. Petersburg:
          Shipovnik, 1911).

SS8:   Aleksandr Gertsen, *Sobranie sochinenii*, 8 vols. (Moscow: Pravda,
          1975).

SS12:   Vladimir Solov'ev, *Sobranie sochinenii*, 12 vols. (Brussels: Foyer
          Oriental Chrétien, 1966–1969).

*SS*13: Vissarion Belinskii, *Sobranie sochinenii*, 13 vols. (Moscow: Izdatel'stvo Akademii nauk SSSR, 1953–1959).

*SS*30: Aleksandr Gertsen, *Sobranie sochinenii*, 30 vols. (Moscow: ANSSSR, 1954–1965).

SSA: Nikolai Berdiaev, *Sub specie aeternitatis: opyty filosofskie, sotsial'nye i literaturnye (1900–1906)* (St. Petersburg: M. V. Pirozhkov, 1907).

SShP: Vladimir Solov'ev, *Stikhotvoreniia i shutochnye p'esy.* Leningrad: Sovetskii pisatel', 1974.

ST: Nikolai Berdiaev, "Smysl tvorchestvo," in *Filosofiia tvorchestva, kul'tury i iskusstva*, 2 vols. (Moscow: Iskusstvo, 1994), 1:39–311.

TCh: Aleksei Losev, "Trio Chaikovskogo," in *Zhizn': Povesti, rasskazy, pis'ma* (St. Petersburg: Komplekt, 1993), 150–271.

TN: Lev Shestov, "Dobro v uchenii gr. Tolstogo i Nitsshe: Filosofiia i propoved'," in *Izbrannye sochineniia* (Moscow: Renessans, 1993), 39–157.

V: Nikolai Berdiaev, *Vekhi: sbornik statei o russkoi intelligentsii* (Frankfurt: Posev, 1967 [1909]).

Zh: Aleksei Losev, *Zhizn': Povesti, rasskazy, pis'ma* (St. Petersburg: Komplekt, 1993).

ZhM: "Zhenshchina-myslitel'," *Moskva*, nos. 4–7 (1993).

FICTION'S OVERCOAT

�֎

Introduction

Why haven't we had a real philosophy and real philosophers? People ask that question in order to cast doubt on the philosophical quality of our national character. Our philosophy, one often hears, is a parasitic growth, it is a bad translation from the German. That opinion is mistaken and shows an ignorance of both Russian and European philosophy.

—Nikolai Berdiaev, "On the New Russian Idealism," 1904

Philosophy should have nothing to do with logic; philosophy is an art, striving to break through the logical chain of deductions, carrying a person out onto the boundless sea of fantasy, of the fantastic, where everything is at once possible and impossible.

—Lev Shestov, *The Apotheosis of Groundlessness,* 1905

We love everything—both the heat of cold numbers,
And the gift of divine visions,
We perceive everything—both Gallic wit
And twilit German genius.

—Aleksandr Blok, "Scythians," January 1918

TO THIS DAY Russian philosophy presents a fascinating and productive challenge to Russian culture. The question of a philosophy relevant to Russian readers was debated across the nineteenth and twentieth centuries, always offering valuable insight into the complexities of Russian writing culture as a whole. Although a passion for ideas is a vital quality of Russian letters, formal, systematic philosophy as it developed in the modern Western tradition often meets with powerful resistance. Lacking an ancient philosophical tradition of their own, Russians express ambivalence toward modern Western philosophy. Although they prize philosophy variously as a crucial component of a modern literary language, as part of the intellectual baggage of a true *intelligent* and a necessary intellectual skill of the well-educated citizen, Russians have largely been skeptical about what they view as an imported tradition that generates one abstract system after another, a practice that speaks more of intellectual hubris than of enduring truth. The most original Russian philosophies build on personal testimony and the psychological drama of human nature, which is also the hallmark of Russian narrative fiction.

This book seeks to submit the rich variety of philosophical thought in Russia to a literary-rhetorical reading, focusing on two themes, one historical and the other textual. The first concerns the historical relationship between discourse and truth, and the second deals with the ways in which the philosopher works within his text to attract resistant readers and to legitimize his philosophical practice. Our story starts in the 1820s with the new perception that Russians needed their own philosophical language as a matter of national dignity. In 1824 the great creator of Russia's modern literary language, Aleksandr Pushkin, lamented that "we [Russians] have grown accustomed to thinking in a foreign language" and that "we have absolutely no metaphysical language."[1] He called on his compatriots to stop the practice of borrowing ready-made French turns of phrase, and to deepen and enrich their own literary language by developing psychological, political, and philosophical expressions. Pushkin's historic challenge implied that some discourses, including philosophy, could convey a more profound and authoritative truth than others do and could lend status to a developing national language.

In an article from 1918—almost one hundred years after Pushkin's call for a Russian philosophical idiom—the young philosopher Aleksei Losev wrote that the point of departure for Russian philosophy was the question: "Does cognition happen only through rational thought?" (RF, 209) He observed that "whoever values in philosophy the qualities of systematicity, logical refinement, clarity of dialectic—in a word, scientific qualities—can ignore Russian philosophy without undue distress" (ibid.). My focus here is this heritage of speculative philosophy and the role it came to play in both private and public life. I seek to show how this particular kind of philosophy grew into a serious medium of cultural exchange in a culture that had largely resisted the classical Greek tradition and its secular European descendants.

Fiction's Overcoat is decidedly not a study of academic Russian philosophy, which until the late nineteenth century was largely imported, derivative, and strongly censored by state and church. Academic philosophy remained dry and descriptive, disengaged from the burning issues of Russian modernity. In the Orthodox theological seminaries the philosophy curriculum was typically limited to a few ancient Greek thinkers, particularly

---

1. A. Pushkin, *Polnoe sobranie sochinenii* (Leningrad: ANSSSR, 1937–1959), 11:21.

Plato, who were respected by the Fathers of the Eastern Church. It should be noted, too, that I deal only tangentially with the relatively well-understood tradition of radical political thought that has so long occupied center stage in the Western study of Russian philosophy.[2]

Although philosophy is an intellectual practice arising through its own particular social-cultural networks and institutions, it is viewed here primarily as a cultural language, a discourse. Like literary art, social commentary, and scientific thought, philosophy uses distinct rhetorical and poetic means to convince readers of the truth of its statements. Every cultural language carries with it an argument, either implicit or explicit, for its own truth-value. At key historical moments cultural languages have competed with one another for authority, especially when a relatively "young" discourse is claiming fuller truth than an older one. For example, the early seventeenth century, the beginning of the modern era, is famous for the dispute between religious doctrine based on revealed truth and scientific theory based on reproducible empirical observation. In their scientific writings Copernicus, Kepler, and Galileo, among many others, implicitly challenged Catholic doctrine and biblical claims to the nature of the cosmos. In Russia of the late nineteenth and early twentieth centuries, a nonscientific form of philosophical inquiry asserted its own authenticity, arguing consistently against the authority of "scientific," systematic philosophies and the cult of science as it had developed in radical intellectual discourse of the second half of the nineteenth century. In the works treated here, specifically Russian philosophical voices, vocabularies, and genres took shape through dispute with other kinds of cultural speech, particularly scientific and poetic discourse. We find here a sustained effort to redefine philosophy, to evaluate its kinds of truth and knowledge, and to accord it a place and a high level of legitimacy in Russian culture.

A central issue in this study is how to define philosophy and how to deploy that definition in our discussion of the strange but alluring phenome-

---

2. See, for example, Isaiah Berlin, *Russian Thinkers* (Harmondsworth: Penguin, 1978). The essays that comprise Berlin's work were published first in the late 1940s and 1950s. See also Edward J. Brown, *Stankevich and His Moscow Circle, 1830–1840* (Stanford: Stanford University Press, 1966); Andrzej Walicki, *A History of Russian Thought from the Enlightenment to Marxism* (Stanford: Stanford University Press, 1979); Martin Malia, *Alexander Herzen and the Birth of Russian Socialism* (Cambridge, Mass.: Harvard University Press, 1961); and Aileen Kelly, *Mikhail Bakunin: A Study in the Psychology and Politics of Utopianism* (New York: Oxford University Press, 1982). For a rare and more recent collection of essays that compare Herzen to an array of European thinkers, see Aileen Kelly, *Views from the Other Shore: Essays on Herzen, Chekhov, and Bakhtin* (New Haven: Yale University Press, 1999). Other studies that canonize the radical tradition include Adam B. Ulam, *Prophets and Conspirators in Prerevolutionary Russia* (New York: Viking, 1977); Abbott Gleason, *Young Russia: The Genesis of Russian Radicalism in the 1860s* (New York: Viking, 1980); and James H. Billington, *Fire in the Minds of Men: Origins of the Revolutionary Faith* (New York: Basic Books, 1980).

non that is Russian philosophy. The problem is that Russian philosophy, which often has been marginalized, follows a path of development different from that of the major European traditions—French and English rationalism and German idealism, and the other philosophies that later emerged from that philosophical bedrock. How, then, does one define philosophy? Is philosophy characterized by a specific hermeneutic line—that is, through its commentary on classical texts that are accepted as "philosophical" and not as literary, historical, sociological, or scientific? Or do philosophical texts identify themselves rhetorically and generically by using styles and forms of writing readily recognized as "philosophical"? Or do we define philosophy by the issues it tackles and the questions it poses?

Clearly we recognize philosophy as a distinct, creative, intellectual practice in all these ways. Existing studies of Russian philosophy have defined and evaluated their subject by criteria external to it, ignoring the inner rhetorical process by which texts identified themselves as "philosophical," clearing a space for themselves in an increasingly complex and contentious Russian writing culture. Thus, for example, nineteenth-century Russians usually understood the term *philosophy* to mean the German academic standard of systematic, logically rigorous argumentation about the nature of the world, human nature, ethics, and knowledge. At the same time they also argued that this overly abstract approach to the hard questions of self, identity, history, and existence was not necessarily "true" and, moreover, had only tangential relevance to Russian life.

Russian intellectuals read or at least informed themselves about everything new in philosophy, whether written by a European or a Russian. In the 1830s and 1840s young intellectuals adored first Schelling, then Hegel and Feuerbach; they knew and debated Chaadaev's arguments about the place of Russia in world history. At the end of that century Solovyov became known as a popular teacher and public speaker. Still, as a group, educated Russian readers tended to doubt the truths set forth in abstract texts and to prefer philosophical debate anchored to a concrete issue or theme. Only at the start of the twentieth century would a substantial circle of Russian readers develop an interest in relatively abstract argumentation. Almost from the beginning, Russian writers developed more passionate forms of philosophizing that thrust the speaking self into the foreground and claim the legitimacy of subjective knowledge and truth. Turning to the epigraphs above, Berdiaev was right in asserting the existence of a Russian mode of philosophizing distinct from European styles. Shestov and Blok put their fingers on the pulse of Russian philosophy: here is a "Gnostic" mode of thinking that draws on all kinds of cognition, logically reasoned and objectively observed, as well as intuited and revealed.

Because speculative philosophy in Russia developed in close contact with literature, *Fiction's Overcoat* takes this particular relationship both as its point of departure and its chief focus. I argue that Russian philosophy in its own original way emerged from the "overcoat" of an already well-established literary culture that offered alternatives to systematic Western philosophy. Part of this story concerns the ways in which poets, particularly Aleksandr Pushkin and Vladimir Odoevsky, and novelists, such as Ivan Turgenev, Fyodor Dostoevsky, Andrei Platonov, and Boris Pasternak, engaged with philosophy. We find that a pattern emerges: there is initial enthusiasm, a process of defining philosophy and its merits, welcoming philosophical discourse as a new and necessary aspect of Russian culture that promised to deepen the credibility and dignity of Russian literary culture as a whole. This initial enthusiasm is then often supplanted by criticism, competition, and finally a creative internalization of philosophical discourse in the framework of fictional narrative. These writers played an essential though not always friendly role in disputing modern Western philosophical models and shaping the discursive character of what eventually became a Russian style of philosophizing. Russian philosophers, in turn, responded to the philosophical models that they found in literary art and formulated their own forms of philosophy that subsequently extended the frontiers of the writing culture. This crucial, complex relationship between philosophy and literature gave rise to a fresh and absorbing speculative philosophy, some aspects of which became influential in Europe in the mid-twentieth century, while others are only now coming to light.

Much recent, post-structuralist philosophical criticism has focused on the "quarrel" between philosophy and fiction. In contrast to traditional philosophical criticism that shows the formative impact of philosophical ideas on literary texts, work by American philosophers such as Martha Craven Nussbaum and Arthur Danto has emphasized the rhetorical efforts within literary texts to resist the influence of formal philosophical thinking.[3] Deconstructionist philosophy has frequently stressed the literary aspects of formal philosophy.[4] Growing in part from these arguments with the traditional discursive hierarchy that asserts the greater truth and authority of philosophical discourse over literary art, *Fiction's Overcoat* focuses on the emergence of philosophy in a writing culture where philosophy previously had been almost nonexistent. An original Russian philosophy sprang not from a quarrel with fiction. Rather, it grew in the discursive space be-

---

3. Arthur C. Danto, *The Philosophical Disenfranchisement of Art* (New York: Columbia University Press, 1986), 1–21; Martha Craven Nussbaum, " 'Finely Aware and Richly Responsible': Literature and the Moral Imagination," in *Literature and the Question of Philosophy*, ed. A. Cascardi (Baltimore: The Johns Hopkins University Press, 1987), 167–191.

4. The canonical example is Jacques Derrida, *Margins of Philosophy*, trans. A. Bass (Chicago: University of Chicago Press, 1982).

tween imported systematic models of abstract thought, with which Russian philosophers generally did consistently quarrel, and narrative, dramatic, and lyric models of fictional philosophizing, with which they interacted in a more subtle manner.

An exploration of the ongoing argument with Western thought that motivates Russian philosophy sheds a bright light on the philosophical tastes that Russian writers and readers formed in the modern age. In contrast to the relatively bland analogies and didactic narratives that post-Cartesian systematic thinkers sometimes use to define their terms, Russians retain the rich metaphorical qualities of poetic language in all kinds of speech genres, including formal philosophical ones. If modern Western philosophers have tended to discredit associative language as overly "subjective," leaving it to religious and poetic use, Russian philosophers routinely appropriate figurative language and literary genres for their philosophical projects, seeing in them the way to profound, nonsystematic, nonrational truths.

To say that philosophy eventually became an independent social-intellectual institution within Russian writing culture would be to lend it too great an aura of solidity and stability. Typically philosophers—for example, Petr Chaadaev in the early nineteenth century and Lev Shestov and Vasily Rozanov in the early twentieth century—have stood at the edge of "proper" thinking and writing. It is more accurate to say that an enduring Russian philosophical style of seeking knowledge and truth developed over seven generations, first through private discussion and later through literary and social debate about Western paradigms of systematic philosophizing.

Indeed, the foremost issue in the Russian debate about philosophy would continue to be a dispute about the value of its truth. Throughout our discussion of philosophical texts it will become clear that the reader's perception and acceptance of "truth" has everything to do with his or her taste for a given style of writing. In other words, style, vocabulary, genre, and voice play a vital role in establishing the truth of one discourse in competition with others. This exercise took place in various forums—ranging from private letters and diaries in the early part of the nineteenth century to literary criticism, fiction, and social commentary at mid-century and, finally, to literary critical essays, collections of fragments and aphorisms, and large volumes of philosophical essays at the turn of the century. At that time, during the three decades before the revolution of 1917, Russian philosophy acquired a clearer shape and definition, and a genuine public presence of its own. Both professional philosophers, for example, Solovyov and Losev, and social-cultural critics who pointedly made themselves into philosophers, such as Rozanov, Shestov, and Berdiaev, produced works that remain fresh and interesting even today both for their ideas and for the innovative styles and philosophical identities they articulated. What we untangle, in short, is the always contested presence of philosophy as an integral, creative part of Russian writing culture.

The first three chapters of *Fiction's Overcoat* examine early- and mid-nineteenth-century efforts to justify and articulate a philosophical discourse relevant to Russian writing culture and to attract a Russian readership, traditionally hostile to abstract, systematic argument. This process is far from linear. Moving through the enthusiastic engagement with Western philosophies of the 1820s and 1830s, for example, in the friendship of the poet Pushkin with the philosopher Chaadaev or in the passionately philosophical student circle of Nikolai Stankevich, we then encounter an eventual rejection of what was perceived to be a stilted "scholasticism" isolated from the relevant issues of the day. In the ensuing two decades this kind of philosophy would be discredited and displaced as a number of other new discourses vied to establish credibility and truth-value—for example, the philosophical fiction of Ivan Turgenev, the political journalism of Aleksandr Herzen and Nikolai Chernyshevsky, and the Orthodox theology of Ivan Kireevsky and Aleksei Khomiakov. Dostoevsky's debate with Chernyshevsky, in *Notes from the Underground,* may be seen as a final step in this early stage. Here we find the emergence of an original kind of speculative discourse, without the label of "philosophy" attached to it. This "underground" discourse would be embraced and developed by later philosophers as the ground for a genuine and original Russian philosophy.

Together with reanimating the discussions and disputes from which Russian philosophy emerged, this book explores the array of textual rhetorical strategies by which philosophers persuade readers of the authority and authenticity of their writing. As we interpret philosophical texts, our focus will be on the creation of the philosophical identity within the text, the "voice" or discursive persona that authors use to legitimize their philosophizing and its claim to truth. Another central issue is the shaping of an implied reader, or reader-in-the-text, through which the philosopher anticipates real readers and builds an audience. A third strategy is to examine the use of metaphors of place and time in the text that locate philosophy as a discourse and a practice essential to understanding and, indeed, living life. One chapter is devoted to each of the five most significant "literary" philosophers of the age, starting in the 1870s with Solovyov, moving on to Shestov, Rozanov, and Berdiaev, and ending in the Soviet era with Losev. What will materialize in the intertwining of style and argument is the complex interaction of "science" and "art" in Russian philosophy.

In order to articulate certain issues they perceived as crucial, Russian philosophers needed to go beyond the relatively unadorned language of formal post-Kantian philosophy. They probed the possibilities for philosophical meaning in poetic tropes and rhetorical figures, particularly metaphor (association of an imperceptible state or experience with a perceptible image), oxymoron (juxtaposition in an adjective-noun phrase of seemingly mutually exclusive qualities), paradox (the juxtaposition of two mutually contradictory statements), and apophasis (affirmation through denial). Just as important, in their search for psychological and mystical insight philosophers mined the existential insight and the implicit values embedded in literary genre—whether lyric, epic, tragedy, or satire—both in their critical work and in their own philosophical styles. Because German philosophies, with the exception of Nietzsche, have not been analyzed in terms of the implications of the literary aspects of their writing, language and form might be seen as the relatively submissive tool of logic for Kant or Hegel and their heirs.[5] This approach lends itself well to the philosophies of Solovyov, Shestov, Rozanov, Berdiaev, and Losev, all of whom went beyond the neutral language and the genres of systematic philosophy. All experimented with style and genre, and clearly found in both an important conduit leading to a principled subjectivity. Our discussion throughout traces the actual impact of this developing philosophical discourse on the modern Russian literary language, eventually making it deeper, richer, more significant, and, in this sense, more "true."

The final chapters of the book are devoted to two novelists, Andrei Platonov and Boris Pasternak, whose chief prose works are the result of complex and very productive disputes with an array of formal kinds of philosophy. Although both novelists displace and discredit the philosophies of their day—both the idealism of the prerevolutionary years and the dialectical materialism of the Stalin years—they also rejuvenate and resuscitate philosophizing as a necessary human activity at the heart of their literary practice.

The deep goal of *Fiction's Overcoat* is to reconsider and reestablish Russia's vital speculative, philosophical culture as a relevant object of intellectual inquiry in the post-Soviet era. When the Bolsheviks came to power, they claimed as their heritage the radical tradition that emerged from

5. See, for example, Berndt Magnus, Stanley Stewart, and Jean-Pierre Mileur, *Nietzsche's Case: Philosophy as/and Literature* (New York: Routledge, 1993). A pathbreaking study of style and imagery in the work of the iconic scientists of the modern age is Stanley Edgar Hyman's *The Tangled Bank: Darwin, Marx, Frazer, and Freud as Imaginative Writers* (New York: Atheneum, 1974). For the most well-known analysis of genre for a nonliterary writing form, in this case historiography, see Hayden White, *Metahistory* (Baltimore: The Johns Hopkins University Press, 1973). It should be noted that, although Hayden White does analyze Hegel's thoughts about historiography and the relative merit of its various poetic genres, he does not actually consider Hegel's own historio-philosophical style. See White, *Metahistory*, 81–131.

Radishchev, the Decembrists, Herzen, and Chernyshevsky, which meant that that tradition was canonized and the speculative tradition occluded. In the 1960s, in English-speaking intellectual circles, Sir Isaiah Berlin established the reputation of the first Westernizing generation of radicals of the 1840s in his pathbreaking series of essays, *Russian Thinkers*. Martin Malia put Aleksandr Herzen on the English-language intellectual map, and Aileen Kelly did the same for Mikhail Bakunin. The arrival of Herzen and Bakunin was subsequently reinforced by histories of Russian social and political thought, such as Andrzej Walicki's *Slavophile Controversy* and *History of Russian Thought from the Enlightenment to Marxism*.

For a short while in the 1960s and 1970s the strong link between the Russian speculative philosophers, particularly Berdiaev and Shestov, and French existentialism brought a degree of popularity to the speculative tradition outside Russian émigré circles.[6] The broader study of Russian philosophy proper was made possible in the 1960s through the publication in English of many cornerstone texts. Beyond the translation of many longer, book-length works, three collections of Russian philosophy in the 1960s made the Russian tradition available to English-speaking students: the three-volume *Russian Philosophy*, Raeff's *Russian Intellectual History*, and Riha's three-volume *Readings in Russian Civilization*.[7] Histories of Russian philosophy were translated into English, for example, Berdiaev's *The Russian Idea* and Zenkovsky's *History of Russian Philosophy*. A 1980s latecomer to this move to establish the Russian speculative tradition in the English-speaking world is *Philosophy in Russia from Herzen to Lenin and Berdyaev* by Frederick Copleston, the author of the multivolume *History of Philosophy*, which omits any discussion of Russian philosophy. Even here, the nonradical, speculative tradition in all its variety did not stand fully on its own but was inaccurately stereotyped as "conservative" as against the radicalism of the radicals. This stereotype has endured insofar as Russian philosophy has survived at all on the radar screen of contemporary Western intellectual life.[8]

Since the fall of the Soviet Union, a silence has descended over the Rus-

6. See, for example, Albert Camus, *The Myth of Sisyphus* (1942; reprint, New York: Vintage, 1955), 24–28; here Shestov (spelled "Chestov" in the English translation), along with Kierkegaard, is heralded as one of the progenitors of "absurd" consciousness.

7. James M. Edie, James P. Scanlan, Mary-Barbara Zeldin, George Kline, eds., *Russian Philosophy*, 3 vols. (Chicago: Quadrangle, 1969); Marc Raeff, ed., *Russian Intellectual History: An Anthology* (New York: Harcourt, Brace and World, 1966); Thomas Riha, ed., *Readings in Russian Civilization*, 3 vols. (Chicago: University of Chicago Press, 1970).

8. The label "conservative" was used by Spencer E. Roberts, ed., *Essays in Russian Literature; The Conservative View: Leontiev, Rozanov, Shestov* (Athens: Ohio University Press, 1968). This misidentification persists in comparative studies, such as Randall Collins, *The Sociology of Philosophies: A Global Theory of Intellectual Change* (Cambridge, Mass.: Harvard University Press, 1998), 779.

sian philosophical heritage. The radical tradition has been generally discarded in view of its association with the failed Soviet experiment. Similarly all Russian "intellectual capital" in general shrank in the 1990s so that even the nonradical tradition the Soviets had repressed was now doubly suppressed in the English-speaking world. Although this legacy is currently being rediscovered as a genuine "usable tradition" among post-Soviet Russians, it has been widely ignored in the sphere of the American superpower.[9]

Another related problem can be found in the way that Western Russianists have traditionally studied philosophy. The study of the interaction of philosophy and literature has generally concentrated on the reception of Western philosophies in Russia, ignoring the Russian contribution to philosophy.[10] These reception histories have described the cultural background for the growth of a Russian philosophy. Such studies, together with Walicki's work, established the reception history of European philosophies, beginning with the French philosophes at the court of Empress Catherine II. Thanks to reception studies we are very familiar with the adverse conditions for philosophizing in Russia. The production and reading of philosophy were mainly practices imported from Europe. Both had been banned in medieval Orthodox Russian writing culture and were strictly controlled by a modern state that wanted modern technology but not the critical thinking and creative imagination that went with it. An all-too-familiar effort was made to limit and control both literary art and philosophy—the imported works as well as the practices, institutions, and texts produced in Russia.[11] We know the long history of literary and philosophical censorship, intrusion and confiscation by the police, arrest, imprisonment—as well as the long prohibition beginning in 1826 of philoso-

9. American research on Russian philosophy since the end of the Soviet Union has not received broad, public attention. See, for example, James P. Scanlan, ed., *Russian Thought after Communism: The Recovery of a Philosophical Heritage* (Armonk, N.Y.: M. E. Sharpe, 1994). See also Marina Kostalevsky, *Dostoevsky and Soloviev: The Art of Integral Vision* (New Haven: Yale University Press, 1997). A stimulating discussion of Dostoevsky as a philosopher has recently appeared: James P. Scanlan, *Dostoevsky the Thinker* (Ithaca, N.Y.: Cornell University Press, 2002).

10. See, for example, Vs. Setchkarev, *Schellings Einfluss in der russischen Literatur der 20er und 30er Jahre des XIX. Jahrhunderts* (1939; reprint, Nendeln, Liechtenstein: Kraus Reprint, 1968); Dm. Chizhevsky, *Gegel' v Rossii* (Paris: "Dom Knigi" i "Sovremennye Zapiski," 1939); A. M. Mlikotin, ed., *Western Philosophical Systems in Russian Literature* (Los Angeles: University of Southern California Press, 1979); B. G. Rosenthal, ed., *Nietzsche in Russia* (Princeton, N.J.: Princeton University Press, 1986); E. W. Clowes, *The Revolution of Moral Consciousness: Nietzsche and Russian Literature, 1890–1914* (DeKalb: Northern Illinois University Press, 1988); B. G. Rosenthal, ed., *Nietzsche and Soviet Culture* (Cambridge: Cambridge University Press, 1994); B. G. Rosenthal, *New Myth, New World: From Nietzsche to Stalinism* (University Park: Pennsylvania State University Press, 2002). Two welcome exceptions are Irina Masing-Delic, *Abolishing Death: A Salvation Myth of Russian Twentieth-Century Literature* (Stanford: Stanford University Press, 1992); and Kostalevsky, *Dostoevsky and Soloviev*.

11. Marianna Tax Choldin, *A Fence around the Empire* (Durham: Duke University Press, 1985).

phy as an academic discipline.[12] In Soviet Russia philosophy was stifled through the exile of major philosophers in 1922, the installation of an almost exclusively Marxist-Leninist curriculum in the universities, and the removal in 1923 of the Western philosophical canon from public libraries throughout Russia.

As an idiosyncratic "history" of Russian speculative philosophy, *Fiction's Overcoat* addresses two "weaknesses" commonly attributed to this tradition—its lack of continuity and its close ties to religion and mysticism. The first difficulty is overcome by drawing attention to the cultural networks, the weave of the nonphilosophical interactions, discussions, and debates that are so essential to the very nature of Russian philosophy and that illuminate the continuity of its themes and concerns.[13] The present study provides a long view of Russian philosophical culture, emphasizing precisely how philosophers disputed established discourses to legitimize personalist views that had hitherto enjoyed little authority in modern Western philosophy.

A broad historical concern delineated throughout is the question of discourse formation and differentiation across an entire era. A secular literary art was the first Western-inspired verbal register to produce original work in modern Russia—followed soon thereafter by historiography. At the start of the nineteenth century secular Russian writing culture formed a relatively homogeneous unit focused largely on literary art. Throughout that century and into the next, moving in a series of ebbs and flows, Russian discourse became far more diverse and disputatious. Over the several generations covered in this study philosophical debate moved in waves of intense engagement with philosophical activity—however "philosophy" came to be defined—followed by equally intense creative displacement of philosophy into nonphilosophical genres—primarily fiction, social commentary, and cultural and literary criticism. I examine the process by which a new philosophical discourse gradually emerged and asserted its own authority in the context of powerful literary and scientific competitors. The figure in the appendix gives a shorthand idea of the lines of dispute within generations and the lineage that develops across generations.

The second perceived shortcoming of Russian speculative philosophy, namely, its proximity to religion and mysticism, is, in part, a linguistic issue. Michel Foucault's concept of discourse can help us frame the issues at stake.

12. A. I. Gertsen, *Byloe i dumy* (Moscow: Khudozhestvennaia literatura, 1973), 2:10.
13. Among the best existing histories of Russian philosophy are N. A. Berdiaev, *Russkaia ideia* (Paris: YMCA, 1946); V. V. Zenkovskii, *Istoriia russkoi filosofii*, 2 vols. (Paris: YMCA, 1948); F. Coppleston, *Philosophy in Russia from Herzen to Lenin and Berdyaev* (Notre Dame: University of Notre Dame Press, 1986); and H. Dahm, *Grundzüge russischen Denkens: Persönlichkeiten und Zeugnisse der 19. u. 20. Jahrhunderte* (München: Berchmans, 1979).

In *The Order of Things* (1966) and *The Archaeology of Knowledge* (1969) Foucault views "discourse" as modernity's defining mode of language use, closely related to the growing dominance from the seventeenth century on of rational scientific thought. In *The Order of Things* Foucault focuses on the emergence of scientific discourses, particularly biology, grammar, and economics. He makes the crucial distinction between kinds of language use in which concepts of truth and knowledge are embedded, singling out two types, each of which, he claims, dominated at an important stage of European history. The first is the premodern language of "similitude" that relies on tropes possessed of the power to reveal the hidden, divinely ordained likeness and unity between seemingly disparate things. This is the language of mysticism, alchemy, astrology, and poetry. The second is the modern scientific language of "representation" in which things are described, defined, and classified by their differences—the language of economics and biology. While Foucault is aware of the strange power and vitality of poetic language, it is scientific discourse that holds the greatest interest for him, precisely because it gained such overwhelming authority in the modern era. His goal is to understand the interaction of these influential discourses within the larger cultural and historical frame of the modern epoch and to explain the ways that they change and how new theories and new focal points establish their authority.

At the start of *The Order of Things* Foucault notes that poetic language—in contrast to alchemy and astrology, for example—was perhaps the only premodern language of similitude to survive the great shift toward modernity in the seventeenth century in Europe. Whereas most modern speech is defined by a particular mode of representation, a specific, simple, and straightforward relation between signifier and signified, poetic speech remains on the "primordial" level of multiple associations leading to some single, unifying insight. It does not signify in the same way but instead "compensates for . . . the signifying function of language."[14] Poetic words themselves are alive, endowed with a magical power. Poetry is that "other" that allows the "being of language" to shine "on the frontiers of Western culture—and at its center—for it is what has been most foreign to that culture since the sixteenth century."[15] The clear division of modern discourse and the premodern language of similitude that Foucault posited for Europe does not hold in the Russian sphere—which is indeed on the "frontiers of Western culture"—where the borders between empirical, philosophical-analytic, and poetic speech are more forcefully disputed.

This situation is brought on precisely by the experience of being on the

---

14. Michel Foucault, *The Order of Things* (New York: Vintage, 1973), 44.
15. Ibid.

valuative, discursive cusp between modernity and the premodern. Shestov brilliantly grasps the difference in mentality between the postenlightenment, scientifically oriented Europeans and the newly "modernized" Russians in this fragment from his existentialist work, *The Apotheosis of Groundlessness* (1905):

> Civilization came to us in Russia suddenly, when we were still barbarians, and immediately assumed the role of animal tamer, first through allure, then, when it was assured of its power, through threats. We succumbed quickly and in a short time swallowed huge doses of the things that Europeans acquired over centuries, gradually becoming used to even the strongest poisons. Because of its [rapidity] the coming of culture to Russia ended up being less than innocent. All a Russian had to do was breathe the air of Europe for his head to start spinning. He interpreted everything in his own particular way, as a barbarian would. . . . People talked to him about railroads, agricultural machinery, schools, self-government, and in his imagination these became miracles: universal happiness, limitless freedom, paradise, wings, etc. And the more unrealizable his dreams became, the more willingly he accepted them as reality.(AB, 355)

Romantic youth and speculatively minded students in Moscow of the 1830s looked to German Idealism for a "realm of pure light" and absolute truth, and for a way to transform the moral space of Tsar Nicholas's police state.[16] Sir Isaiah Berlin writes of the quasi-religious fervor with which European science, biology in particular, was met among the young generation of radicals of the 1860s.[17] Here we find a peculiarly Russian mix of the older, mystical language of similitude and the modern language of representation, in which, in the enthusiastic minds of young Russia, technical or scientific terms seemed to acquire an almost magical power to transfigure the social and natural world. Decades later, in Platonov's dark satire of Soviet collectivization, *The Foundation Pit,* we see the language of dialectical materialism emerge as a magical language inspiring fervent faith.

Russian philosophical modernity has inhabited the edge between mystical, associative, "poetic" thinking and representative, categorizing "scientific" thinking. In the flowering of Russian philosophy around 1900, and beyond into the twentieth century, this conflict led to what we can call, together with the Italian philosopher Gianni Vattimo, a "weak" philosophical discourse. What is meant by "weak" thought is a rich, compelling skepticism about all absolute categories of truth, logic, essential being, knowledge, and identity that both religious and scientific types of discourse often have imposed on a complex world. In weak philosophy these categories be-

---

16. Berlin, *Russian Thinkers,* 141–142.
17. See ibid., 131, 230–232.

come a matter of interpretation and negotiation.[18] Using the logic of poetic tropes and asystematic genres to probe such "self-evident truths," these early-twentieth-century experiments count among the first significant expressions of principled subjectivity or "personalism" that would later become a staple of modernist and postmodernist thought.

18. Gianni Vattimo, *The End of Modernism: Nihilism and Hermeneutics in Postmodern Culture* (Baltimore: The Johns Hopkins University Press, 1988), xxii.

❋
Part One

The Displacement of Philosophy
(1820s–1860s)

Chapter One

The Possibility of a Russian Philosophy: Language and Reader in a New Philosophical Culture (1820s–1830s)

A word can sound only in a responsive environment.

—Petr Chaadaev, "Fragments," n.d.

It is too early for us yet to think about science in the proper and rigorous sense, much less about philosophy, which can take root only in strong, well-prepared soil.

—Vissarion Belinsky, 1840

THERE IS A CLEAR IRONY in the tastes of the nineteenth-century Russian intelligentsia. Although in the course of the century the educated elite became increasingly passionate about ideas and a principled life guided by ideas—perhaps more than most intellectual elites in other countries—they were generally, and for most of their history, resistant to "philosophy," that deeply Western foundation of secular, reasoned knowledge and truth. In his effort at a canonization of a Russian philosophical tradition, Nikolai Berdiaev, in *The Russian Idea* (1946), noted that the nineteenth century was a "century of thought and word." Only in the nineteenth century, in Berdiaev's view, did Russians learn how to "think": "after a long period of no thought [*bezmyslie*] the Russian people finally expressed themselves in word and thought and did so under [the] difficult, stifling conditions" of the imperial autocracy.[1] Although, as Berdiaev argued, external restrictions imposed by the autocracy suppressed philosophical expression, I contend that the strange career of philosophy in Russia had at least as much to do with the internal dynamic of Russian writing culture itself. Among the cru-

1. N. A. Berdiaev, *Russkaia ideia*, in *O Rossii i russkoi filosofskoi kul'ture* (Moscow: Nauka, 1990), 45.

cial issues that shaped Russian philosophizing were, for example, the character of a modern Russian literary language just coming into its own, the sensibility and taste of the emerging Russian readership, and, in particular, readers' responses to abstract, systematic thought.

The first real philosophical "moment" in Russian history took place in the two decades between 1823—when Prince Vladimir Odoevsky formed the Moscow philosophical society, the Liubomudry (Lovers of wisdom), and started to publish his literary-philosophical almanac, *Mnemosyne*—and 1847, when Aleksandr Herzen went into European exile. Although there had been separate philosophically inclined writers—Novikov in the 1770s and Radishchev in the following decades—no culture had taken root. In a sense Empress Catherine II had used philosophizing as part of her guise of the "enlightened monarch." She had corresponded with Voltaire, received Diderot at court, offered Rousseau one hundred thousand rubles, and gladly published the new French encyclopedia when others in Europe would not. More important, however, she had disallowed any serious development of philosophical discourse or philosophical issues in her own land.[2] Novikov's satirical journals were shut down relatively soon after their appearance; Radishchev's biting social criticism in *A Journey from St. Petersburg to Moscow*—inspired by Rousseau's thought—did briefly see the light of day, and then its author was sent into exile in Siberia. While this activity had a strong social impact, it did not spur the growth of native philosophizing. Only in the 1820s, for the first time in Russian history, did Russians perceive the need for a Russian language of philosophy, and the social and cultural spaces for philosophizing.

The 1820s and 1830s were decades of tremendous enthusiasm for European philosophy, German Idealism at first, beginning with Schelling and Kant, later Hegel, and many others still later. This period can be divided into two shorter stages: the very brief, highly optimistic pre-Decembrist period, from 1823 to 1825, and the post-Decembrist period, from 1826 on. The years from 1823 to 1825, before the revolt by Russia's young generation of army officers in December 14, 1825, and the subsequent destruction of the cream of Russia's aristocratic elite, marked a fleeting moment of fervent discussion in high circles about the need to develop a Russian philosophical sensibility and an appropriate language for it. The main actors would be Aleksandr Pushkin (1799–1837) in St. Petersburg and Prince Vladimir Odoevsky (1803–1869) in Moscow. Through his philosophical club, the Liubomudry, and in his philosophical almanac *Mnemosyne,* Odoevsky tried to spur public interest in philosophy. Stating the obvious—"We Russians are

2. Andrzej Walicki, *A History of Russian Thought from the Enlightenment to Marxism*, trans. H. Andrews-Rusiecka (Stanford: Stanford University Press, 1979), 2–5.

not yet rich in philosophical works"[3]—he called minimally for the creation of a reliable philosophy textbook in Russian: "There is no text on philosophy, much less a complete one. There is not even a journal in which even a few pages are devoted to Philosophy so that we might become acquainted with the efforts of the Geniuses, the friends of humanity, who are moving us down the road to that foundation of human knowledge, without which knowledge has no essential significance, just as a body is colorless when it is not subjected to the action of light upon it."[4] After the Decembrist revolt *Mnemosyne* would voluntarily disband.[5] The Liubomudry would continue to meet but would disperse by the early 1830s. Pushkin would spend a significant amount of time in exile. Nevertheless, the call for a Russian philosophy had been heard and would be answered during the 1830s.

The second stage, which came after 1826, was much more colorful, socially diverse, and well populated with gifted analytical minds. Despite university philosophy programs being closed in 1826 in the wake of the events of December, tightly knit groups of students gathered like conspirators at one another's quarters in the deep of night to read German philosophy and to debate philosophical questions. These networks developed primarily at Moscow University, where students were attracted to the lectures of two popular professors: M. G. Pavlov in the natural sciences and T. I. Granovsky in history. During the 1830s certain patterns of social behavior took shape that made a "survival" philosophy possible even in the darkest days of Stalinist rule in the 1930s. These included the small groups of trusted friends, the personal lectures on philosophy in private quarters, and the university lectures that were purportedly on a subject other than philosophy (for example, physics or history) but to the initiated were clearly devoted to philosophical issues.[6]

The major character to bridge both periods and both generations was Petr Chaadaev (1794–1856), an aristocrat and hero of the Napoleonic wars and the first Russian to consider himself a philosopher. His "Philosophical Letter," Russia's first openly "philosophical" essay, was published anonymously in *Teleskop* in September 1836. It shocked educated Russian society with its iconoclastic castigation of Russian history and culture, in part for the absence of a consistent intellectual tradition and the lack of "philosophers." As a result of this publication Chaadaev was placed under house arrest in Moscow and ostracized as a "madman."

During this formative decade philosophical debate became, in a way, a

3. Odoevsky, *Mnemosyne* 4 (1825): 160.

4. Ibid., 161–162.

5. Andrzej Walicki, *The Slavophile Controversy: History of a Conservative Utopia in Nineteenth-Century Russian Thought* (Oxford: Oxford University Press, 1975), 70–71.

6. For a good discussion of the student circles, see Martin Malia, *Alexander Herzen and the Birth of Russian Socialism, 1812–1855,* 64–68.

rite of passage for intelligent young men and a rearguard form of protest against the stultifying police state Tsar Nicholas I had introduced. Students' heated arguments about selfhood, morality, and history warmed and brightened the cold, dark night of an oppressive regime bent on preventing a repetition of December 14. One of the gifted young men of this decade, Nikolai Stankevich (1813–1840), pictured his friend, the future anarchist Mikhail Bakunin, basked in warmth while reading Kant: "I am imagining your comfy room, the table, made according to my design, Kant, the cloud of tobacco, your snout [*rozhitsa*] flushed with thought."[7] Ivan Turgenev's description adds to our understanding of what these circles meant to their youthful members:

> I cannot help repeating: those were hard times; young people nowadays have not had to live through anything like it. . . . You imagine it in your mind's eye: bribery is flourishing, serfdom is as firm as a rock, barracks life occupies the center of attention, there are no courts, rumors about closing the universities are rampant. . . . It is impossible to travel abroad, you cannot get a passport, a dark cloud lingers over all so-called academic life, and here everyone is whispering and the place is crawling with denunciations; young people share neither contacts nor interests in common, everyone is overcome with fear and humiliation so thick you can touch it! So, then you come to Belinsky's place, someone else shows up, then a third friend, a conversation gets under way, and life becomes more bearable.[8]

Reading philosophy, for the first time in Russian history, had now become an essential rite of passage from youth to manhood, the defining experience of one's university years, distinguishing the educated elite from everyone else. In Stankevich words, youth was an "age of insurmountable thirst for knowledge, truth in the powers of the mind, an age of doubting the old, rickety beliefs" (*PNVS*, 292).

The early 1830s, when young university students, such as Stankevich or Vissarion Belinsky (1811–1848), were rushing to read German Idealist philosophy, particularly Schelling, was a time of creative promise. It was only the beginning of philosophical culture in Russia, and more native philosophy would be promised than could be produced. In a letter from 1833 Chaadaev expressed optimism about Russians' native talent for abstract thought: "Like all nations we Russians are now moving ahead at a run, taking our own path, if you like, but we are undoubtedly rushing along. Time will pass, and, I am certain, great ideas, once they have reached us, will find

---

7. A. Stankevich, ed., *Perepiska Nikolaia Vladimirovicha Stankevicha, 1830–1840* (Moscow, 1914), 578. Hereafter cited in the text as *PNVS* with the relevant page number.

8. Ivan Turgenev, *Polnoe sobranie sochinenii i pisem*, 28 vols. (Moscow: ANSSSR, 1960–1968), 14:49. Hereafter cited in the text as *PSSP*28 with the relevant page number.

here soil more fertile than anywhere else for their realization in people's lives, because they will encounter neither firmly rooted prejudices nor old habits."[9] Chaadaev saw the modern Russian mind as a tabula rasa without a cultural heritage. Hence it would easily adapt to Western models.

Our chief question, then, is what was achieved by this passion for philosophy, this pure intellectual energy? Why was there so little philosophical production? And what did this situation mean for the later development of Russian philosophy? I shall argue against the grain that the main hindrance to developing philosophy lay less in the conditions of political and ecclesiastical control than in the dynamics of Russian writing culture of the day, in the literary taste of educated readers, and in the accepted hierarchy of discourses. Granted, strong political forces were working against a successful philosophical culture. Tsar Nicholas I curtailed Chaadaev's famous effort to start a national dialogue, sentencing him to house arrest for publishing his philosophical letter. Granted, too, many of the young men of the 1830s died at an early age and were therefore unable to develop their philosophical powers to the full. Belinsky died in 1848 at the age of thirty-seven, and Stankevich, the charming and brilliant organizer of Moscow's most productive philosophical circle, died in 1840 when only twenty-seven. Many of the best talents of this generation, Herzen, Bakunin, and Turgenev, eventually went to Europe and channeled their intellectual energies in other directions.

In order to understand the forces shaping writing culture, three main issues need to be addressed in the writing process itself. The first is the development of a literary language adequate to express abstract thought. Next is the apprehension and education of an audience willing and able to read and respond to philosophical thought. The third area of concern is the evaluation of philosophy with relation to other kinds of discourse and the perceived value of the kinds of knowledge and truth each discourse asserts. In short, we need to understand the ways in which a broader segment of the educated public beyond a few gifted intellectuals came to accept philosophy as an important and necessary part of Russian writing culture and then became participants in philosophical debate.

The first factor in developing a philosophical culture in Russia was an awareness of a need for a more intellectually articulate language. In 1824, one year before the Decembrist uprising, Pushkin spurred his friends to work toward a "metaphysical language":

---

9. P. Chaadaev, *Polnoe sobranie sochinenii i izbrannye pis'ma* (Moscow: Izdatel'stvo "Nauka," 1991), 2:79. Hereafter cited in the text as *SS*2 with the relevant volume and page numbers.

With the exception of people who work with verse, the Russian language cannot be very attractive to anyone—so far we have neither literary culture [*slovesnost'*] nor books; all our knowledge, all our concepts learned from childhood have come from foreign books, we have grown accustomed to thinking in a foreign language; although the enlightenment of the century demands significant subjects of thought as food for our minds that no longer can be satisfied with brilliant games of fantasy and harmony, learning, politics, and philosophy have not yet been articulated in Russian—we have absolutely no metaphysical language; until now our prose writing has been so little developed that even in simple correspondence we are compelled *to create* turns of phrase in order to explain the most common concepts; and our idleness would sooner express itself in another language where automatic formulas were coined long ago, and everyone already knows them.[10]

In his article, "Trends in Our Poetry" (1824), Pushkin's friend and the coeditor of *Mnemosyne*, Vilgelm Kiukhelbekher, echoed Pushkin's criticisms, mocking Russians' imitations of European expressions that made original thought impossible: "With us everything is a *dream* [*mechta*] and a *specter* [*prizrak*], everything *appears* [*mnitsia*] and *seems* [*kazhetsia*] and *is dreamed* [*chuditsia*], there is only *as if* [*budto by*], *as though* [*kak by*], something indistinct [*nechto—chto-to*]."[11] Continuing in this vein, he added: "From the rich and powerful Russian language some people are trying to distill a small, decorous, sickly sweet, artificially impoverished language adapted for the few, *un petit jargon de coterie*. They mercilessly expel all Slavic expressions and idioms and enrich it with 'architraves,' 'columns,' 'barons,' 'Trauer,' Germanisms, Gallicisms, and Barbarisms. . . . Thoughts and ideas are out of the question [under these circumstances]."[12]

Pushkin launched a campaign to urge his friends to express their ideas in Russian. In a letter of July 13, 1825, to P. A. Viazemsky he remarked that, although he did not really mind Viazemsky's use of gallicisms in his articles, he would have liked to see the formation of a metaphysical Russian language after the French model. As he put it: "At some point people are going to have to say out loud that our Russian metaphysical language is in a barbaric state. God grant that it take shape in the likeness of the French [language]" (*PSS*, 13:187).

Several years later, in the 1830s, Pushkin resisted the current German Idealist style coming from Moscow by articulating a model for a Russian philosophical discourse in the language of Voltaire. In his unpublished article, "On the Insignificance of Russian Literature" (written in 1833–1834),

---

10. A. Pushkin, *Polnoe sobranie sochinenii*, 17 vols. (Leningrad: ANSSSR, 1937–1959), 11:21. Hereafter cited in the text as *PSS* with the relevant volume and page numbers.

11. V. Kiukhelbeker, "O napravlenii nashei poezii . . . ," *Mnemosyne*, 2 (1824): 36.

12. Ibid., 38.

Pushkin praised Voltaire for inculcating into the public sphere a kind of philosophical speech that also completely remade and rejuvenated poetic language. The argument Pushkin makes shows the extent to which he saw writing culture as an enlivening confrontation between various kinds of language usage. It also clearly indicates the direction Pushkin wanted the Russian literary language to take in developing its philosophical capacities:

> Nothing could be more alien to poetry than the philosophy to which the eighteenth century gave its name. [Philosophy] was directed against the ruling religion, the eternal source of poetry for all peoples. Its favorite weapon was cold, cautious irony and crazy, popular mockery. The giant of this epoch, Voltaire, mastered verse precisely as an important branch of human intellectual activity. He wrote his epic [*Candide*] with the purpose of blackening Catholicism. For sixty years he filled the theater with tragedies in which, without concerning himself with the plausibility of the characters or the legitimacy of his means, he forced his characters, appropriately or not, to relay the principles of his own philosophy. He flooded Paris with charming nothings, in which philosophy spoke in a widely accessible and humorous language, one that differed from prose only through its rhythm and meter—and this lightness seemed to be the height of poetry (*PSS*, 11:271–272).

Voltaire, as Pushkin imagined him, revolutionized literary language and revitalized a number of genres. He engaged not only the leading lights of the French literary and philosophical world, Diderot and Rousseau, but all Europe. The point is that Pushkin in the oppressive years following the Decembrist revolt continued to speak out for philosophical discourse as a necessary part of literary life and indeed public life as a whole. He stood implicitly against segregating philosophy within the university walls (on the German model) and for integrating philosophical discourse in the language of the educated public. In this preference for public philosophizing he was following the trace left by Novikov and Radishchev decades before.

The younger generation that came of age in the 1830s generally agreed with Pushkin in calling for a more fully expressive Russian philosophical idiom to enhance a dignified and contemporary national language, putting it on a par with other European literary languages. Their model, however, would not be that of the ironic, worldly, literary French but the more rigorous but unwieldy example of German Idealism, which had been born in the academy. This style ill suited Russian literary taste and very likely contributed to philosophy being discredited and marginalized in the middle decades of the nineteenth century.

Pushkin's campaign for a richer literary language was strongly resisted in some quarters. The idea that Russians should even try to transform their native tongue into a fully dignified European language, capable of expressing abstract ideas and concepts, met with vigorous opposition. Such influential lights as Pushkin's old friend Chaadaev, with whom Pushkin carried on a long correspondence, argued that developing a Russian philosophical language would further marginalize Russia from the mainstream of European history. The main language of European culture, in Chaadaev's view, was French. Surely no one could express ideas as well in Russian. Despite his strong penchant for German Idealist philosophy Chaadaev was a Francophile and a believer in the enlightenment notion of a universal, international language of thought. On this ground he challenged the move to write philosophy, indeed to write almost anything, even personal letters, in Russian. In a letter of April 20, 1833, to A. I. Turgenev—one of Chaadaev's regular correspondents and a close friend who procured philosophical books and later delivered letters for the housebound prisoner—Chaadaev urged his friend to write in French, arguing that French was much more dignified than Russian: "I don't mean to insult you when I say that I prefer your French letters to your Russian ones. In your French letters there is more spontaneity, you are more yourself" (SS2, 2:78). And in a tone demeaning of literary Russian, he continued: "Your newsletters [tsirkuliary] in your native tongue—these, my friend, are nothing but newspaper articles; it's true, they are very good ones, but that is precisely why I do not like them" (SS2, 2:78). And in conclusion: "The French language is your obligatory suit of clothes. You have shed all parts of your national clothing on the highways of the civilized world. So write in French and please don't hem yourself in" (SS2, 2:79). Russian, Chaadaev suggested, was limiting, whereas with French one could spread one's intellectual wings.

Throughout the rest of his life Chaadaev defended what he viewed as the koine of intellectual European culture, the French language. Even two decades later, in the vastly different atmosphere of the 1850s, when the language question had been resolved and Russian writing culture was well on the way to developing its own philosophical idiom, Chaadaev recommended that Aleksandr Herzen write in French. This was particularly inappropriate since Herzen, even more forcefully than Pushkin, took the very opposite stance on the language question from Chaadaev, striving to build a Russian voice capable of theorizing and philosophizing that could be heard in the concert of other national voices of European culture. Nevertheless, Chaadaev persisted: "It would be very good if you succeeded in assimilating with one of the European nations and its language so that you might use that language to say everything that is in your heart. Best of all would be to adopt the French language. Besides, this is quite a simple matter if you read good examples, for no other language lends itself so well to the expression of contemporary issues. It will not be hard for you to part with your native idiom in which you used to express yourself in such a lively fashion" (SS2, 2:255–256).

It should be said that this letter was one of Chaadaev's parting shots. By the 1850s he had largely backed down from his universalist position, an indication of the degree to which the authority of the Russian language had heightened by that time. In 1851, the same year he wrote to Herzen, he wrote in a mollifying tone to Prince Odoevsky, whom we know as a strong proponent of philosophizing in the Russian language. Chaadaev excused himself for writing to Odoevsky in French, but he did so, he explained, "because I do not have the time to write to you in my native idiom, which is less obedient to my pen, or lends itself less well to the epistolary style—it is hard for me to say which of the two" (*SS2*, 2:231).

The question of whether to use Russian for abstract thought was resolved by the generation of the 1830s and 1840s, which included *raznochintsy* or university-educated professionals from various social estates who did not always have a complete universal education. Young men such as Vissarion Belinsky did not know European languages as Russia's aristocrats did. Although this post-Napoleonic generation read and took a passionate interest in philosophy, they had to do so in Russian, a situation that made Belinsky, for one, feel inadequate and poorly educated. All knowledge, in Belinsky's opinion, had to come through Western languages.[13] Thus it was this generation, whether or not by choice, that began the process of developing a Russian philosophical language.[14]

The first efforts to shape philosophical expression in Russian were mocked by the reading public. In his memoirs, *My Past and Thoughts*, Aleksandr Herzen noted that in 1840 philosophical discourse was having a negative impact on conversational language. Herzen described humorously the overwhelmingly bad effect he believed "scholastic" (read: German, academic) philosophical discourse was having on Russian speech and thought:

> Our young philosophers spoiled not only their talk [*frazy*] but their thinking. Their attitude toward life, toward reality, became scholastic and bookish. It was the same kind of scholastic understanding of simple things, of which Goethe had made such ingenious fun in Mephistopheles' conversation with the student [in *Faust*]. Everything that *in fact* was spontaneous, every simple feeling, was raised to an abstract category and conveyed without a drop of live blood, as a pale algebraic shadow. All this was naïve and completely sin-

---

13. Belinsky expressed his sense of inferiority of Russian to Western languages in a letter of August 16, 1937, to Mikhail Bakunin: "What should I study? Art? for that I need to know German and English. Philosophy? for that I need German. History? the same thing. Thus I need to think not about enjoying the inner life of the spirit, the idea, but to prepare myself to make this enjoyment possible" (Vissarion Belinskii, *Sobranie sochinenii*, 13 vols. [Moscow: Izdatel'stvo Akademii nauk SSSR, 1953–1959], 10:172; hereafter cited in the text as *SS13* with the relevant volume and page numbers).

14. Ibid., 38.

cere. A person strolling through Sokolniki went to give himself up to a pan-
theistic feeling of unity with the cosmos; and if along the way he happened to
meet a tipsy soldier or a woman who struck up a conversation with him, the
philosopher did not merely talk with them but defined the essence [*substantsiia*] of these people.[15]

Despite Herzen's mocking response, we find in private letters abundant examples of a smooth, non-scholastic, and perfectly literary philosophical
Russian. For example, Stankevich, in a letter from 1835, delivered an impas-
sioned, if brief, summary of Kant's concepts of pure and practical reason in
normal, modern Russian. To give a sense of the flow of Stankevich's discourse and its integration into normal speech (even in English translation),
I cite a lengthy passage:

> You write that you won't have any rest until you get to the spirit of Kant. To
> that end I will briefly tell you, as well as I can, about his system. By trying to
> read him hurriedly and chasing only after results, you'll just get off track and
> won't get anything out of it. You need to study him, and you have to get used
> to the method of the new philosophy; you need to become firmly convinced
> of his tenets that later became the basis for Schelling's system. You must be-
> come convinced of transcendental and natural philosophy. This firm
> methodological mind smashed the old idols, waved away the specters that
> were hovering around. With his dry critique he prepared the way for
> Schelling's poetry. I bow down before Kant despite the fact that my head
> sometimes hurts from reading him. Here are the main points of his system:
> Our knowledge has two sources—sensuality [*Sinnlichkeit*] and reason [(*rassu-
> dok*) *Verstand*]. Objects are given to us (or are perceived) through the first;
> through the second they are thought. But sensuality and reason have in
> themselves pure, pre-experiential [*antérieurs à l'expérience*, a priori] forms
> that they apply to given objects. The forms of sensuality are space and time;
> the forms of mind—pure concepts or categories. Both are only forms; there-
> fore they require content that nature, which submits to our senses, gives to
> them. Therefore they have meaning only in the realm of experience [*opyt-
> nost'*]. They serve as the basis for experience. They are not derived from ex-
> perience but, for all that, are without external content; they are empty.
> Therefore one cannot use these pure forms to resolve issues that transcend
> experience, for example, issues of God, moral freedom, immortality; one
> cannot use them as an *organon* (tool) for resolving these questions; pure
> forms (that is, space, time, and categories) can only be a *canon* (law, rule for
> thought). (*PNVS*, 583–584)

Stankevich translates easily between German and Russian, finding good
Russian equivalents for German concepts. Whatever other cultural hin-
drances there might be to the development of a philosophical discourse, the

---

15. A. Gertsen, *Byloe i dumy,* 3 vols. (Moscow: Khudozhestvennaia literatura, 1973), 2:13–14

linguistic capability of modern Russian to express philosophical concepts was in place from the mid-1830s on. With the exception of Chaadaev's famous philosophical letter, made public to Russian readers in Russian "translation" from the French in 1836, that discourse now existed hidden from the scrutiny of the censor and the police, primarily in the form of private letters.

This philosophical idiom eventually enriched a number of other budding discourses, which are explored in the next chapter. One early example of a new discourse was the literary critical prose of Vissarion Belinsky (which, granted, was written so hastily that no one took it as any sort of literary model).[16] In his essay, "The Idea of Art" (written in 1841, published in 1859), Belinsky provided a good example of how this philosophical idiom, brought in through translating the German Idealists, was employed in public discourse. He introduced a philosophical vocabulary and portrayed the philosopher in a positive image as the "strict servant of eternal truth and wisdom, embodying truth in his words and virtue in his actions."[17] A most important sign of the times was Belinsky's careful attention to his readers. Although he began his article with a brief excursus on the nature of an "idea," he cut himself short out of deference to readers unused to philosophy:

> All phenomena of nature are nothing more than the partial and particular realizations of the *general*. The general is the idea. What is an idea? According to a philosophical definition an idea is a concrete concept, the form of which is not something external to itself but the form of its development, of its own content. But as the philosophical presentation of our subject is foreign to us, we will try to give a sense of it to our readers with as few abstractions as possible and as many images.[18]

This gesture takes us beyond developing a conceptual Russian language to the much thornier problem of shaping a sympathetic Russian reader. Although readers gladly welcomed literary criticism, they were less prepared to consider aesthetics, which raised a crucial issue for the generation of the 1830s: For whom would philosophers be writing, and who would pay any attention? From the very start the various Moscow circles—the Liubo-

16. In his memoirs Pavel Annenkov noted a lyricism and philosophical tone of Belinsky's first piece, "Literaturnye mechtaniia-elegiia v proze," pubished in 1834 in *Molva*. This tone, he believed, derived from Schelling. P. V. Annenkov, *Literaturnye vospominaniia* (Moscow: Khudozhestvennaia literatura, 1983), 121.

17. Belinsky, *Estetika i literaturnaia kritika v 2-kh tomakh* (Moscow: Gosudarstvennaia Izdatel'stvo khudozhestvennoi literatury, 1959), 457.

18. Ibid., 470.

mudry around Prince Odoevsky, the Stankevich and Herzen circles—were keenly aware that Russia lacked a readership interested in philosophy. All tried through their personal and public channels to justify the study of systematic, abstract thought and to win readers to its cause. The first concerted effort to define philosophy and its importance for Russian readers and writing culture as a whole came in the mid-1820s with the formation of the journal *Mnemosyne* by Odoevsky and the Liubomudry. Almost every issue included some work connected to the popularization of philosophy. In the journal's final issue, before closing down in 1825, Prince Odoevsky openly addressed the problem of the reading public. Russians, he remarked, tend to be afraid of "philosophy" and thus to dismiss it: "until now a number of people consider this science not only to be useless but even harmful."[19] In an effort to bring some notion of philosophy to the reading public, in this last issue he printed a fragment of a dictionary of philosophy that he had been working on for the previous two years.

The contributors to *Mnemosyne* frequently addressed the question of the reader as a central problem in their mission to graft philosophy onto Russian writing culture. With his fragment of the projected *Dictionary of the History of Philosophy* Odoevsky criticized current literary journalists for merely catering to "public taste" without also "trying gradually to attract readers to more elevated interests."[20] "After all," Odoevsky fumed, "we are living in the nineteenth century!" a time when one presumably should be interested in issues more substantial that entertaining doggerel.[21] He went on to browbeat Russian readers as being "deaf and dumb" to what seemed to him the obvious importance of philosophy as the foundation for all human knowledge. He then justified the development of philosophy as the way to national cultural originality: "the only reason that we have up to now been mere imitators in the arts and science is our scorn for philosophy [*liubomudrie*]."[22] Odoevsky argued that "the human spirit, once it has been aroused, has never turned back and has never even halted: throughout the centuries it has not ceased to strive."[23] In good German Idealist style, he recounted that when Greece weakened, the striving, philosophical spirit was taken up in Arabia and thence moved on to Europe. Russians, he was sure, would follow the same path.

In his published philosophical letter Chaadaev insightfully hit on one of the keys to developing a Russian reader interested in ideas namely, that Russian readers generally want ideas to be directly related to material, social re-

19. *Mnemosyne*, no. 4 (1825): 163.
20. *Mnemosyne*, no. 3 (1824): 97.
21. Ibid.
22. Ibid., 162.
23. Ibid., 190.

ality, moral issues, and historical events in order to be meaningful. For the nineteenth-century reader this insight would prove crucial. In that letter Chaadaev said the following about the Russian intellectual character, embracing both general readers and those fervently devoted to philosophical thought: "all of us lack a certain constancy, a certain consistency of mind, a certain logic. We are unfamiliar with the syllogism of the West. Even the best of our heads are filled with something worse than airiness. The best ideas, outside of context and consistency, become paralyzed in our brains as fruitless wanderings" (SS2, 1:327–328). Chaadaev's criticisms of his native land and its lack of a national history worthy of the name was a bombshell that drew the attention of the Russian readership, whether or not they had even read the letter.

Herzen famously called this first published philosophy in Russian history "the last word, in a way, a borderline. It was a shot that rang out in the dark night; whether something had drowned or was announcing its death, or was a signal, a call for help, a harbinger of the morning or announcing that there would be no morning—all the same one had to wake up."[24] Chaadaev had not expected that readers would be so generally and vocally hostile to his work. In a letter to S. S. Meshcherskaia from October 15, 1836, Chaadaev noted the reading public's antagonism to the letter: there had been a great hubbub around its publication in Teleskop, and many readers called for Chaadaev's banishment from the capital (SS2, 2:108).[25] In the eyes of readers he was a traitor to his country.

This hostility toward critical philosophical thinking was an attitude that would draw close attention from many later devotees of philosophy: without a well-disposed educated reader there would be no philosophy in Russia. For example, the most influential instigator and organizer of philosophical study in the 1830s, Nikolai Stankevich, carried on a continual dialogue about philosophy in his personal correspondence with a good friend from St. Petersburg, Ianvary Neverov, who was skeptical about philosophy and its purposes. Stankevich felt that he constantly needed to justify himself. As he wrote to Neverov on November 10, 1835, "You have been making fun of my efforts in philosophy for quite a while now, but these efforts have rescued a great deal in me. [Philosophy] has held my interest more than anything else. Every area of study has seemed one-sided to me unless it had some philosophical significance. I am studying history now but only as a philosophical task" (PNVS, 337). In a more humorous vein, Stankevich wrote to Bakunin

24. Aleksandr Gertsen, *Sobranie sochinenii v 30–i tomakh* (Moscow: ANSSSR, 1954–1965), 9:139. Hereafter cited in the text as *SS30* with the relevant volume and page numbers.

25. For a range of responses to Chaadaev's letter, see P. Ia. Chaadaev, *Pro et Contra*, ed. D. K. Burlaka et al. (St. Petersburg: Izdatel'stvo Russkogo Khristianskogo gumanitarnogo instituta, 1998).

just one week later that he would like to cure Neverov's "St. Petersburg" skepticism about philosophy: "We will go, I will take some water from the Moscow River, we will cleanse him of his Petersburg disbelief in philosophy, we will christen him in our faith!" (*PNVS,* 594). This argument over philosophy was still very much alive the following year. On October 19, 1836, Stankevich sent a wry note to Neverov: "your respect for philosophy, I believe, is worse than hostility" (*PNVS,* 367). By January 25, 1837, the friendship was in serious jeopardy because of the disagreements over the value of philosophy.

An important issue in shaping a Russian philosophical readership was the question of women's attitudes toward philosophy. Although traditionally philosophy was not viewed as part of a woman's education, the need to reach and convince women and the frequency of arguments with female interlocutors about philosophy is a constant theme in the effort to develop a philosophical sensibility in Russia (*SS*30, 22:54). Women were relatively new but important readers in Russia, at least since the time of Empress Catherine II. The empress herself had helped to plant the seeds of interest in philosophizing. Now, in the 1830s, women were perceived by young men to be a formidable challenge to their efforts to legitimize systematic, abstract thought in Russian culture. It is significant that Russia's first generally acknowledged philosopher, Chaadaev, addressed his works to a woman, giving them the title *Lettres Philosophiques adressées à une dame.* He took care to keep this female persona alive and in the reader's vision throughout his letters. Even as late as the sixth (of eight) letters, Chaadaev cajoled his interlocutor, and his readers: "By the way, I remind you, madame, that I am not lecturing you and that these letters are but the continuation of our interrupted conversations during which I have derived so many enjoyable moments and which—I take pleasure in repeating this—have been a true comfort to me at a time when I most needed it" (*SS*2, 1:392).

The generation of the 1830s was keenly aware of a measure of distaste for philosophizing among women friends and relations. In a letter from 1838 to Mikhail Bakunin Belinsky remembered how the Bakunin sisters would laugh at philosophical language used in conversation and personal correspondence: "I remember how they [Bakunin's sisters] laughed at words like *subjective* and *objective,* considering them to be unpronounceable and strange even in our male conversation; I remember how they used to make fun of Natalia Andreevna who would use the word absolute in her letters; in this fun making, in this alienation from such terms, there was a deeply normal nature making itself heard" (*SS*13, 10:302).

In his memoirs, *My Past and Thoughts,* Herzen offered an example of a woman acquaintance in Novgorod who mounted the most significant challenge to his belief in philosophical truth. He remembered a certain L. D.

who had lost all three of her children and had become a life-hating mystic. To the young man her attacks on philosophy were virulent and convincing. Here Herzen pointed to one of the key challenges that Russian women posed to philosophizing—the belief that philosophy and religious faith were incompatible:

> Her attacks on my philosophy were original. She assured me in an ironic tone that all the dialectical supports and fine points were nothing more than a drumbeat, a noise that would help cowards to block out their moral dread. "No philosophy," she would say, "will help you to reach a personal God or immortality of the soul, and you all lack the courage to be atheists and to reject life beyond the grave. You are too human not to be horrified at these consequences. Inner disgust repulses them. So you think up your logical wonders in order to avert your eyes from it, in order to arrive at what religion gives us simply and naively." (*SS*30, 22:26)

Herzen remarked that eventually it was Hegel's and Feuerbach's views on religion that helped him to overcome L. D.'s objections.

Finally, women interlocutors became central to the readership of literary-philosophical dialogues and fictional narrative. Both Herzen, in his collection of philosophical dialogues, *From the Other Shore* (German edition, 1849; Russian edition, 1855), and Turgenev, in most of his early philosophical fiction, made female characters the sounding boards and the ultimate judges for the value of philosophy. In the fifth of the eight dialogues that comprise *From the Other Shore* the interlocutors are a doctor, who defends empirical, scientific discourse and condemns German philosophy, and a woman, articulate and well versed in German and French philosophy, who defends philosophical discourse and an idealistic view of humanity.

As a writer who by his own admission took his literary material from his observations of social life, Turgenev created women characters of wide-ranging scope who anticipated and revealed attitudes toward philosophy among the Russian reading public at large. In early works, such as "The Correspondence" ("Perepiska," 1856), *Rudin* (1856), and *On the Eve* (*Nakanune*, 1859), Turgenev's young women characters in varying degrees engage with the figure of the male philosopher. Since Maria Aleksandrovna, Natalia, and Elena, respectively, begin by admiring the philosophical protagonist and thus casting him in a favorable light, it would seem that Turgenev's goal was partly to create a congenial atmosphere for the gradual popularization of philosophical discourse.

Although the weak development of Russian philosophical writing in the 1830s and 1840s had very much to do with the lack of a committed lay readership, it had most to do with the responses of its most engaged readers, the young men who themselves read and wrote texts, either publicly or privately, in which they defined, evaluated, and made use of this discourse. This raises the most difficult issue of all—Russians' evaluations of philosophical truth in relation to the truth claims of other discourses. The generations of the 1820s and 1830s judged the truth-value both of philosophy itself as well as in relation to other kinds of speech, particularly religious, poetic, and natural scientific. It is in this process of developing a hierarchy that philosophy faded as a discourse in its own right, while also serving the vital purpose of informing other types of discourse that would come to occupy center stage in Russian writing culture. This "gestation" would be a critical stage in the eventual development of an original Russian philosophy toward the end of the nineteenth century.

Against all expectations, even the most devoted enthusiasts eventually grew tired of philosophy, though they did believe that philosophizing and rigorous thought played an important role in their intellectual and spiritual education. Eventually the limitations of philosophy stood out more clearly than its uses and benefits. These early practitioners of philosophy often related philosophy to other surrounding discourses that made competing claims to truth and knowledge. At first, efforts were made either to establish the preeminence of philosophical discourse over other speech or at least to locate it on the same plane with other discourses. For example, one of Chaadaev's concerns in writing the *Philosophical Letters* was to develop as broad a readership as possible and lure his readers into an engagement with philosophical topics. An important factor is that, from the outset, Chaadaev reached his reader through the juxtaposition of two discourses, scientific rationalism and religious faith. Although in the West the two have often been bitter enemies in the struggle for discursive authority, this harmonization would become a hallmark of much Russian philosophy as it developed in the late nineteenth and early twentieth centuries. In his third philosophical letter Chaadaev posited religious feeling as the basis for philosophy, thereby winning the interest of many high-minded readers. As he put it toward the start of his first letter: "Our task is . . . to unfold not the contents of philosophy but rather what is lacking in philosophy. I hope that this will not be beyond our powers. For a religious spirit this is the only means by which to understand and bend human science to one's own advantage. At the same time we need to know how this science is structured, without omitting anything and, if possible, to scrutinize everything in it from the point of view of our beliefs" (*SS2*, 1:356). Clearly religious faith became the bedrock of truth beside which philosophy and other "sciences" were merely a sidebar.

In contrast to the Decembrist generation which, in the persons of Chaadaev and Odoevsky, turned increasingly toward religious belief, the

generation of students of the 1830s, led by Stankevich, lived in complete ecstasy, worshiping philosophy as the source of life and truth. Like his contemporaries, Stankevich started with a synthetic, inclusive vision, seeing
philosophy in close alliance with poetry and religion. Relating philosophy
to poetry, Stankevich wrote in a letter to his friend Neverov: "It stands to
reason that a poet does not say to himself: we are going to develop this or
that thought, for in that case he would have developed it in a logical manner. No, he will more likely relate a fact of life, which touched his soul in a
particular light, without the consciousness that this fact develops into a
great idea" (*PNVS,* 237). Stankevich saw the difference between poetry and
philosophy as one of priorities, in psychological experience as well as in discourse. Despite the fact that a literary work expresses a concept, the poet is
least concerned with articulating that concept. The poet responds to intuitive insight, to the "wonder" that appeared in his soul. His language is that
of revelation and telling, not of logical proof. Stankevich used this conventional aesthetic as a benchmark against which to define the nature of philosophical inquiry, which is quite the opposite of poetry—concept-oriented,
consciously logical, and directed toward deliberate proof. Still, for Stankevich, poetry and philosophy were the two languages that stood closest to reality. As he wrote in 1836 to Granovsky: "Poetry and philosophy are the soul
of what exists [*sushchii*]. They are life, love: beyond them everything is
dead" (*PNVS,* 450).

Like Chaadaev and Odoevsky, Stankevich juxtaposed philosophy to religious teaching, but he still considered philosophy the more authoritative
discourse. Writing to Neverov, in 1833, he noted a small philosophical article
by a priest in *Syn otechestva* (*Son of the fatherland*) and expressed the hope
that the Russian clergy would eventually become involved "with such
things," that is, with philosophy (*PNVS,* 290). Writing again to Neverov in
1834, he expressed a belief with Schelling in the "gradual education of humanity" through philosophy and religion. By the end of the decade, in 1839,
he differentiated between the two more clearly: "Religion is a demand of
philosophy, but philosophy must finish as it began; the first [i.e., religion] is
striving, in the other [i.e., philosophy] must be mastery (I am speaking of
the final form of philosophy)" (*PNVS,* 679). Here, in contrast to Odoevsky,
Stankevich is suggesting that philosophy incorporates religious faith, rather
than Odoevsky's preference that religion incorporate philosophy.

In many other letters to his skeptical friend Neverov, Stankevich en-
thused about the power of philosophy as the keystone that unites natural
science and art. For example, on October 16, 1834, Stankevich called philosophy the "center of the world of knowledge" (*PNVS,* 292). The following
year, in a letter from November 10, 1835, he reiterated the same belief, delin-
eating true philosophy as something Kant and Schelling had newly rede-

fined, making philosophy into something more powerful than mere poetry. Thanks to them, it had become a rigorous, precise "science": "Before Kant, philosophy was only poetry or empty dialectic; from Kant on, it has become a science because it was he who laid the firm foundation for it as the study of mental faculties" (*PNVS,* 338).

At this time Stankevich still believed in the legitimacy and deep truthfulness of philosophical systems: "I have constructed for myself my concept of the truth of philosophical systems: it is conventional, everything is founded on method. Kant showed what the human mind can achieve using reason [*rassuzhdenie*] (and, as well, a critique of our spiritual faculties), the French drew on a belief in the senses and sensory impressions, and Schelling relied on pure self-consciousness and meditation [*sozertsanie*]" (*PNVS,* 317). Writing to Neverov once again on December 2, 1835, Stankevich spelled out the use of the philosophical method: Philosophy is necessary for its rhetorical and logical discipline, which make it possible to persuade other people of the value of one's convictions. "There is no other way," he wrote, "[to persuade] than by bringing [one's convictions] to a certain level of knowledge" (*PNVS,* 341).

Like Stankevich, Belinsky, at least at the start, was a passionate defender of the rigorous, systematic thinking that for him was the essence of philosophy. In his 1836 review of Drozdov's book, *An Attempt at a System of Ethics* (*Opyt sistemy nravstvennoi filosofii*), he used the term *mathematics* when, had it not been for the censor, he could just as easily have substituted the word *philosophy*: "Mathematics is primarily a positive and exact science. At the same time it is not empirical but rather derived from the laws of pure reason, which is the same thing: that $2 \times 2 = 4$ is not a truth derived from experience but brought to experience by the spirit" (*SS13,* 2:242). In a letter of 1837 to D. P. Ivanov, Belinsky made clear the generalizing role of philosophy: no knowledge is useful without its generalized, philosophical context. He wrote, "All partial [*chastnoe*] knowledge lowers and vulgarizes humanity; thought, or the idea, is objective, universal meaning is what should be the focus of humanistic study. Without thought everything is a specter, a dream" (*SS13,* 10:146).

By 1845, four years after he had rejected Hegel's philosophy as a mere justification of the political status quo and had turned to French utopian socialism, Belinsky still admired the rigor of the only philosophy he felt was worthy of the name, German Idealism. "When people speak of philosophy," he remarked, "they always have German philosophy in mind because humanity has no other philosophy. In all other countries philosophy is an attempt of an individual person to resolve known issues about our existence, but in Germany philosophy is a science that has developed historically" (SS13, 8:501–502). Even now Germany continued to be the homeland of philosophical truth.

Despite the ongoing admiration for philosophical rigor and precision, almost everyone in the generations of the 1820s and 1830s eventually backed away from philosophy as the source of ultimate truth and knowledge. Other discourses, other paths to knowledge, were embraced, because they seemed to support an increasingly vociferous national consciousness and to promise needed social change. Already in the mid-1830s Stankevich was beginning to feel that philosophical abstraction by itself was too dry: "Abstract knowledge by itself can dry out one's soul, but it must be the focal point which gathers the rays from all over the broad country of knowledge and, in turn, illuminates it [that country]. I satisfy the most vibrant needs of my soul by studying this science; but I know that it must not be the exclusive subject of my labors, so I devote just as much time to history" (PNVS, 341). He reiterated this thought to his student friend, Vasily Botkin, in a letter from early 1839, in which he criticized the dryness of philosophy: "Thinking requires peace and quiet, spiritual harmony; thought must return to its integrity, gather its strength in the enjoyment of art in the real world. My God! How dry and useless absurd, restless, abstract studies are!" (PNVS, 492).

For Stankevich, philosophy was an all-important stage in life during which he matured intellectually through his efforts to gain an overarching view of human knowledge. Nevertheless, it remained only a stage and not an end in itself. Stankevich called philosophy "a step by which I will go on to other studies, but first I must satisfy this need" (PNVS, 341). As Chaadaev also noted, philosophy itself was not enough, and many Russians would agree that it must be used to animate the study of something more concrete and compelling, whether history, physics, or art.

Another criticism from Stankevich touched on the social and political passivity of philosophers. On June 14, 1836, he had written to the popular history professor, Timofei Granovsky, that philosophy was the basis for all other mental, intellectual disciplines: "Your field is the life of humanity— look for the image of God in this humanity, but first prepare yourself through hard trials—study philosophy!" (PNVS, 447). As before, Stankevich hailed the study of philosophy as an exercise through which one would gain mental discipline. Although this exercise was good and necessary, he associated it also with inactivity. As he remarked to Granovsky in a letter from early October 1836: "All reading is useful only when you go to it with a certain goal, a question, in mind" (PNVS, 450).

Finally, though this is no criticism of philosophy per se, many of these philosophical enthusiasts mocked Russian attempts at formal philosophizing, embarrassed by the lack of discipline and the shallowness of the results. In a very real sense, philosophy still remained something foreign to the Russian mind. Chaadaev wrote to his old acquaintance, Schelling, May 20, 1842, six years after his published letter had met with such anger among real Russian readers: "You probably know that speculative philosophy has long since penetrated to us, that the majority of our young men, in their thirst for new knowledge, have hastened to assimilate this ready wisdom, the various formulae of which give a precious advantage to the impatient neophyte because they spare him the difficulties of thinking for himself" (*SS*2, 2:144).

When writing an 1840 review of *An Introduction to Philosophy* by Professor Karpov, of the Theological Academy in St. Petersburg, Belinsky noted the open hostility among academics to philosophy. Academics, in his view, "direct the blows of their vulgar skepticism against philosophy in particular, even though, by their own admission, they have not only never done it the favor of studying it; they do not even understand its most basic terms which any educated and well-bred European is assumed to understand" (*SS*13, 4:285). He went on to mock the nature of Russian "wisdom": "In our country, which has never participated at all in the development of philosophy, it is natural for philosophical books to appear in which the authors philosophize at will, as they see fit. Taking various opinions and various fragments of concepts, they paste together a colorful kaleidoscope, turn it around and are soothed by the new combinations they see" (*SS*13, 4:287). In 1845, in yet another review of what he saw as a pathetic effort at philosophy, he scoffed:

> There is nothing more amusing than Russian philosophy and Russian books on philosophy. No one treats philosophy as a science; all our philosophers think that, in order to become a philosopher, they need only to want to be one. They do not consider it necessary to study philosophy: it is easier for them to announce that all German philosophers tell lies than to read even one of them. Our philosophers do not understand that we do not even have the soil, the compelling necessity, for philosophy to develop. Our philosophers suddenly, for no reason at all, will get the urge to philosophize a bit, and, since there is no tax for running on at the mouth, the outcome of this unexpected episode of philosophizing is a small book in which everything is said, everything except one thing: why and for whom this drivel was written. (*SS*13, 8:502–503)

In short, having started with a great deal of enthusiasm and love for philosophy and hope for its future in Russia, many intellectuals eventually concluded that philosophy did not fit the Russian character. Although philosophy has never been a popular endeavor, in Russia in the 1830s there was not even a small elite, a thin layer of topsoil on which to found the practice of writing philosophy. The philosophical elite, such as it emerged in small

Moscow and Petersburg circles, was itself of two minds as to the ultimate value of their newfound faith in logic and system.

Chaadaev, the intellectual most clearly defined as a "philosopher," is a case in point. Although Chaadaev made the most concerted effort both in his private letters and formal works to establish philosophy as an authoritative discourse capable of articulating the goals of his society, even he would eventually branch off into religious interests. To start with, in his third philosophical letter, Chaadaev resisted traditional scientific philosophical discourse and, in particular, the tendency to ally philosophy with mathematics:

> Why is it, for example, that mathematical calculations are the highest exaltation of reason [*razum*]? What is a calculation? A mental action, the mechanical work of the mind in which there is no place for the reasoning will [*rassuzhdaiushaia volia*]. Where does this miracle-performing power of analysis come from in mathematics? The point is that the mind here acts in full compliance with a given rule. Why does observation yield so much in physics? Because it overcomes the natural inclination of human reason and lends it a direction diametrically opposed to the normal course of thought: it puts reason in a passive relation to nature. . . . What is the function of brilliant logic, which has given [German] philosophy such gargantuan power? It captivates reason [*razum*], it brings it under the universal yoke of obedience and makes it just as blind and subordinate as that same nature which [reason] studies. (*SS2*, 1:358)

Here Chaadaev offered the first of a great many Russian critiques of human reason. Reason, he believed, is circumscribed by certain rules; it is not reasoning alone that gives systematic philosophy its force. He implied that intuition and religious insight—not reason and logic—are the powers that give the new German philosophy its earthshaking truth-value.

In Chaadaev's discursive hierarchy religion occupied the highest rung, with philosophy just below it. In his philosophical letters Chaadaev argued in accordance with German Idealist theory that philosophy and literature both were outgrowths of religion and stood as the crowning achievements of a developing national consciousness. He remarked in his first letter: "Philosophical and literary development of consciousness and the improvement of mores under the influence of religion is the final stage of this [national] history which one could call sacred, like the history of an ancient chosen people" (*SS2*, 1:335). Chaadaev yearned to see the signs of this development in his own country.

With time, Chaadaev concerned himself less with the hope that a Russian national consciousness would develop and focused more narrowly on religion and religious philosophy. In one of his aphorisms Chaadaev affirmed his belief that mind has its power only because it is in harmony with the Creator and a universal plan:

> If only people would understand that the power of the mind derives not from the creation but from the creator; that it is in harmony with one general plan; that it is not a personal act but stands in relation to a universal act, as every divine emanation does. People would remain perfectly Orthodox and, what is more, would have the advantage over the extreme dogmatic person in the sense that they would have better apprehended the object of their faith. Thus knowledge received through revelation is higher knowledge than that acquired through ordinary reason, but it is in no way supernatural knowledge. (*SS*2, 1:448)

Associative, metaphorical religious axioms of "revelation" and "divine emanation," and a language of faith, coexist here with an effort to build a kind of logical argument for the compatibility of philosophy and reason with Russian Orthodox religion.

There was certainly more than just a philosophical-religious sensibility emerging in Chaadaev's letters. The Russian philosopher was also pursuing a political agenda designed to defend the practice of philosophy under the straightened cultural-political circumstances of the regime of Tsar Nicholas I. Even as early as 1832 this claim was supported in a note Chaadaev wrote to the chief of the tsarist secret police, Count Aleksandr Benkendorf: "I would like for religious feeling to awaken in my country, for religion to emerge from its condition of lethargy in which it is currently buried. I think that the enlightenment which we envy in other countries is nothing more than the fruit of the influence that religious ideas have had" (*SS*2, 1:518). Chaadaev went on to envision a Christian civilization for Russia and then concluded with this observation: "I see with untold sadness that religion with us is completely ineffective" (*SS*2, 1:518). Through the introduction of "ideas" and critical thinking, Chaadaev implied, Orthodox Christianity itself would awaken and become a more ennobling force of enlightenment in Russian society.

After his house arrest in 1836 Chaadaev continued, in his private correspondence, to defend "theology" as knowledge, along with philosophy (*SS*2, 2:126). As in his published letter, so in letters and in his subsequent "Apology of a Madman" ("Apologiia sumasshedshego," 1837), Chaadaev chastised his fellow Russians for their poor intellectual habits, based in part on a religion that had developed no theology of its own but had merely adopted ready-made values. In a letter to I. D. Iakushkin, from 1838, he remarked that Russians are able to think only in momentary, spontaneous spurts because they have not developed historically (*SS*2, 2:129). In "Apology of a Madman" he launched a much weightier attack, claiming that Russians tend not to worry about the difference between deep moral, religious truth and falsehood. In short, to put it bluntly, Russians are liars: "It's true that we Russians have bothered ourselves little with what is true [*istinno*] and what is false. Therefore there is no sense in being angry at society if it was insulted by my somewhat sharp reproach of its weaknesses" (*SS2*, 1:524). Chaadaev's move to ally rigorous philosophical discourse with religious thinking would, of course, eventually become the bedrock of Russian speculative thought. Aleksei Khomiakov and Ivan Kireevsky, in the 1840s and 1850s, would be the next to pick up the torch for a religious philosophy.

The man who exerted the most powerful influence on the subsequent development of Russian writing culture and the place of philosophy in it was certainly Vissarion Belinsky. It was he who first claimed the greater truth-value of literary fiction over philosophical tract. Though he was and remained a great philosophical enthusiast, Belinsky was starting—even before his famous shift away from Hegel in 1841—to move his focus from "pure" philosophy and to argue instead for a philosophical art that conveyed social "truth." It was he, much more than Pushkin or any of the generation of the 1820s, who laid the critical groundwork for a philosophical fiction and philosophical criticism in Russia. As we can see in his letters to his close friend Bakunin in the late 1830s, Belinsky's thinking veered from the abstractions of philosophy and settled on art with its subjective, intuitive, revelatory nature: "I know that I should be striving toward liberation from subjectivity, toward the absolute truth; but what can I do when for me the truth resides not in knowledge and science but in life?" (*SS13*, 10:271). He continued: "In life you are a rationalist and I am an empiricist. You can be satisfied with truth only in consciousness, in philosophical development, in logical necessity; for me it [truth] exists not just in and of itself . . . if it glistens with the rainbow sparkle of an image, then it is mine" (*SS13*, 10:272). Despite his claims to be an "empiricist," clearly he had a keen poetic bent. Belinsky saw truth mediated through the associative, metaphorical language of poetry and fiction.

In his famous epistle to Bakunin of September 10, 1838, Belinsky rebelled decisively against the abstract thinking his friend so touted: "I grasped onto mind, and now onto a kiss, a smile, I gladly shrug off philosophy, science, the journal, thought, everything. The main thing is perception, the excitements of life. . . . You somehow . . . measure thought against life and eternally subordinate life to thought. Life for you is trouble, and that is the source of your continual checks, inquiries, articulations of your every move" (*SS13*, 10:291). Thus Belinsky was already rejecting abstraction as illusion. He expressed his own credo: "A person who lives with his feelings in reality is higher than the person who lives by thought in an illusion, that is, outside reality; and the person who lives by concrete thought in reality is better than the one who lives spontaneously" (*SS*13, 10:315). A person who has a vision that guides his actions in life is better than one who gropes his way through life. Thus Peter the Great, in Belinsky's view, had a firmer hold on reality than, for example, Fichte did (*SS*13, 10:322).

In his unpublished article, "The Idea of Art," written at the time of his philosophical crisis, Belinsky tried to set new standards for a philosophical art, which he designated as "thinking in images."[26] Drawing on Hegel's hierarchy of discourses that places philosophy firmly on the pinnacle, Belinsky saw poetry and philosophy in a mutually fruitful relationship but one that was not always friendly.[27] Philosophy, not poetry, Belinsky asserted, was the primary mediator of truth. More important, however, and in contrast to Hegel, Belinsky then limited the reach of philosophy, subsuming it under what he saw as the greater power of literary art. In his view, art assumes for itself philosophical activities and themes, both transcending mere reason and consciousness and drawing on the even more powerful sphere of the intuitive and the spontaneous:

> Nature originated spontaneously and unconsciously. Historical phenomena, for example, the emergence of languages and political societies [*sic*], formed spontaneously but far from unconsciously. In the same way spontaneity in a phenomenon is its basic law, the inevitable condition in art that lends it its lofty and mystical significance. But unconsciousness not only does not form a part of the necessary equipment of art, but it is inimical and debasing for it. The word *spontaneous* embraces a much broader, deeper, and higher concept than the word *unconscious*.[28]

Here Belinsky emphasized the nondiscursive aspects of poetic language: literary art is nonrational in its meaning and is beyond the bounds of logic and reason in its psychological and spiritual grasp. He deepened this impression as he linked artistic creativity implicitly to religious experience: "Clearly everything is considered to have been created or to be creative that cannot be produced through consideration, calculation, reason [*rassudok*], and will; and everything that cannot be called an invention, but which appears in existence spontaneously out of nonexistence either through the creating force of nature or the creative force of the human spirit must, in contrast to an invention, be called a *revelation*."[29] Belinsky used the religious image of "revelation" to describe the source of knowledge available to poetic intuition. As different in temperament and ideological direction as he was

---

26. Belinsky, *Estetika i literaturnaia kritika*, 456.
27. Ibid., 457.
28. Ibid., 467.
29. Ibid.

from Chaadaev and later Khomiakov, Belinsky showed here a similar predilection for nondiscursive, nonrational language.

In a review from 1846 of a new philosophical dictionary Belinsky concluded the following, perhaps in a more pessimistic tone than the times warranted:

> One cannot escape the fact that philosophy has yet to take root with us in Rus; for the time being this plant is being delivered to us in more or less dry form by our neighbors the Germans—and it has put forth only a few, original, Slavic shoots like the *Lexicon of Philosophical Subjects*. . . . To be perfectly clear, we are not complaining about the poverty of our philosophical writing, although we do hold the opinion that the Russian mind first needs a nudge from outside for its own original development—but so far we have acknowledged neither the possibility nor the need for a nudge in the realm of philosophy. . . . We would just like to remark that, so far, there is no chance for philosophical writing or a scientific philosophical movement in Russia. For now, we would just be happy with the publication of a good-quality compendium, giving perhaps a brief history of philosophical schools. (*SS13*, 9:600)[30]

Over the previous two decades academic philosophy in Russia had been practically destroyed after Nicholas I closed existing departments of philosophy in the aftermath of the Decembrist revolt. Existing academic philosophers, perhaps not surprisingly, had failed to build the apparatus for the serious academic study of philosophy. In addition, the most passionate students of philosophy had moved away from a simple adulation of the new method of thinking to a critical application of this method in other areas of discourse. These included subjects ranging from literary criticism and religious thinking to the development of a discursive poetic language, political journalism, historiography, and theology. Although abstract, systematic philosophical discourse, as such, was being marginalized, it did exert a vital influence as a motivator for other intellectual inquiry.

What, in conclusion, was the "place" of philosophy in Russian writing culture in the 1830s? Were we to believe the later Belinsky or Chaadaev, it would seem that philosophy had no meaningful place at all. Yet it did—and indeed a unique and important one. Mikhail Bakhtin's concept of "chronotope" posits a matrix of time and space imagery, in which every literary text couches its core values and perceptions. This concept can also be applied to nonliterary texts. Every written discourse occupies at least an implicit textual and historical place and time in which it acquires meaning and in

---

30. The work reviewed was *Leksikon filosofskikh predmetov*, ed. Aleksandr Galich.

which it expresses some kind of truth to its users. Outside this constructed framework, discourse has neither use nor meaning. We have considered the hierarchy of emerging discourses in the 1820s and 1830s in which philosophy came to play a role, and in which it articulated clear claims to intellectual authority and moral truth. Another aspect of the cultural position and role of philosophy had to do with the forms of writing, the genres, in which philosophizing happened; indeed the genres in which one engaged in philosophy are crucial to understanding what philosophy became in the Russian context and what role this discourse played. In the 1820s philosophizing took place primarily in private letters and, before the Decembrist revolt of December 14, 1825, essays published in Prince Odoevsky's magazine, *Mnemosyne*. In the 1830s—the locus of philosophizing was in published and unpublished literary essays and reviews. Finally, the place of philosophy as a discourse among discourses is of paramount importance. Russian readers and writers alike preferred writing that was tangibly situated—about history or religion or society. They did not want only abstractions. More important, they preferred the language of tropes and figures to what they perceived as the overly abstract and false language of logic and syllogism.

As we glean from Belinsky's letters, Herzen's novel, *Who Is to Blame?*, as well as Turgenev's early prose, for example, "The Correspondence," thinking philosophically had become a kind of prison house of logic, tying its devotees to a language of ratiocination and idealization that hemmed in their desire to choose and to take a course of practical action. As Stankevich realized, it soon became clear that one system followed on the heels of the preceding one, and none of these systems had "firmness and stability" (*PNVS*, 292). Stankevich, like so many of his generation, felt strongly that the "age of action" had arrived (*PNVS*, 292).

Why did a Russian philosophy not emerge in the heady atmosphere of the student circles of the 1830s? Writing in 1845, the Slavophile Ivan Kireevsky described a phenomenon that helps to answer that question. He remembered when, in the early 1830s, the word *philosophy* was magical, and German philosophy especially seemed like a new world, the discovery of a new America. Everyone was conversant with philosophical language and ideas: "Philosophical concepts have been well disseminated here. Hardly a person does not speak in philosophical terminology; there is hardly a young man who cannot talk about Hegel; there is hardly a book or magazine article where one cannot pick up a trace of German influence; ten-year-old boys speak of concrete objectivity."[31] At the same time young Russians, Kireevsky noted, were looking for mystery, not for strict logic. Moreover,

---

31. Ivan Kireevsky, *Polnoe sobranie sochinenii*, 2 vols. (Moscow: Moscow University Press, 1911), 2:133. Hereafter cited in the text as *PSS*2 with the relevant volume and page numbers.

they tended either to read popular introductions to German thought or bits and pieces of the original. This last reading habit led to a shallow, non-philosophical reception of philosophical ideas and methods: "philosophical rationalists are being molded in our midst—taking on faith [*na veru*] other people's convictions. Yes, the acceptance of other people's convictions is so common that, of several hundred Hegelians known to me, I could hardly name three who in fact have thoroughly studied Hegel" (*PSS2*, 134).

Writing in the mid-twentieth century in his influential history of Russian thought, *The Russian Idea*, Berdiaev articulated what became a generally accepted notion that philosophy in Russia was merely the victim of political persecution. In this assertion he was only partly right. In the 1830s philosophy as a cultural language, as a register of intellectual self-expression, was taking shape but was not yet acceptable to readers and, surprisingly, not even to its greatest advocates. This discourse that had had such a powerful, if socially limited, liberating effect in the stifling atmosphere of Nicholas's police state soon would give way to other discourses that would propose more compelling interpretations of Russia's social and spiritual condition and would lead to more practical courses of action. Berdiaev called the nineteenth century a time of "both inner liberation and intense spiritual and social seeking."[32] In both these avenues, although it would play a key role as a catalyst, philosophy itself would not yet emerge in Russian writing culture as a separate, distinct discourse. Nevertheless, these two decades were the seedbed that bore fruit in ensuing generations. Chaadaev's letter stimulated the Slavophile-Westernizer debates of the 1840s. As a young engineering student, Fyodor Dostoevsky absorbed the Schellingian thinking that wafted in the air of the 1830s. In a still later generation, Lev Shestov would embrace Belinsky's thinking as a point of departure for his own idiosyncratic existentialist philosophy. How it aided in the evolution of new discourses—political journalism, fiction, and theology—is the subject of the next chapter.

32. Berdiaev, *Russkaia ideia*, 45.

Chapter Two

Competing Discourses:
Philosophy Marginalized

We absolutely need philosophy: the whole development of our [Russian] mind requires it. Our poetry lives and breathes by it alone: it alone can lend soul and unity to our young sciences, it will perhaps lend our very life the grace of harmony and balance. But where will it come from? Where can we look for it?

—Ivan Kireevsky, "A Survey of Russian Literature for 1829," 1830

When you are writing a story and you need your hero to speak well and consistently, then a system is a good thing. But when you are alone by yourself—can you really think seriously about a "world view"?

—Lev Shestov, *Apotheosis of Groundlessness,* 1905

ALTHOUGH MOST OF the major writers of the 1840s and 1850s started their student careers entranced by formal philosophy on the German model, all of them ultimately displaced philosophy and found other discourses and genres more suited to their political, aesthetic, moral, and theological concerns. In his book, *The Slavophile Controversy* (1975), Andrzej Walicki argues that German philosophy in the figure of Hegel reached many corners of the empire and exerted a powerful influence on all kinds of Russian writing and thought, including literature.[1] Although Hegel's influence is incontrovertible, another force was also at work: the Russian resistance to philosophical systematicity that Hegel had perfected. The three sections that follow examine three Russian discourses and genres that emerged in part through a discursive dispute with philosophy—Aleksandr

1. Andrzej Walicki, *The Slavophile Controversy: History of a Conservative Utopia in Nineteenth-Century Russian Thought* (Oxford: Oxford University Press, 1975), 287–288.

Herzen's journalistic essay, Ivan Turgenev's philosophical novella, and Aleksei Khomiakov's theological tract.

ALEKSANDR HERZEN AND POLITICAL JOURNALISM

Until the 1840s attempts at publication of original Russian philosophizing met with severe repression from the authorities. In 1790 Aleksandr Radishchev's self-published philosophical travelogue, *A Journey from St. Petersburg to Moscow,* was confiscated and Radishchev sent to Siberia. In 1832 the young student Aleksandr Herzen drafted a short essay, "On the Place of Man in Nature," that was immediately confiscated (*SS*30, 1:13–25). The issue of *Teleskop* in which Petr Chaadaev's philosophical letter appeared in 1836 was quickly appropriated and destroyed. But by the 1840s the publication of philosophical discussion had become somewhat more open. With the appearance of "Dilettantism in Science" ("Diletantizm v nauke") in 1843 Aleksandr Herzen became the first Russian writer to publish a formal philosophical essay and not be punished for it. Herzen won a broad following among students, even convincing one student to change a decision to enter a theological seminary and devote his life instead to "science," by which he meant the philosophical quest for rational, secular knowledge (*SS*30, 9:204–205). With the upheavals in France of 1848 Herzen, who was by then in European exile, became increasingly dissatisfied with philosophy, its truth claims, and its inability to stimulate needed social and political change. By the early 1850s he had turned his energies toward writing essays in political journalism, a genre that would gain increasing popularity among Russian readers. His experience with philosophical discourse would play a central role in defining these generic formations.

Herzen, as an adolescent, had fallen passionately in love with German letters, both poetry and philosophy.[2] He and his closest friend, Nikolai Ogarev, spent long afternoons wandering Moscow's Swallow Hills, talking about friendship, Russia, and humanity, quoting Schiller at length. As a student in Moscow University's faculty of natural science, inspired by his first mentor, Professor M. G. Pavlov, Herzen steeped himself in Schelling. After his first exile in Viatka and Vladimir (1835–1840), he delved into Hegel, now prompted by Stankevich and his circle.[3] In "Dilettantism in Science" Herzen placed Hegel on a par with Napoleon—the general and the philosopher were the two best-known figures in contemporary Europe. He wrote:

2. Martin Malia, *Alexander Herzen and the Birth of Russian Socialism, 1812–1855* (Cambridge, Mass.: Harvard Universtiy Press, 1961), 39–68.

3. Ibid., 202. Herzen and others were arrested for little more than writing freedom-loving letters to Ogarev and being acquainted with students who sang, drunkenly, the Marseillaise while wandering the Moscow streets.

"In this epoch of fitful struggle, of bloody dispute, of barbaric dissolution, an inspired thinker proclaimed that philosophy was based on the reconciliation of opposites. He did not distance himself from people who were at odds with one another. In their struggle he found the process of life and development. In struggle he saw the highest identity that would obviate struggle itself."[4] At the same time that he praised this German professor of philosophy, Herzen rejected academic philosophy per se as a dead, scholastic discipline. He argued instead in support of the nonspecialist philosopher, whom he called a "dilettante," as the ideal sort of thinker who could bridge the gaps between the scholasticism of academic philosophy and the narrow empiricism of science. It was Goethe, a poet and not a philosopher, who impressed Herzen as being this all-embracing nonspecialist.

From the start Herzen sought in philosophy a liberating discourse that would spur active change and development particularly in the life of society. His focus would be less on extending the boundaries of philosophical knowledge than on bringing habits of philosophical reasoning to a wide circle of people and thus inspiring the change he dreamed of. By the late 1840s Herzen shifted from writing popularizing philosophical essays to writing political-philosophical dialogue, for example, *From the Other Shore,* and then to rejecting philosophizing altogether in favor of political polemic. Philosophy, which early on had helped him to articulate his criticisms of dogmatic thinking in general, stimulated this move to political journalism, only then to become its victim. Before considering the reasons for his eventual "rejection" of philosophy, we first examine the allure that philosophy held for the young Herzen.

As with the Decembrist generation whom he fervently admired, Herzen wanted to extend the conceptual reach of the Russian language. And also like that generation he devoted his early philosophical essays to bringing the habit of rigorous philosophical reasoning to Russian readers notoriously resistant to abstractions and speculative systems. Although he poked fun in his memoirs at the stilted, bookish speech of philosophically minded students, Herzen wanted, like Aleksandr Pushkin before him, to integrate philosophizing into educated Russian speech. To that end he moved away from the abstractions of German philosophizing and worked instead toward a concept of philosophy as a "science" powerful enough to theorize and generalize the factual findings of empirical science. In "Dilettantism in Science" he defined philosophy as a "science" (*nauka*) on a par with empirical science (*SS*8, 2:6). In his sequel to "Dilettantism," "Letters on the Study of Nature" ("Pis'ma ob izuchenii prirody," 1844–1846), he solidified the interdepend-

---

4. Aleksandr Gertsen, *Sobranie sochinenii*, 8 vols. (Moscow: Pravda, 1975), 2:36. Hereafter cited in the text as *SS*8 with the relevant volume and page numbers.

ence of the two by asserting that "philosophy without natural science is just as impossible as natural science without philosophy" (SS8, 2:89).

The next step in Herzen's process of redefining philosophy was to link philosophical practice with the notion of being a citizen in a civilized society. Herzen started "Dilettantism" by removing philosophy from the realm of poetic "dreaming"; least of all, in his view, was philosophy a romantic yearning for some eternal other world (SS8, 2:7). Rather, philosophy is valuable primarily for its disciplined reasoning as well as the liberating force of its arguments. Philosophy possesses a totalizing quality, an "extreme all-encompassing character" (SS8, 2:11) that allows it to give as complete an account as possible of whatever subject it addresses. Philosophical reasoning is rigorous and objective, avoiding pathos and individual preference. It has the positive power to bring into a single framework many different points of view to arrive at a consensus.

Of central importance is that Herzen related philosophical discourse to the legal structures of civil society. Even as early as "Dilettantism in Science" one of his chief goals in engaging with and popularizing philosophy was to find a way to bring civil order to the authoritarian Russian autocracy. "The whole project of philosophy and civil culture," he wrote, "is to unfold one mind in all heads. The whole building of humanity stands on this unification of minds" (SS8, 2:12).

To make philosophical reasoning appealing to his readers Herzen pictured it as the hero in a narrative of personal liberation. Philosophical argument, he claimed, is essential for breaking down dogma and all forms of petrified thinking: "in it, as in a furnace, everything hard and petrified that falls into its whirlpool . . . is melted down" (SS8, 2:11). In addition, philosophy answers a deep need for spiritual liberation and satisfies a thirst for meaning (SS8, 2:7). Significantly Herzen believed that philosophy is frighteningly free and requires of its practitioners real intellectual maturity: "Science is the realm of maturity and freedom. Weak people, sensing this freedom, tremble. They are afraid to take a step without guidance. . . . In science there is no one to evaluate their deed, to praise or reward them. Science seems to them like a terrible vacuum, their heads start to spin, and they go away" (SS8, 2:14). It was the promise German philosophers held out for civil society and their sense of spiritual freedom that so attracted Herzen and would utterly disappoint him later when he became disillusioned about the social power of philosophy. But for now, in "Dilettantism," he admired the free spirit of this discourse: "Science has its autonomy. . . . It is free and depends on no authority. It liberates and does not subject anyone to authority" (SS8, 2:19).

Herzen criticized existing German philosophy for not extending beyond the academy and reaching out to change public taste (SS8, 2:39, 50–52)—

and here his philosophical sensibility, like Pushkin's, leaned toward the French enlightenment tradition. By linking philosophy to empirical observation and civil sociality Herzen resolutely divorced philosophy from the academy where, in his view, it had been languishing far too long. Philosophy, he insisted, must be broad in scope. It must, first and foremost, educate the public to behave as citizens. Although it may first develop in the university, it must find wider circles of readers in order to stay vital. "Abstract thought," he wrote, "comes alive in the guild and the group of people who have assembled around it. . . . But once it matures in the guild, the guild becomes harmful to it. It needs to breathe air and see the light of day" (*SS8*, 2:39–40). He remarked further: "The nature of thought is radiant and it belongs to everyone. It yearns for generalization, it penetrates into all nooks and crannies, and it flows out through one's fingers. The true realization of thought is not in a caste but in all humanity" (*SS8*, 2:40). Here again we find that, for Herzen, the very strength of philosophy as a language and a discipline is to change social identity, to alter the way people in society think, talk, and act. It is important to note Herzen's style here. Pursuing his notion of philosophical discourse as a means to social and spiritual liberation, he pictured a philosophical concept as if it were a young man yearning to be free. The concept is currently "bored and feels constrained in lecture halls and seminar rooms. It is anxious for freedom. It wants a real voice in real areas of life" (*SS8*, 2:40). Thus philosophy becomes a metaphor for the desire to break free of the heavy social constraints of Emperor Nicholas's police state.

How to reach the reading public was Herzen's most difficult task. He appreciated that abstract formulations are too difficult for most people to understand and that the philosopher was generally perceived as aloof. Here Herzen, like his predecessor, Pushkin, expressed a preference for the French model of philosophizing over the German form that was pervasive in Russia. The French philosophes traditionally made their ideas more accessible to the educated public: they were specialists without being a priestly "caste," esoteric and isolated. For the French, "science is an open table for all and everyone" (*SS8*, 2:47). They are, in a sense, more democratic, supporting the attitude that "the spirit of striving for truth excludes no one" (*SS8*, 2:47). —

In pursuit of his ultimate goal of bringing philosophy to the educated public, Herzen, in "Dilettantism," heralded the notion of a mediator between philosopher and public, a kind of spokesperson for philosophy. He envisioned a popularizer, a "dilettante," who would make this liberating discourse available to the reading public. The dilettante would be the kind of person who could grasp the theories of the specialists and put their ideas into concrete language for the educated layperson. Dilettantes are the "people of title pages and forewords" (*SS8*, 2:41). Although they are not original thinkers and cannot even plumb the depths of a philosophical idea, they can accomplish something philosophers and scientists cannot: they can transmit both their feelings of enthusiasm for an idea and a version of the idea that will make it meaningful to the reader and can be put into practice. This key point for Herzen would eventually become the basis for condemnation: scientists and philosophers generate ideas, but they do not realize their knowledge in action. Without action in the social realm an idea, for Herzen, was only half-alive. Citing Goethe, his model for the dilettante, he remarked, "a person is not just a thinking being but an acting one as well" (*SS8*, 2:66).

Through his idea of the "dilettante" Herzen created a modern myth of spiritual, and implicitly social, liberation. Staying with mere universals and abstractions is "death" (*SS8*, 2:79). Yet a person in the modern world cannot survive without "science," that is, without philosophy. "A person of lively spirit who has come into the contemporary world," Herzen wrote, "cannot be satisfied without science. Having suffered deeply through the emptiness of his own subjective convictions, having knocked on all the doors to quench the burning thirst of his spirit now stirred, and finding no true answer . . . tormented with skepticism, he throws himself into science" (*SS8*, 2:18).

Again, in "Letters on the Study of Nature," Herzen reaffirmed the poet, not the philosopher, to be the ideal "dilettante" who could make ideas concrete and palpable for the educated public. His model once again was Goethe, and particularly Goethe's hero, Faust (*SS8*, 2:111). In Faust's enlightenment worldview, natural science and philosophy cooperate with each other. Faust arrives at "truth" through a combination of reasoned thought and precise empirical study (*SS8*, 2:106). Each, by itself, is too one-sided. Philosophers, Herzen argued, need to "leave off their crude claims to unconditional power and eternal purity" (*SS8*, 2:95). In contrast, positive science tends to "get lost in an abyss of facts" (*SS8*, 2:96). Each is a branch of one whole tree of knowledge and, as such, they need to cooperate. It is the poet who can make this cooperation a reality.

It is crucial to an understanding of Herzen's concept of language and knowledge to emphasize that he viewed meaning as something that "develops" through rational and empirical tools of thought. The meaning of nature, he argued in "Letters," is not inherent in nature itself. People observing and asking questions construct interpretations and meaning (*SS8*, 2:101). Herzen compared reason to a prism that bends and focuses the light flow of empirical evidence. He noted: "When it is operating normally, reason develops self-knowledge. Enriching itself with information, it discovers in itself that ideal focal point to which everything else is related, that endless form . . . that uses its power to bend toward itself the linear, endless route of empirical development that has no goal . . . there and only there does the real truth emerge" (*SS8*, 2:106). Through the cooperation of natural science and philosophy a fuller meaning, a more complete truth, becomes accessible. This concept of reason differed entirely from, for example, the theory underlying Aleksei Khomiakov's concept of an Orthodox theology. In Khomiakov's thinking higher truth was revealed rather than deduced.

Herzen's early project of harnessing the cognitive forces of empirical sciences and philosophy for social betterment foundered when he left Russia in 1847 and entered into the current social debates and political rebellion in Western Europe. The change came as he worked on his series of dialogues in *From the Other Shore* (written in 1847–1848; first published in 1849 in German) to develop a Russian voice in the European intellectual theater. He now concluded that an irreparable rift existed between philosophy and natural science, on the one hand, and between philosophy and social practice, on the other. He had believed that the ethical and metaphysical promise of German Idealism could be realized in social change, but now he rejected that idea as a mere dream. In 1845–46, in *The German Ideology* (published first in 1932), Marx wrote his famous dictum that "philosophers have only interpreted life in different ways, the task, however, is to change it."[5] At nearly the same time Herzen realized that philosophy had changed nothing:

> We rebel against the natural conditions of life, and submit to every kind of arbitrary nonsense. All our civilization is like that, it has developed in the midst of internecine moral strife; breaking out from the schools and monasteries, it did not emerge into life, but sauntered through it, like Faust, merely to take a look at it, to reflect upon it, and then to withdraw from the rude mob into salons, academies, and books. It has made the whole journey under two banners: "Romanticism for the heart" was inscribed on one, [and] "Idealism for the mind" on the other.[6]

Now Faust, the philosopher and scientist, was no more than a feckless intellectual, no longer the popularizing "dilettante" capable of changing people's minds and liberating behavior.

From the Other Shore, which strongly focused on the questions of discourse and discursive authority, was the pivotal work in Herzen's discursive development. It is a collection of six dialogues with an epilogue to which one more dialogue was subsequently added. Here Herzen argued against

5. Karl Marx, *Die Frühschriften: Von 1837 bis zum Manifest der kommunistischen Partei 1848* (Stuttgart: A. Kröner, 1971), 341.

6. Alexander Herzen, *From the Other Shore* (Oxford: Oxford University Press, 1979), 24. Hereafter cited in the text as *Shore* with the relevant page number.

universal, historically dictated solutions and for individual liberty and personal responsibility. The genre of the work combines the thematic focus on political movements and parties of a political essay and the dramatic tension of a philosophical dialogue, now used to criticize philosophy and separate it from "science," by which Herzen now meant the social and natural sciences. In *From the Other Shore* Herzen submerged philosophical discourse, appropriating it to serve more concrete journalistic ends. Philosophy as a guiding theoretical discourse was discredited.

Herzen's first criticism of philosophy was its isolation from social practice. He argued that social behavior should be the outcome of moral thought. This problem, in Herzen's view, is very much a language problem: philosophical discourse is wrong for social action, because it is simply too difficult for most people to understand. Although philosophers tended in the past to view themselves as the teachers of society, Herzen argued, "their voices did not carry, and besides their language was not one familiar to the masses" (*Shore*, 26). Herzen accused philosophers, and particularly Hegel, of verbal tricks meant to confuse ordinary people: "What finessing, what rhetoric, what circumlocution, what sugaring of the pill the best minds like Bacon or Hegel resorted to in order to avoid plain speaking, for fear of stupid indignation or vulgar catcalls" (*Shore*, 115–116). In other words, philosophical discourse is not only unsuited to mass communication, but philosophers intentionally worsen the situation by using obscure language to make their thoughts even less accessible. In addition, philosophers tend to assume that proof alone is sufficient to convince anyone of the truth of their argument: "People think that it is enough to prove a truth as one would a mathematical theorem for it to be accepted" (*Shore*, 112–113).

Philosophical idealism becomes the object of Herzen's next criticisms. Idealists, he claimed, tend to prefer theory to material fact, even to the extent of ignoring facts (*Shore*, 74, 108). In a move that certainly shows a preference for journalism over philosophy, Herzen asserted that facts are primary and much more difficult and important than theory: "Life is infinitely more stubborn than theory, it goes its way independently of [theory] and silently conquers it" (*Shore*, 136–137). Somewhat later Herzen rejected the language of philosophical dualism, viewing it merely as a disguise for Christian myth with its two separate spheres—one of this world and one of the other world (*Shore*, 136). Philosophical idealism is nothing more than "Christianity raised to the power of logic, Christianity freed from tradition, from mysticism. Its chief method consists in dividing into spurious antitheses that which is indivisible—for instance, body and soul—in pitting these abstractions one against the other, and then effecting an artificial reconciliation . . . it is the Gospel myth of God and man reconciled by Christ, translated into philosophical language" (*Shore*, 136).

Increasingly Herzen seemed to prefer the more concrete and simpler language of natural science, finding it closer to "reality," and thus "truer." Natural science is excellent material "for exercising and sharpening the brain" (*Shore*, 83): "The naturalist is used to watching and waiting and not introducing anything of his own until the time comes to do so. He will not miss a single symptom, a single change; he seeks the truth disinterestedly without coloring it with either his love or his hate" (*Shore*, 83). In later dialogues it is the figure of the physician who becomes, for Herzen, the voice of the person closest to reality: "A doctor lives in nature, in the world of facts and phenomena—he doesn't teach, he learns: he seeks not revenge, but the alleviation of pain" (*Shore*, 102–103). This sort of person is no judge but a careful observer. With this move the truth-value of philosophy in the hierarchy of discourses has plummeted. Herzen called the moralizing and scolding of philosophers merely the "primitive stages of understanding" (*Shore*, 104).

In his disillusionment with the failed revolution of 1848, Herzen abandoned what in his earlier writings was the philosophical side of the alliance between philosophy and natural science. Philosophy had offered the tools for overview and clear evaluation of the facts gathered by empirical methods. Now conscious, thinking people, Herzen argued, could no longer both observe and judge dispassionately. They had to choose: either they could know "reality" by observing but not judging, or they could evaluate and judge, a necessarily emotional, subjective activity that inevitably would skew the facts. In his political journalism Herzen would come down on the side of emotional engagement and editorial judgment.

A question still remained: How could one solve the language problem, the matter of expressing difficult and complex truths and moral valuations in a way that would be accessible to ordinary people? Herzen realized that the newspaper was the most prominent medium of his time. If *From the Other Shore* was his agonized departure from idealist philosophy, it was also his declaration of his freedom from ideological constraint. It would be political journalism, and not theory, that would occupy his energies for the last two decades of his life. In his social commentaries was a discursive currency that any literate person could read. In the early 1850s he wrote his open letter to the historian Jules Michelet, "The Russian People and Socialism" (1851, in French). Soon afterward, in 1853, the Free Russian Press opened its doors in London, and then began his editorship of the very influential, first free serial publications in Russian history, the almanac *Poliarnaia zvezda* (*Polar Star*, 1855–1869) and the newspaper *Kolokol* (*The Bell*, 1857–1867).

In the final dialogues of *From the Other Shore* Herzen arrived at the notion of a disillusioned but self-reliant personality that makes no assumptions about the needs and wants of the masses and who does not dream about an ideal future but lives firmly in the present. He wrote, "If only people wanted to save themselves instead of saving the world, to liberate themselves instead of liberating humanity, how much they would do for the salvation of the world and the liberation of humanity" (*Shore,* 128). He clearly rejected the "objective" generalities of the philosopher or social theorist and was moving toward the stance he had taken as a political journalist, to reach out to each reader, to touch each living, thinking person. Similarly he rejected the dispassionate cynicism of his contemporaries, describing them in this way: "Such absence of feeling, such narrowness of outlook, such lack of passion and indignation, such feebleness of thought" (*Shore,* 145). Political essay writing would allow Herzen all his vintage passion and drama, only now in the context of bringing to the public each act of injustice and corruption as it occurred.

Herzen's decision to devote himself to political journalism came through a clear confrontation with philosophical idealism. Already in 1845 he wrote to his best friend, Nikolai Ogarev, that he really could not stand abstractions: "I am completely lacking in originality of thought, and even in initiative—but I can think quickly and to good effect. I am always stimulated by external events. I hate abstractions and cannot breathe for long around them. . . . I am endlessly drawn to life—physiology and history, the only concrete property of science" (*SS*30, 22:219). As fascinated as he was with all kinds of abstract thinking—philosophy, physics, and mathematics—he knew they were neither his strength nor ultimate goal. His passion from the start was intellectual engagement with current events, with history in the making, which eventually led to political journalism.

In his memoirs, *My Past and Thoughts,* Herzen argued that Russians in general were ill suited to philosophical thought: "An exclusively speculative direction [of thought] is completely opposed to the Russian character" (*SS*30, 9:18). Although he believed that a philosophical education was central to a civil society composed of independently thinking people, he also believed that philosophy itself was useless because it tended to foster passive reading and musing rather than concrete social action. Action was what Russia needed. In this opinion Herzen articulated a view that would often be reiterated, eventually becoming part of a radically "Russian" attitude toward philosophizing: the object of philosophy and theory must be concrete experience; tangible experience must take the upper hand over theory; and, finally, thought must stimulate practice, whether social, political, or personal.

In the end Herzen provided a key to the development of the Russian literary language. As if answering Pushkin's call of 1824, Herzen extended the grasp of literary language, offering an elegant and clear, yet still colorful model for speaking about ideas and theories. In his letter to Michelet, at a

time he was working to create a "Russian" voice to fill the void in the East
that European observers had sensed, he defended the Russian language almost as an artifact in itself: "During the eighteenth century the most important theme in the new Russian literature was the development of that rich,
sonorous, and magnificent language that we use today: a language which is
at once supple and powerful, capable of expressing the most abstract notions
of German metaphysics, and also the light, witty, sparkling phrases of
French conversation" (*Shore,* 197). Still, this was a Russian language proud
of the breadth of its imitative capabilities. Herzen, with his political essay
writing—and Turgenev, Ivan Kireevsky, and Khomiakov after him—would
find Russian forms and words for a particularly Russian approach to the
world. They would not write philosophical tracts, but they would, in response to Western philosophies, develop their own ways of theorizing.

TURGENEV'S ANTI-PHILOSOPHICAL FICTION

Traditionally critics have seen philosophy and fiction coexisting in a
fruitful equilibrium in Russian writing culture. That fiction came to house
philosophical discourse has been easily explained by the weakness of philosophy per se. Critics point to the external, institutional prohibitions against
philosophy. And, as the previous chapter has shown, Russian readers tended
to resist philosophical argument in an abstract form. Despite this homoge-
nizing view we can find many examples of an "argument" between philosophy and fiction. Clearly fiction emerged as the more powerful of the two,
appropriating for its own goals the rhetorical language and rational argument that traditionally marks philosophy in Western writing culture. The
process by which Russian fiction gained the greater authority over Russian
philosophy in the mid-nineteenth century is a discursive, rhetorical one at
least as much as it is a political one.

Some evidence from the late 1820s and early 1830s indicates that
Chaadaev, Russia's earliest formal philosophical voice, made at least two
weak attempts to criticize the state of Russian literary art and to exert an influence as a philosopher on the further course of poetic development. In the
late 1820s one of Chaadaev's implicit aims was to imbue poetry, and particularly the verse of his friend, Pushkin, with greater philosophical depth. In
the early 1830s Chaadaev and Pushkin carried on something of an "argument."[7] Chaadaev had just finished his philosophical letters, and Pushkin

---

7. There is substantial critical literature on this relationship. The fullest discussion I have
found is David Budgen, "Pushkin and Chaadaev: The History of a Friendship," *Ideology in Russian Literature,* ed. R. Freeborn and J. Grayson (New York: St. Martin's, 1990), 7–46. For a full
bibliography of this literature, see *Petr Chaadaev: Pro et Contra,* ed. A. Ermichev and A.
Zlatopol'skaia (St. Petersburg: Izdatel'stvo Russkogo Khristianskogo gumanitarnogo instituta,
1998), 755–756.

was among the first to read them during the summer of 1830 (*SS2*, 2:305–306). In Chaadaev's view, poetry in its conventional form was outmoded. It languished, he argued, "under a pile of old thoughts, habits, conventions, niceties with which, whatever you say, every poet is inevitably saturated, even if he has tried not to be" (*SS2*, 2:70). In the spring of 1829 Chaadaev had chided Pushkin for not reading and studying more. He wrote, "I am convinced that you can bring infinite well-being to this poor Russia that has gone astray on the earth" (*SS2*, 2:66).

It is worth noting that, contrary to his usual advice, Chaadaev urged Pushkin to use Russian in his verse and never French, since he saw the poet as the voice of Russia, speaking not to the world but to his fellow citizens (*SS2*, 2:68). Clearly Chaadaev was concerned with molding a new, more thoughtful kind of reader and saw literary art as the medium for this education.

Chaadaev wanted to teach Pushkin to use his art to speak about substantial (philosophical) issues, and particularly moral questions. In a letter from September 18, 1831, clearly with the earthshaking events of the revolutionary year of 1830 in mind, Chaadaev wrote: "Have you noticed that something unusual is happening in the depths of the moral world, something similar to what is happening in the depths of the physical world? I beg you to tell me what response this calls forth in you? As far as I am concerned, it seems to me that this is ready material for poetry—this great revolution in things; you cannot remain indifferent to it" (*SS2*, 2:69). Chaadaev then vented his frustration, urging Pushkin not to be so lazy and to "probe" his head and heart for weighty subjects to address in his next letters.

By far not the first to do so, Chaadaev expressed a philosopher's envy of Pushkin's poetic gift. Although Chaadaev admitted that he could not write with the force that Pushkin could, he did wish to mold in him a taste for a philosophical poetry: "Oh, how I wish I had the power to call forth at once all the forces of your poetic nature! How I would like to bring forth from it everything that I know lies hidden in it, so that you could let us hear at least one of those songs that our times demand" (*SS2*, 2:70). In his relationship to Pushkin we sense a certain attempt on Chaadaev's part to shape a hierarchical relationship between philosophy and poetry in which poetry takes its thematic direction under the tutelage of philosophy. Chaadaev saw himself as lacking Pushkin's poetic talents but possessing much broader and deeper insight into the nature of things. Thus his goal was to instruct and guide the poetic genius toward a poetic expression of the substantial moral and political questions of the day.

Of course, as we saw in the previous chapter, Pushkin had his own ideas about philosophical language and art. But his, in distinction to Chaadaev's, was a French-inspired model, taken from Voltaire. Philosophical language, as Voltaire reinvented it, as Pushkin stated in the mid-1830s, appropriated literary forms and "spoke in a widely accessible and humorous language, one that differed from prose only through its rhythm and meter—and this lightness seemed to be the height of poetry" (*PSS,* 11:271–272). This worldly, more widely accessible alternative was closer to what Pushkin thought philosophy ought to be. And, in Pushkin's concept, philosophy took its generic direction from fiction.

Chaadaev had other arguments with poetry. One of his unpublished aphorisms summarizes his rather Platonic conclusion that poetry is inferior to philosophy because it flatters rather than tells a truth: "Poetry is given to us in order to join the physical and mental worlds and to flatter the mind with this conjoining" (*SS*2, 1:457). In his seventh philosophical letter he delivered a lengthy criticism of Greek art, which, in his view, distorted the real order of things, putting matters of the flesh above matters of the spirit:

> Here, madam, is one of the most telling examples of mendacity of certain historical notions that are predominant in our time. As you know, the Greeks created from art a very great idea of the human spirit. Take a look at the substance of this splendid creation of Hellenic genius. It is the material aspect of humanity that is idealized and exalted; the natural and lawful order of things was distorted; what should have forever stayed in the lower spheres of the spiritual world was raised to the highest sphere of thought; the action of feelings upon the mind was magnified without measure; the chief marker dividing the divine from the human was erased. (*SS*2, 1:420)

Later in the same letter Chaadaev rejected not only Homer but also Greek and Roman culture and their impact on European thought, because it was alien to Russians. Still he resigned himself to the idea that he must speak this philosophical language, since it was also the language of enlightenment. "Like it or not," he lamented, "one must speak the language of Europe" (*SS*2, 1:433).

In the course of the late 1830s philosophical diction did indeed start to make itself felt in literary fiction. For example, in *A Hero of Our Time* Lermontov paid lip service to philosophical discourse as a signal of intelligence and spiritual depth. The ability to philosophize distinguishes Lermontov's protagonist, Pechorin, from his opponent, Grushnitsky, who represents the typical, chameleon-like "*honnête homme*" of Russian polite society.[8] Here

8. M. Iu. Lermontov, *Sochineniia v 4–kh tomakh* (Leningrad: Nauka, 1981), 4:242–244. The term *honnête homme* is developed in William Mills Todd III, *Fiction and Society in the Age of Pushkin: Ideology, Institutions, and Narrative* (Cambridge, Mass.: Harvard University Press, 1986), 55.

were the beginnings of a different kind of protagonist, one defined by a psychological depth and intellectual substance that went beyond quick wit.

Ivan Turgenev (1818–1883) was Russia's first great novelist to interpolate philosophical discourse into his stories and novels. If Lermontov, in *A Hero of Our Time,* had been the first to intimate the importance of philosophy as a marker of a deep and complex character, then Turgenev took on the challenge and incorporated actual philosophical vocabulary and dialogue in his narratives. Turgenev made philosophical dialogue a central part of what later would emerge as a mainstream Russian tradition of the philosophical novel. In this particular respect Turgenev was the very Russian image of a philosophical "dilletante" of which Herzen had dreamed in 1843.

Although he studied German Idealist philosophy at St. Petersburg University and at the University of Berlin, Turgenev never thought of himself as a philosopher. As his memoirs attest, in his early years he was devoted to "philosophy," that is, German Idealism, but at most as an enthusiast. As he wrote in his "Reminiscences of Belinsky," in the early 1840s "we still believed then in the reality and importance of philosophy and metaphysical conclusions although . . . we were in no way philosophical and did not command the ability to think abstractly, purely, in the German style. In philosophy we were looking for anything in the world except pure thought."[9] Despite his affinity for philosophy, Turgenev soon came to evaluate its truth and importance quite differently from his German teachers. In this shift we find another example of a new Russian discursive hierarchy taking shape, one in which figurative language and associative thinking would typically take the upper hand.

Early on Turgenev tended to enthuse about philosophy (*PSSP*28, 1:153). In a letter to Bakunin of August 1840, written soon after the death of Stankevich, Turgenev reasserted his friendship with him, immediately claiming philosophy as an art, indeed the highest of all arts (*PSSP*28, 1:195–196). As if to reinforce his claim, Turgenev switched to German: "Eine philosophische Überzeugung fassen ist das höchste Kunstwerk—und die Philosophen sind die größten Meister und Künstler" (To state a philosophical conviction is the highest work of art—and the philosophers are the highest masters and artists) (*PSSP*28, 1:196). In contrast, only two years later in 1842, when Turgenev was preparing for his final exam in philosophy in St. Petersburg, he wrote a playful letter, this time to Bakunin's younger siblings, Aleksei and Aleksandr, in which he showed a much less reverential attitude toward his subject. Here he was "devouring" philosophers for his

9. Ivan Turgenev, *Polnoe sobranie sochinenii i pisem,* 28 vols. (Moscow: ANSSSR, 1960–1968), 14:29. Hereafter cited in the text as *PSSP*28 with the relevant volume and page numbers.

exam, Descartes, Spinoza, and Leibniz, as well as Kant and Fichte. In a lighthearted vein he assumed the role of the thinking self, watching "itself" read philosophy. This letter is worth quoting at length to convey Turgenev's attitude:

> Enough about you. . . . I would do better to talk about myself, a more entertaining subject. So:
>
> "I"
>
> am sitting in my armchair in front of the fire and am reading Fichte; here is my train of thought: Wir sollen einen absoluten Grundsatz finden [we should find an absolute grounding] . . . hee . . . hee . . . I should put some wood on the fire (accomplished) . . . das Ich setzt sich als Nicht Ich [the I posits itself as not-I] . . . hee . . . hee . . . I'm sitting in silence under the window of my dungeon . . . after this a whole whirlwind of thoughts . . . (these thoughts are no concern of yours). Fichte behauptet [asserts]—I read these two words twenty-five times in a row and can't understand—finally I shake my head and get to it again . . . I yawn; I stand up—go up to the window and sing: ta-ri-tam, taritam, tarita . . . ra-ra (Grundt's sonata) . . . I look at the snowflakes falling for about ten minutes . . . I amble around the room: I imagine myself a minister—"it's time, it's time"—I sit down once more to Fichte—first I look at the fireplace for five minutes, smiling, then: im Ich ist das Princip sich zu setzen und das Princip—sich auch nicht zu [setzen] [in the I is the principle of positing oneself and the principle also of not positing oneself] . . .
>
> Oh, bliss, bliss, bliss of working unhurried, by oneself, with time to dream and think foolish thoughts and even to write them.
>
> I have a good poem "At the Station"—I'll read it when I come to visit you in Moscow. (*PSSP*, 1:222–223)

The sum total of this "philosophical" self-observation is a lighthearted word game with the German expression "sich setzen," which means both to "posit oneself" philosophically and to "seat oneself" physically. It is revealing that, like many other writers, Turgenev here intimated the foreignness of philosophy to his Russian idiom; every time he started to talk about philosophical ideas he reverted to German. What is still more interesting in terms of Turgenev's evaluation of the different discourses at his disposal is his sudden, final, and serious announcement of his new poem: here poetry is set implicitly above philosophy as the more important endeavor.

Despite his lack of engagement with philosophical speculation, philosophical discourse played a central role in many of Turgenev's early prose works from the 1850s, including "The Lull" ("Zatish'te," 1854), "The Correspondence" ("Perepiska," 1854), and his novella, *Rudin* (1856). Turgenev brought philosophical discourse to a much broader circle of readers, and, through him, it now truly started to become a part of educated speech. He achieved this goal by creating an implied reader through whom he could reach the actual reader.

The "positive" implied reader throughout is an educated Russian, usually a woman who becomes passionately interested in what the philosophizing protagonist has to say. This choice of a female implied reader is significant, since women were often most skeptical about the uses of philosophy. This character gladly listens to logical argument and thinks about the big ethical and metaphysical questions. Around her are always people who doubt the value of philosophy and indeed make light of efforts to explain earthly existence and human nature through grand, logical systems. Turgenev made the case for philosophy partly by using logic to show the weaknesses of its opponents and partly by emphasizing the liberating drama of philosophizing. In short, he used literary means first to legitimize philosophy and then later to undermine it.

In the three works considered here Turgenev first articulates the negative popular attitude toward philosophy and then challenges it. Universally the word *philosopher* is a pejorative term. In "The Lull," for example, a philosopher is popularly seen as something of a "nerd," a bookish person who rejects the pleasures of the senses (*PSSP*28, 6:115). In "The Correspondence" philosophy is treated as something foreign, specifically German (*PSSP*28, 6:176). For example, Maria Aleksandrovna, who corresponds with the philosopher-protagonist, Aleksei Petrovich, is a devoted follower of German romantic culture. She loves to play Beethoven and read German literature. Her neighbors accuse her of "philosophizing," which they associate with false logic and empty paradox. They make fun of her, claiming that she talks in empty phrases, for example, "It's easy because it's hard" (*PSSP*28, 6:176). Her nanny pleads with her to think and speak in a simpler way: "We are simple people, we are guided by common sense; and what do you think, all this cleverness and these books and scholarly acquaintances—where have they gotten you?" (*PSSP*28, 6:177).

In *Rudin* the implied reader's philosophical horizon is quite negative to start with, although in a more complex way. Whether quietly or vociferously, a number of minor characters cast doubt on the credibility of philosophy. There are the quiet heroes of the story, Rudin's former friend, the landowner Mikhail Lezhnev, and his gentry neighbors, Aleksandra Lipina and her brother, Sergei Volyntsev. These people have little time for philosophical theories and live their lives well in the sense that they take good care of their estates and the peasants who work for them. For them philosophy is implicitly a waste of time. The anti-philosophical sidekick who aggressively challenges the truth-value of (idealist) philosophy is the petty bureaucrat, Afrikan Pigasov.[10] This narrow-minded man with pretensions to intellectual perspicuity had once upon a time failed to complete a master's thesis. Afrikan Semenovich is outspoken in his distaste for philosophy as systematic, idealist thinking. Now a provincial "raisonneur," he orients the conversation toward philosophical issues shortly before Rudin's arrival in the country, "Philosophy . . . is the highest point of view! They'll be the death of me—these highest points of view. And what can you see from up there? If you're going to buy a horse, you don't climb up into a watch tower to look it over" (*PSSP*28, 6:255). Resisting idealist rationalism, Pigasov makes a case for purely factual, empirical knowledge. He claims, "all these so-called general considerations [*rassuzhdenie*] and hypotheses, systems— excuse me for my provincialism, I like to cut right to the chase . . . they're no good. It's all acting smart—just to confuse people" (*PSSP*28, 6:260).

Rudin is more complex than Turgenev's stories. Here we find two posi- tive implied readers, enthusiastic young people thirsty for fresh philosophi- cal vistas. They are Natalia Alekseevna, the daughter of Rudin's hostess, Daria Lasunskaia, and Basistov, a young teacher. At the start Turgenev de- picts Rudin in a favorable light when he first arrives for a visit. Rudin—who is modeled in part on the vivacious but controlling and overly abstracted Mikhail Bakunin—appears to possess a magnanimity, eloquence, and fine sensibility that are lacking in others. Rudin soon captivates others of Lasun- skaia's guests with his youthful charisma. His speech weaves together the poetic with the logical and systematic, and has a quality that borders on the mystical: "The very sound of his voice, concentrated and quiet, augmented the charm; it seemed that something elevated, something unexpected even for him, was speaking through him. Rudin talked about what it was that gives our temporal life its eternal meaning" (*PSSP*28, 6:269).

Shown against his philosophical rival, Pigasov, whose narrowly empirical thinking leads him to a jaded materialism and moral skepticism, Rudin seems to offer a genuinely new way to see the world and articulates it well. He possesses "just about the highest of mysteries—the music of eloquence" (*PSSP*28, 6:269), which he marshals to defend systematic thinking against Pigasov's attacks: "Why are you so frightened of that word [*system*]? All sys- tems are founded on a knowledge of the basic laws, the origins of life" (*PSSP*28, 6:262). Through Rudin, Turgenev counters Pigasov's crass materi- alism. He shows that the philosophical method is a potent tool. He argues

10. Although Afrikan Pigasov has the same initials as Pushkin, A.S.P., and his first name also brings to mind Pushkin (who was one-eighth African), it is not clear why Turgenev would want to refer to Pushkin in this way. It is possible to see Pigasov as a travesty of Pushkin's strongly anti-ide- alist attitudes.

by posing questions; he insists on rigor and consistency of argument; and he disproves through exposing the paradox in his opponent's thinking. Not unlike the young Herzen, Rudin turns Pigasov's objections on their head by defending the use of philosophy as a method for interpreting "facts." He asks: "Should one try to convey the meaning of facts?" implying that philo sophical argument is indeed useful as an interpretative tool (PSSP28, 6:260). Rudin brackets Pigasov's crude materialism by persuading most of his other listeners that philosophy is worthwhile as a means for understanding the world and by showing that Pigasov, too, has a form of "philosophy." For example, Pigasov rails against all "convictions": "All this is based on so-called convictions; everyone interprets his own convictions and demands to boot that others respect them. . . . Ugh!" (PSSP28, 6:260). Rudin replies with the question, "then, it would seem, in your view, that there are no such things as convictions?" (PSSP28, 6:261). Here Rudin catches Pigasov in the paradoxical position of having the conviction that there are no convictions. He goes on to show that Pigasov himself actually does have a "philosophy"—of skepticism.

Rudin goes on to question Pigasov's understanding of what a "fact" is. He exposes Pigasov's objectivism, showing that Pigasov, too, relies on subjective experience and feeling. At this point Rudin makes his winning play in favor of systematic thinking: "All these assaults on systems, on general considerations and so forth, are particularly distressing because, along with the systems, people reject knowledge in general, science, and faith in science and, it would seem, faith in themselves and in their strengths. People need that faith; you can't live on your impressions alone" (PSSP28, 6:263). He goes on to clinch his victory, not through reasoned argument but through an emotional appeal to faith and patriotism. In terms akin to Herzen's, Rudin argues that having a consistent, systematic worldview makes one a better citizen: "If a person lacks a sturdy foundation in which he has faith, he has no ground. . . . [H]ow can he give himself an account of the needs, the significance, the future prospects of his people? How can he know what he himself should do?" (PSSP28, 6:263). At this point Pigasov is defeated; other characters favor Rudin. It would seem that the stage has been set for a new faith in abstract, systematic thinking.

Turgenev's novella can be read as a parable about the fate of philosophy in mid-nineteenth-century Russian culture. Gradually philosophy becomes discredited when its defenders evince that same fundamental rift between feeling, thought, and action that so bothered Belinsky, Herzen, and the rest of Turgenev's generation. The self-consciousness that philosophy brings turns out to be a sickness rather than a form of liberation. Dostoevsky has often been credited with articulating the moral problem of "nadryv" or the rift or laceration between moral ideal and subconscious drive.[11] Already in the 1850s Turgenev coined a similar term, *nadlom* or "breakdown," for a slightly different condition of a rift between self-conscious thought and the ability to take action. The word would seem to have appeared first in "The Correspondence" in which the philosophizing student Sergei Petrovich diagnoses the very thoughtful and morally conscious Maria Aleksandrovna as having a "breakdown in her soul [*nadlom v dushe*]" (*PSSP*28, 6:179). Rudin speaks eloquently of the ways in which philosophical self-consciousness helps one to "break the stubborn egocentricity of human character [*nadlomit' upornyi egoizm*]." He defends self-love (*samoliubie*) as something one needs in order to act effectively, but he reviles narrow self-centeredness (*sebialiubie*): "We need something to break down the stubborn egocentricity of our personality in order to have the right to express ourselves" (*PSSP*28, 6:267). It eventually becomes clear that Rudin himself is a person with just such a broken soul, one who possesses the mystery of eloquence, which, it becomes clear, is only a mask for inaction and emotional coldness. The philosopher and his rhetoric, however heroic they may at first have seemed, are shown to be wanting.

In *Rudin* the process of discrediting philosophy happens gradually. Even as Rudin is confronting the cynicism of Pigasov, the narrator and various characters introduce critical or amusing comments about Rudin himself. Volyntsev, who competes with Rudin for Natalia's love, notes that, although Rudin has wonderful eyes, his hands are big and red (*PSSP*28, 6:265). The narrator mentions that, despite Rudin's wonderful rhetorical gift, his hero is unable to tell a good story or make his audience laugh (*PSSP*28, 6:268).

The downward turn starts when Rudin is seemingly at the height of his powers. Sitting in Lasunskaia's drawing room among his newfound admirers, he tells the following parable:

> A king is sitting around a fire with his warriors in a long, dark barn. It is a winter night. Suddenly a small bird flies in the open doors and flies out some other doors. The king notes that this bird is similar to people living in the world: it flies out of the darkness and then flies back into the darkness, having spent only a short while in the warmth and light. "King," says one of the warriors, "the bird will not get lost in the dark and will find its nest." In the same way, our life is brief and insignificant; but everything great is carried out through people. The consciousness of being the tool of those higher forces must eclipse all other joys: in death itself a person will find his life, his nest. (*PSSP*28, 6:270)

---

11. See, for example, E. Clowes, "Self-Laceration and Resentment: The Terms of Moral Psychology in Dostoevsky and Nietzsche," in *Freedom and Responsibility in Russian Literature*, ed. E. C. Allen and G. S. Morson (Evanston: Northwestern University Press, 1995), 119–133.

This brief story belies the impression that we have received of a vibrant, lively, passionate person. Although he may seem to reinforce the idea that people carry out great actions, Rudin actually focuses on death and the insignificance of human life. Already he is starting to preach, and now a message of passive resignation shines through the veil of rhetoric that had seemed so energizing.

While his rhetorical gifts mesmerize and intrigue most of his listeners, even if they do not understand his ideas, the narrator himself turns against him. The narrator first starts with the old language question: Rudin lacks a truly refined ear for language and style. By analogy, Rudin is insensitive to the imported aspects of his thinking that eventually have the effect of bringing out inconstancy in his character. His verbal fireworks will eventually be shown to be mere sophistry. This linguistic line of criticism continues eventually with the conclusion that Rudin's rhetorical talents are foreign and not Russian at all (*PSSP*28, 6:293). The criticisms deepen as we hear about Rudin's past from his former friend, Lezhnev, who points out the failings of Rudin's character. Lezhnev, who seems provincial and lazy but actually turns out to be very hardworking, shows that Rudin is both emotionally and physically a freeloader (*PSSP*28, 6:293).

Ultimately it is Turgenev's female protagonist who exposes most successfully the inconsistency between the philosopher's fiery words and his total inaction. Just as Maria Aleksandrovna in "The Correspondence" eventually brings out the weakness of Sergei Petrovich's character (just as he seemed on the verge of committing his life to her, he leaves her to wander Europe as a theater "groupie"), so Natalia Alekseevna reveals the emptiness of Rudin's words. Natalia Alekseevna is inspired by Rudin's early criticisms of laziness, cowardice, and egoism, and she believes in his desire to act in the name of a good cause. She eagerly absorbs everything he teaches her. Propelled by his words to imagine her life beyond her provincial surroundings, she is ready to follow him to the ends of the earth to work for social change and improve life for other people. Enthusiastically asking him about his various projects, she is repeatedly disappointed. He never carries through with his plans, even something as small as writing an article. Finally, he exposes his worst inconsistency during their secret meeting at Avdiukhin's Pond. Although Natalia is prepared to run away with him to perform great deeds in the name of social liberation, Rudin betrays her by advising her to submit to authority and obey her mother's wishes to return home (*PSSP*28, 6:323). All the implied promise of liberation at the heart of his philosophizing is nothing but a sham.

Ultimately it is neither the cynical materialism of Pigasov nor the verbal pyrotechnics of Rudin but the pragmatic mores of Lezhnev and Lipina that win the day. The story is framed with their good acts: Lipina's kindness to a dying peasant woman at the start and Lezhnev's kindness to Rudin in the end. Although it would seem that philosophy has no place in this world, Lezhnev the pragmatist will defend it: Rudin may be fully discredited, but philosophy per se is not. Some characters, for example, Lipina's brother Volyntsev, attacks Rudin as a "damned philosopher" (*PSSP*28, 6:328). It is now Lezhnev who comes to rescue philosophy. He reaffirms that philosophy as such is not to blame and claims that Rudin is not a true embodiment of philosophy. Nonetheless, Lezhnev delivers the final judgment of philosophy as a part of Russian life. The susceptibility to big ideas of younger characters, such as Basistov and Natalia Alekseevna, suggests that youth is the time of life for philosophy. Philosophy is most useful when one is developing a consistent worldview and wrestling with questions of defining the good and the true, in short, when one is developing rigorous intellectual habits and working out one's system of beliefs. But then, as the pragmatic Lezhnev shows, one must live and act in the real world of work, business, and family—here is where one shows one's true consistency. At the end, as Pigasov snipes at Rudin's memory one last time, Lezhnev remarks: "You attack philosophy; when you speak of it, you can't find words that are scornful enough. I myself don't put much stock by it and can't understand it; but it is not philosophy that is to blame for our main misfortunes! Philosophical cleverness and delirium will never be grafted onto the Russian character; the Russian has far too much common sense for that; but I cannot allow that, in the name of attacking philosophy, one would attack honest striving toward the truth and toward consciousness" (*PSSP*, 6:349). Pigasov is once again discredited when Lezhnev recalls to Lipina how Pigasov used to accept bribes. More significant, however, systematic philosophy has been marginalized for the time being as something un-Russian.

It is important to point out that, even in the early 1840s, philosophically minded contemporaries such as Ivan Kireevsky were well aware of the psychological problems that thinking in pure logical forms brought with it for Russian readers. In a letter to his friend, Khomiakov, of July 1840, Kireevsky mulled over the failure of Western philosophies to establish deep roots in Russia. In this context he mentioned the lack of will that Herzen had also noted and that, with Turgenev, could be called the "Rudin syndrome." Kireevsky wrote:

> My idea is that logical consciousness, when it transfers action into words, life into a formula, does not fully grasp its object but destroys its impact upon the soul. Living in this plan, we live by the plan instead of living in a house; having drawn up the plan, we consider that we have erected the edifice. When we get down to real construction, we find it difficult to carry a stone instead of a pencil. Generally speaking, in our time only the uneducated or those with a spiritual education have will. Since in our time—with or with-

out it—a thinking person must put his knowledge under the yoke of logic, at least he ought to know that this [logic] is not the peak of knowledge and that there is one more step, a supra-logical knowledge, where light means more than a match, where it means life itself, where will can grow along with thought.[12]

Kireevsky believed that only through a philosophy reconciled with religious belief could people overcome this problem of fecklessness.

Despite seeming to discredit his philosophizing characters, Turgenev's philosophical fiction was successful in two ways for integrating philosophy into Russian language and culture. First, as for so many other cultural concepts, such as the "superfluous man," the "new man," "nihilism," or the "nest of gentry," his fiction went far to fix in popular parlance the youthful exuberance of "philosophy"—and also the negative image of *nadlom,* or the "breakdown" that often occurs between ideal and practice. Turgenev did more than any other writer of the 1850s to incorporate philosophical discourse into everyday language, whether negatively or positively. "Philosophy" disappeared as its own genre but was woven thickly into other social, psychological, and intellectual texts and contexts saturating a number of other discourses. Turgenev had dramatized both its limitations and its strengths. Despite his personal enthusiasm Turgenev never really defended formal philosophy but showed instead why a philosophical culture could not yet flourish in the Russia of the 1850s.

IVAN KIREEVSKY, ALEKSEI KHOMIAKOV, AND THE GROUNDS FOR A RUSSIAN ORTHODOX DISCOURSE

Certainly the major outcome of Chaadaev's philosophical letter was the famous debate of the 1840s and 1850s about Russia's present and future that took shape around the two "parties," the Slavophiles and the Westernizers.[13] The Slavophiles, namely, Kireevsky, Khomiakov, and Koshelev, among others, argued against Herzen, Belinsky, and the Westernizers for the reintegration of ancient Russian social and religious traditions into the fabric of contemporary life. From the start of the dispute Kireevsky (1806–1856) and Khomiakov (1804–1860) were predominant among the Slavophiles as their two chief theorists. In devising their theory, they shared a conflicted view of philosophy, which, although diagnosed as the root of the crisis of faith in the West, also became the key to grounding a uniquely

---

12. Ivan Kireevsky, *Polnoe sobranie sochinenii,* 2 vols. (Moscow: Tipografiia imperatorskogo Moskovskogo universiteta, 1911), 1:67. Hereafter cited in the text as *PSS*2 with the relevant volume and page numbers.

13. See Walicki, *The Slavophile Controversy,* 70–71.

Russian religious discourse that would give Russians a voice to be heard and heeded at home and in Europe.

Ivan Kireevsky stands as the strongest link to the beginnings of Russian speculative thought in the 1820s. He grew up among people who read and valued philosophy. Kireevsky's father, a man of the 1780s, who died when Ivan was six, had been a cultivated man, an enlightened conservative who hated Voltaire and was drawn to Freemasonry.[14] Kireevsky's stepfather, A. A. Elagin, was a philosophical enthusiast who loved Kant and brought *The Critique of Pure Reason* with him from abroad. Elagin also translated Schelling. Among Kireevsky's private tutors were the famous Moscow University professor of natural sciences, M. G. Pavlov, and the St. Petersburg University professor of anatomy, D. M. Vellansky. When only a teenager Kireevsky attended the meetings of Odoevsky's circle, the Liubomudry. He attended literary evenings at the home of Z. A. Volkonskaia, and spent a great deal of time reading and discussing philosophy, in particular, the thought of Schelling.

In contrast to the Westernizers who typically found few supporters among women, Kireevsky was fortunate to enjoy the support, and indeed strong influence, of his deeply religious wife, Natalia Petrovna Arbeneva. She guided his thinking away from seeking a theoretical reconciliation between reason and faith to a more concrete effort to define an Orthodox Christian philosophy. Generally the Russian Orthodox Church did not countenance speculative thought. Very strict in her piety, Arbeneva nonetheless tolerated philosophy as long as it did not mock religious belief (*PSS*2, 1:285–286). Natalia Petrovna was shocked at first by Kireevsky's lack of belief when they married in 1834, and she kept to her own rituals. Eventually the married couple started to read philosophy together. After reading Kireevsky's favorite philosopher, Schelling, Arbeneva pointed out that long ago the Greek Fathers of the Church had already articulated many of Kireevsky's most beloved thoughts, and she showed him specific passages. On the sly Kireevsky himself began to borrow his wife's books and absorb their contents. It is important to note that in a female reading culture that resisted philosophical thought Arbeneva and other strictly pious but also learned women played a crucial role in moving Russian thinking in the direction of an Orthodox theology.

The friendship between Kireevsky and Khomiakov marks the first instance in Russian history of an actual, ongoing philosophical dialogue, which lasted almost two decades, between two Russians. This dialogue, conducted both in private and in the public press, was significant in offsetting the repressive effect of the censorship during the reign of Tsar Nicholas

14. Ibid., 121.

I and establishing the roots of the rich religious philosophical renaissance sixty years later. Censored three times in as many decades and barred from a teaching post at Moscow University, Kireevsky was restrained from participating in public discussion. Unlike Herzen and later Khomiakov, he never sought "*tamizdat*" or publishing his writings in the West.

From the very start Kireevsky had a singularly philosophical bent of mind. Although it was he who first tried to reconcile Orthodox religious faith with philosophical critical thinking, it would be Khomiakov who would eventually give fuller articulation to this direction. In contrast to Kireevsky, Khomiakov was a jack of all intellectual trades. He had remarkably broad interests and gained considerable expertise in chemistry, theology, poetry, philosophy, and engineering, among many other subjects.[15] Khomiakov was born into a Moscow patrician family headed by his mother, a religious dogmatic. To quote his friend and student, Iury Samarin, he lived his whole life "in the Church." Samarin claimed in his 1867 introduction to Khomiakov's theological writings that his mentor "represented an original phenomenon of the fullest freedom in religious consciousness, almost unknown in Russia" (*PSS*8, 2:xiv).

Although Kireevsky was the first to work seriously on the reconciliation of reason and faith and was, by most accounts, the more original of the two thinkers, Khomiakov is generally credited with altering the image of the Orthodox Church and according it a new, higher position in relation to Catholicism and Protestantism.[16] According to Samarin, Khomiakov drove home the image of Orthodoxy that since became something of an empty stereotype: in contrast to its Western counterparts that were "tainted" with rationalism and "dead" logic, Orthodoxy was the receptacle of living truth. Samarin wrote: "Now we see the *Church*, in other words a living organism of truth [*istina*], entrusted with mutual love, and outside the Church—logical knowledge separate from the moral impulse" (*PSS*8, 2:xxx). It is this rationalism, Samarin held, that led ultimately to loss of faith. For Samarin, Western theology and philosophy were opposed to the spirit of true mystical knowledge expressed in Orthodoxy.

Although Samarin would seem to have rejected rational discourse out of hand, both Kireevsky and Khomiakov tried to integrate philosophical speech into their projects. Kireevsky would try to incorporate philosophy into a kind of Schellingian religious philosophy, first as such, and later with a specifically Russian Orthodox character. As he wrote in a fragment, first published after his death in 1857, a Russian philosophy "must be the com-

---

15. Aleksei Khomiakov, *Polnoe sobranie sochinenii*, 8 vols. (Moscow: Kushnerev, 1911), 2:x. Hereafter cited in the text as *PSS*8 with the relevant volume and page numbers.

16. Walicki, *The Slavophile Controversy*, 181.

mon cause of all believing and thinking people who are familiar with the writings of the Christian Fathers and with Western erudition" (*PSS2*, 1:270). Khomiakov would first imitate and then criticize philosophical discourse, and finally he would appropriate it in a modified way to justify the emergence of an actual Russian Orthodox theology. The difference between the two lay in Khomiakov's greater knowledge of and attachment to Orthodox tradition and ritual. He would move more strongly than Kireevsky in the direction of "theology," that is, to an inquiry into the nature of the Christian god, working within the framework of Christian texts and doctrine. Kireevsky's interests, in contrast, lay more generally in religious philosophy, that is, in defining a particularly Russian religious psychology and its possible intersections with speculative thinking. The primary concern of both writers was to create an Eastern Christian voice that would be heard at home and, in the case of Khomiakov, by Western theologians (*PSS8*, 2:31). Neither of them rejected philosophy but rather saw it as a building block in a discursive pyramid, the apex of which would be the Orthodox faith in its new theological presence. This process of grounding an Orthodox religious discourse would develop in part through a confrontation with the notion of "philosophy" and particularly the concept of "rationalism."

"Philosophy," for Kireevsky and Khomiakov, was always something foreign and an intellectual practice that Russians tended to accept too simply and uncritically. In 1845 Khomiakov expressed their shared criticism that philosophy in Russia was at most the expression of a Western influence, which its Russian followers merely imitated: "Accepting everything uncritically, good-heartedly, hailing as enlightenment anything Western, any new system or new nuance of a system, any new fashion or nuance of fashion, any new fruit of the leisure time of German philosophers and French fashion designers, any change in thought or life, we have not once gotten up the courage yet, even in the shiest, most polite terms . . . to ask the West: is everything true that is being said?" (*PSS8*, 1:13). Khomiakov compared Russian intellectuals' servile attitude toward European philosophy to the relationship between Aristotelian scholastics and their master, Aristotle: "We never can summon the courage to subject the general grounds or bases of [European] systems to a rigorous interrogation" (*PSS8*, 1:35). This would be Khomiakov's project as he examined German philosophical development in the framework of religious history. In the early 1850s Khomiakov protested against this scholastic imitativeness, "the stamp of scholastic deathliness" (*PSS8*, 1:182) that had bothered Herzen. As Khomiakov put it: "Apparently we have thoughts and feelings, but we neither think with our heads nor feel with our own soul. This is the fruit of that intellectual enslavement to which we have subjected ourselves so proudly and willingly" (*PSS8*, 1:182). Turning away from philosophy as a dead artifact, Khomiakov devoted his energies in the last decade of his life, until his death in 1860, to creating a philosophical-theological voice that would be wholly "Russian," the voice of an Orthodox discourse. Kireevsky echoed this train of thought in a letter from 1852 to the Slavophile A. I. Koshelev (1806–1883): "It is too bad, really too bad, that Western insanity has inhibited our thinking, precisely now when, it seems, would be the time for Russia to say its word in philosophy, to show those heretics that the truth of science is only within the truth of Orthodoxy" (*PSS2*, 1:74).

Kireevsky was the first to articulate the religious turn that would mark Slavophile thinking in general, as an integration of Western philosophy with the Orthodox tradition. During his semester in Berlin and Munich in 1830, Kireevsky found himself most attracted to the issue that would propel the Slavophiles to create a religious-philosophical discourse and eventually an Orthodox discourse and to close the gap between reasoned argument and the need for faith. In Berlin he heard the great German interpreter of the Bible, Friedrich Schleiermacher, whom he called "one of the most remarkable theologians and philosophers, one of the very best professors in Berlin" (*PSS2*, 1:28). Although he particularly admired Schleiermacher's lectures on the life of Jesus Christ and on revelation, he felt frustrated by the professor's unwillingness to attack this difficult area where religious faith borders on philosophical skepticism. "Touching on this analysis of two worlds, one of reasoned [*razumnyi*] conviction and the other of spiritual [*dushevnyi*] assurance," Kireevsky wrote in a letter from March 1830, "he [Schleiermacher] should have torn up all the concepts of their interrelationship, represented faith and philosophy in their opposition and commonality, and thereby in their whole, full existence [*tselostnoe bytie*]" (*PSS2*, 1:31).

Kireevsky, much earlier than Khomiakov, started to articulate the need to account for the relationship between philosophical reason, which trusts nothing and takes nothing for granted, and religious belief, which operates on profound trust in higher truth. Kireevsky was not yet thinking only in terms of Orthodox faith, although he did mention Russian Orthodoxy. Now he rejected the values of the French Revolution, as well as scientific empiricism and its claim to truth. In the eighteenth century, he wrote in his first published article, "The Nineteenth Century" ("Deviatnadtsatyi vek," 1832), "religion fell into disfavor, and mindless lack of faith took its place. In the sciences only what could be experienced through the senses was pronounced to be true and everything supersensory was rejected not only as unproven but even impossible" (*PSS2*, 1:88). Kireevsky hailed the counter-revolution in philosophy brought on by systematic speculative thought (*umozrenie*) that "deduced the whole visible world from one immaterial cause" (*PSS2*, 1:88). He welcomed Schelling's attempts to reintroduce religious thought into the sphere of philosophy. As Kireevsky put it: "True knowledge . . . is outside the scholastic-logical process and is therefore *alive;* it is *higher* than the concept of eternal necessity, and is therefore *positive;* it is more *vital* than mathematical abstraction" (*PSS*2, 1:92).

If Kireevsky was critical of the sole preoccupation of philosophy with reason, finding it a weakness in reason to be limited only to itself, he was still more critical of isolationist sentiments in the Orthodox Church with regard to Western thought. This certainly was a major reason for the official reprimand and closing of his journal, *Evropeets* (The European), following the publication of "The Nineteenth Century." He wrote that "some sort of Great Wall of China stands between Russia and Europe, and the air of Western enlightenment comes to us through only a few openings" (*PSS*2, 1:95). Although he pointed out the positive aspects of Russian Christianity (it is "purer and holier" (*PSS*2, 1:100)), he also indicated what he saw as its major failing: Russian Orthodoxy lacked the heritage of classical antiquity that the West had embraced. This lack, of course, would turn in Russia's favor in later articles, particularly those by Khomiakov, but now and throughout the 1830s Kireevsky regretted this hole in Russian culture. In an unpublished "Answer to A. S. Khomiakov," written in 1839, Kireevsky went on to express regret that Russian monasteries, where the "inner spiritual reason" of the Church Fathers was studied, never expanded to become "universities" for all Russians (*PSS*2, 1:119).

Kireevsky continued to search for a particularly Russian way of integrating philosophy into Russian life. In both his private correspondence and published essays he continually called for a merger of philosophy and religion (*PSS*2, 1:67, 142). His next (and last in his lifetime) major philosophical publication, "On the Character of European Enlightenment and Its Relation to Russian Enlightenment," came in 1852 and brought about the quick demise of yet another journal, *Moskovskii sbornik* (Moscow anthology). Here Kireevsky summarized positions formulated earlier and pressed for a more concerted effort to define a place for philosophy in a Russian tradition that rejected the dominance of Western concepts of "reason" and "rationalism." As before, he reiterated that the sources of a Russian philosophy would have to be the writings of the Fathers of the Church. The natural basis for a Russian enlightenment, however, Kireevsky found not in written texts but in ritual, feeling, and mentality. Russians, he claimed, are distinguished by a "wholeness of spirit" that is enacted in a life lived through prayer (*PSS*2, 1:211). In this article he gave his best summary of the differences between Russia and the West: "In Russia [Christianity] was illuminated on the lampions of the whole Orthodox Church; theology in the West acquired the character of intellectualized [*rassudochnyi*] abstraction— in the Orthodox world [theology] retained an inward wholeness of spirit; there—the division of the force of reason, here—the striving toward [truth] through the inner elevation of self-consciousness toward wholeness of the heart and focus of the mind; there—the search for outward, dead unity, here—the striving toward inward, living [unity]" (*PSS2*, 1:217). Kireevsky appointed a concrete place for philosophy in Russian life in his final article, "On the Inevitability and Possibility of New Sources for Philosophy," published in 1856, just after his unexpected death from cholera. In his very strict discursive hierarchy the truth produced by reasoned thought occupied a place beneath divine revelation: "In the Orthodox Church Divine Revelation and human thought do not mix; the boundaries between the Divine and the human can be crossed neither by science nor by the [theological] teaching of the Church. However much believing thought tries to harmonize reason with faith, it can never accept a doctrine of Revelation as a mere conclusion [produced by] reason, it can never appoint to a reasoned conclusion the authority of a Revealed doctrine. The borders [between the two] are firm and inviolable" (*PSS2*, 1:247). Kireevsky went on to delineate a higher form of reason that needs to "gather into one indivisible wholeness all its separate forces" of logic, ecstatic feeling, aesthetic sense, and love (*PSS2*, 1:249). He then proceeded to delineate a "mythical," three-part hierarchical structure, positioning philosophy with this "higher" form of reason in the middle, as the mediator between revealed knowledge and empirical science: "Philosophy is not one of the sciences and is not faith. It is a general summation and general foundation of all the sciences and the transmitter of thought between them and faith. Where there is faith but no development of reasoned education [*razumnaia obrazovannost'*], there can be no philosophy" (*PSS2*, 1:252–253).

It is curious that here, as before, Kireevsky never cited any specific examples from the frequently mentioned sources in the writings of the Fathers of the Church, with which he was certainly less familiar. The whole argument thus remained quite abstract and relatively negative: the Russian spirit is whole and undivided, in contrast to the Western spirit, and thus it is open to a more healthy form of philosophy. What that philosophy might be Kireevsky could never define. It would be Khomiakov's accomplishment in his published answers to Kireevsky to give flesh to Kireevsky's call for a Russian philosophy and, based on Kireevsky's beginnings, to put together the vocabulary for a Russian Orthodox discourse.

Although Khomiakov saw Idealist philosophy as a potentially useful tool for religious expression, he was much more positive than Kireevsky in his mention of the merits of the Orthodox tradition. From 1852 on, he followed Kireevsky in articulating the path from philosophy to Orthodox discourse. In a review of Kireevsky's article, "On the Character of European Enlightenment" (1852), Khomiakov welcomed philosophy as the mediated knowledge of God: "St. Kliment of Alexandria defended the study of philosophy, saying, 'some things come directly from God, others through mediation. Philosophy belongs to this last category, but I don't know whether one should not say that it came directly from the will of God'" (*PSS*8, 1:201). Khomiakov intimates here that philosophy may even have the authority of a form of speech that is directly inspired by God.

Khomiakov argued frequently, using a "Hegelian" dialectic, that, although philosophy in and of itself had reached its limit, it had also opened the way to its opposite, a nonreasoned but much fuller, more meaningful faith. He wrote: "Philosophy has done a great deed. The rationalism hidden in the Latin religion [*latinstvo*, i.e., Catholicism], and sharply expressed in Protestantism, has finally emerged and perished of its own force in philosophy, thus clearing a space in the human soul and mind for a fuller and more holy Faith, passed on to us from the very beginning of Christian teaching, like pure gold, that fears neither the experience of centuries nor the temptation of tortuous analysis" (*PSS*8, 1:201). Khomiakov reiterated that philosophy, by itself, was not enough to lead one to new faith. It was too bounded by its origins in the Protestant rebellion against Catholicism: "Protestantism itself was the fruit of a rationalist movement. Its forms and rigorous logical approach were the triumph of the rationalism that emerged clearly and consciously from Roman teaching in which it existed secretly and unconsciously. Its deed became clearer, more consequential, and more rigorous. Soon the wraps were off . . . and the Feuerbachs of our time began their destructive work" (*PSS*8, 1:210). Reasoned argument alone, in Khomiakov's view, had led to the attempt to destroy religious faith—as in the case of Feuerbach who argued for the view that people invented God and religious myth out of a psychological need for answers and explanations for existence. Rationalism had now reached its apogee in German Idealist philosophy and, through its self-destruction, opened the way to the restoration of faith. Khomiakov remarked, "The cycle of Germanic philosophy is complete. Hegelism [*sic*], its last conclusion, has been rebuffed and condemned by everyone who is in any way true to its dialectical method" (*PSS*8, 1:267).[17] Later, in "On Contemporary Phenomena in the Field of Philosophy" (1859), Khomiakov made a still stronger statement, explicitly connecting idealist philosophy to renewed faith: "Hegel not only represented the crowning moment of philosophy, but he rehabilitated for Germany if not faith itself then at least a feeling of faith" (*PSS*8, 1:309).

If philosophy, as the acme of rationalism, served the purpose of opening the way to renewed faith, then, Khomiakov further claimed, a new problem arose from the Orthodox side. Reasoned debate and dispute were not part of the Orthodox tradition. Indeed, Orthodoxy remained pure because of its

17. For a similar comment on Kant, see *PSS*8, 2:293.

refusal to engage in debate. In a letter to Samarin, Khomiakov discussed the polemic of the eighteenth-century archbishop Feofan Prokopovich with the Old Believers. Prokopovich allegedly had expressed the belief that Christianity ought not to be "learned" but to have a "fullness of spirit" (*PSS8*, 8:232). Christianity is in no way a "science," nor can it be. According to this view, being literate and in any way well read was the opposite of being pious. Khomiakov finished with the remark that, in Prokopovich's view, theology was at best "negative": its purpose is to discredit opponents, not actively to build faith.

Generally, although Khomiakov would never have agreed that one should not be learned, he did agree that theological polemic is negative by nature. The reliance on polemic rather than unity and harmony was the problem that brought the Western Church to its "downfall," what Khomiakov saw as its eventual loss of faith: theology was integral to the Western tradition of rebellion against existing belief. This was something Protestants inherited, Protestants who "did not restore and, as a result of their intellectual development, could not restore that wholeness and fullness that are the essence of Christianity but were lost in the West from the very moment of the Schism [of 1054]" (*PSS8*, 1:210). Ironically, as Khomiakov began his own disputes with the British theologian William Palmer and the Russian Jesuit Father Gagarin, he argued against polemic as a way of producing truth and knowledge. "To believe in the infallibility of science," he wrote, "indeed, science that has developed its positions through argument, goes against common sense" (*PSS8*, 2:46). In other words, theologians who question revelation as the way to true knowledge and faith are nonsensical.

Khomiakov further criticized reason itself as an expression of hubris, the very opposite of the Orthodox virtue of resignation. In Western Christianity, he argued, "human reason leaped up, proud of the independence of logical self-determination created for it and indignant at the chains that had arbitrarily been placed on it; here are the origins of Protestantism, the legitimate, although disobedient, offspring of the Roman Church" (*PSS8*, 2:54).

As Western Christianity failed, crumbling even in its final expression in German Idealism, Khomiakov imagined a new "enlightenment" that could bring back the wholeness that had been lost (*PSS8*, 1:210). Again following Kireevsky's lead, he wrote: "Whatever lies ahead and is the will of Providence, the verdict is in for Western erudition [*obrazovannost'*], and it has been delivered dispassionately: for the West itself pronounced its own sentence in the most recent conclusions of philosophical thought that became tangled in abstractions and one-sided rationality [*rassudochnost'*]; and we are lucky that we have some bearings and directions in another enlightenment and another area of life and thought" (*PSS8*, 1:212). Khomiakov made a virtue of the fact that abstract thought is alien to Orthodoxy: "From what has been said, it is clear what the foundation of the firm edifice of Russian enlightenment is to be. It is Faith, Orthodox Faith, which, thank God, . . . no one has ever called a religion (for religion can unite people, but only Faith binds people with one another as well as with the angels and the very Creator of people and angels), Faith, with all its life-giving, constructive force, its freedom of thought, and patient love" (*PSS*8, 1:255). Without ever really explaining how, Khomiakov argued that this rather unlettered "enlightenment" could build on the foundations and learn from the mistakes of Western philosophy without being "tainted" by its "logical deathliness": "Only the precise knowledge of earlier schools of philosophy gives one the right to acknowledge their faultiness or lack of fullness and to try to create a new, fuller and more harmonious [*stroinyi*] doctrine. The labor of past generations is not being rejected but is being swallowed and re-created in the new labor of the present generation" (*PSS*8, 1:262).

In his polemic with Western theologians Khomiakov offered some basis for his "Russian enlightenment" and its approach to knowledge. Higher knowledge could be attained only through faith and revelation: "Faith is always the result of revelation, recognized as such; it is the meditation on an invisible fact realized in a visible fact; faith is not precisely creed [*verovanie*] or logical conviction, founded on conclusions: it is much more. It is not just an act of cognition isolated from other capabilities but an act of all the forces of reason, seized and captivated to their very depths by the living truth [*istina*] of the revealed fact" (*PSS*8, 2:61). Khomiakov's attempts to discredit Western philosophy and make a case for an Orthodox philosophy rest more on assertion than on careful argument. As his Westernizing opponent, Herzen, put it in his memoirs, *My Past and Thoughts*, Khomiakov did not keep to the rules of reason and rational argument:

> His philosophical arguments consisted of rejecting the possibility of using logic to get to the truth [*istina*]; he allowed reason the one formal capacity to develop embryos or kernels received, relatively ready-made, by other means (that is, through revelation or faith). If one were to leave reason to its own devices, wandering in the desert and building category after category, it might expose its own laws but could never get to an understanding of the spirit or of immortality, and so forth. (*SS*30, 9:157)

Although Herzen captured the essence of Khomiakov's critique of reason, and despite his quite exact if not very friendly perception, Herzen actually agreed with Khomiakov on one key point. Reasoned speculation in and of itself was completely foreign to the Russian character (*SS*30, 9:18).

What then was the nature of Kireevsky's and Khomiakov's religious discourse? In general, it seemed a language of *representation*, to use Foucault's term. Although it made relatively sparse use of figures and tropes, and was based on logical argumentation, its key terms related to nonempirical forms of knowledge. Foremost among these are such heavily weighted words as *faith* (*vera*), *feeling* (*chuvstvo*), *communion* (*obshchenie*), *collectivity* (*sobornost'*), *revelation* (*otkrovenie*), *inner knowledge* (*vnutrennee poznanie*), and *prayer* (*molitva*). Both men attempted to harness the rhetorical authority of philosophy to articulate a mystical unity binding diverse things together and a mystical knowledge, the knowledge of the "invisible fact" inaccessible to the senses but available to the believing soul in a congregation of believing souls.

In conclusion, although we find the generation of the 1840s generally moving away from formal philosophy as something un-Russian, particularly during the 1850s, we find new rhetorical forms and voices fed by the experience of reading and confronting philosophical positions and methods. The Russian literary language, particularly as Herzen and Turgenev worked it, had extended its reach and depth through these disputes. Although he appropriated philosophical territory for his political essays, Herzen still felt that philosophy as such was part of an essential education in a civil society. Orthodox theology, as Kireevsky and Khomiakov conceived it, would mend the rift between logical analysis and religious faith. It would move away from discourse to a nondivisive, nondisputatious, holistic language oriented toward revelation. In each instance the marginalization and reappropriation of idealist philosophy led to fuller articulation of consciousness and broadened the authority of Russian writing culture as a whole.

Chapter Three

The Parting of the Ways: Chernyshevsky, Dostoevsky, and the Seeds of Russian Philosophical Discourse

> The moment you start narrating something, you stop being a philosopher.
>
> —Fyodor Dostoevsky, *The Idiot,* 1868

THE DECADES OF the 1840s and, even more, the 1850s saw the relegation of philosophy on the German model to a position of relatively little importance, first by the Slavophiles and Westernizers, and then by radical utilitarian Young Russia—Chernyshevsky, Pisarev, and Dobroliubov. The generation of the 1840s—Herzen, Turgenev, Kireevsky, and Khomiakov—used their critiques of German Idealism both to bring philosophical vocabulary and themes into the mainstream and to appoint received formal philosophical discourse to a subordinate position. All eventually made it clear that philosophy was less authentic and authoritative than other discourses—whether political journalism, fictional narrative, or a nascent theology. The radical utilitarians' discrediting of "philosophy"—now understood generally as a semi-poetic, metaphysical meditation that contributed nothing to the causes of hardcore, "scientific" knowledge or of social justice—is given a memorable, if travestied, treatment in Turgenev's novel, *Fathers and Sons* (1862). Philosophy still occupies a space, but it is no longer the central, vital space of the city and the small, secret circles of students on a moral quest. Here it is the quiet space of the garden built by Vasily Bazarov, the father of Turgenev's nihilist "new man," Evgeny Bazarov. The elder Bazarov not only loves to work in his garden "by the sweat of his brow" to improve nature but also loves to come at sunset to meditate. His philosophizing irritates his son Evgeny. Its only use, in Evgeny's view, is on the threshold of death when one needs a source of comfort. Evgeny implies that philosophical rhetoric and reasoning occupy time and energy that would be better used in concrete action aimed at destroying corrupt institutions and invidious customs and traditions. The language that enjoyed authority as the standard of "truth," as Evgeny sees it, is natural science, particularly biology, which he asserts to be true and effective in spurring social change.

If there is a single figure in whom Russia's original philosophical energy was distilled that radiated through the second half of the nineteenth century (in Russia) and the early and mid-twentieth centuries (first in Russia and then in Europe), it is certainly Fyodor Dostoevsky (1821–1881). A member of the generation of the 1840s, Dostoevsky was absent from intellectual circles for most of the 1850s. When he reemerged from his Siberian incarceration in the late 1850s, he had no intention of being seen as a "philosopher." What he did instead, particularly in *Notes from Underground*, was to shift the terms of discursive exchange, to open up the spaces between relatively closed discursive systems of the 1850s.

Before discussing Dostoevsky's vital contribution to the question of philosophy in Russian writing culture, it is important to have a fuller sense of the discursive ambience that he entered after his Siberian exile. By the 1860s Turgenev was only a minor participant in the process of defining, and giving a value to, philosophical discourse. The leader of Young Russia, who now played the central role in this ongoing process, was Nikolai Chernyshevsky (1828–1889). During his early career before his arrest and imprisonment in 1862, Chernyshevsky saw himself specifically as a philosopher. In his articles on the age of Gogol (1856) he plainly adored the philosophical environment that Stankevich and Belinsky had created.[1] He admired their efforts to lay the groundwork for a philosophical literature and implicitly took on the role of philosophical educator for the Russian reading public of his day. The chief goals of his early journalistic writing in *Sovremennik* (The contemporary) were to redefine the meaning of "philosophy" for the present day, to return it to the top of a new hierarchy of discourses, and, finally, to develop a Russian readership able and willing to read and talk about philosophical issues. In these goals he followed in the footsteps of the young Herzen.

The main impression we may have of Chernyshevsky is of a vehement foe of philosophical idealism. What remains in the shadows is that early on he was an enthusiastic champion of philosophy. Following his lifelong mentor, the Left Hegelian Ludwig Feuerbach, he insisted that philosophizing be based on the experience and observation of physical, material reality, which, in his view, was the only true reality.[2] For him philosophy became a power-

1. Nikolai Chernyshevskii, *Sochineniia*, 2 vols. (Moscow: ANSSSR, 1986–1987), 1:246, 272, 274. Hereafter cited in the text as *S2* with the relevant volume and page numbers.

2. See Irina Paperno, *Chernyshevsky and the Age of Realism: A Study in the Semiotics of Behavior* (Stanford: Stanford University Press, 1988), 66–67. Chernyshevsky kept diaries in which he meticulously recorded both his mental and physical experiences.

ful set of tools for theoretical conceptualization, essential for anyone working seriously in any kind of science or art. In Chernyshevsky's review of his own master's thesis, "The Aesthetic Relation of Art to Reality," written for *Sovremennik* under the pseudonym N. P., he offered a considerable critique of the idealist bases for the "sublime" and the "elevated" in art and nature. He rejected idealist philosophy as nothing but dreams and fantasy but endorsed "philosophy" per se as "science." He wrote: "Having acknowledged the weakness of fantasy that diverts us from reality, in its verdicts about the substantial value of various desires of a person, the new views are guided by facts represented in real life and human activity" (*S2*, 1:186).

Chernyshevsky saw his role as that of a philosopher rethinking and reconstructing the "general philosophical building" that had collapsed around the ears of the idealists (*S2*, 1:174). It is important to note that in at least two major review articles (like Belinsky, this was his chosen genre for bringing philosophy to his readers) he clearly placed himself in the context of a philosophical heritage. Although, Chernyshevsky wrote, the history of philosophy is filled with creative hostilities—he cited how Aristotle discredited his predecessor, Plato, and how Socrates disparaged *his* forerunners, the Sophists—there are philosophers who can bring about change even as they acknowledge their debts to their philosophical forebears. "There are," he wrote, "gratifying cases in which the founders of a new system clearly raise the connection of their opinions with the thoughts of their precursors. . . . [S]howing the insufficiency of their precursors' concepts, they also clearly articulate how much these concepts contributed to their own development" (*S2*, 1:186–187). Chernyshevsky clearly counted himself among this latter group: as his "reviewer" put it, "Mr. Chernyshevsky" took pains to show the links between his system and those of his predecessors.

For Chernyshevsky, following in the tracks of Feuerbach, philosophy was "an anthropological science" clearly linked to human, historical processes, and not to some notion of the absolute. In 1860 he wrote his clearest and most publicly resonant statement of his philosophical views, "The Anthropological Principle in Philosophy." Here anthropology was defined in this way: "a kind of science that, whatever part of the living human process it addresses, always remembers that this process and each part of it originates in the human organism, that this organism serves as material that produces the phenomena that [anthropology] examines, that the qualities of those phenomena are conditioned by the properties of the material, and the laws according to which those phenomena arise are special, specific instances of the actions of the laws of nature" (*S2*, 2:228). Contemporary, "cutting-edge" philosophy, Chernyshevsky believed, should be devoted to theorizing and understanding these human processes, and not to a hunt for absolute principles.

At this turning point Chernyshevsky bound philosophy to political action, thus answering Herzen's earlier criticism of philosophy. In "The Anthropological Principle" we see a parting of the ways in Russia between speculative philosophy and politically engaged thought. Chernyshevsky made it clear that philosophy was not just a set of theoretical and conceptual tools but something closer to what we would call ideology—that is, a politically interested system of values meant to promote the goals of a particular group in society. In his view, philosophy has never existed in a vacuum: it has always been connected to, and informed by, political views. "Every philosopher," he remarked, "has been the representative of some political party struggling in his time for predominance over society" (*S2*, 2:147). He reviewed all the German Idealists' political views and concluded: "Their philosophical systems are suffused through and through with the spirit of those political parties to which they themselves belonged. To say that it was different then from now; to say that only now philosophers have started to write their systems under the influence of their political convictions would be naïve in the extreme, and still more naïve would be to make this claim for thinkers specializing in the area of political philosophy" (*S2*, 2:148). The secret agenda of philosophy, Chernyshevsky implied, has been the authorization of some sort of political action. This view provides the turning point at which Chernyshevsky's thought moves rapidly from being speculative and theoretical in nature to being practical, didactic, and ideological, in short, oriented toward specific political and social goals. Still, for Chernyshevsky at this point in his life, philosophy still retains its own character apart from politics.

There is, of course, a problem with this particular critique of idealist philosophy. As we have seen, Chernyshevsky, in Feuerbachian fashion, called the quest for absolute principles merely dreams and fantasies, the very beauty and loftiness of which, by comparison, diminish the value of our imperfect human and natural "reality" here on earth. Chernyshevsky's discrediting of philosophical idealism is ironic. Eight years later, in 1863, the young radical—in his didactic novel *What Is to Be Done?*—would create the character of the liberated woman, Vera Pavlovna, who *dreams,* in one of her four famous dreams, of the utopian Crystal Palace. Moreover, one can certainly argue that Chernyshevsky's new philosophical grounding in "reality" is just as idealistic and absolutist in its own way as various Idealist projects before him had been. He claims a naïve view of reality as being simple and unquestionably true. "In real life," he believes, "everything is right [*verno*], there are no slips, none of that one-sided narrowness of view that bedevils everything people do" (*S2*, 1:167). For the young Chernyshevsky, although all human observation is necessarily flawed, there is an absolute reality that is absolutely true. In effect, Chernyshevsky is exchanging one absolute for another.

Despite his move to intertwine abstract, systematic thought with political interests, Chernyshevsky continued to use the word *philosophy* and to award it, as he defined it, with a leading social and intellectual role to play in civil society. For him, philosophy as a discourse is positioned high on the hierarchy of discourses because it has a general truth-value that is absent in other intellectual activity, whether art or science. In the best of all possible worlds, it indeed informs and molds other intellectual and creative human endeavors. Philosophy is the guide for both literary art, which Cherny- shevsky viewed as the most worthwhile art by far, and for all the sciences, from economics to history to chemistry.

Chernyshevsky is infamous for having subordinated art to "reality." In his view, art is a relatively poor "reconstruction" of reality—material being is rich in variety and detail, and is accessible to the five senses. It is impor- tant to note that Chernyshevsky does not see art as passive "imitation" but rather as an active "reconstruction," "*vosproizvedenie*" (*S2*, 1:156). Cherny- shevsky tore down the pedestal on which romantic theory had placed art as a medium for experiencing the "sublime." From his earliest writing in his master's thesis he also saw literary art as the handmaiden of philosophy—in this he was almost in complete agreement with Aristotle and, to a lesser de- gree, with Plato (*S2*, 1:166–170). In "The Aesthetic Relation of Art to Real- ity" he claimed that a poet worth his salt should not be so concerned with creating the sublime as with "conveying to us his thoughts, views, feelings" (*S2*, 1:122). In this sense, literary art is a form of generalization, a kind of lesser philosophizing. As he put it, art has the "strength of generalization" and the "strength of commentary" (*S2*, 1:153). Later, he made the same point more directly: "If a person, in whom intellectual activity is strongly stimulated by questions arising from observation of life, has an artistic gift, then in his works, consciously or not, he will express a living judgment on phenomena that interest him (and his contemporaries)" (*S2*, 1:163). Chernyshevsky admired this kind of writer who "becomes a thinker and [whose] work of art, while it remains in the realm of art, acquires a scientific meaning" (*S2*, 1:166). It should be noted that here "scientific" still means "philosophical" or "theoretical."

In Chernyshevsky's early discursive hierarchy, although he valued "po- etry" for its power to convey knowledge and information, he modeled his concept of literary art on the sciences. He admired the sciences because the knowledge they produce makes no claim to being "above life" but is firmly rooted in the materials of earthly life (*S2*, 1:170). At their best, these kinds of writing—scientific description as well as literary narration—are a "'Hand- book' for people beginning to study life" whose role is "to prepare one for reading sources [in nature] and then from time to time to answer inquiries" (*S2*, 1:167).

During this period Chernyshevsky placed philosophy higher than any individual science, indeed appointing it the science of sciences. Philosophy provides that essential part of a scientific education that makes a scientist able to formulate theory and to interpret what is being observed. For example, even in 1860, in his article "Capital and Labor," Chernyshevsky railed against economists' "philosophical helplessness." These specialists have no conceptual framework that allows them to draw conclusions from their individual research (S2, 2:18). Indeed, Chernyshevsky was one of the few Russians to call publicly for a real philosophical education that would raise the level of theoretical articulation (S2, 2:52).

This remark brings us to our final point about Chernyshevsky and his importance for the debate about philosophical culture in Russia—the question of a philosophical readership. In brief, Chernyshevsky used all his critical and journalistic powers to create excitement about philosophy. In a review article from 1860 he ranted against the Kiev University professor Orest Novitsky for teaching philosophical ideas in such a manner as to turn students away from the study of philosophy. Similarly, in his sixth article on the age of Gogol, he argued that, although philosophers have the duty to "explain reality," what passed in the late 1850s for philosophy, in his view, failed to explain anything and only served to stir a "general mistrust" of philosophy (S2, 1:277 n.). For Chernyshevsky, philosophy bore the momentous burden of forming people into "genuine, useful members of society" (S2, 1:277 n.). And he was clearly on the lookout for just such a popularizer, a writer who could bring a philosophical perspective and sensibility to Russian readers.

Like Herzen more than a decade before, Chernyshevsky sought various models from European cultures that would show how first a literary education, and then a philosophical one, could create a "historical," self-aware citizenry. In his 1856 article, "Lessing: His Time, His Life and Works," he described Gottfried Lessing as the single German writer who helped to form a reading public with a taste for philosophical thought. Although none of the great Idealists could be said to have their roots in Lessing's work, Lessing did a great deal for what might be called the "sociology" of philosophy: he helped to mold readers who could grasp philosophical concepts. Lessing, as Chernyshevsky put it,

> prepared the minds of his people to receive philosophical thought. Before his time philosophy was a matter for the academy, shunned by society as something not only mysterious but horrifying as well—and as soon as philosophical thought penetrated beyond the narrow circle of regular scholars to the education of the public, it was rejected [by readers] as something opposed to all their convictions and the conditions of their life. But twenty years later the philosophies of Fichte and then Schelling were not viewed that way; on the contrary, society welcomed philosophical doctrines with vibrant sympa-

thy; these doctrines spread rapidly among the public and became part of their convictions. (S2, 1:366)

In his review article of Novitsky's history of religion and philosophy in the ancient East, Chernyshevsky again devoted pages to the process of the public reception of new philosophies. In his opinion a lag time was necessary between the first formulation of those ideas and their acceptance among educated readers. For example, he remarked that France had the most advanced and capable readers: soon, Chernyshevsky asserted, "every Frenchman and Frenchwoman will be a reader" and will "be shaped by the works of first-class people in science and poetry" (S2, 2:234). With this claim he implied that such writers as Novitsky, who knew only how to kill their subject, hindered this same process in Russia.

During the 1850s Chernyshevsky was one of a small number of younger intellectuals to reintroduce the question of philosophy into the public domain; primarily it was the generation of the 1840s who had been the champions of philosophy but who had then become disillusioned with it in ways that stirred the development of new cultural discourses. In his 1856 articles on the age of Gogol, Chernyshevsky expressed deep regret at the loss of interest in philosophical themes in literature: "Philosophical strivings are now almost forgotten in our literature and criticism. We do not want to judge how much literature and criticism have gained from this forgetfulness—it seems, nothing at all—and we have lost a great deal" (S2, 1:274).

Possibly Chernyshevsky saw himself in the role of literary-philosophical popularizer. Although it cannot be claimed that "philosophy" was an authoritative discourse in his influential novel, *What Is to Be Done?*, the notion of the philosophical reader does emerge at crucial points, and (French) philosophy is highlighted for its ability to teach and stimulate social change. For example, in Vera Pavlovna's fourth dream in which she sees the Crystal Palace, the voice that speaks to her knows Rousseau's *Nouvelle Heloise* and welcomes its notion of gender equality.[3] Even as late as 1876, in his didactic letters to his children, Chernyshevsky continued to see philosophy as a key to a complete "general, scientific education," so that specialists would argue intelligently and not "philosophize all over the block" (S2, 2:379).

By the time of his arrest in 1862 Chernyshevsky was no longer a philosophically minded literary critic and an opponent of philosophical idealism, redefining philosophy as an intellectual discipline enabling scientists and writers to theorize. He had become a didactic political journalist determined to make politically and socially conscious citizens of his readers. It is at this point that Dostoevsky resurfaced in Russian public life. He was to re-

3. Nikolai Chernyshevsky, *What Is to Be Done?* trans. N. Dole and S. Skidelsky, with an introduction by K. Feuer (Ann Arbor, Mich.: Ardis, 1986), 373.

shape the discursive dispute in such a way that "philosophy" emerged as a kind of argument about language, genre, and truth. Although Dostoevsky was not the literary popularizer of philosophy Chernyshevsky had hoped for—one who would use his art to mold readers into conscious citizens—he was, far more than Turgenev, the writer who brought serious ethical and metaphysical issues to Russian readers and taught them to think, talk, and write in a new and quite Russian philosophical language.

Coming from his Siberian incarceration and exile in the late 1850s, Dostoevsky confronted new "young Russian" ideological language with his own potent new discourse that drew on poetic, psychological, and religious vocabularies. It is important to note that at no time in his thirty-five-year literary career did Dostoevsky actually identify himself as anything resembling a "philosopher." What is more, he only rarely used the term *philosophy*.[4] Nonetheless, although throughout Dostoevsky's work the language of reason and systematic thinking (particularly as it relates to "science") was secondary to the psychological language of subliminal desire—as has been repeatedly shown in critical commentary—we find here a strong, if sometimes disguised, use of speculative, reasoned argument.[5] And if, as Dostoevsky allegedly quipped, Russian writers of the 1860s and 1870s "came out from Gogol's 'Overcoat,'" then we can say that some of the major, uniquely Russian philosophical discourses of the early twentieth century came largely "out of Dostoevsky's *Underground.*" This contention alone

4. A survey of the use in Dostoevsky's literary works of words with the stem "*filosof-*," for example, *filosofiia* (philosophy), *filosofstvovat'* (philosophize), *filosofski* (philosophically), *zafilosofstvovat'sia* (philosophize too long), *pofilosofstvovat'* (philosophize a little), and so forth, shows fewer than one hundred uses throughout his entire fictional opus. The largest number was found in *The Brothers Karamazov* (twenty) and *The Idiot* (thirteen). Indeed, in *Notes from Underground* the root appears only once: *zafilosofstvovalsia* (I've philosophized too long). I am grateful to the makers of "The Dostoevsky Concordance," http://netra.karelia.ru/Dostoevsky/ and to James Scanlan for bringing this wonderful tool to my attention.

5. See James Scanlan, "The Case against Rational Egoism," in idem, *Dostoevsky the Thinker* (Ithaca, N.Y.: Cornell University Press, 2002), 57–80. Aside from the studies written by Russian philosophers of the Renaissance era, discussed in later chapters of this volume, among the best treatments of Dostoevsky as a philosophical writer are André Gide, *Dostoevsky* (Paris: Plon-Nourritet Cie, 1923); Iakov Golosovker, *Dostoevsky i Kant* (Moscow: Izdatel'stvo Akademii nauk, 1963), an unusually bold speculative essay for the Soviet times in which it was written; Joseph Frank, *Dostoevsky*, 5 vols. (Princeton, N.J.: Princeton University Press, 1976–2002); Louis J. Shein, "Kantian Elements in Dostoevsky's Ethics," *Western Philosophical Systems in Russian Literature*, ed. A. M. Mlikotin (Los Angeles: University of Southern California Press, 1979), 59–69; and V. E. Vetlovskaia, *Poetika romana "Brat'tia Karamazovy"* (Leningrad: Nauka, 1977). Recently two other valuable studies have appeared: Liza Knapp, *The Annihilation of Inertia: Dostoevsky and Metaphysics* (Evanston, Ill.: Northwestern University Press, 1996); and Marina Kostelevsky, *Dostoevsky and Solovyov: The Art of Integral Vision* (New Haven: Yale University Press, 1997).

makes it essential to rehearse the confrontation between discourses in Dostoevsky's formative work of the early and mid-1860s that paved the way for the great philosophical novels. We focus here on the pivotal work from Dostoevsky's early post-Siberian years, *Notes from Underground* (1864). This work is notoriously ambiguous in its genre and type of discourse, and this ambiguity bears within it a deep dispute about the relative truth-value of various genres and discourses. Indeed, here we find a signal expression of that combativeness which would become the hallmark of Dostoevsky's post-Siberian writing. What is intimated particularly in *Notes from Underground*, without being named as such, is a new kind of language use. In the philosophical world it would be Dostoevsky's Russian devotees (Rozanov, Shestov, and Berdiaev) and later European and American admirers (Gide, Camus, and Kaufmann) who would claim it as "philosophy."

Russian writing culture of the mid-nineteenth century, as we have seen, was unusual for the aggressive debate about the truth-value of various types of discourse and the ease with which writers shifted between genres. In both his essays and his fiction Dostoevsky took this general attitude to an extreme. Discursive debate was at the heart of all his work. "Poetry" versus "science" defined the terms of discursive competition in Dostoevsky's fiction, as in many works by or about young Russia of the 1860s. "Philosophy" itself remained relatively unimportant.

Although Dostoevsky treated a number of famous metaphysical and moral issues innovatively, he was very distant from identifying with "philosophy" or even talking or knowing much about established philosophy or individual philosophers. As his erstwhile friend and colleague of the post-Siberian period, the conservative thinker Nikolai Strakhov, commented in his memoirs: "Fyodor Mikhailovich loved these [most abstract] questions, about the essence of things and the limits of knowledge, and I remember how amused he was when I compared his judgments to various views of philosophers whom we know from the history of philosophy. It was becoming clear that it was difficult to think up new ideas, and he took humorous comfort in the thought that his ideas matched those of one or another of the great [philosophers]."[6] Although Dostoevsky did not view himself as a philosopher of any kind, one can better appreciate the meaning philosophy as a concept had for him by examining the ways he used the term *philosophy* in his nonfiction writing. The first mention of philosophy came in a letter of October 31, 1838, that Dostoevsky wrote to his brother, Mikhail. Here he repeated a somewhat vulgarized Schellingian view. He saw mind as a faculty secondary to and weaker than the psyche and spirit: "Thought is born in

---

6. N. N. Strakhov, "Vospominaniia o F. M. Dostoevskom," in *Biografiia, pis'ma i zapisnye knizhki F. M. Dostoevskogo* (St. Petersburg: Suvorin, 1883), 225.

the psyche. The mind is a tool, a machine, driven by the soul's fire."[7] This orientation would remain with Dostoevsky throughout his literary career. In the same letter he insisted on a generally Schellingian high estimation of the powers of poetic language and the close relationship between poetry and philosophy:

> I won't begin to argue with you but I will say that I don't agree with your opinion about poetry and philosophy. . . . You can't posit philosophy as a simple mathematical problem where the unknown quantity is nature. . . . Note that since a poet in the flight of inspiration can decipher God, therefore he fulfills the purpose of philosophy. Therefore poetic ecstasy is philosophical ecstasy. . . . Therefore philosophy is that very poetry, just at a higher level! . . . It is strange that you think in terms of current philosophy. How many useless systems have been born in intelligent, fervent heads. (*PSS*30, 28/1:54).

Dostoevsky, in Schellingian form, was already arguing here against the notion of philosophy as something allied with mathematics and logic, and for the notion of philosophy as a higher form of poetry. Philosophy, like poetry, is metaphysical decoding. The only difference is that philosophy may be higher and more "powerful." It is important to note Dostoevsky's significant distortion of Schelling's view of poetry and philosophy. For Schelling, poetry is elevated by its proximity to philosophy, whereas, in Dostoevsky's view, philosophy is undoubtedly improved by its similarity to literary art. In his own work, of course, he would be true to this opinion: "poetry," that is, fictional narrative and figurative language, would take the upper hand and limit the authority of philosophy. Clearly, in Dostoevsky's mind, poetry was the more powerful of the two.

During his exile in Omsk Dostoevsky expressed a desire to read German Idealist philosophy, apparently for the first time. He wrote to his brother, Mikhail, early in 1854, asking that he send him the writings of the physiologist Karl Gustav Carus (who was also interested in Schelling),[8] Kant's *Critique of Pure Reason*, and, "if you are somehow in a position to send it along with someone, then without fail send me Hegel, especially Hegel's *History of Philosophy.*" He wrote, "My whole future is tied to this" (*PSS*30, 28/1: 173). Strakhov noted, however, that although Dostoevsky indeed had

---

7. Fyodor Dostoevskii, *Polnoe sobranie sochinenii*, 30 vols. (Leningrad: Nauka, 1972–1990), 28/1:54. Note that some volumes of this work have subvolumes; hence these are designated, for example, as 28/1 or 28/2. Hereafter cited in the text as *PSS*30 with the relevant volume and page numbers.

8. Although critics traditionally have thought that Dostoevsky was asking for the Koran, Joseph Frank makes clear that he had in mind the French physiologist Karl Gustav Carus. See Frank, *Dostoevsky*, 2:169. For more information on Carus and Schelling, see Frederick Copleston, *A History of Philosophy*, 8 vols. (New York: Image Books, 1965), 7:1, 179.

Hegel's volume, he never read it. Dostoevsky presented the book to Strakhov as a gift soon after the two met in 1860.[9] Strakhov remarked, moreover, that even in the 1860s the Dostoevskys and their circles of friends were much more interested in French social thought, whereas Strakhov was more inclined toward the German Idealist tradition.

By contrast, Dostoevsky's move toward religious discourse, around the same time as he asked his brother for the philosophical texts, was a great deal stronger and more decisive than his interest in philosophy, and it would shape the uses to which he put philosophical discourse in his later works.[10] Speculative philosophical systems never competed in Dostoevsky's mind with religious dramas of revelation, miracle, and resurrection. Already in his famous letter of early 1854 to N. D. Fonvizina, the wife of the Decembrist, he was constructing what he called his own personal "creed." He admitted that he had been a "child of the age, a child of unfaith and doubt until now and even (I know this) to the moment of my death" (PSS30, 28/1:176). He had experienced a "thirst for faith" which "[grew] all the stronger in my soul the more proofs to the contrary I have in myself" (PSS30, 28/1:176). In his more tranquil moments, Dostoevsky claimed that he had "constructed in [him]self a creed in which everything is clear and sacred" (PSS30, 28/1:176). This creed was, of course, the figure of Christ of whom Dostoevsky intended "to believe that there is nothing more sublime, profound, attractive, reasonable [razumnee], more manly and perfect . . . and that not only is this so, but with fervent love I say to myself that there cannot be [anything better]" (PSS30, 28/1:176).

In the 1860s Dostoevsky's rhetorical efforts were concerned with the defense of "literature" against the onslaught of the radical utilitarians who valued the natural sciences far above literary art. In a letter to Turgenev of October 6, 1863, a few months before writing Notes from Underground, Dostoevsky discussed his plans for his and his brother's journal, Vremia, which he wanted to make "more contemporary, more interesting, and at the same time to respect literature—these are goals which are irreconcilable according to the convictions of many Petersburg thinkers" (PSS30, 28/2:54). He insisted: "We are determined hotly to contest the attitude of dismissal toward literature that is starting [to spread]" (PSS30, 28/2:54). It is worth

---

9. Strakhov, "Vospominaniia o F. M. Dostoevskom," 172–173. See also Linda Gerstein, Nikolai Strakhov: Philosopher, Man of Letters, Social Critic (Cambridge, Mass.: Harvard University Press, 1971), 20–21, 37–60.

10. For more on this fusion of philosophical and religious concerns in Dostoevsky's later works, see E. Clowes, "Self-Laceration and Resentment: The Terms of Moral Psychology in Dostoevsky and Nietzsche," in idem, Freedom and Responsibility in Russian Literature, ed. E. C. Allen and G. S. Morson (Evanston, Ill.: Northwestern University Press, 1995), 119–133.

noting, in addition, that in his letters to Turgenev, who was well read in German Idealism, there was no mention of "philosophy."

"Science," which now usually meant "natural science," was the discourse that fully occupied Dostoevsky's attention by April 1866. Just as he was publishing *Crime and Punishment*, he vehemently attacked the utopian faith of "socialism," moral and political nihilism, and academic natural "science," the last of which, he argued, was not in a position to exert a positive *moral* influence on society. In the spring of 1866 he wrote to the conservative essayist and editor M. N. Katkov:

> All nihilists are socialists. Socialism (and particularly its Russian variant) demands precisely the severance of all ties. They are indeed perfectly sure that they will build paradise right away on a tabula rasa. After all, Fourier was sure that all one had to do was build one phalanstery, and then all the world would immediately be covered with phalansteries; those are his words. And our Chernyshevsky liked to say that all he needed was to talk to the people for a quarter of an hour and he would immediately be able to convert them to socialism. Among our own poor, defenseless Russian boys and girls there is still an eternally present *basic* point on which socialism will be able to build for a long time yet, and that is purity of heart and enthusiasm for the good. There are endless numbers of frauds and wretches among them. But all these little school and university students, of whom I have seen a great number, have so purely and wholeheartedly converted to nihilism in the name of honor, truth [*pravda*], and true usefulness! Indeed, they are defenseless against these absurdities and accept them as perfection. Sensible science [*zdravaia nauka*], it stands to reason, will root out everything [bad]. But when will that be? . . . And, finally, sensible science, even if it does take root, will not be able to pull out the weeds because sensible science is still only science, and not a direct form of civil and public action. (*PSS*30, 28/2:154)

It is in response to contemporary political discourses built on systematizing theories and fervent belief in science that Dostoevsky developed his own discourse from a combination of psychological-religious metaphor, emotionally charged description, and logical argumentation. This discourse, in turn, would help to spur the rich experiment in speculative language that we find in many of Dostoevsky's post-Siberian novels.

It was in his relationship to N. N. Strakhov that Dostoevsky expressed whatever interest in philosophy he may have had, however sparse. In a letter of May 28, 1870, Dostoevsky wrote that he valued Strakhov precisely as a philosophical critic surrounded by critics motivated by radical political theories. "If your criticisms were not available right now," Dostoevsky wrote, "there would be absolutely *nobody* in our whole literary life who would take criticism as a serious and strictly necessary business. There would be no one among the active critics who would at all value the need (and the respect) for a correct philosophical conceptualization of current and past affairs" (*PSS*30, 29/1:124). Later in this same letter Dostoevsky famously professed that "I am a bit weak [*shvakhovat*] in philosophy (although not in my love for it; in love for it I am strong)" (*PSS*30, 29/1:125). It is interesting that Dostoevsky evaluated himself by using the German word for "weak," *schwach,* with a Russian suffix attached to it—showing possibly that he (like Turgenev before him) innately felt philosophy to be something foreign and particularly German. It is also possible that here Dostoevsky, who often preferred French writers and thinkers to German ones, expressed such warmth for philosophical thought in consideration of the tastes of his correspondent, Strakhov, who had professed himself to be a philosophizing critic at least since the 1840s when he participated in circles devoted to studying Hegel and Goethe.

Despite the near paucity of traditional philosophy and philosophical discourse in his personal letters, Dostoevsky did mention philosophy in his notebooks from April 1864 in an interesting and significant context, just at the time of the death of his first wife, Maria Dmitrievna. In that entry he contrasted philosophical materialism, so popular among the younger generation, with "genuine philosophy." "The doctrine of the materialists," he wrote, "is general inertia and the mechanism of matter—which means death. The doctrine of true philosophy is the destruction of inertia—that is, thought—that is, the center and synthesis of the universe and its external form, matter—that is, God—that is, everlasting life" (*PSS*30, 20:175). Here Dostoevsky made clear that real philosophy is closely tied to religion: it frames earthly, material life and makes metaphysical sense of it—indeed mystical sense as well. In contrast, "science," according to Dostoevsky, is correct and reliable, but only as far as it goes: "The confusion and vagueness of our current concepts occur for the simplest reasons: partly because the correct study of nature started quite recently (Descartes and Bacon), and because we have so far collected extremely few facts to be able to draw any conclusions from them at all. Meanwhile, we hasten to draw those conclusions, obeying our law of development" (*PSS*30, 20:175).

In this famous four-page entry Dostoevsky's philosophical meditation was aimed at "destroying inertia" and proving that Maria Dmitrievna's death will not mean the end of their relationship. He tried to make a rational argument to prove to himself that there is life after death and that he would indeed see Maria Dmitrievna again. He built an argument resting on three paradoxes and contradictions, now showing the penchant that marks his later novels for exploring the contradictory terms of a paradox as a way of unfolding deeper truths.

The first is the contradiction between ideal Christian love and the real demands of the human ego. Dostoevsky remarked: "To love another person as oneself, according to Christ's commandment, is impossible. The ego stands in the way" (*PSS*30, 20:172). Second is the paradox that achieving highest selfhood means destroying the individual self. Christ as *the* human ideal embodies the paradox that the highest development of self (*lichnost'*) is to destroy that self by devoting it to all and to every person "wholeheart-edly and without discrimination" (*PSS*30, 20:172). Third, Dostoevsky ap-plied this paradox to all Christian society. Christ's "paradise" means the "mutual destruction" of each and every self, each for the sake of the other: "the law of the ego [*ia*] fuses with the law of humanism, and in this fusion both the ego and everyone . . . mutually destroyed one for the other, also achieve the highest goal of its own individual development, each in a dis-tinctive way. That is Christ's paradise" (*PSS*30, 20:172).

Dostoevsky used these observations to conclude that there must be life after death. Since to achieve Christ's paradise would mean the end of human existence, it cannot be achieved here on earth in the course of this life. Thus, during this lifetime, people can only strive toward Christian communality, sacrificing their egos for the good of other people. "A person on earth," Dostoevsky observed, "is only a developing creature, and is there-fore not finished but transitional" (*PSS*30, 20:173). This characterization of possible earthly goals implies that there must be some end goal, which can-not be reached in this life. Thus there must be a next life in which that end goal can be reached. Since the moral goal of true Christlike love would mean the destruction of human life, as we know it, Dostoevsky argued that this goal must belong to a posthumous life, that "therefore there is a future, paradisal life" (*PSS*30, 20:173). To the distraught Dostoevsky searching for some hope, this logic suggested the possibility that there is life after death.

In conclusion, Dostoevsky implied that "true philosophy" must go be-yond the merely scientific concern with material observation and descrip-tion and with logical argument free of contradiction. It must strive to make sense of all human experience, including the experience of death and the deep opposition between human nature and what people understand to be divine nature. Like Nietzsche, whom he anticipated, Dostoevsky grappled with paradox. Here at the seams of a logical argument is where deeper truth can be apprehended.

These notebook pages cannot be deemed any clear philosophical result or conclusion. They are, however, a preview of that exciting and tragic Dos-toevskian process we so often see in his later novels, a speaking voice on the edge of life and death, suffering at the absurdity of existence and trying to work philosophically toward some meaning, some endurable solution. Al-though the notebook entry in itself is not powerful philosophy, it is a force-ful witness to the need in any philosophy to "think beyond the box" of naïve materialism and to deal with human experience in its least conscious, least reasoned outposts.

In his prose from this period Dostoevsky drew greater attention to the limits of systematic thinking and logical language from *within* a materialist worldview. In *Notes from the House of the Dead* (1860) we find a first, brief consideration of the relative truth-value of personal narrative and impersonal, categorizing, scientific description. In *Notes from Underground* this beginning will develop into a full-fledged critique of both scientific discourse and poetic language. In the second half of *Notes from the House of the Dead* the narrator, Gorianchikov, attempts to categorize types of prisoners and to make generalizations about the Russian character. He soon becomes frustrated with this approach, concluding that abstract, categorizing thinking takes him further away from "reality" and "truth." He asks, "Here I am trying to put our whole jail into categories—but is that possible? Reality is endlessly variegated by comparison with all abstract thought, even its cleverest conclusions, and it does not bear sharp, strong distinctions. Reality strives toward fragmentation. We had our own particular life, however it may have been, and it was not just the official one, but an inner life of our own" (*PSS*30, 4:197). It is the stories of and about the individual inmates that give the truest picture of them as human beings, each with a particular spirit.

In *Notes from Underground* this criticism would be sharpened. In both of these works Dostoevsky chose the free form of "notes" that was popular in the 1850s. But in *Notes from Underground* he used discursive dispute to arrive at a kind of language use that was fresh and, so Dostoevsky believed, at least closer to being "true." On April 2, 1864, he wrote to his brother, Mikhail, about the new kind of work he was writing: "I don't know what will come of it; perhaps it will be trash, but personally I place great hopes on it. It will be a strong and frank piece; it will be truth. Although it may be poor, I dare say, still it will have an impact. I am sure. But perhaps it will come out very fine" (*PSS*30, 28/2:75).[11]

Notes from Underground is unique in Dostoevsky's opus in the sense that it is built in two parts from two very different genres. One is a kind of "anti-scientific" essay that challenges rational and aesthetic constructs by placing them in the context of subliminal desires made hyperconscious. The other part is a narrated confession. The rhetorical style that Dostoevsky finds so much more truthful than the "scientific" cant of his opponents, Chernyshevsky and the materialists, relies on a familiar mixture of paradox, contradiction, and metaphor. Paradox—for example, that pain often is pleasure—

11. Cited in Robert Louis Jackson, *The Underground Man in Russian Literature* (The Hague: Mouton, 1958), 20.

is the hallmark of this work. The same is true for the multiple contradictions that create the capricious tone, especially of the first chapters of part 1. Dostoevsky's own trademark theme of "*nadryv*"—or moral-emotional laceration, the opposition between cherished ideal values and their enactment in real life—presents the central theme binding together the two wholly different pieces of the work.

In part 1 the underground man presents a living Feuerbachian-Chernyshevskian critique of the Schillerian ideal of his youth, the "sublime" and "elevated."[12] He writes: "The more I was aware of the good and all the 'sublime and lofty,' the deeper I sank into my slime and the more capable I was of finally bogging down in it" (*PSS*30, 5:102). High, absolute ideals that place art or an idealized dream above real life, as Feuerbach, Chernyshevsky, and the underground man would agree, do nothing more than to make one aware of the degradation of actual life.[13]

The commentary on *Notes from Underground* has not remarked on the extent to which the underground man *does* use philosophical vocabulary, for example, primary cause (*pervonachal'naia prichina*), secondary cause (*vtorostepennaia prichina*), and ground (*osnovanie*), only to parody it, of course, and show its ineffectuality. First, he criticizes the stupidity of the men of action who "as a result of their limited natures accept the most proximal and secondary causes as primary causes, and thus convince themselves more quickly and easily than other people that they have found the incontrovertible ground of their activity" (*PSS*30, 5:108). The underground man contrasts this mentality to his own which, try as he might to define and accept a primary cause, is given to continual interrogation and disbelief: "And how can I, for example, calm myself? Where are my primary causes on which to lean, where are my grounds? Where can I get them? I practice thinking, and therefore my every primary cause immediately drags along with it another cause, still more primary, and so it goes into infinity. That is the essence of all consciousness and thinking" (*PSS*30, 5:108). The underground man thus creates of the reasoning process a philosophical "mise en abîme" in which one cause contains within it another cause which contains within it yet another—and so on endlessly. There *is* no ground. Although Lev Shestov would invent the concept of "groundlessness" (*bespochvennost'*), the underground man is the first philosophically groundless figure in Russian writing culture.

What the underground man achieves in undermining post-Kantian

---

12. Scanlan, "The Case against Rational Egoism," 552–556.

13. While I agree with James Scanlan that the underground man is, in Scanlan's terms, an "egoist" and not a Chernyshevskian "rational egoist," he does use Chernyshevskian terms to discredit an earlier system of values, the Schillerian "lofty and sublime." See Scanlan, *Dostoevsky the Thinker*, 60–67.

metaphysics, he also achieves with ethics. The underground man ironically finds the ground for "justice" to be the feeling of revenge, that is, the willingness to answer one bad act with another because one has convinced oneself that this answer is "just": "It is said that a person avenges himself because he finds justice in it" (*PSS*30, 5:108). The underground man is more frank and clear-sighted in examining his own motivations: the only reasons he can see for "taking revenge" are his own feelings of malice and anger. He is too honest to insist that any lasting principle can be found in these feelings. Thus he cannot project his bad feeling onto anyone else. He cannot justify his feelings and is left confronting himself at his ugliest moments:

> If I start to avenge myself, I do it only out of malice. Malice, of course, might overpower everything, all my doubts, and, perhaps, might serve quite successfully in the place of a primary cause just because it is no cause at all. But what can I do if I don't even have any malice (which is where I started a long time ago). My nastiness submits once again to chemical dissolution as a result of those damned laws of consciousness. Before your very eyes the object [of malice] evaporates, reasons disappear, the guilty party isn't found, insult is no longer insult but fate, something like a toothache, of which no one is guilty. (*PSS*30, 5:108–109)

The underground man, taught by prevalent thinking to view himself as an agglomeration of physiological mechanisms and sensations, nevertheless finds the chink in the armor of contemporary ethics. If ethical systems are based ultimately on nothing but feeling, and feelings are temporary epiphenomena of physical processes, then they emerge and melt away again according to physical laws. No ethical ground exists.

Finally, the underground man attacks the mathematical bases of contemporary "knowledge." Mathematics was the standard of logical rigor to which Kant wished to hold himself in his philosophizing. Now the underground man's anti-philosophizing makes of mathematical statements—most infamously "two times two equals four"—the stone wall that shuts out "nonrational" human nature with its "*khotenie*," its desire. Of course, the underground man's anti-philosophizing is grounded in the assertion that desire is much more important and necessary for life than reason is. In its ideologized form mathematical reason tries to discredit feeling, imagination, will, and desire. In his well-known anticipation of dystopian attitudes, the underground man fears that "if sometime they really find the formula for all our desires [*khotenie*] and fancies, that is, what they depend on, what the laws of their origin are, how they spread, to what they are striving in one or another case, etc., etc., that is a real mathematical formula—then at that moment people will probably immediately stop desiring [*khotet'*]" (*PSS*30,

5:114).[14] Thus mathematical reasoning, when it is applied to an analysis of human nature, becomes the enemy of human nature. The underground man is glad to embrace life, as dirty as it is, over the "extraction of the square root" (PSS30, 5:115). He is sure that "consciousness, for example, is infinitely more lofty than two times two" (PSS30, 5:119).

The underground man summarizes his moral-psychological predicament as follows:

> As if this sort of stone wall really meant peace and quiet only because it is two times two is four. Oh, absurdity of absurdities! How much better to understand everything, be aware of everything, all impossibilities and stone walls; to be reconciled with not one of these impossibilities and stone walls if it revolts you to be reconciled; to reach by way of the most unavoidable logical constructions to the most repulsive conclusions on the eternal topic—that you are as if guilty of the stone wall, although again it is clear as day that you are not guilty and, as a result, silent and helplessly gritting your teeth, to stagnate voluptuously in inertia, dreaming of the fact that you don't even have anyone to get angry with; you can't find an object for your anger and perhaps none will be found, that here everything is a cheat, a sleight of hand, deception, everything is simply slops—you don't know what is what or who is who, but despite all these impossibilities and deceptions, something hurts and the less you know, the more it hurts! (PSS30, 5:106)

It is this metaphysical, moral, and epistemological prison, in which ironically one can ascertain no hard reality other than one's own desires, that makes the underground man turn against himself and gnaw at himself. Through this voluptuous self-destruction he works toward a different kind of philosophy that takes into account another kind of intellectual, psychological, and spiritual horizon.

Having criticized and circumscribed reason and its discourses, the underground man launches a critique of narrative fiction and literary language. Of course, he asserts the need for narrative. The underground man is a

14. It is worth noting that, although "*khotet'*" and "*khotenie*" are typically translated as "to will" and "will," or "willing," "*khotenie*" can be construed as both "wanting" or "desiring." To translate it as "will" gives the underground man, to my mind, a cast too close to Schopenhauer, although the word usually used to translate Schopenhauer's "will to live" is "*volia*." The difference between Schopenhauer's view and this one lies in the underground man's high valuation of desire as the basis for human striving.

In his emphasis on psychology of thought, Dostoevsky would seem to take a leaf from Schopenhauer's psycho-philosophical arguments about the "will to live" and the strength of pain as a positively existing feeling over pleasure, the absence of pain. Whether he does or not, he devises his own vocabulary of desire that is much more positively evaluated than Schopenhauer's concept of will. Moreover, he rejects the asceticism implicit in Schopenhauer's denial of earthly life and human nature, choosing instead to support and affirm the messy affair of life.

talker who loves to talk about himself. Despite this predilection, he perceives himself as having nothing to "tell" about himself. As Michael Holquist has pointed out, the underground man is a person in search of a story about himself.[15] The underground man says, "Just watch yourself better and you'll understand that that's the way it works. I made up whole adventures for myself and invented a life, just in order somehow to live a little. . . . Another time I even tried to make myself fall in love" (*PSS*30, 5:108).

Although the underground man senses that everyone needs a narrative of self in order to "be" a self, the bad side of the coin is that to one degree or another this narrative of self will always be fabricated. It is not "true." In the case of the underground man, everything he says and purportedly does is fantasy. He admits that many of his words come from books, from fiction. He claims that, although he has been listening to his rationalist, materialist opponents for years and knows their thoughts and words intimately, he "invented" their words in part 1. For this underground man—who is really a fabricated voice of a human subconscious—there is only one reliable, solid ground of "self," and that is his strong sense of self-contempt. Even that is influenced by fictions—exacerbated by years of *nadryv*, of comparing himself to hopelessly high, impossibly superhuman ideals. Everything else is built on the quicksand of moods, shifting plots, imagined relationships, and fabricated systems of value. In the end, he tries to force all these factors to submit to his arbitrary will.

The trouble with literary fiction is that it seems to be inauthentic and improbable, even to the underground man who loves fantasy and sees most forms of rational discourse as either untrue or, if true—as in the case of mathematics and the natural sciences—then wrongly applied to dealing with the human condition. As a child, the underground man read in order to escape his own ugly feelings. Literature seemed to provide a standard of what was "decent" and "correct," and, in this sense, "right" and "real" (*PSS*30, 5:128). Later, when the adult, fully conscious underground man is insulted by an officer, he turns for help to behavior as it is codified in fiction: "The devil knows what I would have given for a real, more correct argument, more decent, more, as it were, literary! I had been treated [by the officer] like a fly" (*PSS*30, 5:128). Although the underground man's sense of honor comes straight from French novels, he realizes that the rest of the world does not share that particular set of values. Most people hold literary diction to be inauthentic. At the bar where the incident with the officer happens, the underground man knows that everyone around would laugh

---

15. Michael Holquist, *Dostoevsky and the Novel* (1977; rpt. Evanston, Ill.: Northwestern University Press, 1986), 54–74.

at him if he were to speak in a literary style: "We still cannot speak of a point of honor, that is, not about honor but a point of honor (*point d'honneur*) unless we use literary language. In ordinary language the concept of a 'point of honor' does not exist" (*PSS*30, 5:129).

The flimsiness of fictional narrative comes out through the underground man's self-lacerations—that is, in the breach between his beloved ideal of the "lofty and the sublime" and his own self-consciously mean, even degenerate feelings. He has fantastic, erotically tinged daydreams that always culminate in some ridiculous expression of the "lofty and sublime": "meanwhile, everything always ended in the best possible way with a lazy and intoxicating transition to art, that is, to the sublime forms of life, fully complete, lifted from poetry and novels" (*PSS*30, 5:133). Reflected here is a consciousness somewhere between Gogol and Chernyshevsky. The underground man's experience supports Chernyshevsky's critique of the sublime and of an art elevated above "real life." And much like Gogol's clerk in "Notes of a Madman," he ends his daydreams with wildly ridiculous, megalomaniac fantasies.

The story the underground man manufactures for the prostitute Liza about her own fate is immediately recognizable as a fiction lifted from a sentimental novel. Even though she is willing to listen, his words sound to Liza "exactly as if they came out of a book" (*PSS*30, 5:159). Once again, we find the source of this sense of literary inauthenticity in self-laceration. A narrative that is not informed by genuine, believed moral feelings is empty. The underground man's true ground, his sense of self-contempt, belies genuine moral feeling. Likewise, the scenarios the underground man creates of Liza's future are motivated ultimately by vengefulness, by an invidious rage against anyone more powerful than he—most recently his schoolfellows, who unceremoniously ditched him. In this first encounter Liza is merely the victim of the underground man's rage.

Through his discursive disputes with rationalist discourse and poetic fictions Dostoevsky strove to develop a relatively authentic form of writing that minutely dramatized feeling and thus conveyed a sense of reality and authenticity. And here we have the difference between Dostoevsky's frank, subjective approach to "real life" and Chernyshevsky's theory-oriented approach, his vague and implausible idealization of "real life." Dostoevsky opted in favor of fictional narrative over philosophical tract and mathematical proof as the form that ultimately yields greater truth about human nature—precisely because narrative allows for the consideration of contradiction and paradox. All the same, fiction as such remains suspect. Dostoevsky chose a form of private writing—personal confession—that, although fictionalized and following in a tradition of sometimes self-serving literary confession, starting with Rousseau, still marshals considerable authenticity.

At the end of his confession the underground man still cannot decide what he has written, though he claims it is decidedly not literature. And perhaps because he has no clear idea about its form, this work gains a high level of authenticity:

> I've at least felt ashamed all the time I've been writing this story, so it isn't literature, but a corrective punishment. Of course, spinning long yarns about how I neglected my life through moral disintegration in my corner, lack of contact with other people, and spite and vanity in the underground are, God knows, not very interesting. A novel needs a hero, whereas here I have collected, as if deliberately, all the features of an anti-hero. All this is bound to produce an extremely unpleasant impression, because we have all lost touch with life and we're all cripples to some degree. We've lost touch to such an extent that we feel disgust for life as it is really lived and cannot bear to be reminded of it. (*PSS*30, 5:178)

The point of this writing has been to regain dignity and authority and to offer the underground man a release: "Writing will lend dignity to [my confession]. There's something impressive about writing things down; it is more conducive to self-examination, and my confession will have more style. It is possible, too, that the very process of writing things down will relieve me somewhat" (*PSS*30, 5:123).

What kind of "new" philosophical discourse did Dostoevsky invent? Certainly it bears a strong resemblance to rational, logical argumentation, but it is also a parody. Rationalist scientific-philosophical discourse has been pushed aside: it is used by a speaking voice loaded with a great deal of psychological baggage—full of resentment, suffering, spite, and desire. This speaking voice has an unusual mind to match, one that has at some time in the past taken seriously the "grounds" of both philosophical idealism and materialism but cannot find a way to live within their strictures. Finally, the underground man is left alone with metaphors to describe his inner condition. These are the familiar images of the piano key, the wall, the mouse, and the sore tooth. These images are far more potent and suggestive than "grounds," "primary cause," "secondary cause," and the like.

The most powerful metaphor in Dostoevsky's collection is that of the "underground," the new philosophical-psychological space in which the underground man talks. We need to ask what sort of space Dostoevsky has created for his new philosophizing voice. The underground is a psycho-philosophical chronotope, a metaphor of the mind and heart, in search of a plot, something that will "happen." This space is the closed, isolated residence of a psychological oxymoron, a "thinking *sub*consciousness" that gazes from below at the functions of mind and reason. The underground man's gaze lends an entirely original perspective on the generally accepted and admired ideas and ideals produced by reason, whether of an idealist or materialist bent. The time associated with the underground is neither past nor future but a bad present, an unbearable earthly eternity alone with one-self in one's own self-made "cave," which, in distinction to Plato's cave, has no outlet to the bright light of the sun of "higher" reason. The underground speaker stands both "inside" and "outside" current intellectual discourse—and never above or beyond logical rhetoric. He objects not to the tools of observation and description, which he himself puts to good use in a parody of scientific materialism in which he describes his own psychic life. Rather, he dislikes the interpretation of social and psychological life, that is, "human" life, in the light of a facile historical and social optimism that is claimed for "science."

The underground is the site of silent watching that, if given an outlet, for example, in private writing, leads to endless emotive babble (*PSS*30, 5:121). But the underground is also a psychic breeding ground for a different sort of "philosophizing," which the underground man freely equates with "fan-tasizing" (*PSS*30, 5:115). Residing in this fantasizing space, he re-embraces fantasy that "science" has rejected as too subjective and unreliable. He be-comes quite breathless and helpless in this rebellion against the confining truths of materialist science: "Gentlemen, excuse me for philosophizing on and on like this [*zafilosofstvovalsia*]; this is the result of forty years in the un-derground! Allow me my fantasies" (*PSS*30, 5:115). At this point he relin-quishes his anti-philosophizing stranglehold on reason and articulates a new, broad realm and subject matter for a different kind of philosophiz-ing—human desire. He finally limits the force of reason and rational facul-ties in the overall weave of the human psyche: "Do you see: reasoning [*ras-sudok*], gentlemen, is undeniably a good thing, but reasoning is only just that and satisfies only a person's reasoning capabilities, but desiring [*khote-nie*] is the manifestation of all life" (*PSS*30, 5:115). And further: "Reasoning just knows what it has had time to learn . . . but human nature acts as a whole with everything that it has, conscious or unconscious, and although it may lie, at least it is alive" (*PSS*30, 5:115). Note that in this insistence of the place of desire in philosophy, Dostoevsky echoed the thought of Ivan Kireevsky that "true knowledge" was more "vital" than mathematical logic. And he anticipated the genuinely new philosophical formulations of the next generation.

The underground man in his psychic, "subconscious" underground (now given a voice and made conscious) comes to the very articulation of *nadryv*, or moral self-laceration, that is Dostoevsky's most original insight about the interaction of an abstract idea and the emotional complex of the human psyche: "desire [*khoten'e*] often and even most of the time completely and stubbornly disagrees with reasoning [*rassudok*] and . . . and . . . do you know, that is healthy and even at times very praiseworthy?" (*PSS*30, 5:115). As a "philosophical" writer, Dostoevsky is best known for showing the ways that philosophy, understood as rational argument about human nature, is belied by practice. He shows how a beautiful, enticing abstract idea is distorted, even betrayed, in its enactment, through the force of ornery human desire. This insight emerges from the space of the underground, which allows one to see reasoning faculties as merely one small piece of the complex phenomenon of human nature.

In his anthropological philosophy Feuerbach laid the groundwork for the idea that humans create their gods—and not the other way around, as religious texts would have it. In response, toward the end of part 1 of *Notes from Underground*, we find the underground man yearning against hope for some indestructible higher goal. From the psychic squalor of the underground emerges its lofty opposite—the desire to strive for something that not only cannot be discredited by human desire but that channels that desire in less self-destructive ways. Here is the yearning for some firm, even absolute ideal and the realization that there may be no such thing. With the underground man we find the seeds of the religious philosophy that would flourish around the turn of the century.

Finally, where does Dostoevsky stand in terms of his discursive preferences? As Adelaida Epanchina, the young artist and daughter of General Epanchin, would tell Prince Myshkin in the novel *The Idiot*, "The moment you start telling something, you stop being a philosopher." Traditionally being a philosopher is something one can only do from a closed position, removed from the affairs of life. A philosopher reasons and teaches. Dostoevsky has changed the rules of the game for philosophizing. Narration, he implies, brings one much closer and makes one more involved in and able to understand the real psychological forces that color our ideals and drive human actions. From the mix of parody and discursive critique comes a discourse that, while distancing itself from "literature," would be a kind of fiction devoted to real-life probing but that also disowns the basis in philosophical materialism and empirical science that informed so much "realist" fiction. Despite his considerable criticism of literature and his additional work as an essayist, Dostoevsky would stay firmly on the side of literary narrative. *Notes from Underground* is a narrative of self and an original search for a new way to philosophize about morality, metaphysics, and human nature. Dostoevsky's major novels would be devoted in part to making psychological sense of that need to reason and theorize, and its role in our lives. Other Russian writers to come—especially Rozanov, Shestov, and

Berdiaev—would call themselves "philosophers" and would give the name "philosophy" to the practice of personal moral quest and the probing of contradictions and paradoxes in one's life. In Dostoevsky they would discover the nexus at which philosophizing became a genuine part of Russian writing culture.

Part Two

The Birth of Russian Philosophy
(1870s–1920s)

✳

Chapter Four

Philosophical Language between Revelation and Reason: Solovyov's Search for Total Unity

Solovyov created an exemplary Russian philosophical language that was striking for its clarity, precision, grace, and simplicity.

—L. Lopatin, "To the Memory of Vl. S. Solov'ev," 1910

IN NOVEMBER 1881, ten months after Dostoevsky's death, the newly minted Doctor of Sciences, Vladimir Solovyov (1853–1900), gave an introductory lecture on philosophy to nonphilosophy students at the University of St. Petersburg. His goal was to give a rationale for philosophy to an audience that might not see the immediate attraction of this subject. Juxtaposing philosophy with science and art, both of which, as Solovyov showed, have obvious uses and attractions, Solovyov made philosophy the hero of a narrative that he called the "liberating process of philosophy."[1] Herzen had

1. Vladimir Solov'ev, *Sobranie sochinenii,* 12 vols. (Brussels: Foyer Oriental Chrétien, 1966–1969), 2:411. Hereafter cited in the text as *SS*12 with the relevant volume and page numbers. In my translations from Solovyov I have translated "*chelovek*" as "person" instead of "man." Although in theory "*chelovek*" can be used as an umbrella term to include women as well as men, in the nineteenth century it was used concretely to mean "men" or "man." Solovyov included women in his project both as interlocutors and as important, active players in the philosophical process. In his biography of Solovyov, S. M. Solovyov cites the former: "About my opinion on the capacity for a woman to understand higher truth, without any doubt she is fully capable, otherwise she would not be a person. The point is that her passive nature *keeps her from finding* that truth, and she must receive it from a man" (S. M. Solov'ev, *Zhizn' i tvorcheskaia evoliutsiia Vladimira Solov'eva* [Brussels: Foyer Oriental Chrétien, 1977], 85). Solovyov remarks that, although there are no women founders of religions (clearly ignoring both Mme Blavatskaia and Mary Baker Eddy), women are the main proselytizers of religion. Having made this claim, however, in his sketch for a theocratic hierarchy Solovyov places women in the second rank by themselves, just behind the few men who have intimate knowledge of mystical reality (Sophia). After that come metropolitans of the universal church, archbishops, bishops, and the like (Solov'ev, *Zhizn' i tvorcheskaia evoliutsiia,* 142).

once pictured philosophy in a similar way in his essay, "Dilettantism in Science," only to leave Russia soon after for a life in exile. Russian intellectual life had broadened and deepened in the ensuing thirty-five years, and now a well-trained Russian philosopher could openly lecture university students in Russia's capital about the beauties and benefits of philosophy. Whereas "liberation" for Herzen had meant not just liberation from dogmatic thinking but the freedom to discuss ideas outside the academy and to put them into practice, liberation for Solovyov would mean the rejection of dogmatic control through critical thought and the gradual deepening of human self-consciousness in the light of divine knowledge. "What has philosophy been doing?" Solovyov asked. "It has been setting human selfhood [*lichnost'*] free from outward violence and lending it inward substance. It has been throwing down all false, foreign gods and developing in people the inner form for the revelation of true Deity" (*SS*12, 2:411–412). In the event this statement sounded too demanding of blind faith, Solovyov hastened to clarify that philosophy uses its old powers of skepticism and critical thinking to examine received truths. Real faith and insight into divine truth come only when one has questioned all received definitions and has achieved for oneself the grounding for a thoughtful, conscious faith. In the conclusion to his lecture, Solovyov remarked that philosophy makes "a person fully human": "realizing the human element in a person, [philosophy] also serves both divine and material elements, leading both into a form of free humanness" (*SS*12, 2:413). In short, philosophy is a gateway between scientific fact and revealed truth that makes a human being more fully conscious as an individual, thinking self.

Throughout the 1880s and 1890s Solovyov's ambitious philosophical goal was to bring all cognitive languages under the umbrella of philosophical "total unity" (*vseedinstvo*). He wanted to go beyond the divide between the abstract rationality of idealism and the scientific positivism of materialist thinking that had been deepening throughout the nineteenth century. At the heart of this project is a serious language problem: Solovyov wanted to synthesize the categorizing, analytical language of modern science with the premodern, revelatory "language of similitude" of religion—and to retain philosophy's liberation narrative in the face of the strongly dogmatic streak in religious language. The goal of this chapter is to discuss the concepts of language implied in Solovyov's project and to show specifically how they work in two "border" genres: in one of his most widely read philosophical essays, *The Meaning of Love* (1892–1894), and in his mystical poetry. The essay was one of two pieces in which the philosopher tried to make his project accessible to educated lay readers. The other was *Three Conversations* (*Tri razgovora*, 1900). The poetry functioned as "other" to reasoned discourse and cast the whole project of achieving total unity into doubt.

These experiments in philosophy are of central importance, because within Russian writing culture Solovyov became the first clear, enduring model for the "philosopher." More than Chaadaev, Kireevsky, Khomiakov, or Chernyshevsky, he was the first Russian writer to think of himself as a philosopher per se, to educate himself specifically as a philosopher, and to make the case for philosophy to a broad Russian audience. He would have a decisive impact on the reading public by stirring philosophical activity in Moscow and St. Petersburg, and by inspiring many in Russia's "Golden Age" of philosophy during the first three decades of the twentieth century.

Although he had encyclopedic interests and wrote in many genres, Solovyov thought of himself as a philosopher in his whole being. Even in his early letters to his beloved cousin, Ekaterina Romanova, he argued and proved his views.[2] In a number of his letters, for example, to the older Slavophile Nikolai Strakhov or to his philosopher friend, Prince Tsertelev, Solovyov appreciated the specifically philosophical nature of their friendship (*P*, 1:52). Moreover, he consciously practiced what he felt it meant to be a philosopher—to work consciously for the union of humanity through everyday recognition of the value of all nations, races, religions, and classes, as well as through exotic, mystical insight into the divine.

Solovyov's academic position as a philosopher ceased in 1881 when he pleaded publicly for the lives of the assassins of Tsar Alexander II. Forced to submit his resignation from his teaching duties at St. Petersburg University, he led an ascetic life. He had relatively few possessions, living at friends' houses or in hotels, giving away most of his money and much of his clothing to poor people. In 1891, for example, he requested that an honorarium from a publication in the modernist journal, *Severnyi vestnik*, be donated to peasants suffering from the terrible drought of that year (*P*, 3:130).

Solovyov's face became embedded in the memory of all who saw him. It had a spiritual aura, like that of an icon. One friend of Solovyov's wrote: "His outward appearance made an enduring impression, like a radiant vision. The mysteriously sublime eyes . . . the high forehead with the visible imprint of thought and worry, the thick, energetic eyebrows, the thick wavy hair, with its remarkable streak of gray, framing the pale face."[3] What is more, his figure and personality left a mark on Russian literature from Dostoevsky to Belyi. Solovyov served in part as a model for Ivan Karamazov and his theocratic thinking in Dostoevsky's *The Brothers Karamazov*.[4] The novel, *The Pass* (*Pereval*, 1893), by the novelist Petr Boborykin, dramatized the growing popularity of philosophy in the early 1890s, partly through the

2. Vladimir Solov'ev, *Pis'ma*, 4 vols., ed. E. L. Radlov (St. Petersburg: Obshchestvennaia pol'za, 1908), 3:81, 88. Hereafter cited in the text as *P* with the relevant volume and page numbers.

3. *Kniga o Vladimire Solov'eve*, ed. B. Averin, D. Bazanov, and E. Pavlova (Moscow: Sovetskii pisatel', 1991), 39. Hereafter cited in the text as *Kniga* with the relevant page number.

4. Marina Kostalevsky, *Dostoevsky and Soloviev: The Art of Integral Vision* (New Haven: Yale University Press, 1997), 100.

Vladimir Solovyov, n.d.

newly discovered Friedrich Nietzsche but also through the presence of Vladimir Solovyov and other neo-idealists.[5] The younger generation of Symbolists, particularly Aleksandr Blok and Andrei Belyi, were at the center of a Solovyov cult in the early years of the twentieth century. Belyi's characters, Musatov in his *Second Symphony* and Nikolai Apollonovich and Dud-

    5. E. Clowes, *The Revolution of Moral Consciousness: Nietzsche in Russian Literature, 1890–1914* (DeKalb: Northern Illinois University Press, 1988), 70–73.

Vladimir Solovyov, n.d.

kin in *Petersburg,* have apocalyptic visions involving the appearance of Solovyov or a Solovyov-like figure.[6]

Although he was very popular as a public speaker when addressing issues of immediate social and political interest, Solovyov's written philosophical works had relatively little impact during his lifetime (*Kniga,* 238).[7] True, on one occasion, when someone borrowed Solovyov's name as a pseudonym for an article on marriage, Solovyov objected vociferously (*P,* 3:186). And there were numerous attacks on Solovyov in the press (*SS*12, 6:481). Nonetheless, after his premature death in July 1900, the attacks ceased, and gradually a new generation of philosophers—Sergei Bulgakov, Sergei Trubetskoi, Nikolai Berdiaev, and later Pavel Florensky and Aleksei Losev, to name only the most famous—hailed Solovyov as their mentor and the forefather of a genuine philosophical culture in Russia (*Kniga,* 238). In 1905 Moscow witnessed the founding of the Solovyov Society, whose membership eventually numbered several hundred.[8]

Throughout his life Solovyov was troubled by the poverty of philosophical culture in Russia. As late as 1888, in his *Russia and Europe,* Solovyov claimed that Russia still lacked a genuine philosophical tradition, and he saw himself as the keystone to a Russian philosophical culture. In his words: "Everything that is philosophical in [nineteenth-century Russian thought] . . . is not in the slightest Russian, and what is Russian in them is not at all like philosophy, in fact not like anything. We cannot point to any real promise of a native Russian philosophy: everything in this line has been an empty claim" (*SS*12, 5:94–99). In a letter from 1890 to N. Ia. Grot, the editor of the recently founded *Questions of Philosophy and Psychology,* Solovyov claimed that Russian philosophy was still so thin that "each thinker is the only follower of his movement and the only representative of his school" (*SS*12, 6:269). Despite this situation, Solovyov noted, in the early 1890s, that "philosophical questions are attracting particular interest, and even metaphysics, which was laid to rest long ago, is making a comeback" among the reading public (*SS*12, 6:277). The soil was prepared for a fuller development of a philosophical culture.

Solovyov was clearly active in encouraging philosophical education and the discussion of philosophical questions. And, despite his complaints, over the preceding decade he had seen considerable improvement in Russian philosophical culture. In the 1870s, when Solovyov was a student and then a teacher, there had been very little in the way of a classical philosophical

6. Ibid., 158, 168.

7. See also S. M. Solovyov, *Zhizn' i tvorcheskaia,* 27.

8. Kristiane Burchardi, *Die Moskauer "Religiös-Philosophische Vladimir-Solovyov-Gesellschaft" (1905–1918)* (Wiesbaden: Harrassowitz, 1998).

Caricature of Vladimir Solovyov in the satirical magazine, *Oskolki*, 1891. The caption says: "Vlad. S. Solovyov, our own Russian homegrown philosopher of philosophers." From *Kniga o Vladimire Solov'eve*, ed. B. Averin, D. Bazanov, and E. Pavlova (Moscow: Sovetskii pisatel', 1991).

education. The theological academies were the only home for a philosophical curriculum that was of high quality, but still it included only classical works. Philosophical instruction at the universities took place at a very low level.[9] In 1879 Solovyov applied to the Ministry of Education to found a philosophical society. He argued that classical education in general would facilitate a better-functioning civil society and could help to prevent the ravages of radicalism. Philosophical education in particular encouraged a more intelligent and well-directed engagement with science (*P*, 3:259). To his disappointment, the proposal was rejected.[10]

When Russia's first philosophical journal, *Voprosy filosofii i psikhologii* (Questions of philosophy and psychology) was founded by Nikolai Grot in 1889, Solovyov passionately supported and defended the journal and its broadly educational goals. In Russia, he wrote, "we need not to prop up various -isms that have lost their credibility, nor to generate new ones that will meet the same fate, but rather [we need] to spread philosophical education and to develop reasonable and conscious views" (*P*, 3:242). When the conservative press, led by the St. Petersburg newspaper *Novoe vremia,* attacked Grot's project, Solovyov led counterattacks with letters to the editor and positive reviews of new articles and books on philosophical subjects. In short, Solovyov helped to create more widespread public philosophical dialogue for the first time in Russian history by taking such debates to the newspapers.

It should be noted that Solovyov helped to create a philosophical culture in a number of other ways. During the early 1890s he served as the philosophy editor for the new *Brockhaus-Efron Russian Encyclopedia,* for which he himself wrote four lengthy entries, on Danilevsky, Leontiev, Hegel, and Kant, and numerous smaller ones. He also translated a number of works of Kant and Plato and indeed, by the late 1890s, had undertaken the project of translating Plato's entire works, of which only a small part was completed at the time of his death.

The nature of philosophical language, its linguistic claim to truth, is an enduring, though implicit, theme in Solovyov's writing. In his earliest work, his master's thesis of 1874, he asserted that philosophizing is an individual activity, not collective or shared by a whole social group (*S2*, 2:5). In the 1870s he referred to two notions of language: language as the absolute

9. S. M. Solov'ev, *Zhizn' i tvorcheskaia evoliutsiia,* 90.

10. When his friend, Kireev, tried again in 1883, Solovyov doubted the success of the undertaking but said that he would support such a society and participate were it to be approved (*P*, 2:112). When the philosophical society at St. Petersburg University opened in 1897, Solovyov was among its first speakers.

Word, variously termed Logos or "*Slovo,*" and language as "discourse," or secular, abstract speech. Solovyov used the words "*diskursivno*" (discursively) and "*diskursivnyi*" (discursive) twice in his master's thesis. The notion of discourse was associated with abstraction, the rational separation of language and concepts from the realms of the subconscious, sensation, and intuition (*S2,* 2:52). In the second instance the term was used to speak of an individualized, analytical thought process and language use that is opposed to religion or language in its general social or communicative functions (*S2,* 2:91).

The notion of Logos or "*Slovo*" is much more fully developed and lies at the heart of Solovyov's project of unifying all cultural languages under the rubric of philosophy. In his unfinished work of 1877, *The Philosophical Origins of Integral Knowledge,* Solovyov referred to the Gospel of St. John to show that Logos, or the Word, is the only origin of existence and knowledge that is "objective," which, in other words, exists for an "other": "In the beginning was the Word, God had the Word, and God was the Word. . . . Everything was born through it, and without it nothing was born" (*S2,* 2:243). The "other" Solovyov generally has in mind is nature. The Word is the mediator between existence, essence, and substance: it is the medium for the revelation of the "super-essence [*sverkhsushchee*]" (*S2,* 2:244, 259). In his *Lectures on Godmanhood* (1878–1881) Solovyov changed his definition, now viewing the Word as the ultimate language that unlocks the nature of things and has the power of revelation. The Word is the expression of that which absolutely exists. It is "God's other" that allows God to act, "to realize God's self, . . . to act in the other, and in this way [the Word] affirms the necessity of the other's existence."[11] Thus the Word is still the mediator that makes it possible for God to exist in the framework of time and space that represents God's earthly "other." It is important to point out that Solovyov, on several occasions, underscores that in no way is the Word to be associated with dogma and with what Bakhtin might have called the "monological" truth of human systems of belief, whether religious or philosophical. The word represents a set of principles that are to be interpreted and realized in the historical moment (*SS12,* 5:421).

For Solovyov, the problem of "total unity"—of bridging the gap between idealism and materialism, and between the ultimate Word and human languages of theology, philosophy, and science—is tightly bound to the possibilities that are inherent in figurative language. Indeed, for a philosopher, he is unusually sensitive to the need to find tropes appropriate to his project. And, here, language as the Word is quite closely linked to poetic language in

11. Vladimir Solov'ev, "Chteniia o bogochelovechestve," in idem (St. Petersburg: Khudozhestvennaia literatura, 1994), 144.

the broad, mythic sense of language that relates the absolute to the historical and relates principle to experience. In *Lectures on Godmanhood* Solovyov
implied a relationship between essence and existence that is metaphorical in
nature: "The very concept of revelation (and religious development, as an
objective [development], must necessarily be revelation) presupposes that
the divine essence [*sushchestvo*] revealing itself is originally hidden, that is, it
is not given as such; however, even here it must exist for a person, since in
the opposite instance its further revelation would be completely incompre-
hensible: therefore it exists and acts, but not in its own definiteness, not in
itself, but in its other, that is, in nature."[12] Here hidden being, unavailable
to human senses, is given sensory expression through language that is not
identical or exact but makes hidden being known in some approximate way.
Both in his early lectures and later, in 1890, in "The General Meaning of
Art," Solovyov saw poetic language as an important conduit through which
the Word could make itself approximately known. He wrote: "the real poet
must necessarily penetrate 'to the homeland of flame and word,' to take
from there the original images of his creations and, as well, that inward illu-
mination [*prosvetlenie*] which is called inspiration."[13] It would be the
metaphorical art of Dostoevsky, who, in Solovyov's view, had found a new
way to close the gap between religion and art, that best represented what
Solovyov was seeking.

Meanwhile, as we will see in *The Meaning of Love,* Solovyov as philosopher sometimes borrowed the metaphorical playfulness and multiplicity of
meaning of poetic language for his own philosophical discourse. Jacques
Derrida's work on metaphor in philosophical texts can help us to appreciate
how unusual Solovyov is among philosophers in the modern era in his high
estimation of metaphorical language. In "The White Mythology" Derrida
argues that Western metaphysicians legitimate their own discourse by controlling the boundaries of metaphor. He writes: "[The] end of metaphor [in
philosophical discourse] is not interpreted as a death or dislocation, but as
an interiorizing anamnesis (*Erinnerung*), a recollection of meaning, a *relève*
[*Aufhebung;* suspension, preservation, derivation] of living metaphoricity
into a living state of properness. This is the irrepressible philosophical desire
to summarize-interiorize-dialecticize-master-*relever* [*aufheben;* suspend and
preserve] the metaphorical division between the origin and itself."[14] In Derrida's view, Western metaphysical discourse traditionally captures living,
poetic metaphor, disappropriates it, and then reconstitutes (re-members) it

---

12. Ibid., 68.
13. Ibid., 142.
14. Jacques Derrida, "The White Mythology," *The Margins of Philosophy,* trans. A. Bass (Chicago: University of Chicago Press, 1986), 269.

in such a way as to aid in two philosophical goals: to define original principles, the metaphysical axioms of natural, physical existence; and to establish
the authority of philosophical discourse as the discourse most able to state
original principles. Although philosophical discourse needs the vivifying
energy of metaphor—the promise of delivering more meaning than what is
embedded in a concrete signifier—philosophers are also wary of the ambiguity, evasiveness, and inability of metaphor to limit its own reach and to
mean precisely that which is intended. The process of recapturing figurative
language and harnessing it for philosophical purposes involves a process of
putting discourses into a hierarchy according to their truth-value. Here it is
the hope of philosophers that philosophical language will emerge as the
most general, the most true, the most authoritative of human discourses, as
it were, the discourse of discourses.

If language and types of language are not always well defined in
Solovyov's writing, the opposite can be said of types of knowledge and their
relative truth-value. Discursive hierarchy is generally pronounced and significant in Solovyov's work. The hidden motivator of everything, of course,
is the Word, Logos, which is most directly "embodied" in biblical language
and, secondarily, in literary art (although it can also find expression in scientific discourses as well).[15] Solovyov's valuation of language implies something like the following schema:

Divine or Ideal language:
Slovo, Word, Logos

Human cultural languages and how they transmit Logos:
Religion—revelation, metaphor
Philosophy—categorization, analysis, systematization
Science—observation, description, analysis of data; creation of "facts"

Philosophy is placed in the middle, along with religion, mediating between
the eternal and the historical, the immutable and the changing. Solovyov
differs from Hegel, however, in that he does not put philosophy at the top
of human cognitive languages. Indeed, religion ultimately stands above philosophy, in Solovyov's estimation. In a letter of 1872 to his cousin, Ekaterina
Romanova, he placed philosophical analysis below religious faith. Discussing Francis Bacon, the early founder of modern science, he commented
that great thinkers have been deep believers: "a little mind, a little philosophy remove one from God, a bit more mind, a bit more philosophy bring

---

15. Solov'ev, "Chteniia o bogochelovechestve," 178.

one to Him" (*P,* 3:73). He added: "Neither science nor philosophy can give such lively conviction [as religion can]" (*P,* 3:75). A decade later he wrote to the schoolteacher V. P. Fedorov that philosophy stands somewhere between religion and science: "When the philosophical mind freely bows before the higher truth of religion, that is worthy meekness—the beginning of higher wisdom. But when the mind falls down slavishly before the facts of external nature and forces philosophy to be a mere echo of natural science, that is not resignation but the humiliation of mind, which brings nothing but mockery to philosophy, even from the scientists whom today's philosophers are so interested in wooing" (*P,* 3:2). Solovyov expressed the same idea in his article, "On the Way toward True Philosophy" (1883), published in the conservative newspaper *Rus'.* Solovyov found both materialism and idealism too skeptical and unproductive, because they reject the "revelation of supernatural and superhuman reality" (*S2,* 2:337). He asserted: "Only by acknowledging given religious truth does our mind receive a firm object [*predmetnyi*] support for its metaphysical work, and it transfers philosophy from the territory of human fabrications to that of divine truth" (*S2,* 2:338).

The place poetic language occupies in this hierarchy is unclear. When it is linked to religious language, as Solovyov believed was the case in the art of Dostoevsky, then it is the highest of all human cognitive languages, combining intuition and revelation (*SS12,* 3:188). At the start of his article, "Beauty in Nature" (1889), Solovyov cites Dostoevsky's famous dictum, "Beauty will save the world." However, most contemporary literary art is secular, and Solovyov was continually drawn to limit its authority. In his three lectures on Dostoevsky (1881–1883), he placed "theory" above literature and made literature into the "object" of theory which theory then shapes and directs: "theory, in explaining its subject as it really is, must open it to the new horizons of the future" (*SS12,* 6:35). Theory, Solovyov claimed, can "see" farther than art and is "neither arbitrary nor fantastic" if it is based on reason and the essence of things as they are revealed to reason (*SS12,* 6:35). Solovyov would continue in this vein in his article, "The General Meaning of Art" (1890), to channel artistic power toward religious and mystical goals of "transubstantiation" (*presushchestvlenie*) of essence into existence. Art is linked to the Christian ritual of transubstantiation: "perfect art . . . must embody the absolute ideal. . . . [It] must animate, transubstantiate our actual life" (*SS12,* 6:90). Here, too, Solovyov viewed art as secondary to philosophy and religion, areas of human activity in which ideas are conceived: "Art in general is the territory of embodiment of ideas, not of their original conception and growth" (*SS12,* 6:90).

Solovyov's main tactic for de-emphasizing the authority of art is to associate it with the lower "outer and visible" realm of human existence, "body," an area secondary to the higher realm of "spirit" with which religion and philosophy are linked. Beauty, Solovyov wrote, is "the embodied idea" (*SS*12, 6:44).[16] The "final task" of poetry is to "embody the absolute ideal not just in the imagination but in actuality" (*SS*12, 6:90). Solovyov thus implies a second language hierarchy within the realm of human cognitive languages:

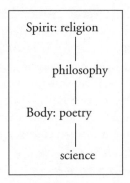

While spirit gives direction and orientation, body provides "facts" and realia (*SS*12, 6:60). Although they represent the lower aspect of sensation and fact, poetry and science are by no means conceived as merely passive, receptive languages. Body is usually treated as an active force: although science is reduced to the realm of producing facts about nature, which philosophy then interprets, poetry particularly must be capable itself of interpretation, enactment, and animation of spirit, even though it is secondary to the idea itself. It will be important to see how in his own poetic practice Solovyov tends to undermine the schemes and hierarchies implicit in his philosophical writing. In a real sense, the tension between the mystical language of his lyric poetry and the rational discourse of his philosophical tracts will not be resolved.

The cultural discourses outlined above function in complex ways in Solovyov's essay, *The Meaning of Love*. This essay was written between 1892 and 1894, when Solovyov had returned to a more publicly active philosophical life, and was published in the new philosophy journal, *Voprosy filosofii i psikhologii*. *The Meaning of Love* may be seen as a serious effort to bring philosophizing to the educated, nonspecialist public. It is written as an essay in social and literary criticism, which then crosses into philosophy. To start with, it disputes the view of love conveyed by Lev Tolstoy in his novella, *The*

---

16. This articulation of the relationship between idea and image is the opposite of Dostoevsky's. Dostoevsky saw the image (particularly of Christ) as the essence of the good. Kostalevsky, in *Dostoevsky and Soloviev* (155–161), and James Scanlan, in *Dostoevsky the Thinker* (Ithaca, N.Y.: Cornell University Press, 2002), 149–151, offer refined discussions of the differences between Solovyov and Dostoevsky on the primacy of ethical goodness and moral beauty.

Kreutzer Sonata (1889). Briefly, Solovyov is critical of post-Schopenhauerian psycho-physiological or behaviorist theories that view love as an illusory sidebar to sexual attraction. Solovyov has many harsh words for the so-called scientific research conducted in the area of love and sex. This research, in Solovyov's view, has an utterly unworthy goal, namely, to define and legitimize a distorted concept of "natural" and "normal" behavior, for example, by making a fetish of the female body and its constituent parts and advocating frequent sexual activity for men (*SS*12, 7:34–35).

For Solovyov, love is the relationship through which a person most completely fulfills the philosophical and spiritual goal of becoming "more completely human," by learning to see the beloved other as a full and independent self. It should be noted at the outset that, in its general discursive orientation, Solovyov's essay is closer to poetry than to science. The proximity of his thinking particularly to literary art can be seen early on in his use of literary examples (from *Romeo and Juliet, The Sorrows of Young Werther,* and others) as sources of the true experience of sexual love more authoritative than contemporary scientific theories of sex.

While the essay operates philosophically in the domain of abstraction, generalization, and theorization, *The Meaning of Love* also occupies the space of play normally reserved for art, in that it experiments with discourse and metaphor. We have noted already that Solovyov uses figurative language much more inventively than professional philosophers traditionally do.[17] Now it will become clear how poetic discourse functions as an important point of departure for Solovyov's explorations into the mystical realm.[18]

Despite the hierarchical nature of Solovyov's evaluation of Logos and human languages, he did show a strongly Russian egalitarianism regarding the truth-value of existing secular languages. Poetry and science, for example, are in general equally good and true, but both are considered inadequate to the problem of revealing ultimate origins and ends. Solovyov comments on existing discourses: "It is obvious that, although they lend substance to separate strivings of the human spirit and meet the needs of humanity, in no way do art, science, and politics convey the absolute, self-

---

17. Some commentaries criticize Solovyov for a dry, academic style. See, for example, Peter Ulf Moller, *Postlude to the Kreutzer Sonata: Tolstoj and the Debate on Sexual Morality in Russian Literature in the 1980s,* trans. J. Kendal (Copenhagen: E. J. Brill, 1988), 285. See also Kostalevsky, *Dostoevsky and Soloviev,* 155–161.

18. See Judith Kornblatt, "The Transfiguration of Plato in the Erotic Philosophy of Vladimir Solov'ev," *Religion and Literature,* 24, no. 2 (summer 1992): 43–44. In "Transfiguration" Kornblatt remarks that one important aspect of Plato's writerly persona on which Solovyov modeled himself was the dual role of poet and philosopher. Solovyov, however, considered his own poetry to be decidedly of secondary importance to his philosophical writing. See Zara Mints, "Vladimir Solov'ev—Poet," introduction to *Stikhotvoreniia i shutochnye p'esy* by Vladimir Solov'ev (Leningrad: Sovetskii pisatel', 1974), Biblioteka poeta, 22ff.

sufficient substance of human individuality [*individual'nost'*]" (*SS*12, 7:32). While they might orient people toward the search for higher truth (*SS*12, 7:13–14), none of the discourses used in educated society, in the philosopher's view, can elucidate the ultimate goal of the transfiguration of spirit and body that he seeks in total unity.

Toward the end of *The Meaning of Love* Solovyov asserts the authority of his mystical-philosophical discourse. He reiterates the inadequacy of poetic and scientific discourses for expressing an evasive "total unity" that will not be captured within their domains. Although he recognizes the authority of poetry in expressing the "inadvertent and spontaneous feeling" of love, he asks, "Is this fleeting revelation enough?" (*SS*12, 7:47). Clearly speaking as a philosopher, he answers his own question with a condescending and resounding no: "This is hardly satisfactory *even* for the poetic sensibility by itself, and the *consciousness of the truth* and the *will to live* certainly cannot be reconciled with it. An infinity that is merely momentary is a contradiction unendurable for the mind, bliss only in the past is suffering for the will" (*SS*12, 7:47). Despite his attraction to poetry, for Solovyov the philosopher, poetic discourse is ultimately limited to emotive speech functions.

In his essay Solovyov creates the space for a mystical-philosophical discourse by treading on the edge of poetic and scientific discourses and showing the limitations of each. Poetry is bound too closely to the passing moment, and science is limited to measurable, empirical evidence and often makes false claims. Despite their shortcomings Solovyov does not hesitate to take from each the figurative and conceptual language needed to establish his "higher" discourse. Probing the possibility of the presence of mystical "total unity" in the material world, he borrows vocabulary and concepts taken from physics to reveal both the borders of science and a mystical reality that penetrates those borders. He writes: "Along with the force of gravity ideal total unity is realized in a spiritual-corporeal way in the world body through light and other related phenomena (electricity, magnetism, warmth), the character of which stands in such stark contrast to the properties of opaque and inert matter, that natural science is forced . . . to acknowledge a special kind of half-material substance which it calls ether. This is weightless matter, that penetrates and is penetrated everywhere—in a word, *immaterial matter*" (*SS*12, 7:54–55).

With the image of "immaterial matter" Solovyov even indicates the central rhetorical figure in his philosophical style, the oxymoron, which permits him to juxtapose opposite spheres of existence. He does not delineate an explicitly *philosophical* discourse per se, but he does create a mystical language that claims authority over scientific description and poetic trope, and marshals these two to aid in articulating ultimate reality in its earthly emanations.

As a second strategy for building and legitimizing a mystical language,

Solovyov criticizes the problematic aspects of competing discourses and the tropic structures embedded in them. As we have seen, the "science" of popular psychology is paramount among the discourses that Solovyov rejects. He argues that psychology breaks down the female other into a series of body parts. In poetic terms, synecdoche dominates metaphor. Sexual feeling, he writes,

> is aroused in many people, almost all of the male sex, largely and sometimes even exclusively by one or another part [of the body] of the other sex (for example, hair, hand, or leg). . . . This anomaly has been labeled fetishism. The abnormality of this fetishism, obviously, lies in the fact that a part replaces the whole, externals replace essence. But if the hair or legs that excite the fetishist are but parts of the female body, then this body in its entirety is only a part of female being [*sushchestvo*]. Nonetheless, none of these admirers of the female body is considered a fetishist, neither are they considered crazy nor subjected to therapy. (*SS*12, 7:35)

One of the original aspects of Solovyov's thought, popular with generations of readers, is his high valuation of the female side of human nature and his concept of androgyny as an expression of the spiritually whole person.[19] The love relationship, Solovyov argues, should be based on *mutual* interaction and dialogue between self and gendered other. The goal is to affirm the absolute worth, the absolute selfhood of the other as well as of oneself. The perception of the human body, and particularly the female body, in terms of synecdoche, or the part in place of the whole, runs counter to Solovyov's own determination to see each human being, male or female, as an integrated whole coherent with total unity.

A number of points should be made in passing regarding the philosophical manipulation of metaphor in *The Meaning of Love*. First, Solovyov makes an implicit distinction between the "metaphysical," the rational grounding of God, and the "mystical," the nonrational, revealed knowledge of God. Already his purpose is different from that of canonical Western metaphysicians, because he is concerned less with marking the territory of metaphysical authority per se than with legitimizing a mystical language. Second, Solovyov, in general, takes almost as his point of departure what, in Derrida's view, Western philosophers try hard to conceal, that is, their de-

---

19. See, for example, Pasternak's reference to *The Meaning of Love* in *Doctor Zhivago* (New York: Ballantine, 1981), 39. For a reading of Doctor Zhivago's response to Solovyov's essay, see Jerome Spencer, "Soaked in *The Meaning of Love* and *The Kreutzer Sonata*: The Nature of Love in *Doctor Zhivago*," in *Doctor Zhivago: A Critical Companion* (Evanston, Ill.: Northwestern University Press, 1995), 76–88. For a discussion of Solovyov's reception among Western feminist theologians, see Brenda Meehan, "A Feminist Reading of the Russian Sophiological Tradition," unpublished paper delivered at the American Association for the Advancement of Slavic Studies, Washington, D.C., October 27, 1995.

pendence on figurative language. The Russian philosopher's "control" of figurative language is *deliberately* looser than that of Descartes, whom Solovyov finds mechanistic. Solovyov consciously both seeks out and creates metaphor, and he enriches his philosophical speech with metaphors from a number of different discourses, scientific as well as poetic. There is a fruitful tension here between spiritual-mystical language and secular discourses. The third point is that this interplay only becomes flat and faded when Solovyov introduces biblical imagery, the traditional symbolism of which he seems, against all expectations, to accept unquestioningly. That this version of total unity contradicts his belief in the diversity of human experience will be seen in his use of New Testament language.

The dominant figure of what will eventually emerge as Solovyov's mystical-philosophical language is very close to oxymoron—a figure capable of encouraging mediation between opposite terms and teasing out the unknowable, the unspeakable, the mystical. We have seen this oxymoronic spirit in the image of "immaterial matter" and will find it again as we discuss another concept taken from both scientific and ecclesiastical discourse, the concept of "syzygy." Throughout, Solovyov defines his concept of sexual love as something of an oxymoron. In his own day *The Meaning of Love* was read very much against the backdrop of Tolstoy's strong opposition of sex and love in *The Kreutzer Sonata*. Within his own text the concept of "sexual love" serves as a mediator between the sexual, corporeal, and instinctual, on the one hand, and the spiritual and mystical, on the other.

Another strategy at work in building an adequate mystical-philosophical discourse is to suspend and preserve the oxymoron of "sexual love" as the essence of this new special language. Solovyov's goal here is to create a new language different from existing secular discourses, one powerful enough to transport us to a more vital consciousness of other people (particularly women). When we learn to see the other person as an autonomous self, we enter into a relation in which we can hope to recapture the spirit of wholeness that is God. Sexual love, for Solovyov, is more than just a topic waiting for its first philosophical treatment.[20] Sexual love is itself constituted as a higher "language," implicitly an expression of Logos or the Word, with all the capacity to shape consciousness—to order facts and to interpret and evaluate experience—that a cognitive language claims. Love is to *be* the very language that articulates and gives value to the wordless subliminal realm of the psyche and links it to the ideal realm, also seemingly wordless to ordinary humans and accessible only through metaphor.

20. In *The Meaning of Love* Solovyov claims to be the first thinker to posit love as the object of philosophical inquiry (39). In "The Transfiguration of Plato," Kornblatt discusses Solovyov's critique of Plato's theory of love and shows how the Russian philosopher transformed his mentor into a "fallen prophet" (48).

An important point is that Solovyov makes a clear distinction between "physical language" (*iazyk*), an instinctive, physiological faculty, and "discursive language" (*slovo*), the conscious use of language linked to Logos or the Word to create meaning and to assign value. Although the notion of love as a language is as old as lyric poetry itself, Solovyov implies that his notion of sexual love is more than mere language: it is a potent weapon for transfiguring and even resurrecting first the private, inward individual spirit, then the physical body, and ultimately the social sphere. As he puts it: "False spirituality is the denial of flesh, true spirituality is its rebirth, salvation, resurrection," and love is the language of true spirituality (*SS12*, 7:40). It is the bridge by which three levels of consciousness—Logos, abstract "discourse" as Solovyov used it in 1874, and earthly experiential language—can all be brought into contact.

Solovyov draws a number of parallels between love and language. Both start as something "natural." And, as has happened with language over centuries, loving behavior will become a higher conceptual language, a bearer of the Word, that enables the transfiguration of individual consciousness and, later, the transformation of social interaction. He writes: "It would be extremely sad if we saw [language] only as a natural process that happens in us inadvertently, if we talked the way the birds sing . . . and did not make of language a weapon for the consistent conveyance of certain thoughts, a medium for achieving judicious and consciously articulated goals" (*SS12*, 7:25). Just as language developed from spontaneous emotive performance into a tool for making meaning of experience and for formulating judgments and articulating goals, so love will become more than a natural feeling of attraction. It will grow into a medium for regenerating the world. Solovyov posits for love an active role not just as the theme of language but also as language itself.

The philosopher then draws a parallel between the uses of discourse in cultural and social development and the uses of love-as-language for personal, spiritual development: "If we adopted an exclusively passive and unconscious attitude toward the gift of conceptual language [*slovo*], science, art, and civil society would not have taken shape, and, as a result of the insufficient application of this gift, physical language [*iazyk*] itself would not have developed and would have remained in a very basic form" (*SS12*, 7:25). He elaborates this point with regard to love:

> Love has the same or even greater meaning for the creation of true human individuality [*individual'nost*] as conceptual language does for the formation of human society and culture. And if in the one area . . . we observe at least slow, but unmistakable progress, at the same time that human individuality from the beginning of history to the present day remains the same in terms of its actual limitations, then the chief reason for this difference is that we are engaging ever more consciously and independently in discursive activity and

in the production of discourse while love stays as before in the dark region of dim affects and inadvertent attractions. (*SS*12, 7:25)

Solovyov claims honors as the first thinker to develop the vocabulary and to articulate the goals of love-as-language, through which a powerful interpersonal ethical and spiritual force could be realized. And what he proposes is much grander than physical and psychological communion. He has in mind nothing less than revealing a new way of being a self and, ultimately, overcoming death. If human selfhood is to develop its full potential, it must do so discursively:

> Just as the true purpose of language lies less in speaking in and of itself than in what is being said—in the revelation of the logic of things through words or concepts—so the true purpose of love lies not in the simple experience of this feeling but in what is brought to completion through that feeling—[the true purpose of love] lies in the deed of love: it is not enough to feel for oneself the absolute significance of the beloved object; one needs really to give or communicate to the beloved that significance, to be joined with the beloved in the real creation of absolute individuality. (*SS*12, 7:26)

Solovyov proposes to achieve his goal through an interactive, interpersonal ethic based on the absolute value of each human being and aimed at the active realization of this selfhood through mutual love.

This concept of higher, conceptual language has important implications for Solovyov's moral philosophy. He appears to move *away* from a morality based on absolute law dictated from above by an eternal will and *toward* a form of perspectivism that incorporates the variety and validity of individual points of view and experiences. Although it is true that sexual love is meant to lead to total unity and to the transfiguration of flesh in the image of God, Solovyov's concept is generally dominated not by *vertical* or hierarchical valuations, dictated by an absolute principle of the good, but instead is strongly *horizontal*, mutually discovered and enacted by "members of opposite sexes able to relate to each other as husband and wife" (*SS*12, 7:22 n. 6). What is remarkable in Solovyov's thinking is the promise of reciprocity and dialogue between self and other that is to lead to a fuller notion of selfhood. The promise of breaking away from a solipsistic egotism that renders all others nothing but an emanation of one's own desire, as well as the liberating possibility of confronting monological absolutism in the ethical sphere, make Solovyov's idea of sexual love an important precursor to Viacheslav Ivanov's idea of "being-in-love" (*vliublennost'*), Rozanov's dialogical engagement of the other within himself, and Bakhtin's idea of answerability.[21]

---

21. For an enlightening discussion of Solovyov as a Russian Orthodox precursor to Bakhtin, see Caryl Emerson, "Russian Orthodoxy and the Early Bakhtin," *Religion and Literature* 22, nos. 2–3 (1990): 109–132. For a consideration of Solovyov's and Nietzsche's impact on Viacheslav Ivanov, see Clowes, *The Revolution of Moral Consciousness*, 134–141.

Solovyov crowns his argument with the rather idiosyncratic, and quite "unpoetic," but richly suggestive metaphor, "syzygy" (*sizigiia*), that successfully works to "reveal" the mystical in the sexual, the religious in the secular, and the whole in the part. This strange term implicitly recaptures in a single word the oxymoronic spirit of "sexual love" and "immaterial matter." Part of its success is that it functions as a concept in a number of disparate, even conflicting discourses, each essential to Solovyov's project. Syzygy (which comes from the Greek term "*syzygia*" or "yoke") is chosen to do what Solovyov would like to see happen in the real world: to "yoke" together what would seem to be "un-yokable." In its various meanings it conjoins physicality and spirituality: the *meta*physical and the *astro*physical with the *merely* physical. With this trope he creates a set of logical relationships, which it is indeed possible, as Solovyov put it, to "think out" total unity (*SS12*, 7:45).

Syzygy in its most common astrophysical sense refers to the points in the orbit of a celestial body—usually the moon—at which that body is in opposition to or conjunction with the sun—at new moon, full moon, or eclipse. In an obscure zoological meaning syzygy refers to sexual intercourse; to quote *Webster's,* it is "the intimately united, even fused condition of certain low organisms during conjugation."[22] And in a note explaining his choice of terms Solovyov emphasizes the mystical, Gnostic sense of syzygy. He writes that syzygy means "combination. I am forced to introduce this new expression since I cannot find another better one in the existing vocabulary. I wish to note that the Gnostics used the word *syzygy*" (*SS12*, 7:57).[23]

In the text Solovyov links the mystical with the social, emphasizing the essay's major themes of reciprocal love and the relative autonomy of individual selves within the community:

> the link [of individual members of society] with whole social spheres—local, national, and, ultimately, with the universal [sphere]—needs to become still more internalized, complete, and significant. This connection of the active human, personal principle with the idea of total unity embodied in the social, spiritual-corporeal organism must be a live *syzygial* one. [The individual must] neither conform to the social sphere nor dominate over it but [rather] coexist with it in loving interaction, to serve it as an active, fertile principle . . . and to find in it a fullness of vitality and potentiality. (*SS12*, 7:57; emphasis added)

22. *Webster's Dictionary* (Springfield, Mass.: Meriam, 1919).

23. See, for example, Werner Foerster, *Gnosis: A Selection of Gnostic Texts,* trans. R. McL. Wilson, 2 vols. (Oxford: Clarendon, 1972–1974), 1:105, 111, 116, 123–124, 139, 152–153. Note that syzygy is indeed a consistent theme in the patristic documentation of Gnosticism. It refers to the notion of coupling between so-called aeons, or worlds, to bring forth emanations from themselves. A pair of aeons is sometimes called a "syzygy."

Solovyov then reinforces the connection between syzygy and his major themes of love, autonomy, and coexistence: "We need above all to relate to the social and world environment as to a real, live being with which we find ourselves in the closest and fullest interaction without ever merging fully with it. This kind of diffusion of *syzygial* existence perfects individuality itself, communicating to it the unity and fullness of life's substance and at the same time elevating and perpetuating the basic individual form of love" (*SS*12, 7:58). As the philosopher uses it, syzygy suggests a conjoining at once of psychological, physiological, physical, social, and mystical-spiritual forces in the name of love and total unity. Syzygy thus becomes the key metaphor for Solovyov's project of total unity: the project of overcoming the dualism inherent in major Western metaphysical systems, the gap between material, contingent experience and the posited unconditional, eternal principle, the sensible world and the mystical realm.

The project of relating part and whole without compromising either would now appear to be successfully completed, were it not for the anomalous way that Solovyov, in the second half of his essay, introduces religious language. The whole project of balancing diverse human experience and total unity is jeopardized, in my view, when Solovyov looks to biblical imagery to deal with the question of gender roles in the totalizing context of *vseedinstvo* (total unity). It is here that one single, and what one might justifiably call "masculine," point of view becomes paramount, and, despite Solovyov's clear efforts to resist it, discursive monologism takes the upper hand: Solovyov starts to preach and set forth one "correct" interpretation of experience. Here the mutual interaction and dialogue promised earlier blend into hierarchy and polarity as Solovyov resorts uncritically (at least, in contrast to his treatment of secular discourses) to traditional biblical images of male and female for symbols of total unity. The *polemical* citation of scientific and poetic sources used frequently elsewhere in the essay now gives way to what can be called *authoritative* citation of New Testament sources. The merging of selves into an ideally androgynous higher self becomes less thinkable, because that higher self is modeled in the image of a clearly *male* God who creates an implicitly female world (*SS*12, 7:45). Woman loses her recently affirmed personhood as she is refigured with grammatically feminine biblical metaphors of passive body: universe (*vselennaia*), Church (*tserkov'*), nation (*natsiia*)—of material to be formed and not as creative spirit capable itself of being a shaping force.

As the division of gender identities becomes more polarized, individual experience and being lose the multiplicity that Solovyov had earlier prized. He reverts to quite traditional gender divisions. The masculine principle becomes characterized as the active, guiding force, whereas the feminine principle is characterized by passivity, docility, and tractability. The female is no longer a person in her own right but a "supplement" (*dopolnenie*) to the male. Although Solovyov does reassert the idea that husband and wife "achieve perfection only through a process of mutual interaction" (*SS12*, 7:42), it is difficult to see how a person can interact with a supplement. The accent is put ever more heavily on the male principle, for example, when Solovyov speaks of "man [*chelovek*] and *his* female alter ego." True mutuality would suggest that there also exists "woman and *her* male alter ego."

Man is increasingly cast in the role of the creator and woman as material to be molded, again on the New Testament model. Just as God created the universe and Christ created the Church, so, by analogy, a man is "obliged to create and mold [*tvorit' i sozidat'*] his female complement" (*SS12*, 7:41). Man is the mediator and conduit of divine force to the female complement, again affirming a hierarchical rather than a mutual, egalitarian structure (*SS12*, 7:42)—or even the triangular structure of ideal androgynous selfhood that Solovyov earlier saw emerging from man and woman in dialogue with each other. Far from achieving true dialogue and interaction between thinking human beings, the female "other" is made into a passive object.

It should be said that this element of *The Meaning of Love* relates to a concept long beloved by Solovyov, the idea of the Divine Sophia. Already in *Lectures on Godmanhood*, Solovyov conceptualized Sophia as the mediating principle between the divine and the human. If the "Word" represents God's essence, then Sophia is God's physical, corporeal emanation. Christ is the synthesis of male and female, of word and body. Throughout his early philosophical career, Solovyov had identified the feminine principle with body. In *The Meaning of Love,* this view of the feminine principle comes into vital contradiction with a more diversified view that the human female is not just body—just the synecdoche of the male imagination—but is a whole spiritual being (*lichnost'*).

The monological quality of this part of Solovyov's treatment of the gendered other contrasts sharply with a response to it nearly twenty years later by Vasilii Rozanov in *Solitaria* (1911). Whereas Solovyov is generally acknowledged to be the greater and far more progressive thinker, one can argue that Rozanov makes headway in confronting an issue in which Solovyov, at least temporarily, becomes mired. Rozanov's work draws groundbreaking parallels between innovative speech genres and new revelations about consciousness, particularly gendered consciousness.[24] In *Solitaria* (1911) he both records and adopts a large variety of voices, including women's voices. Indeed, one may read this work as a sustained probing of

24. For two influential theorizations of the interaction of gender consciousness and genre, see Hélène Cixous, "The Laugh of the Medusa," *Signs* 1(1976): 875–893. See also Jacques Derrida, "The Law of Genre," in *Acts of Literature,* ed. D. Attridge (London: Routledge, 1992), 221–252.

the gendered other within Rozanov himself.[25] It can be shown that Rozanov's listening to women's voices and confronting the female aspect of his own personality are key to finding a structure in this seemingly formless set of fragments and aphorisms. A conscious and deliberate function of this related fragmentation of genre and traditional gendered consciousness will be to question the cognitive languages, both secular and religious, at the heart of contemporary cultural life. Read against *Solitaria,* this weakness of *The Meaning of Love* becomes clear. Despite its radical promise and considerable achievements, *The Meaning of Love* is limited by an unexamined view of gender based on New Testament metaphors. The "*vzaimo-,*" or "mutual," leitmotif of reciprocity and interaction is undermined at important points by the intrusion of a polarized and relatively authoritarian interaction between God and humanity (*SS*12, 7:46).

Despite his difficulties in finding the right metaphors Solovyov ends his essay on an unperturbed, optimistic note, seemingly assured of the capacity of his particular philosophical discourse to use a combination of logical analogy and poetic metaphor to represent at once total unity and individual diversity: "Basing ourselves on firm analogies with historical and cosmic experience, we can assure ourselves that all conscious human reality, defined by the idea of worldwide *syzygy* and oriented toward the embodiment of the ideal of total unity in one or another sphere, . . . actually produces or releases real, electrical, spiritual-corporeal currents which gradually penetrate the material surroundings, animate them, and embody in them images of total unity, living and eternal likenesses of absolute humankind" (*SS*12, 7:60). Human consciousness has a direct, physiological impact on the world of things and transfigures things as symbols of total unity.

The other side of Solovyov's creative-intellectual personality belied this philosophical optimism: he was a first-rate poet as well as a philosopher. His optimistic faith in the power of discourse to penetrate mystical experience was often challenged in some of his most famous poems from the late 1880s and 1890s. In her pathbreaking, Soviet-era introduction to his poetry, Zara Mints argued that Solovyov the poet dealt with the same questions addressed in the philosophical essays but in a way that emphasized structures of imagery and sound.[26] This distinction does not fully hold, since we have shown the extent to which Solovyov the philosopher is willing to use "live" metaphors of light, space, love, and language for the construction of his mystical philosophy. Moreover, we can speculate that at times the poetry

---

25. This point is suggested but not fully pursued in Laura Engelstein, *The Keys of Happiness: Sex and the Search for Modernity in Fin-de-Siècle* Russia (Ithaca, N.Y.: Cornell University Press, 1994), 314–318. For further discussion, see chapter 7 in this volume.

26. Z. G. Mints, "Vladimir Solov'ev—poet," introduction to *Stikhotvoreniia i shutochnye p'esy,* 22ff.

functions as a challenge to the philosophy, providing a venue to express doubt about the adequacy of philosophical metaphor to articulate mystical knowledge.

If Solovyov's philosophical discourse puts the mystical word above a number of secular and religious languages, then his poetry claims unique access to a mystical experience that is beyond all discourse, beyond reason, and, indeed, beyond earthly, sensory experience. Placing itself above all human language, poetry can only hint at this experience. It is important to stress that, in contrast to his philosophical work, here, ironically, Solovyov is *less* concerned with metaphor than with rhetorical figure. The poet approaches the mystical through negation, the subjunctive mood, and through direct address of "thou," the ineffable, incorporeal female other.

In his poetry Solovyov contrasts "wordless" ecstasy and reasoned philosophical articulation. The idea that mystical insight is akin to an erotic ecstasy beyond the expressive capacity of words is first suggested in Solovyov's 1874 translation of a poem attributed to Plato:

> You look at the stars, my bright star!
> O, if I were the heaven, to hold you
> In vast embraces and with a myriad of eyes
> To wonder at you in *wordless* radiance.
>
> Na zvezdy gliadish' ty, zvezda moia svetlaia!
> O, byt' by mne nebom, v shirokikh ob"iatiiakh
> Derzhat' by tebia i ochei miriadami
> Toboi liubovat'sia v bezmolvnom siianii.

(*SShP*, 180; emphasis added)[27]

Mystical experience is conceived in Solovyov's own poetry more as ecstasy, as feeling, than as a process of "thinking." There is no philosophical project of total unity in the poetry, only a private yearning to be conjoined. Indeed, rational thought, when mentioned at all, is treated humorously. In perhaps his most famous poem, "Three Meetings" ("Tri svidaniia," 1898), Solovyov shows a beguiling self-irony, making light of philosophizing and the skittishness of rational faculties in the face of mystical experience. Even in the introduction to the poem, he reminds himself that Sophia, the female image of higher, mystical wisdom that inhabits much of his writing, appeared to him not cerebrally, "not by the effort of thought, oh no!" "Ne myslennym dvizheniem, o net!") (*SShP*, 126), but by the yearning of his soul: "Your image was an answer to the call of my soul" ("Na zov dushi tvoi

---

27. All poems cited are from Vladimir Solov'ev, *Stikhotvoreniia i shutochnye p'esy.* Hereafter cited in the text as *SShP* with the relevant page number.

obraz byl otvet") (*SShP,* 126). The third time he sees Sophia, he hears a voice telling him to travel to Egypt. Here he comments wryly about reason: "Feeling did not even bother to struggle with reason: / Reason was silent as an idiot" ("S rassudkom chuvstvo dazhe ne borolos': / Rassudok promolchal, kak idiot") (*SShP,* 128).

In his poetry, then, Solovyov could convey an inward search for personal mystical consciousness, one purportedly beyond the realm of discourse. A theme in a number of poems from this period is the use and uselessness of words for mystical quest. In a four-line poem from 1892 celebrating the lesbian poet Sappho (each line starts with a letter of her name), Solovyov rails in frustration at the inadequacy of words to express the inner and invisible sphere of feeling:

> **S**omething fairytale-like again was wafting . . .
> **A**ngel or demon, who is knocking at my heart?
> **F**eeling fears to take on form
> **O**h, how *helpless is the cold word!*

> **S**kazochnym chem-to poveialo snova . . .
> **A**ngel il' demon mne v serdtse stuchitsia?
> **F**ormu priniat' moe chuvstvo boitsia . . .
> **O**, kak bessil'no kholodnoe slovo!

(*SShP,* 85; emphasis added)

One of Solovyov's better-known poems, appropriately entitled, "Why Words?" ("Zachem slova?" 1892) conveys a similar idea that the mystical experience of love is beyond words:

> *Why words?* In the azure vastness
> The harmonious streams of the ether's waves
> Bring to you the stormy flame of desires
> And the *mysterious sigh of love falling silent.*

> Zachem slova? V bezbrezhnosti lazurnoi
> Efirnykh voln sozvuchnye strui
> Nesut k tebe zhelanii plamen' burnyi
> I tainyi vzdokh nemeiushchei liubvi.

(*SShP,* 91; emphasis added)

Words are associated implicitly with "the heavy dream of everyday consciousness" and are contrasted to a number of negative adjectives, such as "unearthly" and "unseen," that point to experience beyond the realm of articulation. The things that *cannot* be articulated, finally, are the only "real," valuable things in the world. In one of Solovyov's best mystical poems,

"Dear friend, do you not see" ("Milyi drug, il' ty ne vidish'," 1892 [*SShP,* 93]), the poet asserts that love, the most cherished of feelings, is unspoken:

> Dear friend, do you not feel
> That alone in the whole world
> Only that exists which the heart says
> To [another] heart *in silent greeting.*

> Milyi drug, il' ty ne chuesh',
> Chto odno na tselom svete—
> Tol'ko to, chto serdtse k serdtu
> Govorit v nemom privete?

(*SShP,* 94; emphasis added)

The verbal artifact, the poem itself, is the only verbal medium to be able even to hint at this silent world.

Although Bakhtin famously categorizes lyric poetry as "monological"— we hear only the poet's voice and no others—Solovyov's poetry possesses a certain dialogical quality. Each poem addresses a desired interlocutor, responding to or seeking out some response. By posing questions that remain unanswered, the poet leaves a powerful discursive space open for a female other who is more than just a silent complement to the male poet.

Are these poems, then, exercises in "sexual love," in Solovyov's specific definition of the term? Does the speaker here interact with the speaking voice of the philosophical essay? It becomes clear that the experiences of conceptualizing the mystical and of apprehending and feeling it were never more distant. While these poems are filled with mystical eroticism, they are so in entirely different terms from the essay. In the poems the worldly, social sphere is one to escape from, not integrate into a total vision of the world. The material world is seen as a "bad dream," sense perception only at best a "refraction," a "shadow," an "echo." The poet denies the value of social and worldly experience to a much greater extent than the philosopher does. In contrast to the essay, these poems are much more single-mindedly directed inward toward a sphere beyond sense experience and beyond knowledge that is communicable in discourse to another living person.[28]

At the very least Solovyov's poetry implies a measure of doubt about the feasibility of thinking total unity, recasting the power of reason, the reach of discourse, and the significance of body and material life. Most important, although Solovyov accorded less importance to his poetry than to his phi-

---

28. Kornblatt, "The Transfiguration of Plato," 48. Kornblatt laments that Blok and other Symbolists put Sophia back in heaven, taking away her earthly aspect. Armed with an understanding that they were primarily responding to the poems that they read may help to explain why, indeed, younger Symbolists saw Solovyov's worldview as being more unearthly than it really was.

losophy, the poetry acts as an important counterweight to the philosophy, adding a fresh perspective. We find here a self-ironic persona whose private and provisional quest for love, sorrow, and ecstasy challenges philosophy's hubristic claims to total unity, the belief that human discourse can overcome the rift between personal consciousness, bounded by discrete earthly experience, and the mystical ideal of unity and harmony. Finally, neither poetry nor philosophy wrests full authority from the other. Their differing truth claims and their competing positions concerning the power of discourse are a key to Solovyov's continuing vitality as a thinker.

In 1881 Solovyov had said that philosophy was "setting human selfhood free from outward violence and lending it inner substance"; it was "developing in people the inner form for the revelation of true Deity" (*SS*12, 2:411–412). Philosophy freed a thinking person from dogma and automatic, unreflective behaviors. It fostered a thoughtful, self-conscious approach to life. The goal was not to deny the value of faith but to employ analytical, skeptical thinking to arrive at a faith that would work for a self-conscious individual. The goal of Solovyov's philosophy was to create and deepen *lichnost'* or a sense of a spiritually integrated, individual self. Like his Slavophile predecessors he rejected philosophical rhetoric and logic—syllogism and dialectic—as a merely "human fiction" that did not lead to a higher truth. It was metaphors—the "Word," the language of love, light, and syzygy, among others—that would allow him to work out this spiritual liberation. But in his effort to balance the religious language of similitude and the philosophical discourse of logical argument, Solovyov had to tread a fine line between these living, at times even poetic, metaphors and the relatively worn and deflated symbols of Christian dogma that seemed to dictate a hardened, fixed notion of selfhood and the relationship between selves and between levels of being. Indeed, Solovyov's project works only at the moment when the reader is surprised by the freshness of his imagery and is invited at once to ponder the depth of each metaphor and to work out the logical relationships between its various levels of potential meaning. Only at such a moment—and not over a long span of time—can the creative link, the syzygy, between poetic, scientific, philosophical, and religious languages work.

Chapter Five

Philosophy as Tragedy:
Shestov and His Russian Audience

Shestov is very difficult to understand, not because he writes badly but because of his special way of drawing negative conclusions that most people take for skepticism and pessimism—meanwhile I know of no person more intensely searching for or desirous of truth.

—Gustav Shpet, letter, 1912

The horrors of life hold the guarantee of the future.

—Lev Shestov, *Dostoevsky and Nietzsche,* 1902

Unfinished, disorderly, chaotic thoughts, . . . contradictory as life itself—are these not closer to our heart than systems . . . the creators of which were less concerned with apprehending reality than with "understanding" it?

—Lev Shestov, *The Apotheosis of Groundlessness,* 1905

UNTIL SOLOVYOV'S APPEARANCE in the public arena in the late 1870s, most writers would not have wished to call themselves "philosophers." Those who did generally had the most limited audience among the educated Russian reading public. Solovyov himself became popular less for his systematic philosophical writings than as a riveting speaker. He was famous for his lecture series on divine humanity in the 1870s and particularly for his public address in St. Petersburg in March 1881. In that speech he pleaded for mercy for the assassins of Tsar Alexander II and, as a result, was removed from his university post as lecturer in philosophy. Among his writings his popularizing essays, such as *The Meaning of Love,* his literary criticism, and his mystical poetry found a larger readership than his formal philosophical writings. But building on this beginning, a number of literary critics with strong philosophical interests helped to shape a more philosophically minded readership. Among these were Dmitry Merezhkovsky, Viacheslav Ivanov, Andrei Belyi, and Lev Shestov (Lev Shvartsman, 1866–1938). Of this group only Shestov made the transition to a fully philosophical identity.

Making his publishing debut at the turn of the century, Shestov was the first Russian philosopher to gain real popularity in Russia among both the educated public and the new generation of students, and to be accepted later, in Continental Europe, as a "genuine" philosopher. For a philosopher, his books sold unusually well. His prerevolutionary work, according to one memoir, had the force of an "exploding bomb."[1] Directly after the publication of his first essay on a Russian writer, *The Good in the Teaching of Count Tolstoy and F. Nietzsche* (1899), Shestov became an intellectual fashion. Young people, in their more rebellious moments, would threaten their parents that they would "run amok [*razvratnichat'*] and read Shestov."[2] Vasily Rozanov, writing in 1905 in *Novoe vremia,* hailed Shestov's *Apotheosis of Groundlessness: An Experiment in Adogmatic Thought* (*Apofeoz bespochvennosti: Opyt adogmaticheskogo myshleniia,* 1905) as a truly fresh way of philosophizing. He complained that ordinary philosophers, such as Nikolai Grot, the editor of *Voprosy filosofii i psikhologii,* were "pale specter[s] hanging around real life. . . . [T]hey themselves are skinny, and life itself has grown skinny in their presence."[3] Rozanov loved *The Apotheosis of Groundlessness* because it was "remarkably sincere" in its exposure of the "vanity" of philosophical systems and because it reflected an "idiosyncratic metamorphosis of writerly and philosophical style."[4] Shestov's good friend, the writer Aleksei Remizov, gloated that Shestov had "committed a sin."[5] He had opened a philosophical pandora's box. After reading him, it would be impossible to "return the cover" of steady, stable Kantian philosophy.[6]

---

1. Natalia Baranova-Shestova, *Zhizn' L'va Shestova,* 2 vols. (Paris: La Presse Libre, 1983), 1:71.

2. Ibid. *Tolstoy,* whom Shestov met briefly in 1910, allegedly claimed that Shestov was "a 'literary man' and in no way a philosopher" (Shestov, *Izbrannye sochineniia* (Moscow: Renessans, 1993), 481).

3. V. V. Rozanov, "Novye vkusy v filosofii," *Novoe vremia* (September 17, 1905), 4. Not everyone was so enthusiastic. Iurii Aikhenval'd argued that Shestov was wasting his considerable literary powers. See Aikhenval'd's review in *Russkie vedomosti,* no. 63 (March 7, 1905), 3.

4. Ibid.

5. Aleksei Remizov, "Po povodu knigi L. Shestova 'Apofeoz bespochvennosti,'" *Voprosy zhizni,* 7 (1905): 204.

6. Shestov was the first Russian philosopher to gain genuine recognition abroad, particularly in Germany and in France where he settled in 1921. He enjoyed an international reputation among contemporary professional philosophers, for example, Husserl, Buber, and Levi-Brühl. In the history of philosophy he figures, along with Pascal, Kierkegaard, and Jaspers, in a tradition of philosophical existentialism. See, for example, José R. Maia Neto, *The Christianization of Pyrrhonism: Scepticism and Faith in Pascal, Kierkegaard, and Shestov* (Dordrecht: Kluwer Academic Publishers, 1995).

Oil portrait of Lev Shestov by Parkhomenko, 1910. Courtesy of the Literary Museum, Moscow.

Shestov's great achievement that made him so attractive to Russian readers was the dramatization of philosophy as a tragic but necessary quest after
existential truth. It is this new genre and tone of philosophizing that is examined in this chapter, particularly in *The Apotheosis of Groundlessness,*
Shestov's signature work of the prerevolutionary period. Shestov's writings
are about redefining philosophy so as to assign high value to those moments
of human experience that philosophers usually push to the side—suffering,
illness, and death. In this sense most of Shestov's work is "meta-philosophi-

Caricature of Lev Shestov holding a bottle of porteau, from the diaries of Aleksei Remizov, December 21–22, 1908. From a dream of Remizov's wife: on a field of battle with lots of dead bodies. Shestov picks up some decayed human intestines and says, "Here's an example." Remizov: "These 'decayed intestines' [*ralozhivshiesia kishki*] were typical of Shestov: his passion for 'analyzing' [*razlagat'*], of which he was particularly proud, is here in his hand." From G. N. Slobin, *Aleksei Remizov: Approaches to a Protean Writer* (Columbus: Slavica, 1987), 67.

cal": his chief concern is to define "philosophy"—the nature of "real" philosophical experience and the character of philosophical truth. He takes to
task mainstream "scientific" philosophical views, both positivist and idealist, continually questioning the limits of their authority. Clearly almost all
philosophy is, in some sense, meta-philosophical. But, unlike Shestov, modern philosophers until Nietzsche stayed within an established philosophical
tradition, engaging solely with other philosophers. Philosophers in Russia,
including Shestov, often built their philosophies from the insights of novelists, dramatists, and poets.

From his very first critical work, *Shakespeare and His Critic Brandes*
(1896), Shestov reclaimed literature from the positivists, who devalued it as
a form of mere entertainment,[7] and from the idealists, who treated literary
art as a lesser form of knowledge (*SS6*, 6:56). Founding his thought on his
interpretations of Shakespeare (whom he called "my first philosophy
teacher"), Heine, Tolstoy, Dostoevsky, and Chekhov, and the noncanonical
philosophers Pascal, Nietzsche, William James, and his Kievan friend,
Nikolai Berdiaev, Shestov legitimized an alternative "anti-philosophical"
tradition.[8] He devised fresh and challenging forms of philosophical writing
that intrigued readers and piqued their curiosity. Finally, he turned the current hierarchy of discourses, in which scientific empiricism was accepted as
the "truest" and most authoritative form of writing, upside down, devaluing traditionally authoritative uses of language and re-legitimizing traditionally "weak," non-authoritative ones. The result would be the articulation of a different definition of philosophical discourse and experience that
emerges in a writing tradition that Shestov called "tragic."

For Shestov, "philosophy as tragedy" was a philosophy oriented toward a
candid, personal quest for self-knowledge and for other approaches to
knowing the world. It was a philosophy not meant to preach, teach, or cer-
tify truth; rather, its goal was to probe and articulate the most difficult and
paradoxical human experience. Rejecting the heritage of Kantian metaphysics, it made no claims to total, systematic knowledge. The tragic aspect
of tragic philosophy lay in the concept of the philosopher as a seeker after
wisdom and a risk taker, an adventurer willing to confront the horrifying
aspects of human existence that do not fit in a neat order. This "Dionysian"
figure was depicted as the boldest, most deeply truthful and penetrating sort
of person, who walks the edge of the existential abyss, probing first and final
questions about the meaning and purpose of life, questions that, in the end,

---

7. Lev Shestov, *Sobranie sochinenii,* 6 vols. (St. Petersburg: Shipovnik, 1911), 1:22. Hereafter
cited in the text as *SS6* with relevant volume and page numbers.

8. For more on Shestov's relationship to literature, particularly Remizov, see L. A. Kolobaeva,
" 'Pravo na sub"ektivnost': Aleksei Remizov i Lev Shestov," *Voprosy literatury* 5 (1994): 44–76.

can never be fully answered. There is no guarantee that the tragic philosopher will ever attain wisdom or insight.

Shestov's tragic philosophy was first articulated in his early works, in the prerevolutionary "Russian" half of his career. These works reached and had an impact on audiences in Russia. They include, in particular, *The Good in the Teaching of Count Tolstoy and F. Nietzsche: Philosophy and Preaching* (*Dobro v uchenii gr. Tolstogo i F. Nitsshe: filosofiia i propoved'*, 1899) and *Dostoevsky and Nietzsche: Philosophy of Tragedy* (*Dostoevsky i Nitsshe: Filosofiia tragedii*, 1902). In *The Apotheosis of Groundlessness, Beginnings and Endings* (*Nachala i kontsy*, 1908), and *Great Vigils* (*Velikie kanuny*, 1911) tragic philosophy gained more concrete expression.

Before examining Shestov's concept of philosophy, it is important to ask why precisely *this* philosopher should have been the first to enjoy relatively widespread popularity in a country where readers were so resistant to philosophical writing and strongly preferred literary and journalistic genres. Born in 1866 and trained in mathematics and law, Shestov spent his early twenties working in Kiev, managing his father's very successful cloth manufacturing business. His earliest writings, published in the early 1890s, concerned economic subjects, particularly the labor question. He came to philosophy through a search for a literary voice of his own. He experimented in a number of genres, including literary narrative, literary criticism, and finally philosophy. Although the philosophical genres he chose were noncanonical, not traditionally accepted among academic philosophers, the drama of challenging accepted norms and the quest for a voice of his own certainly appealed to his readers.

Perhaps because Shestov was, at the start, an outsider to professional, academic philosophy (and certainly, as a Jew, an outsider to the new Russian religious philosophy), he was able to articulate the concerns particularly of young readers. As he put it later in life, "It is only because I did not study philosophy at university that I preserved a freedom of spirit."[9] Starting his philosophical career as a literary critic, he implicitly acknowledged the dominant power of the Russian literary tradition and thus found a common ground with his readers who long since had chosen fiction over philosophical tract. From his earliest essays on, Shestov built an image of an implied reader in the text with whom he had an ambiguous but alluring relationship. He wanted to create a kind of philosophy that would speak to an inquisitive lay reader. One can certainly argue that Shestov chose his style of philosophizing precisely with this kind of Russian audience in mind.

The philosophical genres Shestov develops show his concern with shaping a philosophical voice that would appeal to his Russian readers. His phi-

9. Baranova-Shestova, *Zhizn' L'va Shestova*, 1:58.

losophizing emerges from two forms, the literary essay and later the aphoristic fragment. With the form of the critical essay Shestov acknowledges the horizon of expectations of educated readers, only to lead them toward a philosophical discourse. Even in *Shakespeare and Brandes* his orientation is clearly already philosophical, devoted to questions of morality. In this work he attacks Kant's chief idea of the categorical imperative, and finds in Shakespeare a wholly different and much more promising kind of moral philosopher, one who penetrates the criminal's psychological motivations rather than screening them away with moral prescriptions.

Shestov's first two widely read works, devoted to Tolstoy and Dostoevsky, are philosophy disguised as criticism, a combination that resulted in the books selling rapidly.[10] Both books start by addressing and reassuring the reader. *Tolstoy and Nietzsche* begins with Vissarion Belinsky's rejection of philosophy, a position deeply familiar to Russian readers, and then carefully leads the reader to a reencounter with philosophy. *Dostoevsky and Nietzsche* begins with an articulation of Shestov's immediate desire to change the reader's attitude to philosophy.[11] He allays the reading public's fear of "abstract concepts" and "foreign words," criticizing professional philosophy and piquing the curiosity of ordinary readers (DN, 163).

Even in later works such as *Beginnings and Endings* Shestov always reaches out to his readers, sympathizing with their typically negative responses to academic philosophy. He writes: "All those people who came to philosophy for answers to the questions that bothered them came away disappointed if it turned out that they lacked a real gift that permitted them to join the guild of professional philosophers." And further: "Philosophy is concerned with something that could only interest a few people, for many people it seems boring and unnecessary" (*SS6*, 5:154). What specialists have made of philosophy is a kind of glass bead game, a form of "art for art's sake" (*SS6*, 5:160) that does not address the pressing, tragic issues of existence. Raised as they were on the generally antisystematic and yet speculative positions of Dostoevsky and Tolstoy, readers were likely to hear a familiar voice in Shestov's works, to respond to its excitement, and to give it the credence that system-building philosophy could not garner.

Shestov brought his readers to a stance more sympathetic to philosophical thought by speaking to previous Russian objections to philosophy. In his early works he singled out the founder of Russian literary criticism, Belinsky, who in the 1840s had shifted from adulation to rejection of German philosophy in favor of French and English social utopian theories. At the

---

10. Ibid., 63.

11. Lev Shestov, "Dostoevsky i Nitsshe: Filosofiia tragedii," *Izbrannye sochineniia* (Moscow: Renessans, 1993), 161. Hereafter cited in the text as DN with the relevant page number.

start of *Tolstoy and Nietzsche* Shestov quotes at length from Belinsky's famous letter in which the critic categorically rejects philosophy, particularly
Hegelian philosophy. Although it stands on the highest pinnacle of human
history, Belinsky claims, Hegel's thought cannot give a meaningful moral
account of past horrors.[12] Although he sympathizes strongly with Belinsky's
reaction to Hegel, Shestov argues that Belinsky essentially killed the spirit of
philosophy. Philosophy dies precisely with demands like Belinsky's for
moral "payment." Belinsky, Shestov claims, was not interested in the quest
for truth but rather in the establishment of a total moral rule. In Shestov's
view, philosophy arises "from amazement." It comes from curiosity, from
the inner need to seek truth. Thus Shestov responds to what he sees as Belinsky's very understandable and sympathetic yearnings in a way that helps
him to define his own philosophical voice, and also to shift literary criticism
from social critique toward philosophical exploration.

Belinsky's challenge was clearly a significant point of departure for
Shestov in terms of his efforts to delineate a particularly Russian philosophy. His impact worked in two ways. Early on, the figure of Belinsky
marked the beginning of Shestov's serious quest for a philosophical voice
within the framework of the critical essay. Later, in *The Apotheosis of
Groundlessness,* he also marked an important step in the disintegration of
the critical essay into aphoristic fragments. In *Apotheosis,* in the penultimate
aphorism, entitled "The Russian Spirit," Shestov defends the tendency of
Russians to flaunt European traditions and to come up with their own
unique, if rough and uncultivated, critical voice.[13] Belinsky, to Shestov, is
the clear symbol of this spirit:

> We [Russians] do not acknowledge traditions. In no literature has there ever
> been such a challenging struggle with traditions as in ours. We wanted to re-
> examine everything, to reconsider everything in a new way. It goes without
> saying that our boldness is rooted in a completely uncultured belief in our
> strengths. Our Belinsky, a student who never finished university, a person
> who got his knowledge of European philosophy thirdhand, takes the uni-
> verse to court to account for the long-forgotten victims of Philip II and the
> Inquisition. And in this litigation [*tiazhba*] lies the essence and meaning of
> all Russian fiction. (AB, 470)

In Belinsky Shestov finds a stark and refreshing protest against the European tendency toward artifice, the desire to cover up reality with theory, to

---

12. Lev Shestov, "Dobro v uchenii gr. Tolstogo i Nitsshe: Filosofiia i propoved'," in *Izbrannye
sochineniia* (Moscow: Renessans, 1993), 41. Hereafter cited in the text as TN with the relevant page
number.

13. Lev Shestov, "Apofeoz bespochvennosti," in *Izbrannye sochineniia* (Moscow: Renessans,
1993), 470. Hereafter cited in the text as AB with the relevant page number.

give order to nature and cover its true ugliness. He writes: "And so we are faced with a choice between the artistic and consummate lie of old, cultivated Europe, the result of a thousand years of difficult and tormenting experience, and the naïve, unsophisticated simplicity and truthfulness of young, uncultivated Russia" (AB, 472). Shestov sides with neither Europe nor Russia. "But who is closer to the truth?" he asks. "And can there be any talk of voluntary, free choice? Probably not. And probably neither old age nor youth can give us that truth we seek. Does a final truth even exist? Isn't the very concept of truth, the very supposition of its possibility, just the result of the limits—of our experience?" (AB, 472).

Shestov's choice of the aphorism as a philosophical form in *The Apotheosis of Groundlessness* has its roots, in some sense, in Belinsky's protest. Shestov, too, objects to the a priori assumptions typical of Western thought, but he uses more sophisticated tools than Belinsky had. He chooses the aphoristic form as a challenge to systematic philosophy. Having realized that logical consistency and a devotion to the Big Idea came at the cost of freedom of thought, Shestov decides to abandon the critical essay. His thematic point of departure is the image of the aging Turgenev, who, having devoted his whole life to rational social enlightenment, is shaken toward the end of his life by a sudden consciousness of metaphysical groundlessness. At the end the éminence grise of Russian letters writes his relatively weak prose poems and suffers from various uncontrollable maladies, helpless against oncoming death (AB, 330). Turgenev's experience becomes a motif that carries Shestov's overriding concern to show the fecklessness of systematic philosophical constructs in the face of first and final questions.

As he determines to move away from logical argument toward fragmentary insight, Shestov is sensitive to his readers' probable response:

> Risking the wrath of readers and particularly critics who, it stands to reason, want to see in the violation of traditional form nothing more than strange whimsy, [I decided] to put forth my work in the form of a series of externally disconnected thoughts. . . . There is no idea, there are no ideas, there is no consistency, there are contradictions, but that is precisely what I was after, as the reader may have already guessed from the title. Groundlessness, even the apotheosis of groundlessness, . . . my whole purpose was once and for all to get rid of all kinds of beginnings and ends that had been forced on us with such incomprehensible tenacity by all kinds of founders of philosophical systems, both great and small. (AB, 330–331)

In the end Shestov opposes both Belinsky and the Germans in his rejection of all "final" truths and prescriptive worldviews. Contradiction, disorderly thought, incomplete ideas, he claims, are all much more "factual" in that they are much closer to reality than systematic thinking (AB, 331–332).

Shestov himself undertakes neither to "prove" nor to prescribe. Although he makes assertions without proof, most of the time he persuades with self-assured, witty, and nearly always challenging insight. Above all, Shestov draws attention to his own ironical voice, attitude, and mood. The consistency in his work lies in the integrity of his point of view and speaking voice.

Having tempted his implied reader, Shestov turns his attention to "tragic" philosophical discourse. Like many other Russian philosophers appropriating poetic tropes for the purposes of speculative thought, he modulates his voice in contrast to the enlightenment tradition of philosophy and empirical science. His philosophical language is self-consciously figurative. Most important is his use of chronotope, those images of time and space in which philosophizing is embedded.

Shestov employs three issues to articulate the concept of philosophy as tragedy: (1) the difference between "philosophy" and "teaching" or "preaching" (*propoved'*); (2) the distinction between "philosophy" and the philosophical justification of empirical, scientific knowledge; and (3) the difference between "philosophy" and modern "metaphysics" with its claim to absolute truth. Drawing a distinction between philosophy and preaching forms the backbone of *Tolstoy and Nietzsche*. Shestov contrasts preaching with genuine philosophical meditation: "as preachers, both Count Tolstoy and Nietzsche offer us a doctrine that simply closes their inner thoughts from us. Any person who might think of serving the 'good' according to Count Tolstoy's program would be just as foreign to his teacher as the person who would sacrifice himself to the Übermensch would be to Nietzsche" (TN, 139). As Shestov sees it, the preaching philosopher sets forth principles and rules that hide the spiritual doubts and struggles that are the stuff of real philosophy. With his "immoralism," for example, Shestov asserts, Nietzsche stops philosophizing and starts preaching: "Here starts self-protection and self-aggrandizement, the division of people into the higher and the lower, the worthy and the unworthy—in a word, the same thing that existed before Nietzsche" (TN, 152).

When a philosopher preaches, he is, subtly or not, boasting of his own good qualities and finding comfort in this self-adulation: "A person's need to find some point of support is so painful, so deep, that he will sacrifice everything, forget everything, just to save himself from doubt. Preaching, the chance to be indignant, is the best escape [from doubt] that one could ever devise for the raging storm in one's soul" (TN, 153). Shestov explains further: "Wherever the limitations of human strength bring philosophy to a standstill, that is where preaching starts. Ultimately Nietzsche interprets his suffering, his shame, his unhappiness—in short everything that he had to bear in life—in such a way as to give himself the right to crush and destroy someone" (TN, 154). Preaching is a mask that covers the tragic horror the thinking self experiences as it encounters existence: "There, where he experienced the most terrible and exasperating tragedy of life, Count Tolstoy found the poetry of preaching. The same was true for Nietzsche" (TN, 156).

In *Tolstoy and Nietzsche*, as in ensuing works, Shestov grapples with "scientific" philosophy and "science" as areas antithetical to genuine philosophical experience. His criticism is aimed at Kant whose goal, Shestov asserts, was to articulate a priori, synthetic judgments that would form the basis for scientific knowledge (TN, 70). Most important in Kant's effort, Shestov argues, is the theoretical justification for causality in the experimental sciences. He claims that Kant's concept of practical reason and his moral idea of the categorical imperative were "constructed" from this scientific model, "in the likeness of the category of causality" (TN, 70). Tolstoy admires Kant's practical reason, which, as he argued, " 'contained the essence of moral teaching' " (TN, 70). Both Tolstoy and Dostoevsky are too attached to the idea of the categorical imperative which provides, in Shestov's rather more critical view, moral standards of "the good" that have little to do with real moral behavior but against which each person is judged or judges his or her own actions (TN, 71). The older Tolstoy finds Kant's principle of practical reason handy because it gives him, in Shestov's words, "the right to demand of other people that they do as he does, that they live as he does" (TN, 72). Kant gives Tolstoy a mask behind which he can hide from the very painful moral searching of his earlier years.

Relying in part on Nietzsche's critique of systematic philosophy and science (Nietzsche argues that both focus solely on the "normal" and ignore the unique or new), Shestov focuses on the conformity implicit in scientific valuations. In *Dostoevsky and Nietzsche,* he writes: "The chief task of science—and of morality—is to give people a firm basis in life, to teach them to know what exists and what does not, what one may and may not do" (DN, 290). He continues:

> Moral ideas, far more than any other constructs, have lived until now as "premises," culled completely from observations of external human relationships. Moralists have been guided by the same instinctive urge to limit our field of observation that guided scientists when they were creating their theories of natural development. Kant's categorical imperative and Mill's utilitarian principles had just one role to play—to chain people to average, habitual life norms, that were supposed to be fine for all people to the same degree. Both Kant and Mill had a deep faith that the law of morality was just as compulsory, understandable, and close to the heart of each person as the law of causality. (DN, 304)

Shestov supports Nietzsche's observation that science plays a normative role. Science, he points out, focuses on repeated experience and articulates "facts" only from phenomena that can be reproduced. It "takes into account only phenomena that repeat in a certain pattern" (AB, 466). Shestov asserts that "science is useful, there can be no argument, but it has no truths and will never have them" (AB, 466).

In *The Apotheosis of Groundlessness* Shestov mounts a sharper challenge to science, addressed directly to his reader:

> Hold on to your conviction that science is perfect knowledge, and generalize. But if you still have lively eyes and sharp ears—put down your instruments and appliances, forget your methodology and your scientific quixotism, and try to trust in yourself. So what if you do not achieve generally applicable judgments and you actually come to see sheep as sheep? This will be a step forward, perhaps. You will lose the habit of seeing the way everyone else does, but you will learn to see in places where no one has yet seen, not contemplate, but conjure, using strange words to evoke unprecedented beauty and grand forces. (AB, 468)

From his first work on, Shestov argues that philosophy should not be normative. The power of philosophy, in his view, is in the articulation of personal experience and in its speculative breadth, that is, its power to formulate questions.

What bothers Shestov most is the subordinate position that this kind of philosophy-as-science occupies in relation to science. Its truths lack the power of natural scientific truths. First, "scientific" philosophy, in his view, is more concerned with structural harmony (which it never fully achieves) than with facts and reality. In his remarks on Kant, Shestov writes that the German idealist "did not worry how close this or that solution was to reality but was only concerned with the relation it bears to the critique of pure reason—whether it confirms the critique or violates the architectonic harmony of the logical construct" (TN, 71). The outcome of this adherence to the cognitive standards of natural science, he believes, is that philosophy-as-science becomes unnecessary, because science is so much more powerful than such philosophy is. It is able to justify its own findings and conclusions without the apparatus of philosophical theory.

For Shestov, another major shortcoming in science and philosophy conceived as science is the tendency of both to avoid the last questions of life and death. Much later in life Shestov commented that Kant, the epitome of the "scientific" philosopher, "tried to caulk up, and for centuries did caulk, the holes in existence that had been exposed in his very own *Critique of Pure Reason*. But Kant could not give me an answer to my questions."[14] Science, Shestov thinks, "forbids people to be afraid and demands of them a calm at-

14. Baranova-Shestova, *Zhizn' L'va Shestova*, 1:15.

titude toward death" (AB, 379). Scientific constructs, he finds, are the creations of limited minds: "to dampen human sensitivity and to hold reason within the bounds of what may be grasped . . . this is the sort of task that could inspire only a limited being" (AB, 380).

Just as he limits science as a way of arriving at useful, practical truths—which cannot help us with our quest for answers to final questions about human existence—Shestov is even more critical of philosophical metaphysics which, in his view, only offers a fiction of a stable, ultimate, a priori reality that discredits the shifts and turns of real life. Most of the early aphorisms in *The Apotheosis of Groundlessness* are devoted to a critique of metaphysics, which becomes the straw man against which Shestov animates his own view of philosophy and its goals. The "basic inadequacy of human thought," he remarks, "[and the] root of the platonic worldview," is the desire to equate the "real" with the "constant." This shortcoming is then affirmed as the "highest virtue": "the philosopher has a hard time keeping a hold on exciting, capricious life, so he decides that all this is not life but a fiction" (AB, 357). The metaphysician's first concern, in Shestov's view, is to seek metaphysical "comfort" (AB, 462). Moreover, unlike science, which is very close to life and deals primarily in observable fact, idealist philosophical systems make unity and harmony of the system a priority. Facts then become secondary, and the general plan becomes primary. For Shestov, the name of Hegel is synonymous with such negligence of facts. Idealists in general, he claims, try so hard to "understand," that is, to order and interpret phenomena, that they miss the first step of perceiving those same phenomena clearly (AB, 332).

Shestov speaks out repeatedly against philosophers' insistence on eternal truths. Since philosophers cannot even tell what is "absolutely necessary" from what elements are "accidental" (*sluchainyi*) in their own judgments and which elements are the more substantial, he concludes, in *The Apotheosis of Groundlessness,* that "philosophy should quit trying to track down *veritates aeternae* [eternal truths]" (AB, 347). Metaphysics, he points out toward the end of that same work, is at best the "weighing of probabilities": "In the area of metaphysics there cannot be nor should there be enduring convictions. Here the word *durability* loses all meaning. It is appropriate to speak of eternal wavering and vacillation of thought" (AB, 401). And he adds: "If a person proposes a solution to the eternal questions, all it means is that he has not yet begun to think about them" (AB, 409). "The task [of philosophy]," in Shestov's view, "is to teach people to live with uncertainty. In short, the task of philosophy is not to calm but to disturb people" (AB, 347). Finally, he intimates that the greatest literary art has a much firmer grasp on truth than the metaphysicians do: "Isn't it time to forget about conclusions and quarry for the truth, a posteriori, the way Shakespeare, Tolstoy, Goethe, [and] Dostoevsky did, and almost all were poets, that is, simply put, when you want to find something out—go and look" (AB, 460).

For Shestov, then, philosophy is not doctrinaire preaching, and nor is it systematic science or metaphysical construct. His prerevolutionary works offer a "psychology" of philosophy as mental habits and experiences out of which he describes what he believes philosophical experience and activity are. He fundamentally believes that a person begins to think "philosophically" when no path of action is open. As he expressed it in *The Apotheosis of Groundlessness*: "Hopelessness is a solemn and very great moment in our life. Until now people helped us, but now we must rely on ourselves" (AB, 379). And later he adds: "A person begins to think, really to think, only when he becomes convinced that *there is nothing for him to do,* that his hands are tied. That is probably why all profound thought must start with despair" (AB, 409; emphasis added). In *Beginnings and Endings* Shestov refers to the Napoleon in exile on Helena as one who has exhausted all physical opportunities, a prime example of someone ready for philosophy. Genuine philosophy, he remarks, is "the last resort. When material resources have been squandered, when there is no other way to fight for rights that have been taken away, people then turn for help and support which they earlier had avoided" (*SS6*, 5:160–161).

Clearly, in Shestov's view, philosophy is not a science but an art. In *The Apotheosis of Groundlessness* he states: "Philosophy should have nothing to do with logic; philosophy is an art, striving to break through the logical chain of deductions, carrying a person out onto the boundless sea of fantasy, of the fantastic, where everything is at once possible and impossible" (AB, 354). From his earliest work on, Shestov sees philosophy in literary terms, as "tragedy." In *Tolstoy and Nietzsche* he is vehement in his insistence that Shakespeare in his tragedies (Shestov's favorite is *Macbeth*) is indeed a great philosopher who penetrates moral experience and moral consciousness to its depths. He uses his second major work, *Dostoevsky and Nietzsche,* to explore the concept of tragic philosophy. Philosophy as tragedy focuses on those issues in life that philosophers traditionally do *not* want to deal with. In contrast to systematic philosophy, tragic philosophy is based on an acknowledgment of the basic chaos of life: "Laws—all of them—have a regulatory meaning and are needed by a person in search of rest and support. But the first and vital condition of life is lawlessness. Laws are sleep that fortifies. Lawlessness is creative activity" (AB, 404). Whereas metaphysicians, system builders, and scientists try to articulate axioms, rules, and laws, deeper philosophical experience has to do with the phenomena and feelings that do not lend themselves to regularization.

In his move toward a notion of tragic philosophy Shestov relies heavily on the experiences of two precursors, Dostoevsky and Nietzsche, whose approach to speculative thought he views as pathbreaking.[15] Their visions are "underground" visions that acknowledge the role that suffering, illness, and life on the edge of the "normal" play in thought. Responding to personal illness and, in Dostoevsky's case, also the experience of prison, they both counter the normative views of metaphysicians, materialists, and empirical scientists with frank insight into the horror of life: "The wisdom of official wise men has always viewed suffering as something absurd, meaningless, and essentially unnecessary, something one should avoid at all costs" (DN, 320). For both Dostoevsky and Nietzsche the gateway into philosophy was metaphysical hopelessness, and both were capable of deeply experiencing doubt that did not always mask itself in the certainty preaching offered. In *The Apotheosis of Groundlessness* Shestov offers a generalization: "A philosopher is compelled to doubt, doubt, doubt and only then to ask, when no one else is asking, running the risk of becoming the laughingstock of the crowd" (AB, 464).

Just as Shestov is critical of systematic philosophy, so, too, is he against ruling concepts. The key "anti-concept" around which he constructs his

15. The central importance of Nietzsche for Shestov's emergence as a philosopher is indubitable. Shestov first discovered Nietzsche in the mid-1890s while living in Germany. He read Nietzsche first in 1895 and ever more intensely in 1896. Exactly what he read and when we do not know, although the textual evidence from his own first writings amply suggests that he was familiar with *The Birth of Tragedy* as well as with the main middle and late works, particularly *Thus Spake Zarathustra*. Both philosophers began their writing careers within literary critical genres, Nietzsche in classical philology and Shestov in modern European and Russian literature. Shestov had a certain symbiotic relationship with his adopted philosophical mentor, Nietzsche, in that the former helped greatly in laying the groundwork for Nietzsche's wild popularity in Russia. Shestov helped to foster in his Russian readers a feeling for the affinity between the recent Russian literary tradition and Nietzsche's brand of philosophy. The discovery of Nietzsche's works also aided Shestov in finding a philosophical idiom that his nonspecialist Russian audience would not only tolerate but would actually enjoy and rush to read. By 1904–1905, when he was writing *The Apotheosis of Groundlessness,* Shestov had abandoned the traditional long critical essay and was experimenting with the aphoristic style that was Nietzsche's hallmark. Beyond the clear and powerful impression that Nietzsche's style and thought made on Shestov, Shestov developed a dynamic of his own.

The two philosophers differ strongly in their attitudes toward their reader. Although Shestov's style of philosophizing resembles that of Nietzsche in that each claims that his philosophy is not for the average reader, it is clear that one of Shestov's goals is to rouse and "disturb" a broader readership. It is important, however, to distinguish between Shestov's metaphysical anarchism and that of Nietzsche. Shestov, unlike Nietzsche, was careful often to point out that his philosophical quests were not meant to teach anyone anything. His challenge to idealist philosophy and positivist science, he said repeatedly, did not negate the need in the everyday life of society for a stable order and functional truths. In *Dostoevsky and Nietzsche* he agrees that young people especially need guidance from writers and philosophers more traditional in their orientation than *Tolstoy*, Dostoevsky, or Nietzsche (DN, 302). He clearly articulates that he is operating solely in a "philosophical"—that is, a psychological, spiritual, and nonpragmatic—zone and talking about philosophers, not about other people acting out a social or political form of anarchy. Although he is speaking "about people who strive to see, find out, experience as much as possible in life" (AB, 331), he means unequivocally the inner, spiritual sphere.

tragic philosophy is "groundlessness." In contrast to modern European philosophies that are built around a Big Idea, for example, Kant's categorical imperative (which Shestov disparages from his very earliest writings on (SS6, 1:279–282)), Shestov's thought "rests" on what is really a parody of the big idea, the anti-idea of "groundlessness." If all systems need a "ground" or a "foundation," that is, basic ideas or assumptions about the nature of the world, on which to build a structure of ideas, Shestov's thinking denies the existence of such a ground. He calls his thought "considerations founded on nothing but the general supposition that human existence is intelligible" (AB, 388).

Shestov's term *groundlessness* is the metaphysical basis for his idea of philosophy as tragedy. The Russian word *bespochvennost'* is not merely the opposite of *osnova*, the usual philosophical term for "ground" or "foundation." Although "*bespochvennost'*" indicates a parody of metaphysics, the root word in Shestov's term, "*pochva*" or "soil," distantly echoes Dostoevsky's concept of "*pochvennichestvo*," or the idea of "national soil" and national unity of the intelligentsia and the masses. Although in his early works Shestov did not show a strong bond with his Jewish heritage and its lack of a firm national "soil," we might speculate that this "groundless" heritage in diaspora, without a national "soil," may have played some underlying part in Shestov's choice of the term.[16]

Shestov, like his predecessor Nietzsche, is clearly self-conscious and aware that "truth" depends on personal perception and taste. Building taste and style is ultimately more important than a logical system. Here again the reader is on center stage. Philosophy, in Shestov's view, is even more fundamentally about "taste" than it is about "truth." As he puts it in *The Apotheosis of Groundlessness*, "There is no truth—we can only suppose that truth is to be found in changing human tastes" (AB, 396). In other words, truth by itself means nothing and can have no impact unless readers develop a taste for it. As Shestov remarks about Turgenev's experience with metaphysics: "The main shortcoming [of metaphysics] is revealed only by chance: when a person's taste for the dialectical play of the mind is dulled—as with Turgenev at the end of his life, he becomes suddenly convinced of the superfluity of philosophical constructs" (AB, 356). If one wants a type of philosophy—metaphysics, for example—to be authoritative, then one must make it a high honor to study the dialectic. For example, Shestov writes, "people concerned with the success of metaphysics always need public support of the conviction that a taste for the dialectic enhances a person, as witness to

16. For more on Shestov's Judaism, see Judith Deutsch Kornblatt, "Vechnyi zhid: Lev Shestov i russkaia religioznaia mysl'," *Russkaia literatura XX veka: Isledovaniia amerikanskikh uchenykh* (St. Petersburg: Petro-Rif, 1993), 47–57.

the high elevation of his soul" (AB, 356). And he concludes with the ironic advice that readers will take a hypothesis seriously only when it is stated as an unassailable truth, and not simply as a supposition (AB, 360).

Style of argument is the key to building a taste for and establishing the authority of a given kind of thinking. In *Great Vigils* (1911) Shestov formulates his own view of philosophical style: "Philosophy should gain vitality through sarcasm, mockery, alarm, struggle, misunderstandings, despair, [and] great hopes, and it should allow itself meditation and peace only once in a while, so it can catch its breath" (*SS6*, 6:48). If philosophers were only more oriented toward drama, they might come up with visions of the world, which Shestov calls "dreams," that could compete effectively with the empiricist worldview of the science-based style of the day, "realism."

Shestov is keenly aware of the limitations of language and form in the quest for meaning. Because grammar and vocabulary place such strong constraints on what can be thought, much less articulated, language is a problem that must be continually addressed (*SS6*, 5:190). In the writing of his mentor, Nietzsche, Shestov notes the figures that Nietzsche uses to build a sense of philosophical vitality. Nietzsche's writing is sustained by contradiction, keeping its reader continually off balance (DN, 292). Similarly Shestov develops a style animated by oxymoron, paradox, and irony. The term *tragic philosophy,* for example, he views as an oxymoron (DN, 161), as he does *apotheosis of groundlessness.* In both cases the reader is fascinated by the interaction of the two seemingly contradictory terms. In my own view, *apotheosis of groundlessness* is the more successful of the two. Historically it evoked the strongest reactions, for example, from Berdiaev, who welcomed the notion of groundlessness but was disappointed that Shestov, too, was trying to create just another Big Idea.[17] Berdiaev missed the irony of Shestov's "apotheosis," or elevation to divine status, of something that does not firmly exist as a metaphysical "ground." The oxymoron in Shestov's title may be seen as the first volley in the battle with classical metaphysics that comprises the first part of *The Apotheosis of Groundlessness.*

Whereas "scientific" philosophy and metaphysics both place high value on a well-ordered, harmonious system, free from contradiction, Shestov, following Nietzsche and Dostoevsky, glories in inconsistency. Paradox (two mutually contradictory "true" statements) and irony (a statement that means the opposite of the word's face value) particularly form the figurative basis for Shestov's writings. For example, one of his most commonly repeated assertions about philosophers is ironic: that they are able to turn a vice (stolidness) into a virtue (logical systematicity) (for example, AB, 347, 357). One of Shestov's major ironies comes at the expense of metaphysi-

---

17. Baranova-Shestova, *Zhizn' L'va Shestova,* 75.

cians: he notes the conflicting imperatives of these philosophers. Although they are often against material pleasure, they stand up for metaphysical comfort. In an aphorism entitled "Metaphysical Comforts," Shestov asserts that, while metaphysicians "as is well known, mercilessly persecute any sort of eudaemonic doctrine" (AB, 461), they seek comfort (which Shestov understands as a form of pleasure) on a metaphysical plane by proving the existence of God or of absolute a priori truth. As he puts it: "Every metaphysician is much more concerned with *persuading himself* that God exists than with God's actual existence. Once [the metaphysician] has come to believe in God or in incontrovertible metaphysical truth, that is enough for him, even if it turned out that he was wrong. He has found comfort—he wanted nothing more. Otherwise he would have understood that the circumstance that he believes in no way serves as proof of the reality of the object of his belief" (AB, 462; emphasis added). The metaphysician, Shestov continues, "should understand that it is irrelevant whether he believes or not and that the whole point is whether there exists a higher principle or whether we, living people, are eternal slaves . . . of dead laws of necessity. But what does he care! He who has announced himself as the irreconcilable enemy of eudaemonism, wants comfort, comfort, and comfort" (AB, 462).

Shestov's philosophical discourse also represents a clear revolt against descriptive, scientific language. Although he makes wide use of logical figures and again employs scientific discourse itself to analyze the inconsistency of systematic thinking, he strongly favors associative poetic language. Moreover, he is the first Russian philosopher to see this preference in language style—and, by implication, style of thought—as part of a national consciousness. Indeed, it is a cultural dividing line between Russians and Europeans. Europeans, he claims, "have stopped believing in miracles and have understood that the whole task of humanity boils down to establishing life on earth" and, for that reason, "[they] have begun to invent ideals and ideas" (AB, 356). Russians, in contrast, still believe in the literal enactment of miracles and utopian paradise on earth, in part because they were so suddenly and shockingly inundated with Western cultural habits: "Civilization came to us in Russia suddenly, when we were still barbarians, and immediately assumed the role of animal tamer, first through allure, and then, when it was assured of its power, through threats" (AB, 355). What was real in European life was a heady dream to a Russian: "A Russian only had to breathe the air of Europe for his head to start to spin. . . . People talked to him about railroads, agricultural machinery, schools, self-government, and, in his imagination, these became miracles: universal happiness, limitless freedom, paradise, wings, and so forth" (AB, 355).

Shestov sees this gap between Russia and Europe in a way that anticipates Foucault's theories about the grand shift in the seventeenth century from the predominance of magical and poetic language to the increasingly authoritative modern scientific language of definition by differentiation. He writes: "The Russian crawled out of his back-of-the-beyond and headed for Europe in search of the elixir of life, a magic carpet, seven-league boots, and so forth, supposing in his naiveté that railroads and electricity were just the beginning. . . . And all this happened at the same time that Europe put away its astrology and alchemy, and set out in search for positive knowledge that led to chemistry and astronomy" (AB, 356). Shestov wants to keep the door open for the possibilities of magical language, of *zaklinanie* or "conjuring" (AB, 468). Although he himself does not use it, he senses in such language the chance to go beyond mere logical systems to other kinds of insight.

What, then, is Shestov's "tragic philosophy"? Is it simply a critique of existing philosophical systems and an assertion that one can never have metaphysical knowledge? Shestov himself was sensitive to the accusation, made quite often by Berdiaev and others, that he was developing a philosophy that offered nothing more than pessimism and skepticism. Although his early works defended that notion, he increasingly came to differentiate his philosophy from skepticism. In *The Apotheosis of Groundlessness* he stands up fearlessly for the ethos of doubt and inquiry characteristic of skepticism, but at the same time he is aware that consistent skepticism also becomes a system: "An obvious premise: consistent skepticism disproves itself since the negation of the possibility of knowledge is already an affirmation" (AB, 369). Later, in *Beginnings and Endings,* Shestov distanced himself still further from pure skepticism, defining skeptics as "people convinced in the depths of their souls that there is no point in searching because, no matter what, you will never find anything" (SS6, 5:119–120). Still, he urges himself and his reader to continue to search actively (SS6, 5:177). Finally, tragic philosophy is an acceptance of continual change, risk, and search without the guarantee of revelation or insight. In *The Apotheosis of Groundlessness* Shestov shows more concretely what he has only theorized in *Dostoevsky and Nietzsche.*

The question now becomes this: Does Shestov's concept of philosophy as tragedy make *The Apotheosis of Groundlessness* distinctive as a work of philosophy? Or does it remain in the shadow of his philosophical mentors, Dostoevsky and Nietzsche? In my view, Shestov makes concrete and dramatic the experience of a thinking person who can no longer accept the dictates of either positivism or idealism and who must rely on his own wits to find meaning in existence. This consciousness has its roots in Dostoevsky's underground, but it has left the underground to wander the margins and borders of existence.

In *The Apotheosis of Groundlessness* Shestov immediately makes the tragic experience more palpable by situating it amid metaphors of time and space that both affirm the distinct claim of tragic philosophy and lend meaning to its explicit arguments. For example, he envisions scientific philosophy and science as operating in a space defined by relatively closed horizons (AB, 348) and traveling down broad, well-paved roads (AB, 473). Everything is made comfortable and familiar: "[The philosopher] loves large, well-trodden ways on which theoretical thought moves easily and freely . . . dominated by the straight line" (AB, 339). Shestov also imagines the typical philosopher as a "sedentary" (AB, 355), unadventurous sort who stays either at home or in the classroom, the only places where the "order philosophers dream of [actually] exists" (AB, 341).

The tragic philosopher, in contrast to this "office philosopher," takes risks and is willing to cross boundaries. In Shestov's words: "It stands to reason that it is hard to be a good philosopher with the habits of a homebody—and the fact that the fates of philosophy have always been in the hands of professors can be explained purely through the hesitation of envious gods to give omniscience to mortals. While stay-at-homes are the ones looking for the truth—the apple of knowledge will stay on the tree" (AB, 354–355).

"Groundless," tragic philosophy happens in far more uncomfortable but exciting spaces on the edges of human society. It has a plot and is part of a life narrative of ceaseless questing. The first experience Shestov described that counters traditional philosophical "order," which can only inhabit the classroom or the office, is the shaky feeling of the "ground" of firm truth shifting beneath one's feet. He writes: "The firm ground sooner or later slips out from under a person's feet, . . . after that a person continues to live all the same but without ground or with eternally shifting ground, . . . and then he stops thinking that epistemological axioms are truth that does not require proof" (AB, 341). Against the homebody professor, who is powerless to pick the apple from the tree of knowledge, Shestov posits the "homeless adventurers, the natural nomads" who are the real philosophers (AB, 355). These wanderers can never choose the safe "middle road" of material comfort. They are compelled toward a radical solution, going either right or left at the proverbial fork in the road: "The philosopher never chooses the middle road, he needs no wealth, he does not know what to do with money. In either case, whether he goes right or left, nothing good awaits him" (AB, 355).[18] Tragically his inner need to seek his fate presses him toward eventual ruin.

18. In this passage we find a possible private pun. "Ego ne zhdet dobro" means both that "the good" or "goods," that is, "wealth," does not await the philosopher. Only the middle road leads to "goods" or material wealth but, for Shestov, certainly not to "the good." This pun is realized in Shestov's life in that he indeed gave up his job managing the family business and the accompanying wealth in order to follow his path as a philosopher.

In *The Apotheosis of Groundlessness* Shestov offers two main loci of the mind in which genuine philosophizing might take place. While "office philosophers" stay comfortably in their studies, Shestov's philosopher is always somewhere on the edge. In the first of two parts that comprise *Apotheosis* the philosopher wanders on the outskirts of the philosophical city, through the dark, unlit, unpaved streets: "The distant streets of life do not offer those conveniences to which the inhabitants of urban centers are accustomed. There are neither electric nor gaslights, and not even kerosene lamps, the streets are not paved—the traveler must grope his way in the dark" (AB, 342).

About two-thirds into the first part of *The Apotheosis of Groundlessness,* the philosopher becomes bored with "crawling over the earth" (AB, 384). He tears himself away from his philosophical "native ground" (*ot "rodnoi" pochvy*) (AB, 384) and climbs "upward, into the distance, into limitless space" (AB, 384). This move away from one's philosophical homeland prepares the way for the more self-reliant and daring quest of the second part of *this work.*

In part 2, which begins with the epigraph "Nur für Schwindelfreie" ("Not for the faint of heart"), the philosopher wanders the edge of a sheer cliff. To counter the obvious Nietzschean overtones of wandering alone through the Swiss Alps, Nathalie Baranova-Shestova, in her biography of her father, insisted that Shestov actually saw this very sign while hiking in the Alps. He took a path and soon found himself walking along a narrow ledge on the side of a cliff with a sharp drop below and a steep wall above.[19] Indeed, Shestov's image does have a different sense from Nietzsche's mountain scenery. Whereas Nietzsche speaks metaphorically of the great minds of human history as the mountain peaks, he almost never speaks of vertigo or the edge of the cliff. For Shestov, however, the experience of philosophy is akin to the sensation of vertigo, which, instead of being a weakness, becomes a source of strength. It draws us to the abyss of first and final questions that we cannot answer, "to what is unsolved, to mystery—not because we want to resolve . . . to comprehend mystery or, in a word, to understand, to order life. We need to turn away from understanding and to fall in love with horror and disorder [*neustroennost'*]" (SS6, 6:16).

The philosophical voice that emerges in *The Apotheosis of Groundlessness* has its roots in Dostoevsky's and Nietzsche's two "tragic" personae—the underground man and Zarathustra. Despite following these powerful philosophical mentors, Shestov's philosopher successfully asserts his own particular voice. It is tragic neither in the sense of Dostoevsky's underground man, who is caught in the net of an inescapable empiricism and is endlessly spite-

---

19. Baranova-Shestova, *Zhizn' L'va Shestova*, 1:64–65.

ful yet at the same time yearning for a firm ideal, nor in the melodramatic and self-aggrandizing manner of Nietzsche's various philosophical voices. Shestov's philosophical persona is rather self-diminishing and ironic. He deflects attention from himself to the experiences of other writers and philosophers, using them as a foil for his chief philosophical themes of suffering and death. For him, one can never successfully portray oneself as "tragic"— that has to be done by someone else. Indeed, it was his good friend, Aleksei Remizov, who, in his review of *The Apotheosis of Groundlessness,* compared Shestov implicitly to Job in his rejection of hearth, home, and God. Shestov's philosopher instead emphasizes the comic, pathetic, even ugly aspects of philosophizing, a strategy that through contrast brings out the tragic pathos of his experience. In general, Shestov speaks pejoratively of philosophizing not as something heroic or magnificent but rather like being "dunked in the slops" of existential experience (AB, 373).

When speaking of how people expect philosophers to look, Shestov notes that readers often mistakenly expect a kind of celebrity or superhero, an "eagle about to take flight" (AB, 410). In reality, though, in Shestov's view, the philosopher is a comic, pathetic likeness of a person: "A thinking person, above all, is one who has lost his balance in the everyday, but not in the tragic sense of that word. Hands spread apart, feet dangling in the air, a frightened and half-idiotic face, in a word, a most pathetic caricature of helplessness and disorientation" (AB, 410). Shestov's example is the aging Turgenev. Had Turgenev not been tall, handsome, and silver-haired, resembling a patriarch, Shestov argues, as he grew older no one would have paid any attention to him. His prose poems expose the unraveling philosophical experience of the older person facing death, inevitably alone: they are "pale, pathetic, anxious, restless, like a bird only half shot" (AB, 410). Still, weak as they are, it is these momentary musings of an aged man that draw Shestov's attention. Here is the possibility of genuine insight into the end of life.

An image that sets human greatness in a suitably humorous context is Pushkin's famous vision of the poet, who is less than significant but only until he hears the call of the muse (AB, 417). Shestov often points out in his writings that tragedy and greatness are rare but are still an element of *all* human life, not just a few great philosophers and writers. A person is not simply intelligent or simply foolish. Although most of life passes foolishly, occasionally someone penetrates the wall of folly. Even Dostoevsky as a young man was a "scatterbrain" and Nietzsche an "honest, simpleminded, blue-eyed German provincial" (AB, 400). At a certain moment a person becomes aware of a metaphysical lie, that her life has been fabricated by opinions foisted on her as eternal truths. At that point she learns to interrogate and to doubt, despite the consequences. Her doubts and solitude, her inability to convey any of these feelings to another person, comprise the implicit tragic moment. Only now, in Shestov's view, can one hope to find a spark of renewed strength and creativity (AB, 384).

Instead of reinforcing the stature and importance of his main themes, Shestov wryly notes, on a number of occasions, that pain and suffering are themselves boring and repulsive. And Nietzsche argues, in his *On the Birth of Tragedy*, that suffering is something so terrible that we can perceive it only through the mask of Apollonian light and reason. Shestov viewed writing in a similar vein, as a mask that distances the philosopher from the public, and thus makes it possible to articulate suffering in a meaningful way as well as creating a sense of fascination: "In literature one can still sing the praises of despair, hopelessness, incurable wounds—anything you like; after all, it is only literature, that is, it is convention. But to reveal in life one's in-escapable sorrow, to admit to one's incurable illnesses, and the like, means to deal the final blow to yourself, not to relieve your pain. Everyone, even the best people will recoil from you" (AB, 446). Even people who "work you into their worldview" as the object of empathy will avoid you. Shestov, with irony and even cruel humor, suggests that people either remain silent about their deepest pain or "be like Dostoevsky and Nietzsche" and "get into literature" (AB, 446). The implication, of course, is that most people should not flaunt their pain.

What does that mean for Shestov himself? Should he be silent? He would be the first to admit that he is no Dostoevsky or Nietzsche. And he never applies the insights he has into other writers and philosophers to his own experience. Though he certainly does not flaunt his suffering, covering his metaphysical pain with figures and tropes of resistance, he is anything but silent.

The overall structure of *The Apotheosis of Groundlessness* is the final aspect of the work that deserves comment. Although the group of aphoristic frag-ments that comprises the work has neither a clear plot nor drama, there is a sustained movement from a sense of metaphysical crisis in the first part toward confronting that crisis in the second part. Part 1 is written largely in a spirit of revolt against metaphysical order, stability, and dispassionate ob-jectivity. An opening epigraph by Heinrich Heine accentuates this theme: "The world and life are too fragmentary" ("Die Welt und das Leben sind zu fragmentarisch"). At the end of part 1 a coda of aphorisms reasserts the same theme of revolt, as Shestov takes to task a number of well-known contem-porary German philosophers—for example, Oswald Kühlne, Friedrich Paulsen, Wilhelm Windelband, and Alois Riehl—and their "eternal truths." This first part focuses on those moments when one realizes that any worldview is "groundless."

The emphasis of part 2 is on what lies ahead, beyond the metaphysical "truths" that Shestov has shattered in part 1. The epigraph to this part—

"Not for the faint of heart!"—calls on the reader to muster courage. This part, far more than the first, makes some shocking gestures to test the ideal notions of beauty, love, and faith. For example, in the first aphorism, Shestov claims that "eternal love" is fickle under certain radical circumstances. He doubts that a beautiful woman, whose face has been disfigured by acid, will continue to be beloved by the man who has sworn his eternal love. The point is, in Shestov's eyes, that when external conditions change, so do our feelings. Nothing is eternal. With this sort of startling speculation, Shestov hopes to jostle the reader, to make him question so-called eternal or absolute truths. Thus part 2 is about developing greater self-reliance and a willingness to be truly alone. Only then, Shestov argues, can one even hope to uncover a spark of creativity.

In Shestov's tragic philosophy, then, those matters that idealists and materialists have condemned as bad are now an advantage. The acceptance of suffering, the recognition of the mutability of all things, the courage to ask and to doubt—all these embody the possibility of a new creative drive, the energy for deeper insight.

The philosophical personality that emerged in Shestov's Russian period was one that, despite the desire not to attract readers, still invited the bold reader to the ultimate metaphysical challenge. Shestov's questions were easily accessible on some level to educated Russian readers, especially university students. In the 1840s Herzen had called for a philosophical "dilettante" to bring philosophical questioning to the broad public. Once again, in the 1850s, Chernyshevsky had sought a writer who could teach Russian readers to think philosophically. Dostoevsky had been that writer, although clearly not the one Chernyshevsky had had in mind. In the 1890s, it was Nietzsche who seemed to emerge from Dostoevsky's underground and to echo the *nadryv* of Dostoevskian characters. Still, it was Shestov who became the first truly popular Russian *philosopher.* His achievement was to create a sense of passion about philosophical questions, a dramatic philosophical space in which the thinking self broke out of the sedentary isolated life of academic, "scientific" philosophy and became a wanderer, a seeker after inner truth. Shestov challenged his readers to confront the abyss that lurked within them behind fixed values and fictional systems, and to arrive at an authentic, conscious experience of the world.

Shestov often remarked that tragic philosophy, at best, is a momentary phenomenon. People cannot stand the stress of confronting their suffering or that of others. They need the "comedy" of metaphysical comfort. The man who, in a way, realized Shestov's assertion was Vasily Rozanov, the next original philosophical mind to experiment with philosophical voice and genre, and the subject of the next chapter. Although Rozanov held to an oppositionist position—this time not only against metaphysics and science in the abstract but against all rational civil discourse practiced in everyday life—he also held to his own brand of metaphysical comfort. This time it was the invention of a personal, inward God with whom he could engage in life-affirming dialogue. Of all Russia's philosophers Rozanov was indeed the "comedian," the carnival rogue, whose purpose was to scandalize his readers, moving them toward a new, and very risky, awareness of the symbols and rituals of everyday life.

�֍

Chapter Six

Philosophy in the Breach:
Rozanov's Philosophical Roguery
and the Destruction of Civil Discourse

Every movement of my soul is accompanied by some articulation. And every articulation I am inevitably drawn *to note down*. This is an instinct. Is this not the origin of literature (written)? About print there is no thought: and thus Gutenburg came "later."

—Vasily Rozanov, *Solitaria,* 1911

Nietzsche was respected because he was a German and also because he suffered (his illness). But if he had been *Russian* and had ventured *his own* opinion along the lines, "*push* the falling person *still harder*"—he would have been labeled a scoundrel, and no one would have read him.

—Vasily Rozanov, *Solitaria,* 1911

In affirming his opinion that Russia has no history, that is, that Russia belongs in the category of unorganized, ahistorical cultural phenomena, Chaadaev forgot one condition, namely, language. Such a highly organized, organic language is more than a door into history; it is history itself. For Russia, defection from history, excommunication from historical necessity and continuity, from freedom and purposefulness, would be the same as defecting from language. The "falling silent" of two or three generations could bring Russia to historical death. . . . Thus it is really right that Russian history is moving along the brink, the edge, over the precipice, and is ready at any moment to break off into nihilism, that is, into an excommunication from the word. Of all contemporary Russian writers Rozanov understood this danger most viscerally.

—Osip Mandel'shtam, "On the Nature of the Word," 1922

VASILY ROZANOV (1856–1919) has long been recognized as a passionate, if idiosyncratic, thinker, an original practitioner of the Russian language with a humorous, outspoken, and at times outlandish view of life that stood in opposition to mainstream Russian thought and its institutions. At the same time his writing has a distinctly dark side, still not fully confronted by critics and historians. Rozanov is either appreciated as a brilliant critic and essayist, boldly challenging existing cultural institutions and their sexual, ethnic, and religious taboos, or he is denounced as an obscurantist, a racist yellow journalist making unwarranted attacks on the Jews. Although he was an original religious thinker and interpreter of ancient Judaism, in his social commentaries that appeared in the rightist press on the eve of World War I, the opinions he expressed about Jews were unacceptable in a civil society with universalist human values. Little effort has yet been made to find a relation between the two personae.

What seems immediately clear is that Rozanov is a discursive chameleon: the variety of voices in his writing makes it difficult to discern where he stands on any one issue and what he deems to be the truth.[1] Yet he dreamed of being neither a social commentator nor a cultural critic. He wanted to be recognized most as a "philosopher," which few of his contemporaries willingly allowed.[2] This chapter focuses on Rozanov's efforts to achieve a philosophical persona of his own, and on the relationship between this philosophical activity and his journalism. I argue that Rozanov's philosophical voice was founded on a rejection of the civil discourses that had become increasingly dominant in post-emancipation Russian society. This rejection may well have caused a shift in his professional persona as social commentator and feuilletonist, a persona involved directly with civil discourse.

---

1. Anna Lisa Crone, *Rozanov and the End of Literature: Polyphony and the Dissolution of Genre in Solitaria and Fallen Leaves* (Würzburg: jal-Verlag, 1978). See also Emanuel Glouberman, "Vasilii Rozanov: The Antisemitism of a Russian Judeophile," *Jewish Social Studies,* no. 2 (spring 1976): 117–44; Laura Engelstein, "Sex and the Anti-Semite: Vasilii Rozanov's Patriarchal Eroticism," in *The Keys to Happiness* (Ithaca, N.Y.: Cornell University Press, 1994), 299–333; and Brian Horowitz, "Jewish Stereotyping and Jewish Menace," *Shofar* 16, no. 1 (fall 1997): 85–100.

2. See, for example, Nikolai Berdiaev, "O vechno bab'em v russkoi dushe" (1915), in D. K. Burlaka et al., eds., *V. V. Rozanov: Pro et Contra. Lichnost' i tvorchestvo Vasilia Rozanova v otsenke russkikh myslitelei i issledovatelei* (St. Petersburg: Izdatel'stvo russkogo khristianskogo gumanistich-eskogo instituta, 1995), 41–51. Here Berdiaev writes: "Reading Rozanov is a visceral pleasure. It is hard to put Rozanov's thoughts into your own words. In fact, he does not have any thoughts. Everything is embedded in the organic life of words and cannot be torn away. With him words are not symbols but flesh and blood" (41). See also Zinaida Gippius, "Zadumchivyi strannik: O Rozanove," in *Zhivye litsa,* 2 vols. (1925; rpt. Munich: W. Fink, 1971 [1 vol.]), 2:7–92. Gippius remarks, similarly: "Rozanov has no 'thoughts' or what we would usually call a 'thought.' His every [thought] is necessarily also a penetrating *physical* sensation. He is therefore incapable of 'reasoning,' which is something he himself knows" (66).

Rozanov was one of those rare people who experimented in an array of different discourses and whose experiments lend insight into the structural tensions within writing culture in general. At times his writing invited a violent response from his readers and risked the very failure of writing culture by drawing near the edge where physical violence overpowers rhetoric and verbal negotiation. He used contradictory discursive modes—rational argumentation, literary criticism, and social commentary, on the one hand, and nationalist and Orthodox Christian rhetoric, on the other. He also employed a "scientific" and factual style as well as a pugnaciously subjective speaking voice that flagrantly flouted fact. In all his writings he clearly contributed to that late-nineteenth-century anti-Enlightenment, pro-nationalist mood that, in a German context, has been called the "politics of cultural despair."[3] He raised a number of issues and expressed certain views that were very uncomfortable, even unmentionable, for Russia's artistic and scientific communities, challenging the goodness and justice of socially progressive thinking and the truth of rigorous, scientific inquiry. On the other hand, he also confounded his readers by challenging the positions of more conservative intellectuals and by questioning the value of Russia's most conservative national institutions, particularly the Orthodox Church, the tsarist state, and the notion of the Russian *narod* (nation) as an idea of unalloyed goodness.

These discursive antinomies between elite and popular, secular and religious, modern and antimodern ways of writing reached a climax around the issue of Jewish culture and its role in Russian life. The focus of this chapter is Rozanov's treatment of Jewish themes in a variety of discourses, particularly the philosophical and journalistic. In this way I hope to broaden our insight into the ways that Rozanov uncovered the very limits of Russian writing culture and invented a role for himself as philosopher. At the center of the discussion are two of Rozanov's works, both written in the period from 1911 to 1913: *Solitaria* (*Uedinennoe*, 1911) and *Jews and Their Attitude to the Smell and Feel of Blood* (*Oboniatel'noe i osiazatel'noe otnoshenie evreev k krovi*, 1914).[4] Both probed the very borders of the permissible in prerevolutionary writing culture, and the author and both works were ostracized in some way. *Solitaria* was "arrested" for its shocking, near "pornography," and *Blood* was rejected by all publications save the radically conservative Black-Hundreds publication *Zemshchina*. As a result of this latter work Rozanov

---

3. Fritz Stern, *The Politics of Cultural Despair* (Berkeley: University of California Press, 1961).

4. Vasilii Rozanov, *Solitaria* (Moscow: Izdatel'stvo politicheskoi literatury, 1990); and *Oboniatel'noe i osiazatel'noe otnoshenie evreev k krovi* (St. Petersburg: Novoe vremia, 1914). Hereafter these two works are cited in the text, respectively, as *S* and *OEK* with the relevant page number.

himself was "excommunicated" from a number of societies, among them the Solov'ev Society, and it became increasingly difficult for him to find an outlet for his writings.

Solitaria is a work of original "anti-philosophy" told in a nonsystematic stream of consciousness that enables Rozanov to discuss normally taboo themes. In contrast, *Blood* is a work of gutter journalism, a series of articles written from 1911 to 1913, just prior to and during the celebrated Beilis case of 1913. In this case Beilis, a Jewish man, was accused of the ritual murder of a Christian boy, Andrei Iushchinsky. Beilis was acquitted. Like the Dreyfus case in the 1890s in France, the Beilis case became a touchstone for anti-Semitic attitudes in the Russian Empire. In his series of essays Rozanov marshaled contemporary xenophobia, particularly anti-Semitism, in an angry, ugly, and threatening way. In both *Solitaria* and *Blood,* the focus is on Jewish ritual in a way that points to the limits of public discourse and its authority.

The premise of the present discussion is that, although Rozanov earned his living as a journalist, much of his writing was motivated by a lifelong desire to gain credence as a philosopher. For Rozanov, philosophy was the highest and "truest" form of writing. As an older man, well over fifty, now recognized as a columnist and essayist and one of the finest stylists of his day, Rozanov used his philosophical writing in *Solitaria* certainly not to engage in civil discourse but to undermine it. Our chief questions, then, are the following: What does this philosophical attack mean with regard to his attitude toward journalism? Why does a writer with philosophical aspirations write a work such as *Blood*? And what does this writing mean for "philosophy" in Russian writing culture?

The 1890s, when Rozanov was first gathering an audience, was a time of rapid and tension-filled diversification of what had been a limited but homogeneous, if disputatious, writing culture with relatively few speech genres at its disposal. This development can be seen in the emergence of popular and middlebrow publications, writers from the lower-middle strata, the *meshchanstvo,* and the expansion of the popular press.[5] What Rozanov wrote in his 1897 article, "The Democratization of Painting," about the trend toward popularization of culture in nineteenth-century Europe, was

5. Louise McReynolds, "V. M. Doroshevich: The Newspaper Journalist and the Development of Public Opinion in Civil Society," in *Between Tsar and People: Educated Society and the Quest for Public Identity in Late Imperial Russia* (Princeton, N.J.: Princeton University Press, 1991), 233–247. See also idem, *The News under Russia's Old Regime: The Development of a Mass-Circulation Press* (Princeton, N.J.: Princeton University Press, 1991).

also true of early-twentieth-century Russia: "Since the beginning of the nineteenth century, everything is open, everything rushes to the masses, seeking their attention and approval."[6] Scientists, writers, and philosophers alike, even those who scorned the crowd, were all bent on finding an audience. They "use all possible means to appeal to the crowd."[7] Rozanov would both take advantage of and excoriate this popularization of writing.

At the same time elite writing culture was bolstered by the appearance for the first time in Russia of original national forms of philosophizing. For the first time some philosophers and poets, though far from all, deliberately marginalized themselves, spurning the burgeoning crowd of readers and claiming to be the priests and seers of mystical truths. Rozanov, a social commentator who addressed not only highly cultured but also middlebrow readers, was a unique case. As the critic A. A. Izmailov wrote in Rozanov's 1919 obituary: "A feuilleton writer working as a philosopher is nonsense. A philosopher working as a feuilleton writer is one of the greatest foibles of Russian life—not at all bad, however, as long as this philosopher does not write in the idiom of Kant. That combination bore the name Rozanov."[8]

Rozanov's two opposing areas of writing, philosophy and social commentary, typically have mutually divergent readerships and claim widely different forms of authority. These two cultural languages generally occupy separate spheres of a writing culture and have virtually no contact with each other. Philosophy traditionally claims universality, depth of knowledge, and clarity of logic as the basis of its authority, whereas journalism and middlebrow culture largely claim their authenticity because of their large readership, the "truth" thus verified by the taste of the majority. Although Rozanov is sufficiently idiosyncratic as to represent no one but himself, still he indeed embodies both trends in Russian writing culture.

Throughout his writing career Rozanov saw philosophizing as the pinnacle of knowledge. He received a university degree in history and philosophy from Moscow University. Although he became a teacher in Yelets, he continued his work in philosophy. In 1886, at the age of thirty, he published his first work, *On Understanding* (*O ponimanii*), an attempt to create a totally harmonious system of scientific knowledge. Even in this Rozanov's chief concern was the question of the divergent discourses of philosophy and natural science, and how to merge their competing claims to authority and authenticity of knowledge. Neither the academic audience nor the educated

6. Vasilii Rozanov, "O demokratizatsii zhivopisi," in *Religiia. Filosofiia. Kul'tura,* ed. A. N. Nikoliukin (Moscow: Respublika, 1992), 112.

7. Ibid., 113.

8. A. A. Izmailov, "Zakat eresiarkha" (1919), in Burlaka et al., *V. V. Rozanov: Pro et Contra,* 94.

reading public was interested in Rozanov's effort. No one bought his book. One reviewer suggested, unkindly, that Rozanov would have done better had he simply learned German in order to study Hegel.[9]

The continued Russian attitude toward systematic philosophy in general and Rozanov's effort in particular was well expressed in a letter of 1891 to Rozanov from the aesthetic thinker Konstantin Leontiev, who found systematic thinking to be "the beginning of the end."[10] With regard to *On Understanding,* Leontiev wrote: "I am a bit afraid, for, although I am not altogether without the ability to understand abstractions, I quickly tire of that forced and strange consistency and continuity that every philosopher draws me into."[11] And he added, "it is clear, but I am not sure it is true."[12] Rozanov was deeply disappointed by this lack of response to his first attempt at philosophy. As he wrote years later: "If the book had received any welcome at all, I would have remained a 'philosopher' all my life. But the book elicited no response (although it is written with a light touch). So then I went over to literary criticism and essay writing: still, it all felt 'wrong.' It is not the real me."[13]

Dreaming of establishing himself as a philosopher, Rozanov left teaching and moved to St. Petersburg, where he began to make a living and a name for himself with editorial essays and cultural commentary. He was employed as a columnist for the conservative newspaper *Novoe vremia* from 1899 until 1917, when the Bolsheviks shut down the paper. He also published in an array of left- and right-wing journals and newspapers. Although he had shifted course, his interest in philosophy did not wane. What changed was his positive view of systematic, "scientific" philosophy and his new admiration for religious language as the means to universal truth. Like many of the most gifted philosophers at the turn of the century, Rozanov used the genre of literary criticism as a means to disparage systematic reasoning. And for Rozanov, like so many of his contemporaries, Dostoevsky provided the stepping-stone to a new way of thinking about philosophy, truth, and knowledge.

Rozanov's first major work to win public acclaim was one he devoted to Dostoevsky, *The Legend of the Grand Inquisitor* (1894). This work is more than the usual literary-social-cultural critique of the day. It is one of the first in a long line of excellent works in philosophical criticism that would include Shestov's *The Good in the Work of Count L. Tolstoy and Nietzsche,*

9. Cited in A. A. Izmailov, "Vifleem ili Golgofa?" (1911), ibid., 85.

10. Konstantin N. Leont'ev, *Pis' ma k Vasiliiu Rozanovu* (London: Nina Karsova, 1981), 81.

11. Ibid., 60.

12. Ibid., 75.

13. Russian National Archive for Literature and Art, archive no. 419, section 1, item 21, p. 4. Quoted from A. N. Nikoliukin, "V. V. Rozanov i ego mirosozertsanie," in *S,* 11.

Merezhkovsky's *L. Tolstoi and Dostoevsky,* and Berdiaev's later work, *Dostoevsky's Worldview. The Legend of the Grand Inquisitor* gave a sustained critique of reason and its limitations. It also offered a revalorization of religious language. About reason Rozanov wrote: "Pure thought, in its abstract activity, can create only the good [*blagoe*]; and any science and philosophy, when they do not deceive their own nature—are good [*blagi*] and perfect before God and people. The confusion of areas of thought and feeling, the deformation of the first with the second and the second with the first, gives rise to all evil that could ever emit cry against its nature [or] complain about too great a depth of consciousness or the unbridled quality of its passions."[14] Reason, in its pure form, creates the good. When reason merges feeling and will, it then becomes a source of evil.

Religion, not abstract philosophy, provides the language for a total view of existence that, in turn, lends meaning to life experience. Early on in *Legend of the Grand Inquisitor* Rozanov draws attention to biblical imagery: "Biblical images are indeed merely the greatest generalization of the facts that history or philosophy might think up" (*L,* 38). He continues this line of thinking throughout the work:

> Without a doubt, the highest contemplation of human fates on earth is contained in religion. Neither history nor philosophy nor the exact sciences have in themselves even a shadow of that *generality and wholeness* of representation that religion has. That is one reason why people value it so much and why it elevates the mind and enlightens it to such a degree. By knowing the whole and the general, it is easy to orient oneself, to define oneself in the specifics. On the contrary, however many specifics we know—and they are provided by history, science, and philosophy—we can always encounter new ones that cause us trouble. This is the source of the firmness of life, its stability, when it is religious. (*L,* 101)

For Rozanov, biblical language assumes the authority, formerly held by philosophy, to provide the "big picture." Formal philosophy has now been demoted to the discursive equivalent of a social or natural science, able to provide facts but unable to create the large theoretical framework that gives meaning to these facts.

Throughout the middle of his career Rozanov had devoted his energies to a critique of the church and what he viewed as its nihilistic, life-denying values.[15] Now, in *Solitaria,* he turned against all kinds of public discourse,

---

14. Vasilii Rozanov, *Legenda o velikom inkvizitore* (Munich: W. Fink, 1970), 174. Hereafter cited in the text as *L* with the relevant page number.

15. See Anna Lisa Crone, "Nietzschean, All Too Nietzschean? Rozanov's Anti-Christian Critique," in *Nietzsche in Russia,* ed. B. G. Rosenthal (Princeton, N.J.: Princeton University Press, 1986), 95–112.

especially the dominant discourse of "literature." But it would be the discourse of literature from which, and in contrast to, he would build his own philosophical language. Through this confrontation he worked out the intimate philosophical style he is known for and, with it, the realization of a long-cherished identity as a philosopher. Whether he indeed achieved authority as a philosopher is perhaps less important than understanding how his crafting of a philosophical language helped him to assert his own identity as a philosopher. Also at issue is what, if any, impact this philosophical experiment had on Rozanov's career as a social commentator.

The discursive dispute in *Solitaria* can be seen as a kind of "carnival."[16] "Carnival," as Mikhail Bakhtin defined this cultural paradigm, was embodied in the medieval Christian festival of Mardi Gras, and, to a lesser degree, in other festivals that precede periods of fasting. The central character of the festival is the fool who, in the topsy-turvy carnival world, arises from the baser layers of human society to be crowned "king." Through carnival play and merrymaking, the fool-as-king proceeds to turn all social and political institutions upside down, poking fun at their weaknesses. In this atmosphere one is permitted to make subversive remarks that in the framework of ordinary life would be punishable as insubordination. This symbolic revolution is comically represented by the human body, which is also turned upside down, in such a way that private parts replace public features of the face and head. The carnival pageant ends with the restoration of traditional order.[17]

In Rozanov's work, and most radically in *Solitaria,* we have a kind of carnival that revolves around the critique of civil discourse and opens the way for a new philosophical "anti-discourse." Rozanov adopts a carnival persona who undermines the existing *modern* hierarchy of institutions and discourses, and the authoritative truths implicit in them. He makes fun of public, civil discourses—the press, positivist science, rational, systematic philosophy, and realist literature. Corresponding to this process of upending the public sphere and opening the private sphere is a series of images of private, sexual parts—particularly those of the female body, that have been taboo but are now accorded remarkable attention. This moment of revelation marks the instant when Rozanov establishes his own philosophical voice. What makes this particular carnival process modern is its openness and lack of resolution. Unlike the medieval order, the modern order with its civil discourse will never be reinstated and legitimized anew in Rozanov's work. Indeed, Rozanov's revolt will be carried out to the sphere of social commentary where civil discourse will be mocked, but never reinstated.

16. This idea is mentioned in Anton Sergl, *Literarisches Ethos: Implikationen von Literarizität am Beispiel des konservativen Publizisten V. V. Rozanov* (Munich: O. Sagner, 1994), 105.

17. M. M. Bakhtin, *Rabelais and His World,* trans. H. Iswolsky (Cambridge: MIT Press, 1968), 81–84.

How does the carnival persona appear in *Solitaria*? Rozanov easily pictures himself as fool, rogue, and outsider. He writes: "Maybe I am a 'fool' (there are rumors to that effect), maybe I am a 'rogue' (that's what they say): but, until me, no one had that *breadth* of thought, that *boundlessness* of 'opening horizons,' in the way that I do. And 'everything came to me of itself'—without appropriating from anyone even one iota. Amazing. I am simply an amazing person. ([written] on the sole of my shoe; bathing)" (*S*, 68). True to the brash carnival fool, Rozanov is at once self-aggrandizing and ironic about himself. And, significantly, he identifies this persona with the right to challenge traditional, established ways of thinking.

An important aspect of Rozanov's carnivalesque persona is the irony he expresses about himself and his painfully self-conscious, nonauthoritative demeanor. He continually calls into question the legitimacy of his status as a thinker by drawing attention to his physical appearance, his looks, clothes, and name. His goal is to make light of the traditional image of the philosopher, one that is so familiar from Nietzsche's philosophical persona—masculine, unmarried, serious, and aloof from the everyday. Rozanov, by contrast, plays the philosophical buffoon. He points out in himself what is traditionally "other" and alien to philosophy—the feminine, comic, ugly, and the everyday, banal conditions of his life. Rozanov is quick to acknowledge how "feminine" in nature he is, which completely goes against the grain of popular contemporary thinking on gender, from Nietzsche to Otto Weininger, and the general misogynist tenor of his intellectual circle. Early on, in *Solitaria,* he records the comment of his young relative, Nina Rudneva: "The only thing about you that is masculine are your trousers" (*S*, 27).

One of the most famous carnivalesque passages in this work deals with Rozanov's last name and is worth citing at length in order to appreciate the tone in which he writes:

> My last name is surprisingly offensive. It is always with such a feeling of alienation that I sign my articles, "V. Rozanov." If only it were "Rudnev," "Bugaev," anything. Or just the plain Russian "Ivanov." Once I was going down the street. I looked up and read: "Rozanov's German Bakery." Well, so that's how it is: all bakers are "Rozanovs," and therefore all Rozanovs are bakers. What are fools with such a ridiculous last name to do? (*S*, 33)

And further he writes:

> I suspect that "Briusov" is constantly glad of his name. Therefore
> WORKS BY V. ROZANOV
> does not appeal to me. It even sounds odd.
> VERSE BY V. ROZANOV
> is totally unthinkable. Who would "read" such verse?

"What do you do, Rozanov?"
"I write verse."
"Idiot. You'd be better off baking buns."
Naturally. (S, 33)[18]

Rozanov then moves from grumbling about his un-philosophical last name to his unbecoming looks and his lack of masculinity: "Not only was I given such an unnaturally revolting last name, miserable looks were thrown into the bargain" (S, 33). He continues in the same vein: "My face is red. I have a shiny, unpleasant kind of skin. . . . As a schoolboy I had fire-red hair that stood up on end but somehow not in a noble "butch" (a sign of masculinity) but rather in a kind of rising wave, totally absurd, I never saw anything like it" (S, 34).

Although Rozanov worries about being attractive to women, he concludes that his physical ugliness is the reason for his spiritual depth: "No woman *will ever fall for me, not one*. What's left? *To retreat into myself, live with myself and for myself* (not egotistically, but spiritually), *for the future*. In some roundabout nonsensical way, my outer ugliness was a reason for becoming spiritually more profound" (S, 34). He notes gratefully that the only woman who ever liked him was his "friend," his common-law wife, Varvara Rudneva.

The persona Rozanov adopts most consistently is that of the Dostoevskian character type, the "insulted and injured." Although he has been dealt unfavorable conditions and qualities in his life, as an intelligent, thinking person, he must make the best of it. Despite the rich sense of humiliation he brings to the contemplation of himself and his life, he must confront a complex inner nature, torn with resentment toward those he believes have more influence than he.[19]

In his role as the carnival fool Rozanov launches his radical critique of public discourse. His position as carnival philosopher "below" the sacred cows of civil society allows him to recognize and point out their least attractive aspects. It is important to repeat here that in *Solitaria*, in contrast to a number of his earlier works, the objects of this carnivalesque "revolution" are secular, and relate to intellectual and state institutions. He begins by criticizing the technological foundation of modern writing culture, the printing press. This invention, he argues, takes away all sense of individuality and selfhood (*lichnost'*): "It is as if this damned Gutenberg licked all the writers with his bronze tongue, and they all lost their souls 'in print,' they

18. Rudnev is the last name of Rozanov's second wife. Bugaev is the given last name of the Symbolist poet Andrei Belyi. Ivanov and Briusov refer, respectively, to the Symbolist poets Viacheslav Ivanov and Valerii Briusov.

19. E. Clowes, "Vasilii Rozanov als philosophischer Nachkömmling von Solov'ev und Nietzsche," *Solov'ev und Nietzsche: Ein Jahrhundertsbilanz* (Frankfurt: Peter Lang, 2003), 413–423.

Oil portrait of Vasily Rozanov by Parkhomenko, 1910. Courtesy of the Literary Museum, Moscow.

lost their faces, their character. My 'I' is only to be found in manuscripts, indeed, the 'I' of any writer" (*S,* 24). Here is Rozanov's first attempt to justify a private anti-discourse.

He then delivers a broadside attack on all public discourse. In his view, publicly shared language is no more than prostitution. This passage, too, is worth citing at length, as it illuminates the range of Rozanov's project:

An undoubted part of prostitution, "against which everyone is powerless to struggle," is the thought: "I belong *to everyone,*" that is, the same thing that is

Visiting card with photograph of Vasily Rozanov, no date. Courtesy of Russian State Archive for Literature and Art, Moscow (RGALI).

a part of the way a *writer,* a *politician,* a *lawyer* think; or a bureaucrat "at the service of the state." Thus, in one way, prostitution is the "most social phenomenon," to a certain degree the prototype of *social-mindedness* [sotsial'nost']—and one might even say that rei publicae natae sunt ex feminis publicis [republics are born of public women], "the first states were born of women's instinct to prostitute themselves." . . . On the other hand, a prostitute's psychology is really the essence of an actor, writer, lawyer, even a "pater who sends *everyone* to the afterworld," that is, a psychology of indifference to "everything" along with an affectionate attitude toward "everyone." "Do you desire a funeral or a wedding?" asks a priest, who just came in with a calm, indistinct smile, ready to express either "congratulations" or "condolence." A scientist, inasmuch as he *publishes* his work, a writer, inasmuch as he sees his work into print—are, of course, prostitutes. . . .

In essence, it is quite metaphysical: "My most private things I give to everyone." . . . What the heck is this: you could kill, you are so indignant, or you could . . . fall into endless meditation. *As You Like It,* as Shakespeare puts it. (*S,* 29–30)

Thus publicly shared speech is less concerned with truth than with pleasing the audience. Remember, in reading these passages, that Rozanov was certainly among the most published writers of his age; his *Collected Works* were intended to number fifty volumes. He never ventures to question his role as a social commentator, but, being one, he might be the first to admit that he, too, is a prostitute.

Rozanov then treats each separate discourse ironically. One discourse that receives a great deal of attention is the language of science and "positivism." Rozanov remarks: "Positivism is true, necessary, and even eternal, for the moment; but only for a distinct segment of the population. 'Positivists' need positivism; the point is the 'positivist,' not 'positivism'; here, as everywhere, the person is there before the theory" (*S,* 46). Science may be true for the moment, and for a very small portion of humanity; but, according to Rozanov, it does not have lasting value. It is worth noting that Rozanov uses the short form of the adjectives, "true, necessary, eternal"—"*istinen, nuzhen i dazhe vechen,*" denoting the short-lived, temporary conditions of scientific truth.

Journalism, the medium by which Rozanov made his living, receives some derision, at times more bitter than his mockery of science. He writes: "Newspapers, I think, will eventually go the same way as the 'eternal wars' and the 'tourneys' of the middle ages, etc. For now they are supported by the notion of 'universal education' which people want to make 'mandatory'" (*S,* 24). Journalism is just a passing fashion that something else will eventually supersede. What most infuriates Rozanov, however, is the movement of literary art toward journalism.

Rozanov reserves his most enduring mockery for the discourse he views as making the most authoritative use of language in Russian writing culture, namely, literature. It is important to note that at the turn of the century Russian literature was indeed being canonized as the pride of Russian culture, as its most commanding writing form. Rozanov himself had contributed to this process, for example, in his work on Dostoevsky, but now he challenges this canonization. Literature, he argues, does not deserve to be honored. It is no longer "poetry," which is "deep," but rather a rational discourse. Rozanov finds Russian literature of the last two hundred years generally "insubstantial and shallow." Eighteenth-century literature is only about "helping the state" (*S*, 36). In the nineteenth century literature focuses on gentry life, "*pomeshchichii byt*" (*S*, 36). He finds nothing universal in the literary works of the last generation. It is just talk, "*prazdnoslovie*" (*S*, 38), just "a young virgin and a student debating about God and social revolution" (*S*, 36)—it all comes "out of the student 'smoking lounge' . . . and the narrow, poor bed of a prostitute" (*S*, 36). Literature, particularly over the last few decades, in Rozanov's view, has capitulated to the demands of journalism, of reporting and rhetoric, and no longer has its own identity. Rozanov has no patience for populist writers like Nikolai Nekrasov, Gleb Uspensky, or Mikhail Saltykov-Shchedrin, who have used literature simply to lead the young and idealistic toward the illusory goals of revolution (*S*, 63).

Indeed, he questions whether one should even pay attention to this kind of literature: "Why does all this *matter?!*" (*S*, 36). No one becomes deeply absorbed in any of the ideas being debated: writers "write a little," and readers "read a little" (*S*, 36). He singles out Tolstoy (whom he normally derides) for kind words. Of all the writers of his generation, Tolstoy deals with themes Rozanov sees as essential to the spiritual health and vitality of Russian culture. He is the "great exception . . . who treated *the family, the laborer, the fathers with respect*" (*S*, 37). Tolstoy does not just talk about work but actually labors himself.

Yet even this "lived literature" is not profound. The philosopher Rozanov of the second half of *Solitaria* places himself above Tolstoy: "Tolstoy . . . when I spoke with him, by the way, about family and marriage, about sex—I saw that he was confused in all these matters, the way a schoolchild copying out words gets "i" and "y" confused [*putaetsia mezhdu* "и" i "й"], and really he doesn't understand a thing, except that one must "abstain." . . . [He shows] neither analysis nor synthetic ability, nor even any thought, it's all exclamations. You can't interact with this; it's something *imbécile*" (*S*, 72). Tolstoy, in Rozanov's eyes, may be better than most realists of his generation, but he is unable to think, to formulate an idea.

Rozanov calls for a different kind of literature: "I say that we should weep not over the conditions of our lives but over ourselves. This is a totally different project, a different direction, a different literature" (*S*, 37). He believes that each person must write and read the book of his or her life. In other words, each person should concentrate on knowing only him- or herself instead of focusing on the social and natural conditions that form us from the outside. As he expressed it in a later work, "Before Sakharna" {"Pered Sakharnoi," summer 1913): "Properly speaking, there is only one book that a person is obliged to read attentively—this is the book of one's own life."[20] And, in his view, each life is unique. He reflects on *Solitaria*: "Every person, properly speaking, is obliged to write a *Solitaria*. This is the only legacy he will leave to the world and that the world might receive from him, and the world has a right to receive it. 'All the rest has no substance'— and all the rest that he could have written or said is only partly true; what is 'true' [in all that writing] is not in his power, not in his knowledge" (*RFK*, 327). In other words, once a writer publicizes his books and seeks an audience, how his writing is understood depends on the reader. The real source of writing and literature is not the desire to become publicly known. Rather, it derives from silence and the psyche's desire for private self-articulation. Rozanov suggests that this kind of writing most resembles prayer (*S*, 46).[21]

This writing has less authority than authenticity, which comes from its proximity to everyday language and the frank nature of an individual talking to her- or himself or to a very close, trusted person. Another important aspect of Rozanov's attack on public discourse is that he appropriates space for a specifically Russian type of philosophy from discursive territory in Russian writing culture traditionally belonging to literary art.[22] In this intimate sphere one can perceive oneself "thinking." Rozanov writes: "I feel good both when I am alone and when I am with everyone. I am neither a loner nor a person who thrives on social contact [*obshchestvennik*]. But when I am by myself—I am full; with others I am not full. I am really bet-

---

20. *Religiia. Filosofiia. Kul'tura* (Moscow: Respublika, 1992), 326. Hereafter cited in the text as *RFK* with the relevant page number.

21. Much has been said about the ways that Rozanov's "intimate" writing fragments anticipate new trends in Russian literature—from Gor'kii's diary to the Futurists to Mikhail Prishvin's diary, and on to late Soviet underground writers, Abram Terts with his *Voice from the Chorus* and Venedikt Erofeev's *From Moscow to Petushki*. See Crone, *Rozanov and the End of Literature*, 121–126. See also Andrei Siniavskii, *'Opavshie list'ia V. V. Rozanova* (Paris: Sintaksis, 1982), 276; Venedikt Erofeev, "Vasilii Rozanov glazami ekstsentrika," in *Ostav'te moiu dushu v pokoe* (Moscow: Izdatel'stvo KhGS, 1995), 149–164.

22. By contrast, this type of fragmented and aphoristic writing in German writing culture has belonged to philosophy. In German romantic and neo-romantic thought, from Schlegel to Nietzsche, antisystematic thinking pushes back the borders of what can be spoken about, and thus theorized and thought. See, for example, Rodolphe Gasché, "Foreword: Ideality in Fragmentation," in Friedrich Schlegel, *Philosophical Fragments*, trans. P. Firchow (Minneapolis: University of Minnesota Press, 1991), vii–xxxii.

ter off alone" (*S,* 47). Rozanov loves and gives new significance to what might be called "sub-literary" writing, that is, private letters (*S,* 27), one's own manuscripts (*S,* 24), and prayer (*S,* 46).[23] He is the first thinker to appropriate these genres as venues for philosophical discourse, viewing them as a kind of writing that fosters understanding, that is "deep" and thus worthwhile. Despite his carnival veneer, "depth" and meaning are of increasing concern to Rozanov in *Solitaria.*

What is deep, to which Rozanov assigns special meaning through his carnival roguery, is actually his own long-developed approach to faith and religion. One of his major points, explored throughout his works, is that religion gains meaning and vitality from ritual that transfigures the profane, the earthly, the corporeal into the sacred, the divine. For him, the profane is always linked to the sexual organs which then, in some secret, unspeakable way, are transformed and embedded with divine meaning. Rozanov's favorite subject on this account is the role of circumcision in Jewish ritual as a blood sacrifice that brings God's love and protection. Indeed, circumcision is the key image he chooses for the ritual conjoining of the profane and the sacred. In an early experimental piece, "New Embryos" ("Novye embriony," 1901), he writes of Abraham: "God 'circumcized' someone he cherished [*zavetnyi*] at his most 'intimate' [*zavetnyi*] point. As they are betrothed and married, husband and wife conjoin 'intimately' [*zavetno*], that is, in the most secret, intimate, cherished [*zavetnom*] realm of their selves [*ia*]. That is why the ancient conjoining of humanity to God through Abraham is called a 'testament' [*zavet*] and not a 'pact' [*dogovor*] nor 'union' [*soiuz*] nor 'agreement' [*uslovie*]" (*RFK,* 234). Here the words *zavet* and *zavetnyi* are used in all their multiple meanings to link the idea of a sacred covenant or testament and the most intimate, taboo aspects of human life. They are implicitly much deeper and more meaningful than similar words commonly used in civil society to denote an alliance or legal agreement between people, such as *pact, union,* or *agreement.*

It should be emphasized that in much of his writing Rozanov's notion of religious ritual contains essential aspects of the carnival. It merges the low, comic, and profane with the sacred, serious, and blessed. He explores with brash, carnival boldness what is taboo at both ends of the spectrum, both the divinely unspeakable and the base and equally unmentionable. He then brings them into close proximity to each other.

The structure of *Solitaria* turns on Rozanov's effort to identify himself as

---

23. In an article on Solov'ev from 1905 Rozanov had the following to say about the truth of letter writing: "The 'literature of private letters' always seemed to me personally to be the most interesting and valuable. . . . [T]his literature is valuable because nowhere else except the private letter can you find those imperceptible things in a person or writer that are essential to his character" ("Iz starykh pisem. Pis'ma Vlad. Serg. Solov'eva," *Voprosy zhizni,* nos. 10–11 [1905]: 378).

a different kind of philosopher. His first step in the first half of *Solitaria* is to criticize currently authoritative civil discourses. His second step, directly in the middle of the work, is to break the bounds of that kind of speech by entering the realm of the sacred and taboo. Having cleared this barrier, he devotes the second half of the work to defining himself as a "philosopher." The traditional critical discussion of *Solitaria* either sidesteps or condemns the second step, the description of the mikveh, the ritual bath that married Jewish women take after menstruation and that in premodern times men could use after intercourse.[24] It is not by chance that the mikveh passage occupies a marked position at the exact center of the work. It is the gateway from a merely critical treatment of civil discourse to a creative development of a philosophical persona.

Rozanov frames his meditation on the mikveh in a conversation with a student, Rebecca, who immediately tags the mikveh as taboo. She is embarrassed even to say the word: "That is an *indecent* word, and in Jewish society it is impermissible to say it aloud" (*S,* 40). Rozanov immediately suggests an explicit link between shame and holiness, by asking: "But isn't the mikveh—*holy?*" To which Rebecca replies, "Yes, it is *holy.* . . . That's what we were taught. But its *name* is *indecent* and one never says it *aloud* or in the company of *other people*" (*S,* 40). Rozanov then becomes excited, realizing once again the genius of Judaism in its ability to affirm the most vulgar, "dirty" things—those closest to life itself—conceptualizing them as the human connection to the divine. The "indecent" is the mask of inwardly sacred qualities. Rozanov contrasts this mentality to a Christian psychology for which the indecent "goes into the sphere of 'sin', the 'bad' [*durnoe*], the 'nasty' [*skvernoe*], and the 'revolting' [*gadkoe*]" (*S,* 40). In other words, the indecent, and particularly the sexual, is segregated in the realm of the devil.

Rozanov focuses on the life-affirming aspects of ritual bathing. He first describes a mikveh relatively accurately: how it looks, what sort of water can be used, and how women must bathe in it. Then, in a passage that is pure Rozanov, he imagines the old Jewish man who built the mikveh—who could easily be Rozanov's alter ego—going down to the bath area after everyone has left. He lights candles and rejoices that, "with this [ritual purification] all Israel will live, and eternally, if they do not abandon it." Then the imaginary Jew continues: "I am lighting a sacred flame here because nowhere, if not here, is the air so suffused with the bodies of Israel, and they all [the women] breathed this air, breathed and swallowed it, and now it is running as an aromatic and visual stream in each person's veins and is giv-

24. Thanks to Bernice G. Rosenthal and Daniel Breslauer for information about the mikveh. Information also comes from: "Mikveh," *Encyclopedia Judaica,* CD-ROM edition, Version 1.0 (Judaica Multimedia, 1997).

ing birth to images and desires that move and unite all Israel" (*S,* 41). The old man affirms once again the transfiguration of the shameful into the divine: "God is mikveh, for he *purifies* . . . Israel" (*S,* 41).

The passage then becomes outrageous as Rozanov transfers the rather alien rite of the mikveh to the surroundings of a high-society ball. By surprising and violating readers' expectations in this way Rozanov hopes to "have us feel the soul" of this ancient ritual and to animate its central idea, as he sees it:

> Let us silently imagine our ball. Movement, conversations, "news," and "politics." The luxury, the ladies' gowns . . . the row of halls with white columns and walls. And now one of the guests, [one] of the cavaliers . . . tired of dancing goes into a side room: and seeing a bowl on a table full of cool water, forgotten and unneeded, warily looks around, pushes the door to, and, taking out his somewhat aroused member, immerses it in the cold water . . . "till it cools down."
>
> He is doing the same as Jews do in the mikveh. (*S,* 41–42)

The next scene has a young lady performing a similar act—and again it is compared to Jewish ritual.

I should note that neither of these acts, as Rozanov imagines them, resembles the Jewish mikveh. Although married women must use the bath for physical cleanliness, and men may, the mikveh exists solely for the purpose of intentional purification, which places the emphasis on the spiritual rather than the physical. Moreover, for ancient reasons of cleanliness, the mikveh itself may not be a movable vessel, such as a bowl, and the water may not be drawn but must flow from a "natural" source, whether rain, well, river, or sea. Still, none of these considerations has anything to do with Rozanov's point. Lest this passage seem needlessly vulgar, shocking for its own sake, Rozanov immediately comes to his main point, the renewal of life. Again he describes an elderly Jewish man who witnesses these events. The man takes the water and blesses it with a prayer, which Rozanov then makes into *his own* prayer. The Jew says to himself:

> Let them dance. That foolishness will pass. I am praying for the things that they will need in old age, *for health, for the continuation of life;* for life itself to be *fresh, strong;* . . . for those parts they plunged into [this water] and washed *never to be diseased.* Oh, they know nothing now because they are in love— and they talk about service and ranks. I have done all that and don't need anything: I know how *joy in life depends on this part never to become blocked or dull or weak.* . . . I am foreign to them all: but I pray to my Secret God that with the whole *World,* all of *them,* He preserve and bless these parts, for the eternal fertility of the world and for the flourishing of the whole earth which He, the Good One, created. [to which Rozanov adds:] Amen. (*S,* 42)

Clearly this startling juxtaposition of the ball and the mikveh is pure Rozanov. Indeed, the "defamiliarization" of the ball in the Shklovskian sense makes us think of sexuality in a fresh way. Traditional mikveh is concerned with cleanliness and holiness, whereas Rozanov focuses on affirming the corporeal and particularly the sexual as sacred. One may well ask, what, if anything, keeps this passage from being merely crass? The answer lies in Rozanov's own sense of wonderment at being in the presence of something sacred, something higher than human, which finds its expression in human sexuality.

For all the sexual "awakening" of Russian letters in the early twentieth century, this is easily one of the boldest pieces. It goes beyond Artsybashev's *Sanin* or Verbitskaia's *Keys of Happiness* because of its explicit and outlandish conjoining of the vulgar with the loftiest and most sacred of feelings. Rozanov reveals the link between two levels of taboo: sexuality—which is traditionally shameful and unmentionable, and which he revalues as honorable and good)—and the divine, God and life, which are exalted and sacred, and also unspeakable. He does this in a most alienating and unusual way by drawing two startling images of cultural "otherness," being Jewish and being female—the image of a Jewish woman purifying herself.

Having expressed his own cherished idea, Rozanov returns to affirming his identity as a philosopher. This identity clearly emerges from the carnival atmosphere of irreverent mockery of earthly authority and reverent adulation of the unspeakable. Rozanov's project as a philosopher is to probe what is taboo and to demolish discursive walls. On the page following the mikveh passage, Rozanov calls himself a "psychopath" and "decadent," and revels in these "abusive epithets" that, to him, are "labels for poets and philosophers" (*S,* 43). He even takes pride in having been the first in his circle in the 1880s to use these terms. Although, in Rozanov's time, the term *psychopath* was used to demean poets and philosophers, to Rozanov it suggests psychological keenness and sensitivity (*S,* 43). Philosophy, for Rozanov, is not about the systematization of human knowledge and truth but, rather, about the "enormous *deepening* of human nature" (*S,* 43). Philosophy is penetrating rather than totalizing. This idea of philosophy supersedes the classical view of philosophy as reasoned knowledge, as science. Later Rozanov admits humorously that he failed in traditional philosophy in his first work, *On Understanding:* "Oh, my sad 'experiments.' . . . Why did I want *to know everything?* Now I won't die in peace as I had hoped" (*S,* 56). Even as he laments, he also breaks free of this first effort and leaves his failure behind.

It is important to realize that Rozanov's ironic attitude toward himself permits him to forego all outward claims to authority and to turn "philosophical" language from discourse into a more free-wheeling realm of linguistic play and intellectual experiment. Bursting the bonds of systematic thought as well as the rules of polite discourse, he can reposition the boundaries of language. He frees himself to write in a way that existed previously only in oral speech. In the process of creating a space for his unusual style of philosophy, he first demotes Russian literature to a form of journalism and then claims poetic territory for himself. His language, as it emerges in the second half of *Solitaria*, combines aspects of psalm-like, religious, and lyrical speech to discuss the experience of thinking: "I lose my breath thinking. How pleasant it is to live in this state of breathlessness. It makes living my life amid the thorns and tears a real pleasure" (*S*, 49). As he says, quite melodramatically: "For twenty years I have been living in uninterrupted poetry. I am very perceptive, although I stay silent. I cannot remember a day when I did not notice something deeply poetic and, on seeing or hearing something . . . inwardly a tear of ecstasy or tenderness welled up inside. That is the reason I am happy. And probably because of it I write well" (*S*, 60). What is novel about Rozanov's brand of philosophizing and sets it apart from most other philosophers, except Shestov, is that he does not try to "teach" anything to anyone. It is nondogmatic and nondidactic. His point of departure for a new philosophy is the ontological premise: "I am not necessary" (*S*, 51). Here again he disputes the philosopher's public authority and his need to make his thought useful, to teach something. In this Rozanov resembles his contemporary, Shestov. Rozanov's philosophy, like Shestov's, resides, by choice, outside that public sphere of political rebellion and moral resistance that nineteenth-century Russian letters have dramatized. He prefers his own plain, unpretentious, unremarkable realm of private, "domesticated" speech.[25]

Retaining his own rebellious, carnival resistance to philosophical didacticism, Rozanov insists that he cares not one iota about truth and goodness, understood as publicly held and shared values. He claims not even to know how to spell the Russian word for morality, "nravstvennost'" (*S*, 55), and he does not care about truth and lies or taking responsibility for his thoughts and ideas (*S*, 62). Moral character is particular to each individual:

> More than anything by old age one is tormented by an incorrect kind of life: and not in the sense that "I didn't get to enjoy things much" . . . but that I did not do *my duty*.
> The idea of "duty" started to come to me, at least, only with the onset of old age. Before, I always lived "by some motif," that is, by my tastes and appetites, by "what I feel like" and "what pleases me." I cannot even imagine

---

25. The term *domesticated* is particularly apt because it captures the way that "discourse," which is normally understood as public use of language laden with ideology, can be viewed as "private." The term comes from Stephen C. Hutchings, "Breaking the Circle of the Self: Domestication, Alienation, and the Question of Discourse Type in Rozanov's Late Writings," *Slavic Review* 52, no. 1 (spring 1993): 67–86.

such an "outlaw" as myself. The idea of "law" as "duty" never entered my mind. I just read the word in dictionaries under the letter "D." But I never knew what it was and never was interested enough to find out. "Duty was thought up by cruel people to keep down the weak. And only a fool obeys it." That was more or less how I thought . . .

But I always felt *pity.* But that, too, was an "appetite" of mine; and then there was gratitude—as my *taste.* (*S,* 62)

Everything about Rozanov's philosophical persona turns topsy-turvy the model of the true philosopher that Nietzsche described—male, European, single, standing above the rest of humanity on the metaphorical mountaintop, in dialogue only with the few great thinkers in history. And Rozanov's anti-philosopher occupies a territory that is in no way traditionally associated with Nietzsche's philosopher. Rozanov loved to note down, at the end of his fragmentary thoughts, the place where they occurred to him and where he wrote them down. Rather than writing on white paper, he writes on any scrap, even, on one occasion, on the bottom of his shoes (*S,* 68). He writes in low or banal places, in the toilet, in the train, at his hobbies. These spaces he inhabits are appropriate for a carnival philosopher—they correspond to base or at most ordinary, middling human functions, never elevated ones.

Despite his emphasis on privacy of thought, Rozanov has strong national interests. He wants his philosophy to count as a form of "Russian" philosophy. He creates a territory for it that contrasts with the social thought of the second half of the nineteenth century. The roots of this earlier form of Russian thought emanate from two areas, moral preaching and political nihilism. Most fundamentally they are found in Tolstoy's idea of public "nonresistance to evil": " 'Nonresistance to evil' is neither Christianity nor Buddhism: it really is the *Russian element*—the 'even nature' of the East European plain" (*S,* 49). To this passivity he contrasts Russian nihilism, the second locus for a Russian philosophy: "The only Russian rebels are the 'nihilists': and here I am extremely curious to see how it will end; that is, how this sole Russian *rebellion* will finish. But this explains the force and significance as well as the stability and persistence of nihilism. 'We need to rebel someplace, anyplace'—and for eighty million Russians it is 'necessary.' Their bones have gotten tired of just 'putting up with it' " (*S,* 49). Rozanov as a "Russian" philosopher differs sharply from these precedents: he is private and intimate, not at all socially oriented. He is an outsider to civil society; instead, he presents a voice for the voiceless lower layers of civil society, for the "insulted and injured."

Rozanov sanctifies his domestic realm of philosophy by bringing to it his own private God. He explains what makes his private religious philosophy different and modern compared to the Old Testament relationship between God and Abraham: "Abraham was called by God: I myself called God. . . .

There is the whole difference" (*S,* 50). From his study of Judaism Rozanov has appropriated a passionate, personal interaction with his God. What is new is that he has rescued God from philosophical nihilism by personally needing and calling to God. He feels his ordinary realm to be held, protected, and "warmed" by continual contact with his God with whom he carries on an ecstatic, psalm-like conversation: "My God! My eternity! Why does my soul jump so when I think about you. . . . Your hand holds everything: I can feel constantly that it is holding me" (*S,* 49).

What is the result of Rozanov's discursive, philosophical carnival? Has he reestablished the ancient (and quite un-Russian) discursive hierarchy of Plato and Aristotle by reasserting philosophy as somehow the "truest" form of writing? If so, then he did it with a decidedly new twist that annexes literature, poetry, and religious speech and rejects traditional universalizing, didactic philosophical system building and its links to modern civil discourse. It appears that philosophy, in this new animation, lacks the broad sweep of Kant's system or Hegel's or Nietzsche's world-crushing anti-system or the social urgency of the Russian radicals or Tolstoy. It most resembles Nietzsche's thought in its emphasis on private self-confrontation and self-knowledge. With Rozanov we have a modern carnival that does not reestablish an old order but, instead, insists on a new disorder in which authenticity, if not authority, is accorded the privacy of one's home and one's own thoughts. This orientation is quite new to Russian writing culture, which, since the late eighteenth century, has consistently turned its gaze outward toward social issues. Private speech, which, until Rozanov, is not a discourse because it is for oneself alone, and its most ecstatic form, religious prayer, are, for Rozanov, by far the most meaningful and truest form of human speech.

Although Rozanov enlivens his anti-discourse by keeping it open-ended—without a final, authoritative word, without insisting on his own legitimacy or identity, without preaching to anyone—he also risks the difficulties of self-will, moral anarchy, and plain public irresponsibility. His decidedly new philosophical speech, so original in its openness, becomes troublesome when we set it against his social commentary, a civil discourse he greatly reviled and yet brazenly used and abused. Here Rozanov diverges strongly from philosophical precursors, such as Nietzsche, who, for all their colorful and risky language, never crossed discursive barriers from the elite to the public and middlebrow domain. It is this discursive promiscuity that makes Rozanov so contradictory and difficult to grasp.

When we juxtapose *Solitaria* and *Blood,* both written close to the same time, we are forced to confront anew Rozanov's strongly divergent treatments of Jewish ritual—so intimate and suggestive in *Solitaria,* and so raucous and threatening in *Blood.* Rozanov's increasingly anti-Semitic tone grew even more strident through the encouragement of a new friend in these years, the conservative Christian philosopher Pavel Florensky, who is credited with turning Rozanov toward Russian Orthodox piety. Recent research has shown Florensky to be anti-Semitic as well as hypocritical. Afraid to have his name publicly associated with the anti-Semitic Black Hundreds, Florensky penned two appendixes to *Blood,* which his friend, Rozanov, then agreed to publish, at Florensky's request, under his own name.[26] Despite this misguided association, Rozanov's attack on civil discourse remains inseparable from his own writing experience. What did this anti-Semitic volume of articles mean for Rozanov's efforts at authentication of a private, philosophical discourse in *Solitaria*? Did the Rozanov in *Blood* also participate in a carnival setting? If so, in this case the carnival fool himself was now uncrowned and dethroned. He had lost his playful edge and had become furious and vulgar. He was indeed again making a mockery of journalistic writing but now unintentionally, from inside the genre. In his treatment of religious themes, he had lost sight of the bonds between the sacred and the profane, and was pointing out only what he thought were the physical, shameful, even revolting parts of ritual practice.

In fact, although he was undermining serious journalistic writing, it is hardly likely that Rozanov intended to play the carnival fool in *Blood*. Instead, he was in the role of his most consistent persona, the "insulted and injured," resentful of the power of civil discourse to create opinion and genuinely worried that modern civil discourse had no grasp of the true meaning of the deep and old religious rifts against which it purported to defend society. In these essays, he sounded distressed, angry, and vengeful. In my view, with the 1913 Beilis case mentioned above, in which a Jewish man was accused of the ritual murder of a Christian boy, the antinomies in Russian writing culture—and in Rozanov's own writing—reached a crisis. Religious discourse was at odds with secular, intellectual discourse. Ancient religious language (Jewish) was at odds with modern religious speech (Rozanov's version of Christianity). Middlebrow, popular scientific discourse was at war with elite, "expert" discourse. Rozanov violated the rules of civil discourse and, in so doing, went beyond language and its power to negotiate order, inviting, instead, physical violence channeled at Jews and intellectuals.

---

26. See V. V. Rozanov, *Sakharna,* ed. A. N. Nikoliukin (Moscow: Republika, 1998), 438. This volume also includes a reprint of *Blood* and new materials from the Florensky archive. Michael Hagemeister and Efim Kurganov have been working on the relationship between the two and the issue of Florensky's anti-Semitism. See, for example, Michael Hagemeister, "Wiederverzauberung der Welt: Pavel Florenskijs Neues Mittelalter" *Beiträge des Florenskij-Kongresses, Potsdam, 2000* (Zürich: P. Lang, forthcoming); Efim Kurganov, "Rozanov i Florenskii: Problemy messianizma," *Zvezda* 3 (1997): 211–220. See also E. Kurganov and H. Mondry, *Rozanov i evrei* (St. Petersburg: Akademicheskii proekt, 2000).

In *Blood* Rozanov's social commentary becomes suspect and finally loses its authority. He uses vulgarized science based on unproven evidence. He claims early on to have proven scientifically and incontrovertibly the existence of ritual murders: "We can consider that the question of ritual murders of Christian boys by the international leaders of Judaism has been answered in the affirmative, using the same thoroughness, precision, and plausibility that one would use to prove a geometrical theorem" (*OEK,* viii). Rozanov cites scholarly articles at length and then argues with them. He claims to disprove their contentions but, in fact, he asks very odd questions and draws unjustified conclusions. His own arguments are extremely murky and remain unsupported. In contrast to his preface cited above, he writes that Christian boys *are not sacrificed* in the present day (*OEK,* 125). However, Jews are nevertheless irresistibly drawn to blood and have a need for blood sacrifice (*OEK,* 126). By concluding that this sacrifice *could* happen, it is only a small jump in logic to claim that it *did* happen. Elsewhere he argues that only a Jew would have been able to wield the rhomboid-shaped instrument that allegedly pierced the young Iushchinsky's temple. This weapon, according to Rozanov, was used in Jewish practice to slaughter cattle and drain their blood (*OEK,* 68) and thus was perfect to use for a human sacrifice. So if not Beilis, Rozanov reasons, then some other Jew had to have committed the killing (*OEK,* 85, 136). Claiming to have proven that Jews indeed commit ritual murders of Christian boys—contrary to what he argued eleven pages earlier—he goes on to reassert the earlier claim that Christian boys are not currently sacrificed. Finally, in a bewildering third round of opinion, he concludes that, although Beilis clearly did not commit the murder, another Jew did.

Probably Rozanov's most successful rhetorical tactic to lend credibility to his argument is to cite letters from distressed readers whose views support his own. These letters, more than any of his other "scientific" data or supposedly rational argumentation, appear to add validity to his argument by suggesting that his view is a prevalent and popular one.

True to his usual writing style, Rozanov's attitude toward his subject is far from objective and scientific, despite his insistence that this series of essays indeed employs a "scientific" method. His tone is, by turns, abusive and admiring of Jews and Judaism. For example, he characterizes Jews as being both masochistic and sadistic. They are masochistic, he contends, because they "like" blood and thus wish to be near those who oppress them (*OEK,* 25). Later they are said to be sadistic: Jews are beasts of prey and love the blood of the (Russian) "lamb" (*OEK,* 149). But then, at another moment, Rozanov expresses admiration for Judaism as a religion "of universal interest," a source of "science, religion, and philosophy," which is "much

higher and more general than 'the incidents on the street' and the disrup-
tions 'of our day'" (*OEK*, 58).

Most troubling of all, Rozanov's angry and confused rhetoric in *Blood*
seems to invite the man in the street to vent his rage with his fists. Toward
the end of the work he again lashes out at the Jews: "Oh, don't be so jubi-
lant, Jews. . . . Iushchinsky will come back to haunt you! He will be remembered in your chronicles" (*OEK*, 115). He then broadens the rift between the Russian peasant mob, on the one hand, and Jews and
intellectuals, on the other: "The uneducated Russian people will not yield
a child's blood to you. This is all the more so because the clarity, the moral
clarity of a child's blood, 'has weighed the fate' of our 'ruling intellectual
class' and has sent them to hell. That's how it will be. You are enjoying
your last moments of joy" (*OEK*, 116).[27] Still later, after being reminded of
a "decadent" evening at the home of the Jewish poet Nikolai Minsky,
where everyone tasted human blood, he launches into an even more virulent demonizing of Jews: "You are *nothing* at all. And although you lick
droplets of Christian blood—you lick your chops even at decadent
séances and in dark Lithuanian forests . . . we are not frightened of you,
and all of your successes have come only because we have been gripped by
'our Russian laziness' and our Russian mindless, sheep-like 'herd' mentality. But Christ did not die in vain. Christ won out and crushed you"
(*OEK*, 150).[28]

An important convergence between this work of gutter journalism and
Solitaria is that both strike out against the Russian intelligentsia and the
rather fragile, if combative, civil discourse that had developed in intellectual
circles and then in the public sphere since the Great Reforms of 1861. *Blood*
marks the functional limits of civility: at times, in his angry outbursts
against the secular intelligentsia, civil society, and the Jews, Rozanov actually desires the failure of public discourse and invites physical, violent inter-
vention by the mob, the people on the street. He suggests that the intelligentsia are blind to the fact that Jews are not really "modern" but are still
guided by their ancient religious instincts and rituals: "All this the rational-

27. This comment sounds disingenuous coming from Rozanov who, in *The Legend of the
Grand Inquisitor*, argued that the suffering of children is part of original sin and that children are
not absolutely pure and innocent (107).

28. Berdiaev's memory of this incident undermines Rozanov's position still further. In his
philosophical autobiography, *Samopoznanie* (*Self-Knowledge*), Berdiaev remembers the evening at
Minsky's as an innocent if embarrassing time at which a Jewish woman pricked her finger. What
was actually embarrassing about the evening, in Berdiaev's view, was the obvious intellectual and
spiritual fecklessness of those present and their inability to find any serious goals toward which to
channel their intellectual searchings. See *Samopoznanie* (Paris: YMCA, 1983), 179.

ists and positivists 'do not allow,' while the mystics 'demand' it. . . . There is an astonishing *mole* that 'breathes underground.' Beware, gentlemen on the street: the sacred procession of ancient days is coming" (*OEK*, 96).

In *Solitaria* Rozanov made his famous comment as to why Nietzsche could never be considered a *Russian* philosopher: "Nietzsche was respected because he was a German and also because he suffered (his illness). But if he had been *Russian* and had ventured *his own* opinion of the sort, '*push* the falling person *still harder*,'—he would have been labeled a scoundrel, and no one would have read him" (*S*, 49). This remark appears prophetic in light of the aftermath of the Beilis case and Rozanov's outburst against what progressive social opinion held to be a downtrodden ethnic group. Although some critics insisted that Rozanov, in *Blood*, was somehow *protesting* Russian racism and the demonizing of an entire people, his colleagues in both journalism and philosophy rejected him. He had difficulty getting his feuilletons and editorials published, and his erstwhile philosophical confreres expelled him from the St. Petersburg Religious-Philosophical Society.[29] Many viewed him as a kind of vulgar realization of Nietzsche, as standing "beyond truth and falsehood."[30] Thus, as Rozanov foresaw, when he, as a Russian writer, did try, as the German Nietzsche had, to "venture *his own* opinion of the sort, '*push* the falling person *still harder*,' " he was indeed "labeled a scoundrel" and an outsider.

I have attempted in this discussion to suggest the fragility of Rozanov's philosophical language by viewing it not in isolation but in the context of his other writings. Scholars have argued that Rozanov enriched and intensified the private language of self through the domestication of public discourse. This process has permitted him to overcome contradictions between the private and the public and to "reground" philosophy as a "private" discourse.[31] This seeming harmonization, however, clearly does not hold in the context of his feuilletons and social commentary. In *Solitaria* and *Blood*, both written, as I have indicated, in the same period, the gap between religious and secular, and between elite, philosophical discourse and middlebrow, journalistic discourse, has never been greater. Indeed, the authenticity of the one breaks down in the face of the other. In *Solitaria* Rozanov has debilitated journalism as a discourse, and in *Blood* he ignores the notion that he is even interested in exploring his inner self, his own private discourse. In his works

29. A. A. Smirnov, "O poslednei knige Rozanova," in Burlaka et al., *V. V. Rozanov: Pro et contra*, 219.

30. Ibid., 217.

31. Hutchings, "Breaking the Circle of the Self," 79.

Rozanov unlocks the deep rift between a radically conservative religious discourse (so backward that at times it actually seems "modern" and indeed is threatened by what seems to be a hostile recurrence of "ancient" religious ritual) and an enlightened discourse, with its competing value system that negates the power of religion and asserts a brand of social equality and liberty which Rozanov hates. One feat Rozanov does achieve in his philosophy-as-carnival and then in his journalistic practice is to illuminate the ruptures that underlie civil discourse, only then to deal with them angrily and irresponsibly: rather than trying to analyze these ruptures, he dramatizes them.

This juxtaposition of two cultural languages enables us to approach, from a different angle, the point that the poet Osip Mandelshtam was making in his essay, "On the Nature of the Word" (1922). Rozanov did more than just sense the edge of language and the precipice beyond it: we now see that toward the end of his career he actually danced on that edge and dared to fall into the abyss. Further, his hypercritical attitude toward rational civil discourse may be seen as the reverse side of a deep sensitivity to what he believed is the life-giving strength of metaphorical, mythical language. The ancient myths of "covenant" was far more powerful, he believed, than the modern discourse of "contract." He was certain that reasoned argument was skin deep at best and that the profound language of religious quest was powerful and binding. What he failed to understand is that all language has only limited authority. It is the intensity of feeling, and the degree of frustration and anger, that tips the scale away from spoken communication toward mob violence. "Rozanov the philosopher" pushed all stylistic and thematic limits, unleashing taboo themes for consideration, but also unlocking a Pandora's box of such premodern themes as cultural clannishness, ethnic rancor, and religious hatred. "Rozanov the philosopher" may well have created this crisis himself for "Rozanov the social commentator."

Although Rozanov, as discursive rogue, used all kinds of genres to attack civil discourse, the latter was perhaps unworthy of his carnivalesque writings. Civil discourse was relatively little developed in Russia compared to its advance in Western societies. It was both oppressed by the tsarist state and unsupported among the broad reaches of the Russian population. Clearly Rozanov recognized, even during this historical period of burgeoning literacy and literary and philosophical rebirth, how greatly at risk Russian writing culture remained, if not from the state then from its own radical practitioners. In his modern-day carnival, Rozanov did not reinstate the dethroned "king" of civil discourse; instead, in all his writings, both his philosophical works and his feuilletons, he continued to pound away at the "king." Vasily Rozanov, the discursive chameleon, embodies at once the uses and abuses of philosophy and the fragmentation of Russian writing culture on the eve of World War I.

Chapter Seven

Philosophy as Epic Drama:
Berdiaev's Philosophy of the Creative Act

Berdiaev is no "philosopher," if by philosophy one means building systematic objectively grounded world views. But he is undoubtedly a genuine thinker; he always has a multitude of new, original ideas; he can view things from his own point of view and above all possesses rare qualities of love for the truth and inner independence without which there could be no original intellectual creativity.

—S. L. Frank, "Philosophical Echoes," 1910

I hear that the Russian reading public is in love with Berdiaev. He is someone we need to smash and not just his philosophy.

—V. I. Lenin, letter to G. V. Plekhanov, July 30, 1901

IN OUR EXPLORATION of prerevolutionary philosophical discourse we have seen that philosophies are informed by a distinct literary-generic sensibility. Whereas Solovyov tended toward a mystical-lyrical sensibility, Shestov was clearly of a tragic mind and Rozanov wrote in a satirical, melodramatic tone. Nikolai Berdiaev (1874–1948), in contrast, wrote in a characteristically epic style. "Epic" philosophy may be described as a philosophy that builds an influential public presence, reaching across the breadth of intellectual discourse and reconstructing a significant history of philosophical development. In short, epic philosophizing is important both as a tradition and as a major contemporary discourse, not just for a small circle of like-minded people but also for the well-educated public. In Russia, philosophizing in an epic vein meant taking on the much deeper tradition of political polemics. Always defending philosophy as a socially significant discourse, Berdiaev, in one of his last philosophical essays, *On Freedom and Slavery* (1939), reworded Marx's condemnation of philosophy: "In my philosophical existence I never desired merely to know the world; the desire for knowledge went hand in hand with a desire to change the world."[1] Berdiaev, perhaps more than any philosopher before him, attempted to make Russian philosophy a permanent aspect of Russian writing culture in a variety of ways.

As a philosopher Berdiaev had a complex and self conscious view of philosophy that placed him somewhere between Russia's literary philosophers, Shestov and Rozanov, and the conventional religious philosophers of his generation, Semyon Frank and Sergei Bulgakov.[2] Although at times he did defend systematic philosophy and logical discourse as values in and of themselves, he was more sensitive than Frank and Bulgakov to "Russian philosophy" as a problem. It is significant that he defined his philosophy in relation to Shestov and Rozanov, as well as to novelists, but carried on no debate whatsoever with his fellow religious philosophers, Bulgakov and Frank. Clearly, for the younger philosopher, the literary philosophers were more vital and important.[3]

Throughout his career Berdiaev tried hard to develop a public space and historical presence for Russian philosophical discourse. Through the building of public institutions beyond the still rather weak academy and the tightly knit circles of philosophizing young people—almost invisible to the public—he helped to win for Russian philosophy a larger audience than it had ever had. He used the networks of modern writing culture—the newspaper and journal press, publishing houses, critical literature, and large public gatherings—to create a public philosophical voice. In addition, he strove in much of his writing to flesh out a history of Russian philosophy, showing that, beyond Solovyov, who was well known in educated circles, Russia indeed had a continuous philosophical past.

1. Nikolai Berdiaev, *O rabstve i svobode cheloveka (Opyt personalisticheskoi filosofii)* (Paris: YMCA, 1939). Hereafter cited in the text as *RSCh* with the relevant page number. In 1845–1846, in *The German Ideology* (first published in 1888) Marx wrote his famous dictum that "philosophers have only interpreted life in different ways; the task, however, is to change it" (Karl Marx, *Frühe Philosophische Schriften* [Stuttgart: A. Kroner, 1971], 341).

2. It is noteworthy that Frank strongly opposed Berdiaev's philosophical dialogue with fiction. In 1917, writing in *Dusha cheloveka: opyt vvedeniia v filosofskuiu psikhologiiu (The human soul: An introduction to philosophical psychology)*, he called this link "philosophical decadence":

Where philosophy openly identifies with poetic inspiration, religious faith, or moral proselytizing, as happens, for example . . . with a certain young and talented Russian thinker who absolutely denies any link between philosophy and science, and identifies [philosophy] with pure, independent creativity, similar to art—this is a real philosophical fall from grace; this is genuine philosophical decadence. (Cited in A. A. Ermichev, ed., *Berdiaev, pro et contra* [St. Petersburg: Izdatel'stvo russkogo khristianskogo gumanitarnogo instituta, 1994], 536–537.)

3. Although Shestov and Berdiaev remained close friends throughout their adult life, their philosophical approaches were very different, and they disputed into the 1930s, in Paris. See Berdiaev's review of Shestov's *Na vesakh Iova: Stranstvovanie po dusham* (Paris: Sovremennye zapiski, 1929), in *Put': Organ russkoi religioznoi mysli* (Paris), 18 (September 1929): 88–106.

Berdiaev created a language of philosophy that was much simpler and more accessible to a lay reader than the idioms of Solovyov's mystical system or Rozanov's anti-discursive, carnivalesque procedure of watching himself think. Berdiaev's discursive goals would not be so different from those of his friend, Shestov—to define philosophy as a language and as an approach to knowledge between "science" and literary art, adding to that his own effort to create a publicly visible and "normal" space for philosophy.[4] As accessible as Shestov's essays and aphorisms were, Berdiaev may have drawn a larger crowd than his friend partly because of the even greater simplicity and the ordinary expository structure of his writing.

Berdiaev was possibly even more concerned than Shestov with legitimizing his own kind of philosophical language. Although he viewed his writing as "nondiscursive"—he claimed he was unable to "prove" anything—he nonetheless wanted to base the authority of his contentions on logical argument. Unlike Solovyov before him and Losev later, Berdiaev was far from the mystical language of similitude, the "Logos" as a powerfully magical higher word able to shape the object it denotes. Instead, he was unique for his passionate, rhetorically vibrant "speaking voice" which, it can be shown, enabled him, more than any other philosopher in prerevolutionary Russia, to create a broad resonance for Russian philosophy among the educated public.

This chapter has two goals: first, to show how Berdiaev expanded, to genuinely epic proportions, the space and time in which Russian speculative philosophy operated; and, second, to examine his heroic "mythos" of philosopher as leader in a time of cultural and social upheaval. To these ends we first explore the chief journalistic and philosophical works of his Russian period, and then we examine his final work, his philosophical autobiography, *Self-Knowledge* (*Samopoznanie*, 1949). With this work Berdiaev made his last, best effort to reaffirm the legitimacy of Russian philosophy as a public discourse, to fix in Russian historical memory the elusive image and experience of a specifically Russian philosophical self, and, above all, to leave behind an alternative to the version of history that the Bolsheviks, and then Stalin, enforced.

Like many philosophers, Berdiaev was drawn to literature early in life, both as a reader and potential writer. Berdiaev differs, however, in the clear tone of regret at his lack of literary aptitude. Having a literary gift was obviously highly desirable. In *Self-Knowledge,* Berdiaev admitted that he did not have a literary temperament. He had tried early on to write novels "of a

---

4. Despite their similar goals, Shestov and Berdiaev would have very different definitions of "science." Whereas Shestov had Kant and systematic, rational metaphysics in mind, Berdiaev thought of "science" in terms of radical Marxist theory—the reliance on social sciences, economic and social history, and sociology.

philosophical kind" and claimed that he had lots of ideas for novels.[5] Clearly he saw his failure to write novels as a serious shortcoming, for he spent considerable time explaining why he could not write literature. He decided that, although he had "qualities that every fiction writer needs" (*SMPZ*, 34), he was too "dry" (*SMPZ*, 39). A lyrical sensibility was "repressed" by a kind of "secretiveness" in his character that hindered him in articulating feelings other than anger (*SMPZ*, 51). This intellectual attachment to fiction, nonetheless, was of primary importance in forming Berdiaev's philosophy. His approach to thinking "was always existential, as they now call it, it expressed the struggles of my spirit, it was close to life . . . without quotation marks" (*SMPZ*, 36).

Berdiaev began reading German philosophy as an adolescent, when he found Kant's *Critique of Pure Reason* and Hegel's *Philosophy of Spirit* in his father's library. In contrast to most academic philosophers, whom he called the "scholarly estate," Berdiaev saw philosophy as the "search for profound truth [*istina*] and the process of unfolding the meaning of life" (*SMPZ*, 50). Reading Kant and Hegel helped him to form an "inner world," a self with a separate sphere of thinking and interpretation that lent depth and meaning to his life (*SMPZ*, 51). However, despite this early engagement with German idealism, it was Dostoevsky whom Berdiaev claimed as his first serious philosophical mentor.[6] As he put it in *Dostoevsky's Worldview* (1921), it was Dostoevsky's formulation of philosophical issues in the minds of fictional characters that first sparked his imagination: "My earliest awareness of philosophical issues was linked to Dostoevsky's 'cursed questions'" (MD, 8).

In *Self-Knowledge* Berdiaev significantly all but ignored one of his earliest intellectual loves, Karl Marx, whom he began reading as a student in 1894 (*SMPZ*, 131). Writing in exile in France while other Russian exiles accused him of being a Soviet sympathizer, Berdiaev devoted much more attention in his autobiography to Kant and Dostoevsky. In fact, the young Berdiaev, who inherently mistrusted the existing social order, found inspiration in Marx's thought. Although Marx was still being read in the early 1890s as an economic theorist, this young romantic understood that Marx's theories could offer a path to both social revolution and personal liberation (*SMPZ*, 122). In his autobiography Berdiaev reduced his early elation with Marx's work to a mere intellectual point of departure for later developments. Although his experience as a Marxist had kept him from becoming an "abstract thinker" and had made him want to live and practice his ideas, now,

5. Nikolai Berdiaev, *Samopoznanie* (1949; rpt. Paris: YMCA, 1983), 25, 34. Hereafter cited in the text as *SMPZ* with the relevant page number.

6. Nikolai Berdiaev, "Mirovozzrenie Dostoevskogo," in *Filosofiia tvorchestva, kul'tury i iskusstva*, 2 vols. (Moscow: Iskusstvo, 1994), 2:8. All citations in the text, hereafter cited as MD with the relevant page number, are from volume 2.

late in life, he ascertained that by his very nature he could never have become a "Marxist." He did not fit easily into groups of any kind, feeling constricted, even stifled, by the Russian radical mentality that, as he put it, demanded total conformity (*SMPZ*, 133). Arrested in 1898 and exiled to Vologda until 1902, he came away from the experience already fusing Marxism with a strongly personalist philosophical idealism. His erstwhile radical comrades now attacked him for his new critique of materialism.

Berdiaev's philosophical identity took shape very much in conflict with his intellectual surroundings. To judge from his earliest writings, such as *Subjectivism and Individualism* (1901), in which he gave a thorough critique of the aging populist thinker N. K. Mikhailovsky, Berdiaev's own thought took shape in his disputes with radical ideologues. Living in St. Petersburg in the first decade of the twentieth century he associated with other renegades from Russian Marxist circles, for example, Petr Struve and Sergei Bulgakov, who were also trying to find a common ground between Marxism and idealism. However, judging from his autobiography, a deeper positive identity emerged as a result of particular experiences: first, from reading Russian literature early on—particularly Dostoevsky, Lermontov, and Tiutchev—and later reading German Idealist philosophy, Ibsen, and Nietzsche, and still later from his association with Russian Symbolist poets and theorists.

Indeed, essential to his philosophical development was the close acquaintance he developed with certain literary Symbolists. Among these were Dmitry Merezhkovsky, the critical and creative leader of the older generation of Symbolists; Zinaida Gippius, the only poet Berdiaev claimed ever to have liked; Viacheslav Ivanov, the theoretical candlepower behind Russian Symbolism; and Andrei Belyi, whom Berdiaev valued as a marvelously talented novelist. In this company Berdiaev met the writer whom he prized by far as the most gifted of the age, Vasily Rozanov. In his encounters with these people—and particularly Merezhkovsky and Rozanov—Berdiaev arrived at the key themes of his mature philosophy: the affirmation of the human body as a source of creative energy, in which the human and the divine would intertwine, the concept of "freedom," and, even more important, the idea of the "creative act."

What, then, is philosophy for Berdiaev? Clearly it is a "creative act" involving the disciplined process of shaping a conscious self. This process involves the mental and verbal struggle to make sense of life and its conflicting intellectual, moral, and cultural needs and attractions. For example, Berdiaev is attracted to the struggle for social and political liberation. He is viscerally drawn as well to personal, spiritual growth in opposition to the restrictions the social community imposes. Philosophy is, most notably, about developing consistency of character, personal integrity, which one carries throughout life, in both private and public spheres. For Berdiaev,

Nikolai Berdiaev, Dorlys, Paris, n.d. From Lidia Berdiaeva, *Professiia: Zhena filosofa* (Moscow: Melodaia Gvardiia, 2002).

that means resisting all forms of ideological and political tyranny. Many times, for example, the irascible and sometimes dictatorial Berdiaev exhibited a heroic fearlessness in facing down his potential executioners, tsarist or Bolshevik, and a stout willingness to be thrown in jail for insisting on his right to be free and to resist conformity. Just before his exile in late September 1922, for example, he underwent a final interview with Feliks Dzerzhin-

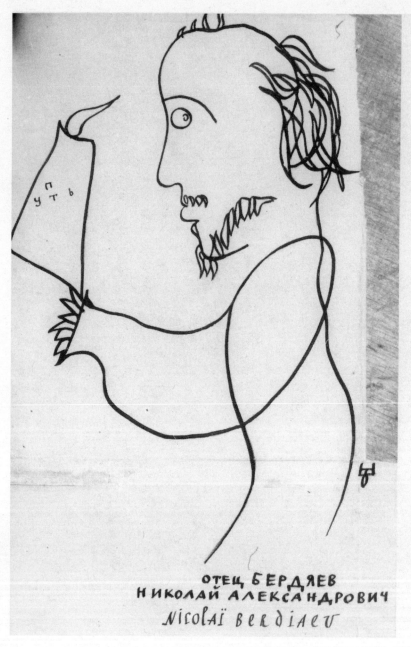

Caricature of Nikolai Berdiaev by Aleksei Remizov, n.d. Courtesy of RGALI.

sky, the fanatical captain of Lenin's secret police, the Cheka. In an even saltier version of Iury Zhivago's bold, confrontational critique of Antipov in Boris Pasternak's novel, *Doctor Zhivago,* Berdiaev took the bold step of lecturing Dzerzhinsky on the philosophical grounds for rejecting Bolshevik power.[7] Thus, for Berdiaev, philosophy is more than an abstract logical system; rather, it is a set of principles that allows one to confront the circumstances of one's life in a meaningful way. Least of all is philosophy a system of absolute values that occupies some timeless sphere—as philosophical idealists would traditionally have it. Philosophical views can and do evolve, and they clearly affect our identity and our behavior.

Berdiaev's prerevolutionary efforts to create a public voice for philosophy directly challenged the traditional rejection of philosophy by politically engaged intellectuals. These political commentators and critics of various stripes—all with their intolerant polemics—had seized the so-called public sphere. Before the 1890s there had been no room for careful, logical, theoretical discussion. Throughout most of the early nineteenth century, although there are notable exceptions, philosophy had generally operated in the realm of closed circles and oral disputes. Now, in the first years of the twentieth century, Berdiaev asserted a public identity for himself, precisely as a *philosopher.* As such, he insisted on the right to a public forum for critical discourse. His first efforts in this direction appeared as separate articles in journals and newspapers between 1901 and 1906 and were later collected in the book *Sub specie aeternitatis* (1907).

In the 1870s public forums gradually opened for public discussion. We recall Vladimir Solovyov's well-attended lectures on divine humanity. Now, in the early twentieth century, large associations were founded, such as the Religious-Philosophical Meetings in St. Petersburg and the Solovyov Societies in Moscow and Kiev.[8] These voluntary organizations had hundreds of members who attended the frequent meetings. In the late 1880s philosophy gained its first print forum, *Voprosy filosofii i psikhologii,* founded and edited by Nikolai Grot. This journal and others—*Poliarnaia zvezda, Novaia zhizn', Put',* and *Logos*—all put Russian philosophy on the intellectual map, enabling it to reach a broader span of the educated reading public. Of course, an even greater number of people read the newspapers, such as the conservative *Novoe vremia,* to which Rozanov contributed a regular feuilleton. In addition, major published volumes of philosophical essays, partic-

---

7. Aleksei Velidov, "Nikolai Berdiaev—arest i vysylka," *Sovershenno sekretno,* 8 (1991): 2–3.

8. Two excellent studies of philosophical societies are Jutta Scherrer's classical work, *Die Petersburger Religiös-Philosophischen Vereinigungen: Die Entwicklung des religiösen Selbstverständnisses ihrer Intelligencija-Mitglieder (1901–1917)* (Berlin-Wiesbaden: O. Harrassowitz, 1973); and Kristiane Burchardi, *Die Moskauer "Religiös-Philosophische Vladimir-Solov'ev-Gesellschaft" (1905–1918)* (Wiesbaden: O. Harrassowitz, 1998).

ularly *Problems of Idealism* and *Landmarks*—to which Berdiaev contributed—participated fully in all public networks of writing culture and
actively challenged the claim of the radicals that only political rhetoric and
social theory deserved public attention. For example, *Landmarks* (1909), a
publication that defied the basic values and assumptions of the radical intelligentsia, enjoyed five editions and sold about fifteen thousand copies, an
astonishing number for a work of philosophy. Further, it provoked hundreds of published reviews, public lectures, and discussions. As a result
thousands of Russians, who may not even have read the volume, knew its
general themes and positions.

Berdiaev was involved with nearly every one of these enterprises, as
founder, leading contributor, or editor. During the cold, hard years of the
civil war he increased his activity as a public lecturer, writing and publishing
a number of books, for example, *The Philosophy of Inequality* and *Dostoevsky's Worldview,* as well as contributing essays to the collected volume *Out
of the Depths* (1918).[9] With the help of Lev Kamenev, the Moscow Communist Party boss, Berdiaev found a building in which to house his Free Academy of Intellectual Culture (*Vol'naia Akademiia Dukhovnoi Kul'tury*),
which functioned until his exile in September 1922 (*SMPZ,* 277). Here he
and others taught seminars to hundreds, even thousands, of freezing, hun-
gry students, unemployed professional people, as well as workers thirsty for
intellectual sustenance. The range of subjects was broad and included Dostoevsky, theosophy, magic, philosophy of religion, and philosophy of history. A lecture on Spengler and his apocalyptical theories of history drew
crowds so enormous as to block the street outside the building, and police
worried that the floor of the lecture hall would collapse under the weight of
the audience (*SMPZ,* 277). After the civil war Berdiaev actually held an official academic position as professor of philosophy at Moscow University
until the philosophy department closed in 1922.[10] In January 1922, when
the Russian Academy of Aesthetic Sciences (*Rossiiskaia Akademiia Khudozhestvennykh Nauk*) was reopened, Berdiaev served as an active member of the
philosophy department, which was headed at the time by the phenomenologist Gustav Shpet.[11]

9. Christopher Read, *Culture and Power in Revolutionary Russia* (New York: St. Martin's, 1990),
70. Interestingly, for our subject, Read notes that the articles in *Out from the Depths* are much
more "otherworldly" than previous philosophical volumes. As he puts it, "While a violent revolution was taking place, the analysis of it in this volume was based on the writings of people such as
Gogol' and Dostoevsky and rarely on observation of the actual events occurring at the time" (70).

10. *Russkaia filosofiia: slovar'*, ed. M. A. Maslin et al. (Moscow: Respublika, 1995), 543. In 1922
nearly the entire law and philosophy faculties of Moscow University were expelled from the Soviet
Union.

11. A. V. Vadimov, *Zhizn' Berdiaeva: Rossiia,* 2 vols. (Oakland: Berkeley Slavic Specialties,
1993), 1:227.

In *The Republic* Plato exiles free-speaking poets from his ideal state. In Lenin's new "republic," it was the philosophers, deemed incapable of being "reformed," who were exiled. After September 28, 1922, when Berdiaev and dozens of other philosophers and academics were forced to leave the country, philosophizing assumed its former sociological patterns of behavior. It existed only in the underground and behind various academic facades, for example, classical studies (Shpet), literary theory (Bakhtin), and aesthetics and musicology (Losev), and eventually only in tiny, tight circles of trusted friends (Pasternak).[12] The early Stalinist camps provided another forum in which lively philosophical debate continued, and even that fell silent as philosophers were executed (among them Shpet and Florensky).[13] As these examples show, Berdiaev was correct when he remarked in *Sub specie aeternitatis* that the radicals showed the same tendency to despotism and tyranny as the unjust tsarist functionaries whose order they wanted to overthrow. In the end, Lenin and then Stalin imposed the same fate that Tsar Nicholas I brought on Russian philosophy, but in an even bleaker form. If the Gendarme of Europe repressed Russian philosophical activity, Lenin and Stalin "murdered" it.[14] Berdiaev was a major player in keeping philosophy alive— even if only for five years—and toward the end he was probably *the* central figure in Moscow struggling to maintain a free, public voice of principled, philosophical opposition to the Bolsheviks.

Berdiaev was equally concerned to construct a Russian philosophical heritage as to increase its contemporary visibility and resonance. Clearly a philosophy that had its own tradition, its own founders, enjoyed greater authority than one that had to reinvent itself with every generation. From 1904 on, in a number of venues, Berdiaev recast Russian intellectual history as the gradual liberation of the thinking self from intellectual and spiritual bonds. He wrote studies on intellectual figures he considered noteworthy. For example, he wrote an article about Konstantin Leontiev in 1905 (ex-

12. One list of the exiled philosophers that I have seen is in Karl Schlögel, *Jenseits des grossen Oktober : das Laboratorium der Moderne; Petersburg 1909–1921* (Berlin: Siedler, 1988), 481. Schlögel lists eight philosophers: Berdiaev, E. Trubetskoi, I. Il'in, B. Vysheslavtsev, F. Stepun, N. Losskii, I. Lapshin, and L. Karsavin. To these names must be added S. Bulgakov, P. Bitsilli, Vl. Veidle, S. Gessen, N. Glubovskii, V. Zen'kovskii, P. Miliukov, P. Novgorodtsev, E. Radlov, P. Savitskii, V. Sezeman, P. Sorokin, E. Spektorskii, P. Struve, N. Timashev, P. Uspenskii, G. Fedotov, G. Florovskii, S. Frank, B. Iakovenko, to name the best known.

13. The émigré philosophy journal *Put'* (Paris) published an anonymous letter to Berdiaev in June 1930 (issue no. 22), purportedly from a young philosopher in the north of Russia (possibly from a labor camp) who wrote of the terrible loneliness he felt in the spreading philosophical wasteland of the Soviet Union.

14. Klaus-Dieter Eichler and Ulrich Johannes Schneider, eds., *Russische Philosophie im 20. Jahrhundert* (Leipzig: Leipziger Universitätsverlag, 1996). This volume contains excellent discussion of many aspects of philosophical life (and death) in the Soviet era. See, particularly, the paper by Vladimir Malakhov, "Über 'russische postmoderne' Philosophie," 58–70.

panded into a book in 1922) and a book about Khomiakov in 1912, as contributions to a monograph series on "Russian religious thinkers" published under the aegis of *Put'*.[15] Berdiaev most famously reappropriated Dostoevsky, whom he claimed as perhaps *the* major Russian philosophical mind and the precursor to his own generation of philosophers (MD, 142). In *Dostoevsky's Worldview* (1921), he presented Dostoevsky's views in terms of ontological and ethical categories, such as "person" (*chelovek*), "freedom," "evil," and "love," as well as the Solovyovian categories of "divine humanity" (*bogochelovechestvo*) and "human divinity" (*chelovekobozhestvo*). Dostoevsky, Berdiaev argued, was more important as a precursor to idealist Russian philosophy than Solovyov who "challenged abstract [European] metaphysics in too abstract a manner" (MD, 144). Dostoevsky, in contrast, gives metaphysics new significance and life by showing metaphysical concepts and meanings taking shape in the minds and hearts of his fictional characters—not imposed from without as an abstract system.

Once in exile, Berdiaev and a number of other philosophers of the Russian Renaissance wrote entire histories of Russian philosophy. By that time, of course, there was no hope of having an impact, since philosophical culture in Russia had been destroyed. However, it was these histories that were among the first works to be reprinted in post-Soviet Russia, for example, Berdiaev's *Russian Idea* (1947; 1990) and *The Origins of Russian Communism* (1937; 1991) and Zenkovsky's two-volume *History of Russian Philosophy* (1948–1950; 1991).

Another tactic Berdiaev used to enhance the authority of Russian philosophy was to diminish his radical competitors' claims to Russia's future. In many of his works, including his earliest articles in *Sub specie aeternitatis* and *Landmarks*, he contended that the radicals were, in general, intellectually limited. They were bound by a life-denying, ascetic mentality that has its roots in Russian Orthodoxy, which itself had fostered only the poorest of philosophical cultures. This meager intellectual heritage suggested to Berdiaev that contemporary radicalism itself could leave only the poorest of intellectual legacies. Later he would develop a whole counter-history of Russian radicalism in *The Origins of Russian Communism,* a work that portrays Bolshevism as the uncultured, nihilistic, ascetic legacy of traditional Russian Orthodoxy.

Berdiaev took on the radical tradition throughout the early years of his philosophical career. He challenged their disdain for literary art and their anti-philosophical attitudes. His most significant public confrontation came in the lead article of *Landmarks,* "Philosophical Truth [*Istina*] and In-

---

15. Nikolai Berdiaev, *Aleksei Stepanovich Khomiakov* (1912; rpt. Westmead: Gregg International Publishers, 1971), v. Hereafter cited in the text as *ASKh* with the relevant page number.

telligentsia Truth [*Pravda*]." Citing Solovyov's famous parody of radicals' logic and ethics—"man came from the ape; therefore we must love one another"[16]—Berdiaev portrayed radicals as people interested in an oddly grounded social justice but not in deeper truth. Radical discourse, he argued, was akin to intellectual fakery. In contrast, philosophy is defined as the "school of love for truth," which embraces human creative force (*V*, 8). In Berdiaev's view, the radical intelligentsia generally preferred "distribution and leveling" over the "interests of [economic] production and [cultural] creative action." Whether the field was philosophy or business, both were considered "immoral" and somehow a betrayal of the interests of the "people" and their "cause" (*V*, 2–3). Moreover, he accused the radical intelligentsia of tunnel vision: they rejected any thought that could not directly be applied to their ideological goals, and thus they impaired the development of a rigorous speculative culture. Berdiaev ended his critique by claiming the preeminence of philosophy as the very "organ of human self-knowledge" (*V*, 21), devoted to understanding individual consciousness as well as social and collective consciousness.

The third tactic Berdiaev employed to expand the historical horizons of Russian philosophy was to lay claim to the future. Russian philosophy, he argued, was based on the notion of a free, conscious, and creative self that has metaphysical as well as social and political dimensions.[17] Particularly in what he considered was his first fully philosophical "manifesto," *The Meaning of the Creative Act* (*Smysl tvorchestva*, 1914), he foresaw the development of a Russian philosophy free of abstraction and scholasticism, fully connected to life and its struggles. This philosophy would be founded on the "creative, self-overcoming, transfigurative nature of knowledge."[18] By nature, only this "revolution of the spirit" could discover the truth through struggle and "creative acts."

This new public, historically developing epic philosophy would provide the forum in which Berdiaev could develop a number of major themes. These included a serious analysis of the Russian radical mentality and its shortcomings, outlined just above; a reassessment of the deep riches of Russian literary art; and the concept of a national philosophical culture. In *Sub specie aeternitatis* Berdiaev was much more optimistic than his precursors in his view of the possibilities for a philosophical culture in Russia. He foresaw

16. Nikolai Berdiaev, *Vekhi: sbornik statei o russkoi intelligentsii* (1909; rpt. Frankfurt: Posev, 1967), 9. Hereafter cited in the text as *V* with the relevant page number.

17. Nikolai Berdiaev, *Sub specie aeternitatis: opyty filosofskie, sotsial'nye i literaturnye (1900–1906)* (St. Petersburg: M. V. Pirozhkov, 1907), 185. Hereafter cited in the text as *SSA* with the relevant page number.

18. Nikolai Berdiaev, *Filosofiia tvorchestva, kul'tury i iskusstva*, 2 vols. (Moscow: Iskusstvo, 1994), 1:64. Hereafter cited in the text as *FTK* with the appropriate volume and page numbers.

a formal Russian philosophy that was more than the "parasitic growth" or "bad translation from the German" that it traditionally had been (*SSA,* 162). He pressed on: "I hold out the hope of showing that the embryos of Russian philosophical thought are qualitatively higher than contemporary European philosophy, which has grown shallow and fragmented. These [embryos] hold the promise of an independent and fruitful philosophical creative activity" (*SSA,* 158). Berdiaev admitted that "grave barriers stand in the way of its development," but that, in time, Russian philosophy would certainly flourish (*SSA,* 162).

Along with this epic canvas, on which he pictured the development of philosophical culture in Russia, Berdiaev created a philosophical discourse that was accessible and attractive to a broad array of readers, both Russian and European. Of all the philosophical idioms considered in the present study, Berdiaev's was the least figurative. He was no longer troubled by the conflict between the magical similitude of words and objects and the scientific representation of an object by a word. His speech was the dramatic, verbal gesture of a "speaking self" in the process of defining itself. For Berdiaev, philosophical language was neither mere rhetoric nor abstract syllogism; rather, it was dramatic and assertive, a speaking voice confident of its intuitive insight.

In a number of works important to his formation as a philosopher, Berdiaev devoted considerable attention to the grounds for the authority of philosophical language. Particularly in his last work, *Self-Knowledge,* he defended his mode of writing and thinking as "nondiscursive." Discourse, he wrote, is meant to persuade. His own thought, in contrast, was "intuitive and aphoristic": "My thought has no discursive development. I do not know how to develop and prove. And those things seem unnecessary. I value and love Kant very much. I consider him the greatest of philosophers. But Kant's thought is overgrown with a schoolish-scholastic rind that always struck me as superfluous and harmful, muddying his ingenious thought" (*SMPZ,* 96). Kant, Berdiaev claimed, came to his major ideas intuitively. Logical proof exists "not for the person who knows [*poznaiushchii*] but for other people" (*SMPZ,* 96). It is nothing more than a rhetorical device meant to persuade people. At other times, however, Berdiaev openly admitted that, despite his lack of trust in analysis, he did make use of logical discourse, insisting, nonetheless, that it is secondary (*SMPZ,* 103–104).

This stand against what Berdiaev called discursive reasoning was articulated in 1914 in *The Meaning of the Creative Act.* His discussion in this work of Thomas Aquinas and the scholastic beginnings of scientific philosophy couches his project in the language of an epic liberation narrative. Scholastic philosophy was first a "handmaiden" of theology and then eventually became the "age-old slave of a foreign overlord," science. He continues his thought: "Philosophical consciousness is eternally muddied . . . by the false desire to be science, an area with goals alien to philosophy."[19]

In the defining chapter of *The Meaning of the Creative Act,* entitled "Philosophy as a Creative Act," Berdiaev further expands his critique of "discursive" thinking, and, by inference, of "science," to mean all observation and interpretation limited to the given, physical world:

> Discursive thinking as such embodies an inexorable [*neotvratimyi*] necessity, coercion, and inevitability, a vicious circle. Discursive thinking, left to itself, falls under the power of bad infinity. . . . Discursive thinking is a formal, automatic apparatus brought into motion by forces that lie outside it. In the end, discursive thinking is merely the tool of intuition that launches and completes [the process]. . . . Discursive thinking is an apparatus wonderfully adapted to manipulating the world as it is given to us. Here [in discursive thinking] one is obliged to adapt to necessity in the world as it is. Only people who have lowered their intellectual interaction to mediocrity seek the exclusive support and grounding of their knowledge in the mediocrity of discursive thinking. They see the justification of knowledge in necessity. (ST, 58)

Berdiaev's point approximates that of Shestov's in the latter's critique of systematic philosophy. The "discursive" mind is locked to the observation of the "given" world and to the rules of logic. Berdiaev does not deny the usefulness of these tools but argues that they are enhanced if one employs other human faculties, namely, intuition and imagination. In short, Berdiaev, like his friend, Shestov, is not arguing benightedly against factual, logical proof; instead, he is insisting that it has a limited role and should not be the sum total of the quest, in religion, philosophy, and art, for human values.

Thus discursive thinking, for Berdiaev, is an "unfree" form of thinking, bound by rules of logic that do not allow us to expand our consciousness, to imagine other options beyond the "necessary," beyond that which already is. It forces certain paths of thinking that, while adhering to the rules of logic, may or may not be true in a deeper sense. Like his confreres, Berdiaev argues for the power of intuition. In *The Meaning of the Creative Act,* he writes: "Philosophical intuition seems less generally binding than scientific discursive thinking, because it has a lower common denominator, it is more generally accessible. In fact, intuition is sympathetic adaptation [*simpaticheskoe vzhivanie*], it is an investigation into the world, into the essence [*sushchestvo*] of the world and therefore presupposes communality [*sobornost'*]" (ST, 59). Despite his strong emphasis on individual intuition, it should be noted that Berdiaev brings a social aspect to this new valorization

---

19. Nikolai Berdiaev, "Smysl tvorchestvo," in *Filosofiia tvorchestva, kul'tury i iskusstva,* 2 vols. (Moscow: Iskusstvo, 1994), 1:48. All citations in the text, hereafter cited as ST with the appropriate page number, are from volume 1.

of intuition by saying that, in order to penetrate the inner nature of the world, one needs some form of check on individual intuition. What is needed is a community of intuition for which Berdiaev borrows Khomiakov's term, "*sobornost*" (ST, 59).

In *The Meaning of the Creative Act,* Berdiaev makes the outlandish claim that, in philosophy, "what is proven is what is imposed, inevitable, inexorable," and, further, that "dependence on proofs is a slavish dependence" (ST, 69). Although these claims may seem ludicrous and willful, they are meaningful if we understand that Berdiaev's philosophical goals are speculative. His aim is to explore new ways of thinking about familiar objects, values, and relationships. He leaves it to others to prove or disprove them. Given the degree to which Berdiaev's insights have served as the framing device for literary and historical study, both of which are traditionally attached to documents and facts, at least in the theoretical and speculative realm he may be said to be right.[20]

Persuasiveness in philosophical language is produced, according to Berdiaev, through crystal-clear, assertive statements that strike at the heart of an issue: "In philosophy, what persuades and infects is the perfection of formulations, their sharpness and clarity, the light that emanates from them, and not proofs and conclusions." Further Berdiaev writes: "Philosophy presupposes interaction [*obshchenie*] on the grounds of first and last intuitions and not middling proofs and discursive thought" (ST, 70). In contrast, contemporary "scientific," discursive philosophy, such as that of Hermann Cohen or Edmund Husserl, "kill" their human subject and create a situation in which not people but philosophy "philosophizes" (ST, 71).

The real point about the character of genuine philosophizing, for Berdiaev, is its autonomy at any cost: it must be no one's "handmaiden." It must be free of external authority. In Berdiaev's prerevolutionary writings the alliance between philosophy and literature—another cultural language susceptible to domination—soon becomes paramount. This alliance becomes the next step in the epic liberation of philosophy from "foreign overlords."

Although Berdiaev is the least "literary" of the philosophers considered in

20. For example, the concept of early-twentieth-century Russian culture as a "Russian Renaissance" comes from Berdiaev and, to my mind, offers a much more positive term for the period than D. S. Mirsky's label, "The Silver Age." Even though Berdiaev did not coin the term *Russian idea,* he certainly popularized it, and it is generally associated with his name. The notion of the "revolution of moral values" and the "revolution of the spirit" that motivates a number of books on turn-of-the-century culture both come from Berdiaev (for example, Bernice G. Rosenthal and Martha Bohachevsky-Chomiak, *The Revolution of the Spirit* [Newtonville, Mass.: Oriental Research Partners, 1982]; Clowes, *The Revolution of Moral Value: Nietzsche in Russian Literature* [DeKalb: Northern Illinois University Press, 1988]; and Joanna Hubbs, *Mother Russia: The Feminine Myth in Russian Culture* [Bloomington: Indiana University Press, 1993], xv).

the present study, he is also the most famous and internationally recognized of twentieth-century Russian philosophers. His strong acknowledgment of literary traditions and models makes all the clearer the extent to which the fertile Russian philosophy of Russia's strongest philosophical age emerged "from the overcoat" of literary precursors. Like Struve and Bulgakov, Berdiaev emerged from the environment of discursive, social commentary that marked early Russian Marxism. Nonetheless, the key to his developing philosophical persona was his decade-long association with poets and critics around the Merezhkovsky circle, Ivanov's Tower, the St. Petersburg Religious-Philosophical Society, and the Moscow Solovyov Society. During this time he discovered another literary philosopher, Friedrich Nietzsche. In Berdiaev's writing we can see a creative process in which he defined his own philosophical voice in contrast to Merezhkovsky, Ivanov, Rozanov, and Shestov. It was from Merezhkovsky and Ivanov, in particular, that he appropriated the vocabulary of human creativity. Even his eventual turn to God and religion happened through these Symbolists' aesthetic sensibility oriented toward human creative agency. Although Berdiaev's epic sensibility, his affirmation of struggle and conflict, found its first expression in Marxism, major Berdiaevian concepts of "freedom," "selfhood," and the "creative act" have their source in the creative ferment of the Symbolist circles.

In *Self-Knowledge* Berdiaev admitted the importance of these literary ties: "The creative surge at the start of the century enriched me, [offering] new issues and refining my thinking" (*SMPZ,* 165). In his St. Petersburg period during the first decade of the twentieth century he granted a great deal of authority to the human self, the human will, and intuition. Now insistence on objective approaches to knowledge struck Berdiaev even more strongly as the death of creative, productive agency. The articles in *Sub specie aeternitatis* clearly mark this shift from a "scientific" orientation toward philosophy to a literary, creative one. He started openly to defend Russian literary art as the preeminent form of writing in Russia, the only one that could be considered first-rate: "Russian literature is our national pride. It is our only contribution to world culture" (*SSA,* 157).

Of central importance to his philosophical genealogy is Berdiaev's insistence, expressed in his work "On the New Russian Idealism" (1904), that the roots of Russian philosophy were not in Orthodoxy but in literature: "The most recent idealist trends [in philosophy] are forecast in the whole history of Russian literature. In [literature] are grounded the deepest philosophical and religious yearnings. It may be that the task of Russian philosophy and social commentary is to work out the themes [first raised in] Russian literature" (*SSA,* 158). Berdiaev's goal by 1905, in "Culture and Politics," was to close the gap between progressive political-social theory and cultural creativity, thus endowing creative intuition with even more importance.

Whereas radicals in their "arithmetical fanaticism" measured literature by mathematical yardsticks, Berdiaev argued that, "in Pushkin, Lermontov, and Gogol, and, above all, in Dostoevsky and Tolstoy, we see real creative agency [*tvorchestvo*], higher mathematics, the seeking and creating [*sozidanie*] of higher cultural values" (*SSA*, 278).

The project of "philosophical anthropology," or a free, person-based philosophy of the creative act, started for Berdiaev not with Feuerbach or Chernyshevsky but with Kant, and was strengthened through an embrace of literary art. In 1902, in "Ethical Problems in the Light of Philosophical Idealism," Berdiaev articulated the central value of human selfhood and self-consciousness. Here he relied on Kant, who saw an individual person as a "goal itself" that "has absolute value because it has eternal spirit" (*SSA*, 71, 73). No one person is necessarily better than any other. In Berdiaev's view, "people are equally valuable because they share one and the same spiritual nature" (*SSA*, 73). Berdiaev drew additional support for this beginning of a personalist philosophy from Nietzsche, who protests "against the abasement of the self [*ia*] in ethical systems" (*SSA*, 74). Berdiaev asserted that "progress" from an ethical-philosophical point of view could be measured in the "liberation of the human self [*ia*] from external bonds" (*SSA*, 81). Later this rather youthful outburst was better articulated in terms of an ethical shift in which externally imposed laws would be replaced by those that are conceived and imposed internally, that is, those to which one is committed.

In *The Meaning of the Creative Act* Berdiaev calls this focus on the human subject an "anthropodicy," or justification of human goodness through good acts despite the existence of evil (*ST*, 46). He insists on his "anthropology," a dualistic view of the world in which only a person as a knowing, self-conscious subject—and not as an object defined externally through theory, myth, or law—can have real meaning. Such a person is capable of apprehending meaning through philosophy: "A philosophizing person cannot avoid affirming the special meaning of the human self in the world" (*ST*, 77). And conversely: "If a person views himself as one of the outward, objectivized things in the world, then he cannot be an active knowing subject—and philosophy becomes impossible" (*ST*, 77). Finally, an "anthropological philosophy," as Berdiaev defines it, "has to do not with the fact of the human self as an object of scientific knowledge (biological, psychological, or sociological) but with the fact of the human self as the subject of higher self-knowledge, with a fact that is beyond nature and the material world" (*ST*, 81). Although Berdiaev frequently implied he was a mystic, this definition of philosophy as opening other worlds should not be seen as mystical. Rather, it implies a distinction between culture and nature. Culture is a human-made realm endowed with the products of the human imagination and intellect, outside physical nature and the bare facts of physical needs. This view is supported by later comments. For example, in *Dosto-evsky's Worldview*, Berdiaev embraced Dostoevsky as a writer who "opens up new worlds" of human possibility (MD, 10). It is such worlds that take human life beyond mere natural existence, beyond necessity, that are the goal of what Berdiaev called "creative acts."[21]

Berdiaev already began to build a theoretical foundation for the concept of the creative act in his essay, "A Critique of Historical Materialism" (1903). The context for his idea is human culture, in which the most obvi-ous creative acts are those in the realm of literature and art. At the heart of this first attempt is the axiom that the thinking, creative self acts in history and contributes to the meaning of history (SSA, 116). Whereas for Hegel and Marx the point of departure for a philosophy of history is an external force, respectively Spirit and the idea of the economic base, Berdiaev, rather more like his Russian predecessor Herzen, posits, as his point of departure, the human self (*lichnost'*), although now, in contrast to Herzen, the self is a "spirit that creates the higher pleasures of human culture as the goal of his-tory" (SSA, 118). Here once again he limits the authority of "science," which in this instance means Marxist sociology, by asserting that "science is not fated to penetrate the mystery of human creative activity since it has no ac-cess to the realm of freedom" (SSA, 131).

In *The Meaning of the Creative Act*, Berdiaev draws on Merezhkovsky's idea of the Third Testament—a new Christian era that would successfully merge the creative genius and earthliness of paganism and the basic cosmol-ogy of Christianity with its promise of resurrection. Berdiaev's goal is to posit a three-part division of the history of human moral consciousness. The three eras are those of law, grace and redemption, and creative action. Berdiaev writes: "the [era of] law initiates the struggle with evil and sin, [the era of] redemption completes this struggle, and in [the era of] free creative activity a person is called to create a new and fabulous world, to continue God's creative work [*tvoren*]" (ST, 114).

The creative act, in Berdiaev's view, develops through dialogue between God and a person. God created the world and now awaits a creative re-sponse from people, an "anthropological revelation of the creative act" (ST, 112). Modern, self-conscious people, aware of their freedom and accepting of their ethical responsibility, continue the divine "matter of creative ac-tion" by creating other "worlds"—that is, cultural spheres that are only tan-gentially related to nature and necessity (ST, 114). The creative act is "co-creation with God" (ST, 136). Berdiaev has a very ambitious assignment for

21. "Creative act" is the chief way I have chosen to translate Berdiaev's term, "*tvorchestvo.*" *Tvorchestvo* can mean creativity, creative work, or creative act or action. I will generally use the lat-ter two terms because they impart the sense of willed act or agency that Berdiaev has in mind.

the creative act: "making another existence, another life, breaching 'this world,' [breaking through] to another, from the chaotically ponderous and hideous world to the free and sublime cosmos" (ST, 218).

Art, and more precisely literary art, serves Berdiaev as an initial model for the "creative act." In this reception of another register of cultural speech Berdiaev uses the predictable tactics of first appropriating artistic creation, and then delimiting and discrediting it, to build his own legitimacy and authority as a philosopher. He first allies himself with major writers of the past, Dante and particularly Dostoevsky, as well as with contemporary Symbolists and nontraditional philosophers such as Shestov and Rozanov. In *The Meaning of the Creative Act,* Berdiaev sums up the strengths and weaknesses of artistic creation. It is closest to what he sees as the "essence of the creative act": "Art is the creative sphere as such. . . . The essence of artistic creative activity is victory over the weight of necessity. In artistic activity [*khudozhestvo*] a person lives beyond himself, beyond his weight, beyond the weight of life. Each artistic creative act is a partial transfiguration of life" (ST, 217).

For all its force, however, artistic activity by itself is not enough. It suffers from the tragic rift between the artistic articulation of the goal and its realization in human practice. Berdiaev remarks, "Artistic creativity does not achieve ontological results: the ideal, not the real, is created; symbolic values—not real existence [*bytie*]" (ST, 218). For example, the greatest poets, Dante and Goethe, use symbols to point to a higher reality, which, however, they cannot actually create or even re-create. Dante's rose, for example, may symbolize higher reality, but by itself it cannot create new being; it cannot engender a real rose (ST, 229). By then, chiding Ivanov and various Symbolist attempts at theurgy for missing this essentially tragic flaw of art and culture, Berdiaev dismisses art and claims a higher level of creativity for philosophy (ST, 334).

A new, free philosophy, the "creation of values," Berdiaev asserts, is the product of a modern human consciousness that has passed through the gauntlet of morality as law and then redemption (ST, 256). The *major* creative act is a philosophical self that is capable of world-creative acts. Enhancing this conceptualization of the philosophical self is the chief goal of Berdiaev's work from 1914 on. In *On Freedom and Slavery: An Attempt at Personalist Philosophy* (1939), he summarizes this idea of selfhood: "Selfhood in an individual person is a victory over the determinism of the social group. Not a substance [*substantsiia*], the self is an act, a creative act. . . . The self is an activity [*aktivnost'*], resistance, victory over the heavy weight of the world, the celebration of freedom over the slavery of the world" (*RSCh,* 23). It is this notion of philosophy as creative act that Berdiaev seeks to realize both in his life and in his work. Hoping to achieve what writers cannot, to enact new being, he reenacts his own philosophical self, his own greatest creative act, in his final work, *Self-Knowledge.*

Certainly Berdiaev's efforts to extend the public reach of philosophical thinking and speech may be called a "creative act," in that they were part of his own life struggle to know himself, to create an integrated philosophical self, and to plant the seeds of unconventional values in Russian culture and society. In this regard, *Self-Knowledge* may be seen as Berdiaev's final philosophical creative act. He finalizes his own philosophical persona, one based on Russian literary characters, and leaves a document of the philosophical type that he wanted his philosophy to encourage—heroic and free, yet irascible, arrogant, and at odds with his surroundings; fearless and resistant to all forms of despotism, yet despising the "mediocrity" of democratic civil society. Along with Rozanov's "little man" persona and Shestov's persona of the wanderer at the edge of the cliff, this public persona is a possible Russian philosophical self.

Berdiaev is very particular about the genre he has chosen for *Self-Knowledge*. Readers of this work are sometimes disappointed that it does not contain more historical detail, closer to Herzen's *My Past and Thoughts*.[22] Instead of inscribing himself in a historical-autobiographical tale filled with lived and observed fact, Berdiaev appropriates for philosophy what might be seen as a "paraliterary" kind of writing, that is, a writing form on the border of literary art. From this autobiographical border genre Berdiaev can project a philosophical "speaking voice" that educated Russian readers will hear. He is determined that his readers view his philosophical testament as unusual, indeed extraordinary, not as a memoir, confession, diary, or autobiography in the usual sense. If it is an autobiography at all, then it is a "philosophical autobiography, a history of spirit and self-knowledge" (*SMPZ*, 5–6). Key events are not set out as a chronological story, particularly in the first half when Berdiaev moves back and forth between his youth and later moments in his life. The second half is chronologically narrated but often omits dates and other sequential, historical markers. Moreover, Berdiaev shifts frequently between historical event and philosophical generalization. He focuses on intellectual encounters and conflicts, each a creative act during which he becomes even more fully "who he is."

Self-Knowledge might be compared in some ways to Nietzsche's *Ecce Homo.* Both are concerned with leaving the verbal trace of a living philosophical personality. Although each tells a story of an intellectual and spiritual development, the similarity ends there. Nietzsche's tone is elevated, hyper-cheerful, and self-aggrandizing, and, above all, endows him with a mask of a Dionysian self, suffering, tragic, and yet self-regenerative. He

22. Vadimov, *Zhizn' Berdiaeva: Rossiia*, 5.

places himself beyond contemporary life; only future readers can hope to understand his voice. His self-description focuses on the physiological and spiritual aspects of his self-image, his physical and moral "health," the process of his spiritual self-liberation. In contrast, Berdiaev's philosophical self-portrait highlights the figure of the philosopher as an epic actor in a social, cultural, and historical context. It is less a lengthy apostrophe to himself, as *Ecce Homo* is, than a description of a particular historically embedded consciousness in which historical events are present not for their own sakes, or for the sake of "accuracy," but are completely intertwined with the personal process of "becoming oneself."

This philosophical autobiography is meant specifically to be a creative act, although not a fiction. Berdiaev explains: "This book I have written about myself contains no inventions. It is philosophical cognition and an interpretation of me as such, and my life. This philosophical cognition and interpreting is not memory of the past, it is rather a creative act completed in a moment of the present" (*SMPZ*, 6). Berdiaev does not bare his soul but makes himself and his "fate" the subject of philosophical knowledge, of "*samopoznanie*," which is the "need to understand oneself" and "to make sense of one's type and one's fate" (*SMPZ*, 6).

What "sense" does Berdiaev bring to his life? How does he capture the flow of experience in the image of a person who believes that as a philosopher he can achieve something new? His efforts focus on answering two questions: What does it mean to be "free," and what does it mean to be "creative"? To Berdiaev, being "free" means to be in some sense "other" to one's social and cultural environment, and yet deeply committed to and involved in that environment. For example, although Berdiaev is proud that he is from an aristocratic family, he generally dislikes elites and claims to get along better with workers, sectarians, people outside educated society (*SMPZ*, 16). Although he often mentions that he wants no followers (and here we are reminded of Nietzsche), yet he fondly recalls the massive audiences that attended his lectures in Moscow and Petrograd during the civil war (*SMPZ*, 38).

Berdiaev strives to overcome the corporeal and material side of life, which he views as "reactionary," and to realize the spiritual, which he claims is "revolutionary." And, on that basis, he creates from the "ego" (*ia*), that is, the biological and psychological self he was born with, a philosophical self (*lichnost'*). He claims that from his earliest youth he saw himself as a "philosopher." It is important to note that instead of reminiscing and recounting specific incidents from his youth, he deals in philosophical issues. He divides this part of *Self-Knowledge* into sections, each dealing with an emotion or drive to which he imparts philosophical meaning: yearning, rebelliousness, pity, spiritual conflict, and eros. Reading philosophy and thinking philosophically helps the young person to "rise above the every-day" and "free [himself] from the oppressive yearning of 'life'" (*SMPZ*, 57). He then claims that his originality as a philosopher lies in the fact that he sees "freedom," and from there "creative activity," rather than "existence," as the foundation of philosophy (*SMPZ*, 60).

As a philosopher, Berdiaev describes himself bombastically as a "libera-tor" (*emansipator*), making him sound almost like the Tsar Liberator Alexander II (*SMPZ*, 60). Although it might seem so, he does not have in mind any kind of social or political emancipation. He agrees with the Grand Inquisitor that most people do not want political freedom. Instead, he links freedom with a personal process of overcoming the "temptations of freedom," as Nietzsche's Zarathustra would put it, with going beyond "free-dom from" and conceiving a goal, a "freedom for" (*SMPZ*, 62). From his earliest years on, Berdiaev asserts that "my philosophical thought was a struggle for liberation and I have always believed in the liberating character of philosophical cognition" (*SMPZ*, 103). Throughout his philosophical au-tobiography he enumerates a number of stages through which he passes on his way to becoming a free philosophical self. This narration gradually gains the trappings of myth, and Berdiaev becomes the mythical hero.

The first of these stages is Berdiaev's youthful infatuation with Marxism. Here he learns in practice that the revolutionary intelligentsia does not love freedom. He realizes that they have tendencies that could easily lead from liberation back to despotism (*SMPZ*, 65). He rejects any group that chooses its members according to a certain strict "faith," because this practice snuffs out "independence of self, creative activity" (*SMPZ*, 65). From this experi-ence Berdiaev comes to understand freedom in two ways. First, freedom is "my independence and the act of defining my personality from within." Second, freedom is "my creative force, not the choice between good and evil placed before me, but my act of creating good and evil"—and thereby be-coming responsible for that good and evil (*SMPZ*, 67). Thus freedom en-ables creative action and insight into truth.

Berdiaev resists the idea that freedom could mean individual anarchism. In his view it leads to a form of sociality, a way of being in society that is not authoritarian and hierarchical. He uses Khomiakov's term, *sobornost'*, to mean a social union of free selves that have broadened themselves to the "superindividual," to general shared experience (*SMPZ*, 68). Nonetheless, this social idea receives short shrift as Berdiaev turns once again to the liter-ary force that is so powerful in his philosophical character. If there is a *sobor-nost'* with which he might ally himself, it is the loose association of relatively free and creative selves that he discovered among the Symbolists and their circles when he moved to St. Petersburg in 1902. When Berdiaev discusses his philosophical experiences in St. Petersburg and later in Moscow, his tone

changes. Suddenly his descriptions of his literary and philosophical contemporaries are much more extensive, as if he had abruptly discovered other
"selves" who, like him, had opened within themselves an inner realm of
self-consciousness and had "expanded," as he puts it, into a kind of sociality
with other selves that one could, indeed, call *sobornost'*.

As he discusses these literary circles, Berdiaev remarks that Russia "was
sent a lot of gifts" (*SMPZ,* 158). He remembers and describes each person
separately, Merezhkovsky, Gippius, Rozanov, Ivanov, Belyi. Whether or not
he agrees with their views—and usually he does not—he appreciates their
significance in themselves and for his personal and philosophical growth.
Yet even here the social issue remains very much alive. In the course of the
decade preceding the revolution Berdiaev becomes disillusioned with these
circles and with the failure of the theurgic principles of Symbolism to renew
the physical world. He witnesses the devolution of Symbolism into a silly
mysticism (*SMPZ,* 179–180). Berdiaev regrets that these gifted people were
so isolated from the rest of the populace and made no effort to open a wide
avenue to Russian society as a whole.

At this point, sometime around 1910, Berdiaev claims to have achieved
what other intellectuals of his circle had not. He tried to form contacts with
people of other social strata. He experienced a religious conversion and a
kind of "going to the people." He spent time with the sectarians and God-
seekers (*bogoiskateli*), with "wandering Rus"—the Immortals (*bessmertniki*),
the Baptists, the Evangelists, the Old Believers, Flagellants, Tolstoyans—in
taverns in Moscow's wild "Yama" neighborhood (*SMPZ,* 227). All the while
he admired regular folks, some of them unlettered, who thought their way
to some form of salvation. Although at first he liked their independence of
mind and the beauty of their "folk language," he soon saw a lack of freedom
in their thinking. Like the Marxists in Berdiaev's earlier years, these people
were intransigent, insisting on only one way to salvation—their own way.
For Berdiaev, they are too dogmatic and intolerant (*SMPZ,* 227).

By the outbreak of World War I, when finishing *The Meaning of the Creative Act,* Berdiaev, looking back on his life in *Self-Knowledge,* concludes
that real freedom culminates in the performance of outward, tangible creative acts, not necessarily cultural acts or writing of some sort. Berdiaev, like
Shestov and Rozanov before him, decides that the meaning of life is in an
ongoing dialogue with God. For him, in contrast to his two older contemporaries, the God with whom one converses is not an inwardly conceived
God but rather an outward force, and the dialogue consists in part in answering God's demands for people to undertake outward creative action
(*SMPZ,* 241). It is worth repeating that Berdiaev calls each of these human
acts an "anthropodicy," a "justification [of humanity]" and a "person's answer to God" (*SMPZ,* 240). In this way the doors to the new, free, and cre-

ative stage of history are opened, and people can deal with their sins through the performance of creative acts in history (*SMPZ*, 243).

Berdiaev's final push toward freedom is his resistance to the Bolshevik Revolution with its blindly egalitarian ideology. He sees in the revolution a "lack of positive creative force" (*SMPZ,* 260); instead of the forced social equality of Bolshevism, he opts for the idea of "social truth founded on the dignity of each self" (*SMPZ,* 265). With this in mind he starts to teach and lecture, not in order to join the "academy," which he still reviles, but as a way to participate in a social dialogue with thousands of people. Finally, for his fearless and loud defense of personal autonomy in the face of brutal tyranny, Berdiaev is "excommunicated" from the new Soviet republic, only to find himself fully "free"—but now without the necessary social-cultural context for his philosophizing. He has lost the battle to keep philosophy a viable language within the newly forming Soviet culture. Now he becomes the internationally known "European" existentialist whom we have known throughout the latter half of the twentieth century. He insists that he is a philosophical "representative of selfhood that has risen against the power of the objectivized 'general' " (*SMPZ,* 335).

Why is Berdiaev's creative act of liberating himself memorable? How is he, as a philosopher of freedom and of the creative act, better than his Bolshevik competitors, for example, Vladimir Lenin, whose creative act was truly epic, to liberate all Russia from a repressive tsarist regime (and who, it should be added, was busy writing Berdiaev and his kind of philosophy out of Russian history)? Berdiaev notes, in *Self-Knowledge,* that Lenin was a relatively uncultivated person: "Philosophically and culturally Lenin was a reactionary, a horribly backward person," which meant that his "revolution brought about a genuine pogrom of high Russian culture" (*SMPZ,* 172). In *The Origin of Russian Communism*(1937), Berdiaev remarks that Lenin "did not recognize inward principles [in people]; he did not believe in spirit and the freedom of the spirit."[23] Berdiaev would be the first to agree that Lenin was not a philosopher; he never attempted to know himself, and he opened no sphere of inner freedom. Therefore his actions were fated to be part of a historical vicious circle, a "bad infinity." Just as Berdiaev had foreseen in his earliest work from 1901, the "liberation" that the radicals helped to bring about soon turned into a resurgence of oppressive rule, far more oppressive than its predecessor. Always in the opposition, Berdiaev continually offered a bold, principled critique of dogma and tyranny, and supported the positive philosophical value of intellectual freedom. In *Self-Knowledge* he helped to fix in Russian writing culture an important precedent, that of a fearless,

23. Berdiaev, *The Origin of Russian Communism* (Ann Arbor: University of Michigan Press, 1993), 127.

articulate, *public* philosophical voice speaking in defense of the freely searching, creative self.

Despite the heroic goal of *Self-Knowledge*—to keep alive the memory of a philosophical culture that had been erased in Russia—there is a deeply ironic, even tragic, as Berdiaev would have seen it, aspect to his philosophical self-portrait. Like all cultural artifacts, Berdiaev's last work participated in what might be called the ironic ontology of the true creative act. In *On Freedom and Slavery* he articulated the tragic disconnection within any creative act between creative plan and the actual historical outcome.

> There is an incongruity between the creative act, the creative plan, and the creative product. The creative act is a fire, and culture is the cooling of the fire. The creative act is upward flight, a victory over the weight of the world-made-object, over determinism; the product of the creative act in culture is already pulled down by gravity. The creative act, the creative fire, is in the realm of subjectivity, but the product of culture is in the realm of objectivity. So cultural life knows that same unfamiliarity, that exteriorization of human nature. (*RSCh,* 106)

The resultant artifact—in this case, a book about one's intellectual life—is not the main point of the creative act. It is merely a dry shell, a trace of a moment when the self acted freely and creatively and thus realized its existence. What we think of as "culture" is just the detritus, the dead imprint of such creative acts. The moment of creative uplift, a moment in which the self resists the demands of conformity, can never be fully recaptured.

One may then ask: Why would anyone even bother to try to document something that can never be relived, that, by inference, cannot inspire others to free themselves and thus lacks any historical impact? For Berdiaev, philosophical autobiography, perhaps more than any other genre, has the possibility for conveying a sense of the living process. The voice of the philosopher reverberates in such a work, an emanation almost of creative energy. Moreover, philosophical autobiography can preserve the memory of a moment from being lost at a time when those in power are determined to force people to forget it. While Soviet ideologists were condemning Berdiaev and other philosophical competitors to oblivion, Berdiaev kept the creative act of this particular Russian philosophical self in memory and perhaps made it possible for another individual at another time to gain energy from it. As with all tragedy, the death of a philosophical culture contains the seeds of new life and energy that can later reemerge.

Berdiaev achieved a great deal in his philosophical career. His philosophy capped a century-long development of Russian philosophical discourse that, resisting systematic scientific language, emerged from the "overcoat" of Russian fiction. He pulled Russian philosophy from its semi-private circle of psychological and spiritual concerns into the public sphere of civil debate, and he led the successful effort to challenge radical visions of Russian history and society. In this effort, with regard to Russian philosophy, he affirmed its dignity by laying the groundwork for its *history,* and he also widened its actual authority in *current* public debate about Russian history itself. In his autobiography he left the first Russian imprint of a *philosopher* as a historical, indeed an "epic," figure.

What is perhaps most significant about Berdiaev's legacy is its remarkable durability, even in the murderous atmosphere of Stalinist Russia. Fully aware of the consequences, university students, even in the dark years of the late 1940s, found Berdiaev's books, among those of other philosophers, in private collections and secondhand bookstores.[24] By the late 1980s, when philosophy was "returned" to Russia, Berdiaev was among the most sought after philosophers. His concepts of the self and the creative act are at the foundations of philosophical anthropology, and his paradoxical thinking has enlivened philosophical debate about Russian history.[25] Moreover, among the post-Soviet reading public, a popular notion of "our Berdiaev"—the Berdiaev who propounded freedom of self in the face of powerful social and political restrictions—has made itself felt.[26] Against all odds, Nikolai Berdiaev, the epic philosopher, helped to establish in the heritage of Russian writing culture an important precedent, that of a fearless and articulate public voice in defense of the freely seeking, creative self.

24. M. K. Mamardashvili, "Mysli pod zapretom," *Voprosy filosofii* 4 (1992): 70–78.

25. P. S. Gurevich, *Fenomen cheloveka* (Moscow: Vysshaia shkola, 1993); Grigorii Pomerants, *Strastnaia odnostoronnost' i besstrastie dukha* (Moscow: Universitetskaia kniga, 1998), 471–473.

26. Berdiaev, *Tvorchestvo i ob"ektivatsiia* (Minsk: Ekonompress, 2000), 3.

Part Three

The Survival of Russian Philosophical Culture (1920s–1950s)

Chapter Eight

Image and Concept: Losev's "Great Synthesis of Higher Knowledge" and the Tragedy of Philosophy

What is philosophy if not the hope of making sense of the givenness of the world, therefore, creatively tearing away from it?

In image and concept are found collapse and schism; here is a disconnected contemplation of thingness.

—Aleksei Losev, *Music as a Subject for Logic*, 1921

If ancient tragedy was diverted from its course by the dialectical desire for knowledge and the optimism of science, this fact might lead us to believe that there is an eternal conflict between the theoretic and the tragic worldview, and only after the spirit of science has been pursued to its limits, and its claim to universal validity destroyed by the evidence of these limits, may we hope for a rebirth of tragedy.

—Friedrich Nietzsche, *On the Birth of Tragedy from the Spirit of Music*, 1872

IN 1935 ALEKSEI LOSEV (1893–1988) wrote to his philosopher friend, A. A. Meier: "After a whole life of philosophizing I find myself once more asking: so, what is philosophy? Just as when I was thirteen years old in school. Philosophy used to seem to me to be such a wise, even sublime Urania [the muse of astronomy], whose gaze alone made me happy for long stretches of time and made me forget human beggary."[1] Losev continued in the same frustrated tone: "So, what is it? Science? Art? Life itself? . . . The Lord forgive me, but what kind of science can it be?! It's a mockery, a pure mockery of science. With philosophy you cannot teach anyone anything. Every idiot has his own judgments: and there is no authority, not even the

---

1. "Perepiska A. F. Loseva s A. A. Meierom," *Nachala*, 2–4 (1994): 47.

police, to make people think correctly."[2] Finally, he cried out: "What does philosophy have to do with anything?"[3] And this outburst came from a person who had devoted his whole life, from adolescence on, to the pursuit of philosophy. Philosophy meant everything to him. Now he compared himself to Chekhov's comical pseudo-philosopher, Epikhodov, in *The Cherry Orchard,* and complained that that "hysterical lady," philosophy, had sapped all his energy. By 1935 the Russian philosophical Renaissance, with its wonderful innovations and inquiries, had ended, and, as this chapter will show, its last great voice was in crisis.

Born in 1893, Losev was among the youngest of the prolific group of Russian philosophers that emerged at the turn of the century, and he had among the broadest interests and was the most prolific of them all. By 1930, just five years before the letter to Meier, quoted above, Losev had published no fewer than eight books on philosophical topics, ranging from music, poetry, and numbers to myth and the mystical philosophy of the name. His philosophical ambition had been to marry these areas of inquiry into a total theory of knowledge. His project came to an abrupt halt in 1930, however, when he was arrested for ignoring the Soviet censor and publishing an uncensored version of his book, *The Dialectics of Myth* (*Dialektika mifa*). He spent the next three years first in Butyrki Prison and then in the north at the infamous White Sea Canal project where he was subjected briefly to slave labor and was forced to undergo political reeducation in the Marxist-Leninist mold. In 1932 the OGPU, the secret police, confiscated his entire library together with unpublished manuscripts, translations, and ongoing work. At this time he wrote to his wife, the astronomer Valentina Sokolova, that he doubted he would be able to "return to scientific work" and reconstruct his project.[4] Losev was allowed to return to Moscow in 1933, his full civil rights restored to him, but under the condition that he not engage in philosophical activities. This stipulation thrust the philosopher into despair. In 1934, in a letter to the famous Leningrad pianist, Maria Iudina, he vented his frustration at his "philosophical isolation" and invited her to imagine herself in the awful situation of being "absolutely prohibited from playing music."[5]

To complete the picture of Losev's philosophical crisis, in the early 1930s he felt an overwhelming urge to write narrative fiction. As he wrote to his wife from the labor camp: "The last few months I feel in my soul something completely new that I don't think I ever wrote to you about. At times—ac-

2. Ibid., 47.

3. Ibid., 51.

4. Aleksei Losev, *Zhizn': Povesti, rasskazy, pis'ma* (St. Petersburg: Komplekt, 1993), 376. Hereafter cited in the text as *Zh* with the relevant page number.

5. "Posledniaia glava: pis'ma A. F. Loseva k M. V. Iudinoi," *Moskva* 8 (1993): 178.

tually very often—I feel a surge of various dense and lush artistic images that weave together into whole fantastic stories. I feel the incredible need to write stories like those of Hoffmann, Poe, and Wells" (*Zh*, 410)—in a style he would later call "nightmarish." From 1932, when he was in the camp, to 1941, the start of World War II, he wrote more than ten stories and novellas, none of them published until the 1990s. Although one could certainly argue that he shifted to prose fiction out of necessity, one might also contend that, when the Soviet authorities shut the doors to writing and publishing philosophy, internal characteristics of his philosophical project may also have led him in this direction. Why he made this shift and what it meant for his valuation of philosophy is the focus of this chapter.

Losev is central to our consideration of Russian philosophy because, for all his overweening ambitions for philosophical discourse and despite its partial failure, his project was the last significant philosophical cry in favor of non–dialectical materialist thought in Soviet Russia. Losev is an essential figure in Russian writing culture, as important, for example, as two other giants of the Stalinist philosophical underground, Pasternak and Bakhtin. He was the only prominent philosopher physically to survive the Stalin era. In addition, he both preceded and nearly outlived the Soviet Union itself, having died in May 1988 at the age of ninety-five, well after the announcement of *glasnost'* and *perestroika*. In post-Stalinist Moscow he became a legend in his own time, a historical link to prerevolutionary culture. A popular teacher of classical philology at the Lenin State Pedagogical Institute in Moscow, he was surrounded by a loyal circle of students, some, for example, V. V. Bibikhin, eventually developing careers as academic philosophers at the Institute of Philosophy of the Soviet Academy of Sciences.[6] To many in the 1960s and 1970s, Losev kept alive the hope for a kind of nondogmatic philosophy, free of Marxist-Leninist dialectical materialism.

At the heart of this chapter is the question of the nature and value of Losev's philosophical idiom. His philosophical discourse wavers between a number of truth claims. On the one hand, it purports to be an overarching meta-discourse designed to marshal all cognitive forces to penetrate the depths of original Logos, the divine Word that empowered the creation of the cosmos. On the other hand, at times, as in his letter of 1935, Losev expresses doubt as to the relevance of philosophy for describing any reality or for making any serious claim to knowledge. What is problematic for Losev is the use of rational, categorizing discourse to apprehend hidden, mystical realities.

Let us first look into Losev's philosophical project of the 1920s. We are

6. Among Bibikhin's writings see, for example, *Iazyk filosofii* (Moscow: Progress, 1993); *Novyi renessans* (Moscow: Progress-Traditssiia, 1998); *Slovo i sobytie* (Moscow: URSS, 2001).

Aleksei Losev, 1961. Courtesy of A. A. Takho-Godi.

given some insight in a letter Losev wrote to his wife, Valentina Mikhailovna, from the labor camp in 1932, while in the depths of despair at losing his library. He wrote: "I stand like a sculptor in a studio that is filled with various plans, models, and building materials but that has not one finished statue in it. I haven't created anything, although I was at the point of creating something big and important, and I was just entering that mature age when I would have reached the culmination of all my work" (*Zh*, 404). Losev felt that he had barely gotten a start on his grand plan when it was taken from him. A hint as to what this project might have been is offered in a much later recollection about his interests as a young man devoted to the field of philosophy. Although he believed that, in Russia, philosophy was an area in which one could never hope to make a living, early on he had decided to persist in it.[7] Clearly, throughout his life, he saw himself first and foremost as a philosopher. Writing in 1981, he recalled his boredom with the academic philosophy program offered at Moscow University by his professors, G. I. Chelpanov and L. M. Lopatin. Like almost all his precursors,

---

7. Aleksei Losev, *Mne bylo 19: Dnevniki. Pis'ma. Proza,* ed. A. A. Takho-Godi (Moscow: Russkie slovari, 1997), 78. Hereafter cited in the text as *D19* with the relevant page number.

Losev found philosophy in a synthesis of reasoned argument and poetic image. He discovered the "genuine subject of philosophy" when he saw Richard Wagner's opera cycle, "The Ring of the Niebelungen," at the Bolshoi Theater. Writing later about Wagner's theory of opera, he openly revealed a key to his ambitious philosophical project. Emphasizing Wagner's interest in mythology, Losev remarked: "According to Wagner [in his article, "Opera and Drama," 1850], intellect and feeling are synthesized in fantasy, and fantasy brings the artist to a miracle. In drama this miracle is none other than its mythology."[8] For Losev, too, the chief object of philosophical analysis would be "myth," understood as a basic pre-discursive language that is embedded in every value-related utterance, whether abstract theory, scientific proof, religious supplication, or poetic expression.

Although Losev never clearly stated the aim of his philosophical project, in his novella, "The Woman Thinker" ("Zhenshchina-myslitel'," 1933), he mentioned the notion of a "great synthesis of higher knowledge."[9] Losev's project can also be deduced from the goals of his disparate works from the 1920s. Judging from the breadth of themes of his eight books and the statements they contain, his goal appears to have been to apprehend the experience of mystical ecstasy by developing a total theory of cognition. This theory would include all basic cultural and scientific discourse—mathematics, biblical language, poetry, and the "pre-language" of music—under the umbrella of philosophical discourse.[10] Knowledge would go well beyond the limits of rational logic practiced in modern Western philosophy. The eight books published toward the end of the 1920s bring into the mix various cultural signs, whether musical notes, mathematical numbers, or words. All are symbols through which one might apprehend some surface aspects of the deeper, mystical reality of the "name."

For our purposes, the two key works of the 1920s are *The Philosophy of the Name* (*Filosofiia imeni,* 1927) and *The Dialectics of Myth* (*Dialektika mifa,* 1930). In the former Losev offers a structure of the inner reality of the cosmos and, with it, a hierarchy of language types and levels and the kind of knowledge they can lead to. Here he states his theory of the "name," which he develops from such ancient and medieval mystics as Dionysus the Areopagite and Nicholas of Cusa, whose works he studied and translated into Russian. He links the name to the notion of an essential "Word" emanating

8. Aleksei Losev, "Istoricheskii smysl esteticheskogo mirovozzreniia Richarda Vagnera," *Estetika Vagnera* (Moscow: n.p., 1978), 294. Cited in *Filosofiia. Mifologiia. Kul'tura,* 504.

9. Aleksei Losev, "Zhenshchina-myslitel'," *Moskva* 4–7 (1993), 7:114, 7:118). Hereafter cited in the text as ZhM with the relevant volume and page numbers.

10. See also A. A. Takho-Godi, "A. F. Losev: Zhiznennaia i tvorcheskaia sud'ba," in *Vladimir Solov'ev i ego vremia* (Moscow: Progress, 1990), 687.

from an inaccessible "essence."[11] In three other works, *The Dialectics of Artistic Form, The Dialectics of the Number in Plotinus' Work,* and *Music as a Subject for Logic,* Losev relates his overall epistemology to three different types of language. For example, in *Music as a Subject for Logic* he focuses on "pure musical existence" as an unstructured pre-language,[12] (M, 656), which he sees, along with Schopenhauer, as being closer than other human languages to apprehending the essence of the world (M, 668). Each book, in its own way, anticipates the final work of the 1920s, *The Dialectics of Myth,* in which Losev posits that myth—understood as a personalist system of values embedded in all texts—is at the foundation of all knowledge, whether discursive, revealed, or poetic. Myth gives us a basic orientation to reality. Ultimately Losev's analysis of myth leads him to that most sought after experience, namely, a miracle, "ecstasy," "being."

What is Losev's conception of "philosophy"? What makes it, for him, an authoritative discourse? In brief, he views philosophy as a flexible, broad, yet rigorous discourse that both absorbs and analyzes all other kinds of language and the forms of knowledge they articulate. Philosophy derives its authority, in his view, from its capacity to bring many other, diverse layers of human discourse into a meaningful relationship.

This view of philosophy is elaborated from Losev's very earliest years and can be seen in the ways that he builds his idea of a Russian philosophical tradition. It is also evident in his philosophical vocabulary and style. Although he first started to think and write on the question of the nature of philosophy in the summer of 1912, Losev left few clear definitions of what he meant by philosophy (*D19,* 316). When he does define it, his descriptions tend to be intentionally contradictory. In a diary from 1912 he wrote that philosophy is the "child" of both "time" and "eternity" (*D19,* 45). Philosophy is the "queen of all sciences, religions, art" but also their "servant" and "slave" (*D19,* 45). He also said that philosophy has its own "epic" story that tells of its "separation and isolation" as a form of wisdom from other areas of knowledge. He remarked in this early diary that philosophy expresses "our relation to the world," particularly in the areas of "aestheticism [*sic*] and morality" (*D19,* 47). Finally, he always viewed philosophy as a part of philology: it is always oriented toward the study of words, values, and consciousness.[13]

The years of war and revolution saw intensified philosophical activity on Losev's part, and increased interest in an idealist form of philosophizing.

---

11. Aleksei Losev, *Filosofiia imeni,* in *Samoe samo* (Moscow: Eksmo-Press, 1999), 153. Hereafter cited in the text as *FI* with the relevant page number.

12. Aleksei Losev, "Muzyka kak predmet logiki," in *Samoe samo* (Moscow: Eksmo-Press, 1999), 656. Hereafter cited in the text as M with the relevant page number.

13. A. A. Takho-Godi, introduction to *D19,* 5.

After graduating from Moscow University in 1915, during World War I and the revolution, Losev was immersed in philosophical activity, in the philosophical institutions that had come to life in Russia. He attended meetings of the Solovyov Society, Moscow's chief philosophical association, and the Lopatin Philosophical Circle, and he gave a talk at the Psychological Society of Moscow University on "Eidos and Idea in Plato's Works." Until 1921, the year it closed, he was associated with Berdiaev's Free Philosophical Academy. After the major philosophers were exiled in 1922, Losev remained in Russia. At the time he was not yet established as a philosopher and apparently posed no perceptible threat to the new Soviet regime. During the 1920s he taught aesthetics at the Moscow Conservatory and was active at the Academy of the Arts (Akademiia khudozhestvennykh nauk). He also carried on his interest in religious philosophy and the philosophy of the name in a small circle that included his wife and a number of priests and lay friends.[14]

During the 1920s Losev coined his own brand of philosophy—"dialectical phenomenology."[15] His particular approach draws on Plato, Edmund Husserl, and Ernst Cassirer, as well as a number of Russian philosophers, particularly Vladimir Solovyov and Pavel Florensky.[16] Losev strongly resists the Soviet tendency to divide philosophy sharply either into idealism or materialism—a move he finds too limiting.[17] He believes, first and foremost, that philosophy ought to describe an object in human consciousness as precisely as possible. As a phenomenologist, Losev is concerned with the interaction of mind and material objects; as a mystic, he focuses attention on a rationally unknowable essence and its relation to the material world.

One of the major concerns of Losev's early years was to define the Russian philosophical tradition. In 1918 he wrote and submitted an article entitled "Russian Philosophy" (a German translation was published in Zürich the following year, without his knowledge). In this article he posits a Russian tradition devoted to the question: "Does cognition occur only through rational thought?"[18] He immediately distinguishes the Russian tradition from the Western: "Whoever values in philosophy qualities of systematic

14. For more information on Losev's religious activities in the 1920s, see the biography and memoirs written by A. A. Takho-Godi, *Losev*, vol. 742: *Zhizn' zamechatel'nykh liudei* (Moscow: Molodaia gvardiia, 1999), part 3, 129–184.

15. Takho-Godi, "A. F. Losev," 701.

16. James P. Scanlan, "A. F. Losev and Mysticism in Russian Philosophy," *Studies in East European Thought* 46 (1994): 263–286.

17. Aleksei Losev, *Dialektika mifa*, in *Filosofiia. Mifologiia. Kul'tura,* ed. A. A. Takho-Godi (Moscow: Izdatel'stvo politicheskoi literatury, 1991), 109, 116. Hereafter cited in the text as *DM* with the relevant page number.

18. Aleksei Losev, "Russkaia filosofiia," in *Filosofiia. Mifologiia. Kul'tura,* 209. Hereafter cited in the text as RF with the relevant page number.

thinking, logical refinement, clarity of dialectic, in a word, scientific qualities [*nauchnost'*], can ignore Russian philosophy without undue distress"
(RF, 209). If one looks from a Western perspective, Losev claims, Russian
philosophy is a kind of anti-philosophy: "Almost the whole of Russian philosophy gives the impression of having a pre-logical, pre-systematic or, better put, a supra-logical, supra-systematic bent" (RF, 209). Beyond a limited
number of works by academic philosophers, there is no systematic Russian
philosophy. Losev writes: "The rest of Russian philosophy is thoroughly intuitive, one could even say mystical; it is a creative act [here Losev uses
Berdiaev's term *tvorchestvo*] that has neither the time nor, generally speaking, the inclination to refine the logic of its ideas" (RF, 209). Characterizing
Russian philosophy as a continuation of the all-inclusive, mystical tradition
of the Eastern Christian fathers of the Church, Losev claims for Russian
philosophy a structure of thought profoundly different from European traditions (RF, 212).

He derives his philosophy in a traditionally "philosophical" way, through
dispute with, and appropriation from, other philosophers. Only occasionally does he draw on poetic texts or use poetic language to enhance the authority of his discourse, as do other philosophers considered here. He cites
Russian thinkers numerous times—beyond Solovyov he refers to Florensky,
Rozanov, and the only truly successful Russian academic philosopher,
Nikolai Lossky. Solovyov was Losev's first philosophical love. Florensky was
a close friend who performed the marriage ceremony for Losev and
Sokolova in 1922. Losev admired Nikolai Lossky as a rare example of a good
academic among Russian philosophers. Rozanov aroused a sense of fastidi-
ousness in Losev, and he also became a focal point for anti-Semitic expression on Losev's part. For example, in *The Dialectics of Myth* Losev refers to
Rozanov's philosophy as "petit-bourgeois Judaistic [*sic*] mysticism" (*DM*,
78). Of foreign philosophers, besides Husserl (*FI*, 32; *DM*, 39) and Cassirer
(*DM*, 39), Losev cited and alluded to Nietzsche only occasionally but under
important circumstances, which are discussed below (*FI*, 42; M,
698–699).[19]

Losev's own philosophical vocabulary combines concepts from Plato,
Solovyov, and Husserl. From Plato he builds notions of eidos (image) and
logos (word), as well as his ontological view, based on *hyle* (nameless matter)
and the *meon* (unformed chaos). From Husserl he takes a phenomenological approach to philosophy and builds on Husserl's use of the concept of

19. Losev devoted an article to Cassirer that was probably written sometime in late 1926 or 1927
but was published only in 1993: "Teoriia mificheskogo myshleniia u E. Kassirera," *Simvol* (Paris),
30 (December 1993): 311–336. Losev lectured on this material in November 1926.

eidos.[20] Solovyov's ideas of divine humanity, total unity, and Sophia (also developed by other Russian thinkers such as Pavel Florensky) are ubiquitous in Losev's work. In "Eros in Plato's Thought" (1916) he relies heavily on Solovyov's reading of Plato. He refers to the central Solovyovian idea of divine humanity, the ideal, Christ-like self that mediates between earthly human existence and the divine. He speaks of Plato's "divine-human path" in his inadvertent groping toward resurrection and transfiguration.[21] Later, in "Russian Philosophy," he speaks of "divine-human logos" (RF, 217).

The same is true of the Solovyovian concept of "total unity," the idea that the world is not a homogeneous unity but a unity of disparate but mutually necessary parts.[22] In "Eros in Plato's Thought" Losev argues that Plato was groping toward but never arrived at "total unity" in his concept of "holy Eros," through which "gods and people are conjoined" and the Eros "of birth in beauty for immortality" (EP, 207). In the early 1920s, in the first part of *Music as a Subject for Logic,* Losev describes music as the medium through which "concrete total unity" can be apprehended (M, 702). Music destroys our usual temporal and spatial concepts and opens up new possibilities for the experience of the unity of opposites—"eternal tormenting enjoyment, the interpenetration of joy and sadness, the synthesis of joys and terrors" (M, 702).

Sophia is the third major Solovyovian concept pervasive in Losev's early work. Sophia is a concept of mediation between unknowable divine essence and earthly existence. With Losev, as with Solovyov, Sophia is female in nature and linked strongly to earthly, corporeal existence. In "Russian Philosophy" Losev sees Sophia as the embodiment of Logos or the original cosmos-creating "Word." In his foreword to *The Philosophy of the Name* he is outspoken in his criticism of any philosophy that remains in the realm of abstraction. He goes so far as to call the work of traditional philosophers "trash" if they do not relate abstract concepts to concrete notions of "body" and human experience (*FI,* 37). He uses the term *Sophia-ness (sofiinost')* to

20. Losev wrote about Husserl in *A Passion for the Dialectic* (*Strast' k didalektike* [Moscow: Sovetskii pisatel', 1990]: "From him I came to understand eidos as a direct and spontaneous but still logically and structurally well-founded given [*dannost'*]" (16).

21. Aleksei Losev, "Eros u Platona," in *Filosofiia. Mifologiia. Kul'tura,* 204. Hereafter cited in the text as EP with the relevant page number.

22. For a review of Russian concepts of total unity in the broader span of Western history, see S. S. Khoruzhii, "The Idea of Total-Unity from Heraclitus to Losev," *Russian Studies in Philosophy,* 35, no. 1 (summer 1996): 32–69. According to Khoruzhii, "total-unity is a category of ontology, designating the principle of the internal form of the perfect unity of the many, in accordance with which all elements of the many are identical with one another and identical with the whole but at the same time do not merge into an undifferentiated and total unity but rather form a special polyphonic structure" (33).

refer to the body and corporeal experience in its quest for spiritual meaning, which he calls the "logic of corporeality" (*FI*, 192).

Losev thus came from a Russian tradition of religious philosophy that had taken shape in the course of half a century and had its own vocabulary. As with Solovyov, Losev's own broadly conceived philosophical idiom occupied a border territory, claiming to operate in both spheres of poetic, metaphorical language and scientific discourse. Philosophy was meant to mediate between art, science, logic, and religious seeking (*D19*, 105). Perhaps it is no surprise that, for Losev, the focus of philosophical inquiry is language, and the meanings and values inherent in language. In his first major philosophical work, *The Philosophy of the Name*, he writes that all science should not only use words but should be about words, since "there is nothing more embedded with meaning than the word" (*FI*, 150). He claims that the word, language, emerges "high up on the ladder of existing things" (*FI*, 150). It is not mere unformed chaos (*meon*) but comes from the "energeme of the essence" (*FI*, 146). Losev also claims that the word is "essence in the process of being understood, being comprehended through reason [*razumevaemyi*]" (*FI*, 150). Indeed, words and things are, on some level, identical: "The word is the thing itself understood in reason" (*FI*, 165).

Losev's works are energized by a passionate quest for the marriage of layers upon layers of modern discourse and much older religious, mystical, poetic, and musical languages. Even in his earliest work he proposes a hierarchy of languages, at the top the most powerful and "true" and at the bottom the most limited. The highest language is the hidden, mystical Word, Logos, or *Slovo*—as it was with Solovyov. This is the language of divine, ultimate being (*D19*, 215). Among languages accessible to people is the "image-oriented" or "eidetic" language, poetic language being the most accessible of all. This type of language is powerful because it can apprehend emanations from the essence, its "energies," "given in its alogical commemoration" (*FI*, 130). "Eidos" is like an icon. It is grasped wholly and intuitively, not analytically or sequentially. Eidos is the "picture of meaning," the "manifested iconic face [*lik*]" (*FI*, 112, 117).

Abstract, logical discourse occupies an ambiguous position in Losev's hierarchy of languages. Toward the start of *The Philosophy of the Name*, "logos" (with a small "l"), or logical, conceptual language, is only a tool, whose "tentacles" make it possible for the mind to apprehend an object. Small "logos" is not directly related to essence, as eidetic language is (*FI*, 116–117). This language of the mind, scientific discourse, is functionally secondary to eidetic language. Whereas the eidos gives expression to the whole, logos is the basis for rational discourse—it permits us to perceive discrete objects and multiple parts. It is based on grammatical structures and inter-relationships. Eidetic language, by contrast, can give the initiated person the whole of a thing, without analysis or fragmentation into its parts.

Despite his high valuation of conceptual language, Losev prefers nondiscursive, figurative language. However, instead of using it openly as a tool, he frames it as an object of logical discourse. He describes this poetic, mythic language through logical discourse, hoping to gain further insight into it. Along with Cassirer, who was working on similar ideas at the same time but without the mystical agenda, Losev characterizes mythical language as having a magic power. In an unpublished paper, "E. Cassirer's Theory of Mythical Thinking" (1926), Losev writes: "Names do not designate but act and exist in and of themselves. This is true particularly of proper names. A person's name expresses his most essential and most private qualities."[23] Losev's view of mythical language and its power differs from that of Cassirer in its focus on divine-human selfhood, or *lichnost'*, in which this power is embedded.

More strongly and self-consciously than his Russian predecessors, Losev posits the eclectic mixture of cultural languages in modern discourse—with its rational, linear rhetoric and its simple representative relation between word and thing—and the much older "magical," metaphorical language with its insistence on the dominant mystical power of the divinely begotten word. In *The Philosophy of the Name,* written in 1927, one year after the Cassirer piece, Losev writes: "The nature of the word, it would seem, is magical. We call a name the energy of the essence of a thing" (*FI*, 169). Although logic, definition, dialectic, and concept all help us to describe the nature of mystical language and the knowledge it imparts, they cannot help us achieve the experience of mystical truth, the knowledge that there is an essence. Thus the philosopher remains outside this realm of truth.

On the very next page of that work, however, Losev seems to change this order. The following is his list of discourses that constitute the "element of object and language" (*predmetno-iazykovaia stikhiia*): (1) the "purely *logical* stratum, which gives us categories of the concept, the judgment, the deduction"; (2) the "purely *eidetic* [stratum], which gives categories of the existing [*sushchee*], of difference, of identity"; (3) the "*artistic* where the same categories would produce metaphor, epithet"; (4) the "*grammatical* where we would be able to formulate dialectically the categories of noun/name, verb"; and (5) the "*rhetorical, stylistic, and hyletic* (or logic of the *meon*)" (*FI*, 170). In this hierarchy he places the logical stratum above all else, followed by the

23. Aleksei Losev, "Teoriia mificheskogo myshleniia u E. Kassirera," *Simvol* (Paris), 30 (December 1993): 320. Hereafter cited in the text as EK with the relevant page number.

eidetic or image-oriented, the iconic, and ending with the "hyletic," which relates to base matter. Rarely is Losev so positive, even implicitly so, about logical discourse, which is the basis for scientific argument.

Natural-scientific discourse, in contrast to abstract logic, is, for Losev, unambiguously limited and faulty. From his earliest diaries and articles he views "science," whether the modern natural sciences or post-enlightenment Western philosophy, as being generally too isolated in its "little part of reality" (*D19*, 45). He finds modern philosophy odd in its resistance to mysticism and poetry: "In its constant struggle with medieval mysticism the new philosophy has torn itself away from the dark, chaotic bases of reason and consciousness, from its irrational, creative, cosmic soil" (RF, 214).

In *The Dialectics of Myth* Losev gives several examples of what is wrong, in his view, with modern Western philosophy and natural science. He writes at length about Descartes and Newton. Both, in Losev's view, are devoted positivists, and both implicitly assert the dominance and power of scientific reasoning over mythical or mystical revelation. Both seem to deny the presence of myth in their thinking—something Losev takes pains to correct. For him, every mode of thought is informed by a "mythology," namely, a view of the world and a system of values. Losev claims, for example, that Newton's mechanics are founded on a "mythology of nihilism." His mechanical theory of the cosmos is "built on the hypothesis of a homogeneous, infinite space. The world has no limits, which means that it has no form. For me, that means it is formless. The world is an absolutely homogeneous space. For me, that means it is absolutely flat, inexpressive, without perspective. This world breathes of unbelievable boredom" (*DM*, 31). He concludes with a Dostoevskian image: "What is this if not a black hole, not even a grave or a bathhouse with spiders in it, because both of those are at least more interesting and warmer and bespeak something human" (*DM*, 31). Here, and throughout his work, the philosopher resolutely positions himself and his opinions in the center of the discussion. His central concern is to convey a committed, personalist (*lichnostnyi*) image of the truth.

For all the deep antimodernity of Losev's position in relation to modern physical sciences, it is intriguing to note that his attack on natural science shares some key points with "postmodernist" critiques of such people as Jean-François Lyotard in *The Postmodern Condition*.[24] Both men note the indebtedness of scientific, rational theory to narrative, nonscientific thought for assigning value to what has been observed or constructed. For example, in his discussion of Newton, Losev points out that, although Newton's theory by itself, in its abstract form, may have few mythological

24. Jean-François Lyotard, *The Postmodern Condition* (Minneapolis: University of Minnesota Press, 1989), 7–8, 23–27.

elements, any application or interpretation of it must indeed be mythological in character in that it imparts an implicit value system to its listeners (*DM*, 31).

In general, despite a clear attempt to hold philosophy apart, Losev tends to ally philosophy much more closely with poetry than with science. Even as a young student he senses that poetry is closer to "reality" (*D19*, 131). In addition, and particularly in his philosophical writings, he implies that philosophical language is closely linked to the metaphorical language of religious mysticism. In "Eros in Plato's Thought," he joins in the Solovyovian tradition, believing that philosophy's truth claim is based on religious revelation. To be completely true, philosophical discourse must embrace revealed truth (EP, 189, 192). In "Russian Philosophy" he continues this line of argument that philosophical language must be based on more than mere logic and rational rhetoric. It is oriented toward divine Logos and the tradition of "Eastern Christian logism" (RF, 216): "Russian philosophical thought which developed on the basis of Greek and Orthodox representations—which in turn were largely appropriated from antiquity—puts Logos at its foundation. Ratio is a human quality. . . . Logos is metaphysical and divine" (RF, 215). Although he would eventually abandon metaphysics, Losev's belief in concrete manifestations of the divine and the miraculous in earthly things would remain throughout his life.

Losev appears to be constructing a philosophy that makes use of poetic language rather than relegating poetry to the realm of mere invention, entertainment, or object of philosophical inquiry. Early on, in "Russian Philosophy," he writes that Russian writing culture is different from that in the West in its high valuation of literary art. He emphasizes this contention by claiming that Russian philosophy is really embedded in fictional form. Indeed, he prefers the notion of a poet-philosopher to the idea of an abstract theorist. In the same work he comments on European writing: "The times of the poet-philosophers Plato and Dante are gone forever," and in the new philosophy "an understanding of poetry as pure invention [*vymysel*] and entertainment has taken root" (RF, 214). (This claim, relying on Kant, seems unfair: one has to wonder how Nietzsche, who certainly appropriated poetic language for his philosophical inquiries and to whom Losev would allude a number of times, would fit this generalization.)

Having supported the concept of the poet-philosopher in early works, Losev then wants to distance himself from eidetic language in later practice (*DM*, 59–61). In contrast to his earliest published article, "Russian Philosophy," in works of the 1920s Losev devalues literature in comparison with myth. In *The Dialectics of Myth*, which is Losev's most thorough effort to describe eidetic language, he argues that poetic language is different from mythical language. Although they are closely allied, literary art is not as "real" as myth. He claims, for example, that fantastic beasts such as centaurs are part of "genuine reality" for pre-Homeric Greeks. They are substantial, corporeal, and alive for the people in the culture that engendered them. By contrast, poetic words do not convey "real things" but offer a "mediated reality" that is one step removed from direct experience (*DM, 65*).

Losev is very critical of traditional philosophical devices, such as syllogisms, that are used to relate the specific to the general, the part to the whole. He calls them the "sickly excrescence of existence, its fall from grace and its dungeon" (M, 698). In his own writing he makes effective use, instead, of rhetorical and poetic devices. Despite his often hyper-systematic philosophical argumentation, he unexpectedly turns away from his painstaking efforts at exact definitions. At these moments, which are always central to convincing his reader, he relies on emotional force. Similarly he appeals to belief, to impression, and to image, that is, to nonabstract, nonlogical forms of persuasion. He claims, at the start of *The Dialectics of Myth*, that one cannot understand myth unless one lives it and believes in it (*DM*, 23, 39). Here, too, his subject matter is nonlogical: he focuses on nonlogical or pre-logical structures of myth (EK, 313), symbol (*FI*, 106, 109, 152ff.), and even miracle, calling miracles a subject for philosophical, "phenomenological-dialectical" analysis (*DM*, 159). Myth becomes a "miraculous person-oriented [*lichnostnyi*] story related in words" (*DM*, 171).

The main rhetorical structure of Losev's philosophical style is the dialectic, and his chief rhetorical device, closely related to dialectic, is apophasis or affirmation through denial. Losev calls the dialectic the "logic of contradiction" (*FI*, 33) that allows one to find the connection between abstract reason and living reality. The dialectic "embraces living reality," unlike other tools of logic (*FI*, 33). He goes so far as to call dialectic the "rhythm of reality itself" which is "obliged to be the system of naturally and inevitably deduced antinomies . . . and the synthetic conjoining of all antinomian constructions of meaning" (*FI*, 33). For Losev, the dialectic is the "genuine and only possible philosophical *realism*" (*FI*, 36; emphasis added).

Losev joins a long mystical tradition in using the rhetorical figure of apophasis. He defines everything by saying what it is not, and then he proceeds to compare the two terms. For example, in *The Dialectics of Myth* his chapter headings always read: "Myth Is Not Fantasy, Fiction, or Invention," "Myth Is Not Ideal Existence," "Myth Is Not a Metaphysical Construct," "Myth Is Neither Schema Nor Allegory," "Myth Is Not Poetry," and so forth. Apophasis has particular significance for Losev—as oxymoron has for Solovyov—as a figure that allows one to see into deeper wholeness behind palpable oppositions. In *The Philosophy of the Name* Losev says that symbols allow one to say something about the "*energeia*" of the "essence," that is, one can at least apprehend the energy flowing from essence, even if essence itself is locked away from human understanding (*FI*, 106). Here logical discourse, which relies on grammatical relations more than on trope and figure, is inadequate, and the use of figures is required: "Beyond it [*energeia*] is hidden a certain unsolved X which, of course, somehow is available in its energies . . . but which is eternally hidden from analysis and is the inexhaustible source of all kinds of new discoveries. The more strongly this mystery is manifested, the more symbolic the emerging image is" (*FI*, 106). He calls this procedure the "logic of myth" or the "logic of symbol" in distinction to analytical logic. Its key element is apophasis, which is negation or denial inherent in the word: "The more supercharged this element of the word is, the more possibilities for meaning it embraces, all the while remaining in its structure the most ordinary word" (*FI*, 106). The apophatic word becomes highly compressed and rife with meaning.

One such word, in *The Dialectics of Myth,* that is compressed through apophasis is *light.* For Losev, as for Solovyov, the image of light conveys layers of meaning and is an expression of a hidden, mystical "essence" breaking through to material reality. Images of light emerge in various forms and places throughout Losev's writing. Often they are associated with the mystic's ecstasy of anticipating and apprehending the light emanating from the essence of God. Perhaps the strangest and most revealing of Losev's commentaries on light, first noticed by George L. Kline, is the discussion of the electric light bulb in *The Dialectics of Myth.*[25] Here, in an idiosyncratic and at times vulgar way, Losev excoriates the invention of the electric light bulb, largely, one might speculate, because it represents a mechanistic worldview that replaces natural flame and thus denies the power of spirit, symbol, and miracle:

> Boredom is the genuine essence of electric light. It is akin to Newton's infinite universe. . . . One cannot love by electric light; one can only scrutinize one's victim. One cannot pray by electric light, but only show one's promissory note. A barely flickering icon lamp is the product of orthodox dogma. . . . It would be just as absurd and nihilistic for a believer to put a light bulb in front of icons as to fly in airplanes or put kerosene in the icon lamp instead of olive oil. It is absurd for a professor to dance, a socialist to fear eternal torture or to love art, a family man to eat in a restaurant, or a Jew not to be circumcised. It is just as absurd and, most important, nihilistic for a believer to replace the living and fluttering flame of a candle or lamp with the trivial abstraction and cold fornication of vulgar electric light. (*DM*, 59)

The repeated denial of the goodness and truth of the electric light bulb through the use of the words *cannot* and *absurd* might be called an extended

25. George L. Kline, "Losev, Aleksei Fedorovich," *Routledge Encyclopedia of Philosophy*, ed. Edward Craig, 10 vols. (London: Routledge, 1998), 5:830–831.

apophasis. On one level Losev is almost certainly making "light" of Lenin's famous dictum of the early 1920s that Soviet power was equal to the Communist Party plus the electrification of the entire country. More important, for Losev, electric light denies the possibility of fulfilling one of the goals of his philosophy: to apprehend evidence of the human-divine and the revelation of the divine in language and in physical reality. Modern technology is based on a purely empirical view of the world that ignores the divine. In turn, Losev rejects objects like light bulbs created by modern technology.

Clearly there is a problem in Losev's concept of philosophical language. Logical discourse by itself lacks the power to penetrate and express mystical truths, but, as we found in Solovyov's quest for total unity, it is not apparent what kind of philosophical language might be powerful enough. Already in 1919 Losev saw in Russian philosophy another variant of the age-old Russian struggle for its own identity between East and West. He wrote: "Native Russian philosophy represents an indisputable struggle between Western European abstract ratio and Eastern Christian, concrete, divine-human Logos and is a ceaseless, ever ascending comprehension of the irrational, mysterious depths of the cosmos by means of concrete and living reason" (RF, 217). This attempt to use several different kinds of language leads ultimately not to the conjoining Losev hoped for but to a schism. Here is a first hint at the rift within Losev's concept of philosophy that will ultimately break apart in his stories of the 1930s.

Losev himself understands this problem. In *The Philosophy of the Name* he asks whether it is "too arrogant to use the goals of the dialectic to relate to the life of the essence [*sushchnost'*] of the name, *directly, without further reservations*" (FI, 105). He continues: "Let us not forget that all our deliberations [*rassuzhdenie*] are carried on in [the medium of] abstract philosophical concepts that adhere to the 'laws of logic' at the same time that we ourselves, operating with such concepts, are positing the inevitability of the emergence of the essence beyond the sphere of these 'laws of logic'" (FI, 105). In other words, essence, that "principle immanent in things," is inaccessible to the limited resources of logical discourse (RF, 215). The paradox of Losev's position is this: he uses logical discourse to get at this deeper, mystical "Logos" or "Word" that is beyond the bounds of logic and its grammatical structures.

This difficulty leads to interesting interventions of poetic speech in the otherwise super-systematic texts of this philosopher who tended to hold real poetic practice in low regard. One example is the passage on light considered just above. Eventually his inability to bridge the gap between logical discourse and the languages of poetry, music, and religion leads to the dominance of literary writing in the 1930s. Before embarking on a discussion of this interaction, it may be useful to ask how Losev, who argues that there is no competition or dispute between cultural languages, actually deals with languages that compete with his hyper-technical brand of philosophical discourse.

As we have seen, Losev complicates Solovyov's hierarchy of discourses by adding a layer of mythical language as a mediator between everyday discourse and Logos. He also adds a layer of musical pre-language that is troubling for any philosophical discourse to grasp and define. At the start of "The Phenomenology of Absolute or Pure Music" (the first essay in *Music as a Subject for Logic*) he differentiates a phenomenological description from an artistic one (M, 648). While a phenomenological description might use and discuss artistic images, "it does not itself consist of artistic images and does not operate with them" (M, 648). The goal of a phenomenology of music, then, is to construct the "live musical object in our consciousness," using exclusively "abstract concepts and not artistic images" (M, 648). Losev tries to clarify the difference between concept and image: "eidos" itself, as we have seen, is not an abstract concept but a "living visage [*lik*]." The "concept" of this "nonabstract, living visage of an object [*predmet*]" is an abstract definition and is thus the tool with which a philosopher must work (M, 648).

Having made this claim, Losev ends his essay conflicted about the relative value of image and concept. Against expectation, he inserts a short narrative with what he calls a "mythological view of music." This piece is about a woman, a nameless, Sophia-like "She," who plays the piano brilliantly, and a philosopher, a male "I," who listens to her and describes his responses. Purportedly a "little known German writer" is the author of the piece (M, 697). Losev adds disingenuously that, as a philosopher, he cannot be a part of these "crazy delights of youth" (M, 697). Even though his purpose would seem to be to establish the authority of a philosophical idiom independent of literary art, it becomes clear that he cannot do without poetic figure, narrative, and the illusion of personal experience that literature can offer. By resorting to poetic speech to convey the experience of music, he breaks his own rules of phenomenology.

Losev's purpose in this short end piece is to impart to his reader what an experience of pure music might be. In a mystical-expressionistic style, the philosophical narrator recounts, in tasteless purple prose, his experience of Dionysian ecstasy as he listens to "Her" play the piano. The music produces in the philosopher a sensuous synaesthesia of sounds and colors, of "blinding lights and mysterious noises," of "sounds glowing crimson and pink" (M, 697). Here Losev's conflicted interaction between literary art and philosophy—between image and concept—fades into relative unimportance next to the much more pronounced interaction between reasoned philosophical discourse and the musical pre-language that is beyond his philosophical grasp. The narrator tells us that, while "She" plays, the philosophical self experiences a "disappearance of categories of mind and all its definitions" (M, 698). What is more, he proclaims, in the sphere of music intellect and its operations are gone (M, 698). There is only a sensuous unarticulated ecstasy, the *hylé* or unconscious, unarticulated matter. To express this sensation, Losev borrows a key image from Nietzsche's *Thus Spoke Zarathustra,* proclaiming that, when he listens to this music, "a god dances in me" and "a dance is in my soul. . . . I feel like springing higher and higher" (M, 698–699).[26] Instead of being the overarching, authoritative discourse that also brings together diverse cultural languages, philosophy pales and fades away when confronted with musical performance.

This small interlude is a signal of things to come in the 1930s after Losev had spent three years in prison and in a labor camp for publishing the uncensored *Dialectics of Myth.* He had been banned from teaching, writing, and publishing philosophy. He had also lost his entire philosophy library and working archive. Now, in despair, unable either to write or publish formal philosophy, he turned to narrative fiction as an outlet. Among the predominant themes of his novellas was the confrontation of philosophy and music, which, along with mathematics, were to have been the main pillars of his "great synthesis of higher knowledge." The narrator of these five novellas is an arrogant and quite ungifted philosopher and music critic, Nikolai Vershinin, a stand-in, ironically, for Losev himself. Vershinin's name is rooted in the Russian word *vershina,* or "summit." His name suggests that he, as a philosopher, stands on the peak of human knowledge. Like his creator, Vershinin is searching for the inner, mystical unity of all life and all levels of language. "Music, mathematics, and philosophy," he claims, "are one and the same."[27] Abstractly analytical, Vershinin seeks the deeper principles through which music engenders life. Music is the "inwardly created element of self-arising existence [*samovoznikaiushchee bytie*]" (TCh, 161). When he hears music, he senses the proximity of the divine Absolute, which he thirsts to apprehend: "What could be deeper and sweeter than cognition [*poznanie*] of life? It is music that lends vision and sharpens the ear. People have grown too used to viewing cognition as a difficult, abstract, and boring process. But how desirable, how absorbing cognition of life is, in fact! And music is the method for this cognition, the way to enter into the inner meaning of reality" (TCh, 217).

The plot of the Vershinin novellas, minimal as it is, is an embellishment of the narrative sketch in "The Phenomenology of Absolute or Pure Music." It usually focuses on a passionate encounter between Vershinin the

26. Compare Nietzsche's *Thus Spoke Zarathustra,* trans. W. Kaufmann (Harmondsworth: Penguin, 1981): "I would believe only in a god who could dance"; "Now I am light, now I fly, now I see myself beneath myself, now a god dances through me" (41).

27. "Trio Chaikovskogo," in *Zhizn': Povesti, rasskazy, pis'ma* (St. Petersburg: Komplekt, 1993), 150. Hereafter cited in the text as TCh with the relevant page number.

philosopher and an extraordinarily gifted woman pianist. Perhaps inspired by Solovyov's view of love, Losev intends to show a man and a woman in love merging together and attaining a higher consciousness in which the whole is far greater than the sum of its parts. The difference here is that the characters are far from being successful representations of flesh-and-blood people. Rather, they mimic the two languages of philosophy and music, which, Losev hopes, can join in some way to apprehend a much more profound awareness of the cosmos. However, as Losev wrote to his wife in the early 1930s, his literary imagination was oriented toward the "nightmarish." In Losev's mystical terms it is dark, chaotic matter, the *hylé*, and primal chaos, the *meon*, that impose themselves on the philosopher's fragile reason. In the Vershinin novellas both characters are manipulative and chilly, and, although offers are made from both sides, the love relationship never coheres. The outcome is indeed nightmarish, usually involving some sort of abuse, even murder. The story always ends with personal disaster and the failure of higher consciousness. Indeed, neither Vershinin nor the performer is portrayed convincingly enough even to seem capable of higher understanding. Whatever wisdom is attained comes from insight into psychological chaos.

It is curious that Losev, like Solovyov before him, tended to lessen the authority of his literary efforts, in this case, rightly so. In a letter of February 17, 1934, to the pianist Maria Iudina, Losev lamented his prose as an "act of weakness."[28] He wrote that he hoped his stories would lead to an "act of strength," which certainly meant a return to his grand philosophical design, the "great synthesis of higher knowledge." Losev, it should be noted, was honest about the poor artistry of his fiction, but perhaps flattered himself by thinking that they were "three-quarters philosophy" and "one-quarter idea-oriented [*sic*]."[29] Although it is easy to see them as little more than showcases for philosophical dialogue, with very little plot and character development, they are extremely informative for what they can tell us about Losev's philosophical mind-set at the start of the Stalinist terror.

In these works, as in the literary sketch in "The Phenomenology of Absolute or Pure Music," the real discursive competition is between the primal musical pre-language that Losev theorized in *Music as a Subject for Logic* and reasoned critical discourse. With Schopenhauer, Losev valued music as the most profound art, more profound even than poetry. In *Music as a Subject for Logic* he describes music as the "ocean," the "alogical musical element" from which are "born logos and myth" (M, 697), a strong claim indeed. Music, in his view, is "beyond the bounds of the categories of the human mind" and becomes for him, as for Schopenhauer, a link to mystical reali-

---

28. *Moskva*, 8 (1993): 178.
29. Ibid., 172.

ties (M, 705). In "The Woman Thinker" (1933–1934) his philosopher-narrator, Vershinin, again touches on these same themes. Music promises to lead us into the magic and mystery of the ancient, hidden realities of the cosmos.

Surprisingly, given his high valuation of music, in *Music as a Subject for Logic* Losev relates music to the lowest, most chaotic level of being, the *meon*. He calls it *hylé*, or matter, and describes it as follows: "The eidos of music has shown us its essence, and this essence is qualitatively unarticulated [*neskazannyi*], unmanifested [*nevyiavlennyi*], and unformed, unnamed matter [*giletichnyi*]" (M, 656). Music is unformed energy in itself, which, nonetheless, is a precondition for the formation of meaningful sound and utterance. What emerges in Losev's narratives, but is absent from his philosophical essays, is that the musical medium is closely attached to Dionysian tragedy. Musical ecstasy is transformed into furious passion, and the individual selves of both musician and philosopher are shattered by the disconnection between sexual passion and the drive of analytical reason to dominate and control chaos.

In the two novellas examined here, "Chaikovsky's Trio" ("Trio Chaikovskogo," 1933) and "The Woman Thinker" ("Zhenshchina-mysli-tel'," 1933), music is that deep root of knowledge that Vershinin seeks to penetrate and understand.[30] In "Chaikovsky's Trio," which is set on a country estate on the eve of World War I, Vershinin studies the brilliant, dramatic piano performances of the genius, Natalia Tomilina. Unlike the "She" of "The Phenomenology of Absolute or Pure Music," Tomilina is physically unappealing, a woman in her mid-thirties, full-bodied and matronly. Her name is rooted in the Russian verb *tomit'*, "to suffer sensually." In Tomilina sensuality, has been sublimated as technical musical expression and philosophical thought about music. Vershinin exaggerates her power as a "thinking architect in music, a great tragic philosopher in performance" (TCh, 206).

It is curious here to note that Vershinin goes against all the traditional stereotypes concerning women and philosophy that we have encountered and will encounter in Russian writing culture. Although historically it is far from true, traditionally, as we have seen, women are portrayed as being hostile to philosophy. In contrast, Vershinin exclaims, "Woman—this is music, this is delight, this is speculative thought [*umozrenie*]" (TCh, 220). Similarly, in "The Woman Thinker," Vershinin is fascinated by the famous, also middle-aged pianist Maria Radina, a character very likely based on the celebrated pianist of the 1930s, Maria Iudina.[31] He writes, "Radina thinks,

---

30. The first critical treatment of these recently discovered works is Elena Takho-Godi, *A. F. Losev: Ot pisem k proze, ot Pushkina do Pasternaka* (Moscow: Dialog MGU, 1999).

31. Maria Iudina was famous not only for a majestic, aggressive style of performance but for her outspoken defense of religious and cultural freedom. A fanatical convert from Judaism to Russian Orthodoxy, she was banned from teaching at Leningrad Conservatory and often from performing.

knows, and penetrates with her knowledge"; she is "not [just] a mediator but a powerful, mighty thinker" (ZhM, 4:100). Radina is creative, aggressive, and capable of bold interpretation: "Her thought is her existence; her thinking is power, might, creativity. When she thinks, she creates new worlds of miracles and mysteries, and our outer self turns to vapor and dissolves" (ZhM, 4:102).

Perhaps echoing Tolstoy's "Kreutzer Sonata," music, in both novellas, predictably unleashes violent subconscious sexual drives. In both works the pianist asks Vershinin to marry her. At first he refuses, because he is far more interested in unearthing the musical secrets of the brilliant performer than in loving the actual woman. In the end, the pianist's personal drama is always more compelling than the philosopher's ratiocinations. Eventually Vershinin himself falls in love only to be rebuffed in some shocking, demeaning way. In "Chaikovsky's Trio," when Vershinin decides he really is in love with Tomilina, she rewards him with a physical beating.

Both novellas end with philosophy and the philosopher fading in the face of passionate life relationships. Losev often repeated the thought that nature and real life do not "need" philosophy. Nature is indifferent to abstract cognition. In both works philosophical seeking is bracketed in the context of Vershinin's relationship with real women, each longing to be accepted not just as a musical genius but also as a whole, integral self. Ironically, though Losev's philosophy is about the realization of one's whole spiritual self, his fictional substitute, Vershinin, tends to see only the technical side and not the spirit, the musical performer and not the entire personality. Both Tomilina and Radina seek a fulfilling relationship with a man who sees in her more than just a great performer of Chaikovsky, Bach, and Beethoven. They want genuine caring and understanding, not just to be under a critical microscope. Radina says: "I am a self [*lichnost'*]. I am a person and I want a human relationship, not just a musical one" (ZhM, 6:114). Through her years of performing she feels she has lost her sense of selfhood (ZhM, 6:115). Having earlier been just like Vershinin in her almost religious faith in music, she is now disillusioned:

> My whole life I thought that all those sonatas and fugues, etudes and preludes, that all those were just like a curtain hiding genuine, full life, as if the threshold of some wonderful sanctuary where heavenly visions would descend and I would be overcome with a happy ecstasy of genuine grace. And how chastely I related to all this. . . . And what came of it? Here is your re-

---

She was known to interrupt her own concerts in order to recite poems by banned poets, for example, Boris Pasternak. Stalin admired her playing and even sent her a generous sum of money for performing a Mozart piano concerto. She wrote to thank him and to tell him that she had donated the money to her church and would pray that God might forgive him his terrible sins. See Solomon Volkov, *St. Petersburg: A Cultural History,* trans. A. Bouis (New York: Free Press, 1995), 365–368.

sult: I am disgusted, I am irritated now when I have to say something or think about music. I see now that Bach . . . cheated me most cruelly, most savagely. . . . As it turned out, Bach just lured men to me, who gazed licentiously at my body, trembling with desire. (ZhM, 6:117)

Radina wants only to take revenge on music. Thus she plays the fool, claiming not to know the first thing about theory and claiming to prefer the popular nineteenth-century French composer of operettas, Jacques Offenbach, to J. S. Bach: "Here is my answer to Bach. . . . I think that an operetta—yes, a clever, lively operetta—that attempts to do nothing more than raise one's spirits and to offer some little comfort, is better than these cumbersome and solemn forms in which everyone places their hopes and from which no one gains anything" (ZhM, 6:117).

In both novellas the ongoing competition between philosophical discourse and musical pre-language is bounded by larger historical events that crowd them out. At the end of "Chaikovsky's Trio" the estate is bombed and destroyed by German invaders at the onset of World War I. Everyone is killed but Vershinin, who is wounded and ends up in a field hospital. He hears the conversations of the soldiers around him, most of them contemptuous of the Russian intelligentsia. At the end, Vershinin sinks into a stupor. The wider circle of human life continues, indifferent to Vershinin's seemingly futile search for higher mystical insight.

At the end of "The Woman Thinker," one of Radina's erstwhile admirers shoots her. When none of her retinue comes forward, Vershinin at least makes sure that she has a proper burial. That night, completely overwrought, he lies down to sleep and has three dreams in which he fulfills his wish to achieve the great philosophical synthesis, which he could not do in his waking life. Of course, in the end, even these efforts fail, since they are only passing dreams.

In the finale Losev's protagonist ultimately rejects philosophy. He returns to a simple, basic form of spiritual life that has nothing to do with the complexities of philosophy and musical composition. Vershinin awakens in a fever. When his nurse arrives to comfort him, she says a simple prayer. He then calms down and falls into a deep, healing sleep. Whereas all the high cultural languages have failed, the simple language of a traditional prayer brings Vershinin tranquility.

What, then, does the writing of fiction bring to Losev's view of philosophy? It frames the great synthesis in various life settings to show its failure in real life. Vershinin himself is an arrogant young man, bent on using people for his own intellectual ends. In his search for meaning, his ideas do not relate to real people's emotional needs. Selfhood is in no way developed or deepened. Fiction provides the framework in which abstract philosophical discourse self-destructs.

The exercise of writing these artistically meager stories brought to a head the tragedy that was apparent since the early 1920s in Losev's synthetic philosophy. Although he remains an important if idiosyncratic voice in the Russian tradition of personalist philosophy, his attempt at a grand synthesis of rational and mystical knowledge falters between rational speech and the meonic pre-language of music. He tries to find a solution to overcome the difficulties that the young Nietzsche finds, in *The Birth of Tragedy,* between Dionysian tragedy, with its roots in music, and the optimistic, scientific age ushered in by Socrates, who repressed within himself the power of music. For both philosophers, music is an expression of something primal and sub-rational—whereas for Nietzsche it expresses primal suffering and terror, for Losev it conveys a cosmic level of chaotic being that escapes verbal articulation. For Nietzsche, music is the powerful generator of the tragic text, which itself conveys the deepest values of a culture, and analytical philosophy is deeply inimical to the tragic spirit of music. During Socrates' time, Nietzsche argues, the dramatist Euripides shifted the focus of tragedy from Dionysian horror, transgression, and the subsequent shattering of the illusion of the integral moral self to mere melodrama. Nietzsche holds Socrates responsible.

Quite the opposite happens in Losev's philosophical career. In his works philosophical discourse acknowledges its own inability to penetrate the profound suffering and chaos at the heart of great music. Just as the philosopher is incapable of apprehending more than the technician in the pianist—and not the integral, complex, suffering human self—so the tools of philosophy can help only to analyze form and cannot penetrate the deeper essence. They cannot explore the unshaped being that is the essence of music. With Losev, Nietzsche's hope for a new tragic culture after the failure of scientific optimism found new expression. As with Solovyov, this tension in Losev's philosophy between scientific discourse, the magical-metaphorical word, and music, as well, is never resolved. It is this tension in Russian mystical philosophy that makes it different from modern Western philosophy and richer in experimentation with genre and language.

A Russian colleague has called Losev an "unrealized thinker" (nesostoiavshiisia myslitel').[32] That assessment is largely true, and it is tragic in the most profound sense. Losev was an unusually erudite person who became a bearer of culture, and he was arguably one of the best historians of ancient philosophy in the twentieth century. He was a beacon in the Soviet philosophical underground. His life represents the destruction of a culture—indeed, its own self-destruction from within. Given Losev's exceedingly high

---

32. The remark was made by the philosopher Vasilii Podoroga in a conversation from August 3, 2000.

expectations of philosophical discourse and its power, it is not surprising that philosophy would eventually fall to a more modest position. Yet, in his novellas, we witness the failure and self-destruction of philosophy in the face of vast, hostile events that were far more powerful than philosophy. Philosophical culture shrank to its earlier forms: in Losev's clique we find a new version of the closed, tight circles of the 1830s. Philosophy as a public discourse would die in Stalinist Russia. But philosophy as a basic speculative discourse would survive in the literary art of Andrei Platonov and Boris Pasternak.

Chapter Nine

The Matter of Philosophy: Dialectical Materialism and Platonov's Quest after Questioning

Platonov is a treasure trove for philosophy.

—Vladimir Malakhov, Russian Academy of Sciences, 1996

ON JUNE 21, 1921, Lev P. Karsavin, the well-known and highly regarded philosopher-rector of Petrograd University, delivered a public lecture on the subject of free will. One year later, on August 18, 1922, he was arrested. Among the evidence against him in his trial was a brief review of his recent book, *Noctes Petropolitanae*, published August 9, 1922, in *Kommuna* by the young proletarian writer Andrei Platonov (A. P. Klimentov, 1899–1951).[1] By late September 1922 Karsavin, like so many other Russian philosophers and writers who did not accept the totalitarian tactics of the Bolsheviks, had been deported from the new Soviet state.

Andrei Platonov was a major Soviet writer and supporter of proletarian ideals who also, by most accounts, loved philosophy and loved "to think."[2]

1. I. A. Savkin, "Na storone Platona: Karsavin i Platonov, ili ob odnoi ne-vstreche," *Tvorchestvo Andreia Platonova: Issledovaniia i materially. Bibliografiia* (St. Petersburg, Nauka, 1995," 153.

2. A great many claims have been made for Platonov's status as a philosophical writer—indeed, a writer who, in another time (and, it could be added, a wholly different writing culture), could have been a philosopher. Platonov has been compared to Sartre as an existentialist (Thomas Seifrid, "Writing against Matter: On the Language of Andrei Platonov's *Kotlovan*," *SEEJ* 31, no. 3 [1987]: 370–387). Parallels have been drawn between Platonov and Heidegger in their concerns for the basic relationship between "thinking" and "truth" (Mikhail Zolotonosov, " 'Lozhnoe solntse': 'Chevengur' i 'Kotlovan' v kontekste sovetskoi kul'tury 1920–kh godov," in N. V. Kornienko and E. D. Shubina, eds., *Andrei Platonov: Mir tvorchestva* [Moscow: Sovremennyi pisatel', 1994], 246). Platonov has been called the "most 'metaphysical' . . . of all our writers" (V. A. Kovalenko, "Stanovlenie svobody [o romane A. Platonova 'Chevengur']," in *Andrei Platonov: Issledovaniia i materialy* [Voronezh: Izdatel'stvo VGU, 1993], 19). His views have been described as radical materialism and radical idealism in the same breath (Sergei Bocharov, "Veshchestvo sushchestvovaniia [Vyrazhenie v proze]" [1968], in Kornienko and Shubina, *Andrei Platonov: Mir tvorchestva,* 112).

In this antagonistic encounter between the old, Russian-European and the new, virulently anti-philosophical Soviet writing cultures, the young Platonov had at once struck a hostile attitude toward established Russian "philosophy" and revealed a strong interest in philosophical matters. In his review of *Noctes Petropolitanae* Platonov rejected "metaphysics." Karsavin's treatise on love, he claimed, showed no familiarity with "real life," creating a bookish, abstract ideal of his subject. "The whole book," he wrote, "is a mishmash of concepts of a worn-out, rotten brain. The author has no idea about real human love. Love to him means religion, philosophy, literature, anything you like except the cry of the future, the movement of seed [*dvizhenie semeni*], warmth, courage, physical strength that wipes out [older] generations that are no longer fit—[in short,] the work of the sun."[3]

Seifrid characterizes Platonov as an "ambivalent idealist writing under materialist hegemony" ("Writing against Matter," 377).

Equally broad claims have been made as to Platonov's responses to philosophical precursors. Most reception studies have failed to establish a firm philosophical "genealogy." The most frequent claim has been for a total impact of the thought of Nikolai Fedorov on Platonov. Although many critics have made the case that Fedorov's work provided powerful philosophical mentorship to the young writer, the case has sometimes been overstated (Mikhail Geller, *Andrei Platonov v poiskakh schast'ia* [Paris: YMCA, 1982]; Ayleen Tesky, *Platonov and Fyodorov* [Amersham: Avebury, 1982]; and Svetlana Semenova, *Nikolai Fedorov: Tvorchestvo zhizni* [Moscow: Sovetskii pisatel', 1990], 364–368). More convincing arguments have been made for Platonov's attraction to and skepticism about specific aspects of his philosophy, for example, Fedorov's views on honoring one's forebears and overcoming their death through technological means (Thomas Seifrid, *Andrei Platonov: Uncertainties of Spirit* [Cambridge: Cambridge University Press, 1992]; Zolotonosov, " 'Lozhnoe solntse,' " 256; and L. Liubushkina, "Ideia bessmertiia u rannego Platonova" (1988), in Kornienko and Shubina, *Andrei Platonov: Mir tvorchestva,* 178). Other, weaker claims have been made for Platonov's readings of the scientist Vladimir Vernadskii, the anarchist Petr Kropotkin, Friedrich Nietzsche; all the claims, however, remain unsubstantiated (for example, Kovalenko, "Stanovlenie svobody," 23–26).

Other philosophical influences have also been claimed. One tantalizing mention of a philosophical interest comes with Viktor Shklovskii, in *The Third Factory* (*Tret'ia fabrika*), who spent a day talking to Platonov and claims that Rozanov repeatedly came up in the conversation (Elena Tolstaia-Segal, "Ideologicheskie konteksty Platonova," in Kornienko and Shubina, *Andrei Platonov: Mir tvorchestva*). No real textual evidence for such an interest has yet been established, and one has to wonder whether Shklovskii, who wrote a major piece on Rozanov and was himself influenced by the idiosyncratic philosopher, was not projecting one of his own interests onto the young Soviet writer.

Another important link that has been difficult to establish is Platonov's reception of the Bolshevik thinker Aleksandr Bogdanov's organizational theory known as tectology. One study finds in Platonov's narratives a Bogdanovian interest in two areas: one is the general principle of organization throughout all spheres of life, and the other is Bogdanov's understanding of cognition as the harmonization of the physical and the psychic (Tolstaia-Segal, "Ideologicheskie konteksty Platonova," 52–54). Another study pursues these parallels between the two writers, particularly their desire to overcome the divide between the abstract and the concrete, to merge the conceptual and the practical, and to resolve the philosophical split between body and matter, on the one hand, and mind and consciousness, on the other (Zolotonosov, " 'Lozhnoe solntse,' " 257). These discussions seem too imprecise to prove that Bogdanov had any specific influence on Platonov. Indeed, these were some of the main themes of the 1920s, when Marxism-Leninism and the emerging ideology of "dialectical materialism" were increasingly dominant.

3. Savkin, "Na storone Platona," 162.

Here the young writer seemed to reject both conventional philosophy and the writing culture of which it was a part. Although he sounded brash, strident, intolerant, and unphilosophical, in keeping with the new rulers and regulators of Russian writing, four years later he would write to Voronsky, the editor of *Krasnaia nov'*, that his "passion for thinking and writing" was "guilty" for his move to Moscow.[4]

Andrei Platonov's thinking was very much in keeping with anti-idealist intellectual currents of the day—what was becoming the vitriolic dialectical materialist dogma that would stand for philosophy during the first four decades of Soviet history. The early 1920s saw a two-pronged struggle for philosophy in the new Soviet state. First came the establishment of dialectical materialist "philosophy" as the officially approved mode of philosophy in the Soviet Union. This move was carried through, first, with the destruction of traditional departments of philosophy at Russia's major universities, the institutionalization of various Soviet schools and journals for the study of Marxism, and the armed arrest and expulsion of noted "idealist" philosophers. Second, in journals and newspapers a debate flared up about the need for any philosophy at all in the new state.[5] Various Bolshevik intellectuals argued vociferously against philosophy in the new culture. Perhaps the most infamous of these is the article, "Overboard with Philosophy" ("Filosofiia za bort"), written in 1922 by two crude materialists, Emmanuel Enchmen and S. K. Minin.[6] The authors claimed that philosophy was passé and that the true ideology of communism was the "ship of science": "In fitting out and trimming the ship of science we must take care to throw overboard not only religion but also the whole of philosophy."[7]

Of much greater importance to Platonov personally was the impact that two thinkers had on him, namely, Nikolai Fedorov (1829–1903), the newly published nineteenth-century "guru" of science and technological utopia, and Aleksandr Bogdanov, the creator of a scientific-industrial organizational theory and founder of the Proletarian Culture (Proletcult) movement. Like other Bolsheviks, Bogdanov believed that philosophy as such had outlived its day and must now be replaced by practical science and scientific theory. Fedorov was much more voluble on the subject of philosophy and its general place in the ranks and categories of knowledge. In *The Philosophy of the*

4. V. Eidinova, "K tvorcheskoi biografii A. Platonova: po strannitsam gazetnykhi zhurnal'nykh publikatsii pisatelia 1918–1925 gg.," *Voprosy literatury* 3 (1978): 214.

5. David Bakhurst, *Consciousness and Revolution in Soviet Philosophy from the Bolsheviks to Evald Ilyenkov* (Cambridge: Cambridge University Press, 1991), 25–59.

6. E. Enchmen and S. K. Minin, "Filosofiia za bort," *Pod znamenem marksizma* 11–12 (1922). According to Bakhurst, this article was first published in a provincial journal (Bakhurst, *Consciousness and Revolution,* 28 n. 6).

7. Cited in Gustav A. Wetter, *Dialectical Materialism,* trans. P. Heath (Westport, Conn.: Greenwood, 1958), 130. See also M. B. Mitin and P. F. Iudin, "Novye problemy marksisko-leninskoi filosofii," *Pravda,* June 7, 1930.

Common Cause Fedorov launched a thorough critique of Western philosophy, particularly the German Idealist tradition. He defended a holistic, Gnostic understanding of knowledge that embraced observable fact, logical deduction, and mystical and intuitive kinds of revelation.[8] Still, unlike Bogdanov, he argued that philosophy does play a role. It is the necessary "negative" that precedes resurrection.[9]

Unlike slightly older, philosophically minded writers who bridged the gap between pre- and postrevolutionary culture, such as Zamiatin or Pasternak, Platonov only rarely mentions "philosophy" as a discourse. Nonetheless, philosophical concerns about truth and meaning are central to him. This chapter focuses on Platonov's response to dialectical materialism as it was "canonized" in the late 1920s. His response, in my view, is a key to one of his finest fictional works, *The Foundation Pit,* written from late 1929 to early 1930, precisely at the time of the most heated debates among Bolshevik academics about dialectical materialism. Although he rarely discusses language itself, Platonov has a great deal to say about the vocabulary of dialectical materialism and, in particular, the concepts of matter, consciousness, dialectical change, and party loyalty. His concept of philosophy as a particular use of language emerges as he defends the activity of "thinking" from the coercion implicit in the idea of party loyalty. In this light his work serves as a safe box for philosophical questing that has also provided a point of departure in the late Soviet and post-Soviet period for the revival of philosophical activity in Russia.

As is true of so much connected with Platonov's biography, the evidence of the writer's philosophical education, that is, what he read and when he read it, is sparse and somewhat conflicting. In his letters, early articles, and well-known stories, he showed a basic concern for philosophical categories of truth and consciousness but without mentioning that "outmoded" term *philosophy*.[10] When he spoke of discourses or categories

---

8. Since his ultimate goal is the resurrection of past generations, quite unphilosophically utopian and socially and technologically proactive, Fedorov must find some theoretical basis elsewhere. As he admits in *The Philosophy of the Common Cause,* "resurrection is the most unphilosophical of concepts: resurrection assembles, restores, and brings everything back to life, whereas philosophy divides and makes abstract [*otvlekaet*] and thus mortifies; in the end, philosophy makes not only restoration just a thought, that is, the most abstract thought, but with its meditative, sedentary, inactive life it turns even the outward, existing world into a representation, a merely psychological fact, a phantom" (N. F. Fedorov, *Sochineniia,* 2 vols. (Moscow: Mysl', 1982), 317). He argues that Western philosophy is too isolated from other kinds of knowledge and thus eventually, with the appearance of Nietzsche, becomes locked in solipsism (*Sochineniia,* 1:72, 426). Such philosophy is a "play with concepts and ideas" that are "only the dreams of the philosophical imagination and real only as psychic states" (426).

9. See Fedorov, *Sochineniia,* 1:317; all the same, Fedorov calls philosophy the necessary "negative," "dissecting moment" that precedes resurrection and the destruction of death.

10. M. A. Dmitrovskaia, "Problema chelovecheskogo soznaniia v romane A. Platonova 'Chevengur,'" in *Tvorchestvo Andreia Platonova: Issledovaniia i materialy. Bibliografiia,* 39, 42.

of knowledge, it was typically those of science, art, and religion. It is a cliché, but nevertheless true, that Platonov was deeply in love with technology, machines, and mechanics. He was equally enamored of science and scientific theory. In one letter he wrote insightfully about what distinguishes science from other discourses: science, he said, is more an expression of human power over the world than a mode of pure knowledge and truth.[11] It is a way to conquer nature. Despite this enthusiasm, in two unpublished articles, "Light and Socialism" ("Svet i sotsializm") and "On Love" ("O liubvi"), he showed a strong concern about the limits of scientific discourse, particularly its inability to satisfy the human need for faith in an ultimate truth.[12] He argued here, as in his story, "The Innermost Man" ("Sokrovennyi chelovek," 1928), that, although socialism must destroy traditional religion, it must also replace it with something more secure than mere scientific knowledge. Without establishing some belief system, he warned, the new Soviet state would be confronted with a revolt of the heart.

The question now arises as to whether Platonov can be said to have used a "philosophical" discourse in any sense of the word. Most philosophically or theoretically inclined critics have had much to say about the quality of Platonov's style. Sergei Bocharov was the first to discuss Platonov's "philosophically awkward turns of phrase."[13] Citing Nietzsche, Elisabeth Markstein notes that the point of departure in Platonov's style is "his concern with destroying from the inside that great fortress of concepts, those 'great rafters and beams of concepts.'"[14] The focus of this tearing down of philosophical language has more recently been captured in the term *ideologeme,* that is, the politicized abstract language used by the party and in the new proletarian "philosophy," dialectical materialism.[15] In my view, Platonov's particular definition and use of philosophical language emerges in his philosophical parody of official dialectical materialism.

Certainly Platonov's philosophical language takes as its point of departure the concepts and assumptions at the heart of dialectical materialism as it emerged in the late 1920s. This was a time of heated debate between two groups, the Deborinites who followed the thinker A. M. Deborin, author of the book *An Introduction to Dialectical Materialist Philosophy* (1916), and the Mechanists, one of whose leaders was the former Menshevik Liubov Aksel-

---

11. Andrei Platonov, *Gosudarstvennyi zhitel'* (Moscow: Sovetskii pisatel', 1988), 565.

12. Both articles appeared ibid.

13. Bocharov, "Veshchestvo sushchestvovaniia," 10.

14. Elisabeth Markstein, "Der Stil des 'Unstils': Andrej Platonov," *Wiener Slawistisches Almanach* 2 (1978): 136.

15. See, for example, Lev Shubin, "Gradovskaia shkola filosofii," in Kornienko and Shubina, *Andrei Platonov: Mir tvorchestva,* 214; and A. M. Abramov, "Nad stranitsami povesti *Kotlovan*," *Andrei Platonov: Issledovaniia i materialy. Bibliografiia,* 48.

rod.[16] The core of the debate concerned the nature of matter and how we can know it. The enthusiasm the Mechanists expressed for the natural sciences matched that of the newly trained Soviet ideologues of the early 1920s. The Mechanists believed that empiricist techniques used to study the natural sciences were adequate for apprehending all aspects of the world and of human experience. They tended to argue that philosophy was superfluous. In contrast, Deborin and his followers supported the view that the methodologies of the social sciences were just as important as those of the natural sciences for perceiving and defining what was "real."

The differences between these two views were more in emphasis and degree than in substance. The Mechanists finally suffered a political defeat in 1929 at the Second All-Union Conference of the Marxist-Leninist Institutes of Scientific Research, when the Deborinites claimed that the Mechanists were politically revisionist. This labeling reinforced a trend that had begun at the very outset of the Soviet period, that of settling philosophical problems by political means. However, in April 1930, Deborin himself was discredited in the infamous "article of the three," published in *Pravda* by a new group of "Bolshevizers," M. B. Mitin, V. Ral'tsevich, and P. F. Iudin, who basically claimed greater "partiinost'," or party loyalty, as the reason for their "philosophical" superiority.[17] Predictably they had Stalin's personal backing.

Although Platonov was not directly involved in this debate, he certainly followed it. In *The Foundation Pit,* written just at this time when critical thinking was being harnessed to the will of party leaders and the atrocities of collectivization were just starting, Platonov gave his own evaluation of this rapid shift from dialectical materialism as a type of philosophy—preferable in his view to philosophical idealism—to dialectical materialism as ideology. As will become clear, he was particularly critical of a simpleminded insistence on the primacy of matter, the class-oriented concept of the "dialectic," and the party's control of philosophy. He remained squarely on the side of philosophical materialism—in the basic sense that he assumed that matter precedes consciousness, and in the sense that all his characters are atheists who assume no higher subjectivity in the organization of the world. It was in this short novel where he isolated what, for him, made any and all "philosophy" so essential.

To begin, it will be helpful to summarize the main concepts of dialectical materialism as it emerged in the late 1920s and early 1930s. Although attributed by all Soviet ideologues to Marx and Engels, *dialectical materialism* is itself a Russian term. First coined by Plekhanov, it then found its way into

---

16. For a scathing contemporary review of Deborin's book, see P. Blonskii's review, *Mysl' i slovo* (Moscow: Leman and Sakharov, 1917), 1:413–415.

17. Bakhurst, *Consciousness and Revolution*, 47.

Lenin's vocabulary.[18] Stalin used the term in 1906 and 1907 in his series of newspaper forays against Georgian anarchists, entitled "Anarchism or Socialism?"[19] The Stalinist "canonization" of dialectical materialism crystallized the early 1930s in the obsequious pseudo-theorizing of Iudin and Mitin. It is significant that Mitin subsequently became one of the chief editors and writers for the philosophy sections of the first *Great Soviet Encyclopedia.* Started in the late 1920s in a cooperative publishing house, the first edition of the *Great Soviet Encyclopedia* was finished only much later under the control of the state publishing house for encyclopedias. Among the longer and politically sensitive articles were those on "philosophy," published only in 1936 in volume 57, and on "dialectical materialism," published in 1935 in volume 22. It is from Mitin's contributions to the *Great Soviet Encyclopedia* that we take our "textbook" version of dialectical materialism.

In a vulgar simplification of Marx's early critiques of German idealist philosophy (we recall his dictum that "philosophers have only interpreted life in different ways; the task, however, is to change it"), Stalinist dialectical materialist theory conceptualized the history of formal philosophy in militant terms as a "struggle" between "idealism" and "materialism."[20] "Idealism," or any kind of philosophical dualism, was defined as the belief that consciousness or spirit precedes matter and in some way causes matter to come into being. "Materialism," in contrast, was defined as the view that matter is all there is. Being is prior to thinking. In contrast, consciousness is fully dependent on matter, existing merely as the property of highly organized matter.

The battle between philosophical idealism and materialism is ultimately seen as a foil for the deeper, more basic class struggle that is the motivating force of human history. Dualist systems tend to serve the established, conservative ruling class, whereas materialism in some form has always been the basis for revolutionary, innovative ideology. In the present historical moment, idealist philosophy is politically passive and, it is claimed, creates a convenient mask to cover the deep structural rifts within bourgeois society and, particularly, the split between physical and mental labor.

Dialectical materialism, of course, is claimed as the intellectual territory of the proletariat. In the history of philosophy, according to Mitin, dialectical materialism itself was not "philosophy." Rather, it represented a new phase, not of philosophy but of "understanding philosophy." He meant that

18. *Russkaia filosofiia: Malyi entsyklopedicheskii slovar'*, ed. A. I. Aleshin et al. (Moscow: Nauka, 1995), 163.

19. I. V. Stalin, "Anarkhizm ili sotsializm?" *Sochineniia*, 13 vols. (Moscow: OGIZ, 1946), 1:294–372.

20. Karl Marx, *Die Frühschriften* (Stuttgart: Kröner, 1971), 341.

the authority of traditional philosophy had now been diminished and could no longer be considered the "science of sciences." Metaphysics and traditional ethics were now dead, because their claims to an absolute origin of being and the notion of eternal, a priori consciousness had been disproved.[21]

It is important to point out that in this new theoretical soup the difference between matter and consciousness is not erased. As Mitin wrote, consciousness is "a step in the development of matter [*materiia*], the property of highly organized matter, and between them exists not an absolute but a relative opposition."[22] What he means by "relative opposition" is never explained. The point he is making is that consciousness cannot exist outside material existence and, indeed, is determined by the conditions of material, that is, natural and social, existence. It is interesting to note, however, a distinct inconsistency in Mitin's dialectical materialism with its claims to be rid of absolutes. In this canonical dialectical materialism, matter has now gained the status of the "eternal," without beginning or end.[23]

This remark brings us to a third crucial concept in dialectical materialism—after "matter" and "consciousness"—the concept of the "dialectic." In this theory all phenomena are interconnected. The world is in a continual state of change and development that occurs through the resolution of contradictions, of opposing truths. Stalin, in his slight newspaper theorizing of 1906, had the following to say about the dialectic: "Dialectics say that there is nothing eternal in the world . . . concepts of justice change as does the truth itself."[24] This relativist ethical stance, in the party's view, eventually came to mean that, to paraphrase Dostoevsky's thought, "God does not exist, so everything is permitted."

The shifting character of truth and justice leads to fluidity and lack of accountability, which, in turn, makes the concept of "party loyalty" (*partiinost'*) the hinge on which all forms of authorization or legitimization turn. This move, too, is a Russian contribution to materialist philosophy and is at the heart of the Leninist concept of "*partiinost'*." Lenin, Mitin tells his readers, decided that philosophy has a "party-oriented" (*partiinyi*) nature. Ironically, even though idealism was supposedly disproved and was dead, the Stalinist ideologue still calls for "struggle" with idealist tendencies. This "militant theory" is viewed as a way to effect social change.[25] The way to destroy idealism and its supposed falsehoods is to destroy class-based society. Class war will pave the way for a total victory of dialectical materialism in

21. *Bol'shaia sovetskaia entsyklopediia* (Moscow: Gosudarstvennyi institut "Sovetskaia Entsyklopediia," 1936), 57:487.
22. Ibid., 57:447.
23. Ibid., 22:135.
24. Stalin, *Sochineniia*, 1:304.
25. *Bol'shaia sovetskaia entsyklopediia*, 22:120.

the area of thought. The result will be social and cultural harmony between physical and mental types of labor. Left unspecified is whether "harmony" would mean Gorky's dream of factory workers reading the poetry of Shelley or Platonov's darker vision, expressed in *The Foundation Pit,* of dumb, disenfranchised workers with their "lips baked together from silence," their mouths dry and sealed from long, speechless hours of hard labor.[26]

Thus, having tried to destroy the bases of traditional philosophy, dialectical materialist theory politicizes philosophical language and tries to bring it completely under the control of the Communist Party. In other words, in the party-controlled atmosphere of the 1930s the "general line" of the party became the "truth." To complete this picture of total ideological control, the encyclopedists crown Lenin, the brilliant political theorist, and Stalin, a gifted political strategist, as "philosopher-kings." Philosophers have been expelled from this "republic" of dialectical materialism, and philosophy, understood as critical interrogation of the bases of knowledge, as seeking answers that science and religion cannot provide, has also been banished.

In this intellectually constricted atmosphere, literature once again became the discursive mode in which philosophizing was preserved. As every critic points out, Platonov's works are all laden with characters that think, doubt, wonder, and question. In my view, this pattern becomes most generalized in *The Foundation Pit,* in which the discourse is most clearly that of "philosophy," how we think and how thinking affects what we do in the world. Although Platonov is obviously satirizing Stalinist visions of the perfect society with a number of dystopian scenarios—particularly a building site for a workers' home and a newly collectivized farm—he is also participating in the deadly debate of 1929–1930, in which real philosophical dialogue ceased and totalized ideology took its place. It is in his response to dialectical materialism that Platonov most fully sets out a philosophical discourse of his own.

Despite his dismissal of traditional metaphysics and his small contribution to the destruction of fragile Russian philosophical institutions, Platonov by no means rejects the basic philosophical character of human beings and their need to ask questions about the nature and meaning of existence. Just as Platonov's characters are "wanderers," so, too, are they "wonderers." All his best characters, Pukhov in "The Innermost Man," Dvanov in *Chevengur,* and almost everyone in *The Foundation Pit* who is not a demagogue or party organizer, have a visceral need to wonder, think, and ques-

26. Andrei Platonov, *Kotlovan,* in *Gosudarstvennyi zhitel',* 115. Hereafter cited in the text as *K* with the relevant page number. Cf. Letter from Gorky to Kuskova, cited in *La vie amère de Maxime Gorky,* in E. Clowes, *The Revolution of Moral Consciousness: Nietzsche in Russian Literature, 1890–1914* (DeKalb: Northern Illinois University Press, 1988), 253.

tion. Whether one is literate or well read does not matter. This very need is precisely what the party organizers would like to obliterate.

In *The Foundation Pit* Platonov reflects on how the Stalinist "philosophy" of dialectical materialism monopolizes writing culture. The only written documents mentioned are political in nature: the notice that the worker Voshchev is being fired; the directives the collective farm activist receives; and the grammar book that is being used to teach the children at the new collective farm, the Party Line (General'naia Liniia), how to read. As far as the political activist is concerned, "words are there to make policy and slogans" (*K*, 165). As we find in the scenes at the "reading hut" at the collective farm, writing is the domain of dogma, of monological pontification. Its vocabulary is largely constructed of foreign roots that magically and mysteriously are linked to revolution and power. For instance, the women and children who are learning to read and write the alphabet are given the following words as examples: for "a," "avant-garde, activists, allelujah-criers, advance, arch-leftist," and so forth; for "b," "Bolshevik, bourgeois, . . . bravo-bravo-Leninists," and so on (*K*, 165). The activist actually goes against Lenin's orthographic reform and teaches his pupils the old style of retaining the hard sign at the end of words that end in a consonant, because, as he puts it, the hard sign "makes for toughness and precision of formulas" (*K*, 165). It is interesting to note here, in passing, that Platonov is mocking the resurgence of a mentality that accepts something akin to Foucault's magical, premodern language of similitude. Language comes alive in *The Foundation Pit* and is itself a key to opening a new communist universe.

In one short episode we find a private form of writing: the engineer Prushevsky receives a card from his sister and writes a letter in return. The only items communicated are the most formulaic greetings and news. In terms of "discourse" they are important only in that they show the extreme diminution of private life and family life in this new socialized, collectivized society.

The thinking and wondering that we associate with philosophy takes place only in the oral sphere, in conversation, or in the completely private realm of inner speech. The narrator of *The Foundation Pit* remains close to the most self-conscious characters, those with the greatest inner life. He focuses predominantly on their inner articulations, their attitudes, doubts, and questions. Voshchev and Prushevsky receive the most attention, and others, such as the foreman, Chiklin, and even the two political organizers, Safronov and the activist, are shown to have occasional private moments of self-consciousness and self-doubt.

A political rhetoric based largely on dialectical materialist assumptions (social and historical determinism, class struggle, proletarian domination, party loyalty) permeates all language, whether oral or written, for example, over the radio, in speeches political organizers give. The conflict between political discourse, which is founded on foreign cognates, and the private philosophical "discourse" of individual characters, which is thoroughly Russian, is, from the very first paragraph, at the forefront of *The Foundation Pit:*

> On the thirtieth birthday of his personal life Voshchev was given his walking papers from a small machine factory where he had been getting the means of his existence. In the release document it was written that he was being fired from production as a result of the growth in him of weakness and thoughtfulness amid the general tempo of labor.

> [V den' tridtsatiletiia lichnoi zhizni Voshchevu dali raschet s nebol'shogo mekhanicheskogo zavoda, gde on dobyval sredstva dlia svoege sushchestvovaniia. V uvol'nitel'nom dokumente emu napisali, chto on ustraniaetsia s proizvodstva vsledstvie rosta slabosil'nosti v nem i zadumchivosti sredi obshchego tempa truda. (*K,* 108)]

Here the "general tempo of labor" (*obshchii temp truda*), announced and determined from above, conflicts with Voshchev's "thoughtfulness" (*zadumchivost'*), his need to make sense of his life so that the labor he performs will be meaningful. "*Temp,*" a foreign word, stands out in contrast to the private and Russian "*zadumchivost'*" that keeps Voshchev from being simply a cog.

The relationship between consciousness and matter is a vital concern to Platonov. As Seifrid has shown, Platonov is squarely in the materialist camp, but a question remains to be answered: *Which* materialist camp? He certainly disagrees with the Leninist-Stalinist notion that inner life, consciousness, thinking, and questioning are merely class-oriented and socially determined. And he will have a great deal to say about the two difficult terms at the center of dialectical materialism, *matter* and *consciousness.* Bocharov argues, in his pathbreaking article, "The Stuff of Existence" ("Veshchestvo sushchestvovaniia," 1968), that, for Platonov, matter and consciousness will become contiguous spheres.[27] The most exalted meanings derive directly from the most concrete things and actions. Metaphysics is to give way to physics. Seifrid, in contrast, has argued that, although matter for Platonov is the basis of existence, and spirit or consciousness derives from physical properties, material things and bodies themselves become the prison wardens of the spirit.[28] This thought could be redirected to the ossified, formulaic *words* that, in my view, become, for Platonov, the prison house of the thinking consciousness. Here it is *consciousness* itself that turns into stiff, unyielding *matter* when it is captured in slogans and set phrases. An examina-

27. Bocharov, "Veshchestvo sushchestvovaniia."
28. Seifrid, "Writing against Matter."

tion of concrete uses of these two concepts, "consciousness" and "matter," in *The Foundation Pit* can help us understand Platonov's approach to thinking and to "philosophy."

Significantly the philosophy of "materialism" is mentioned right at the outset of the narrative, as members of the factory committee explain to Voshchev why they cannot defend his case: "Happiness will come from materialism [*materializm*], Comrade Voshchev, and not from meaning" (*K*, 109). Here "meaning" is treated as something unnecessary; one should simply believe and perform. Here Platonov immediately makes it clear that interaction between materialism and meaning will form one of the key points of tension in his criticism of the new Soviet ideology of dialectical materialism. He sets up opposing meanings of *matter* and *consciousness,* with the result that various ironies and paradoxes inherent in the two terms are exposed. He ends with an argument not for a specific position on any single issue but for a position of openness to questioning and truth seeking. Above all he rejects the habit party activists have of crushing wonderment through dogma and of ossifying thought into one final, total assertion of "truth." In addition to everything Platonov achieves in his satire of dialectical materialism, he also shows that its primary weakness is its inability to confront the issue of what it means to say that something is "true."

"Matter," in *The Foundation Pit,* is depicted, first and foremost, in terms of "nature," the only "reality" in materialist theory. Platonov's narrator seems to distinguish three areas of nature: organic nature, inorganic nature, and the human body. Organic nature—the trees and the grass—is perennially "tired," and the stones and clay of inorganic nature are empty, boring, and sad. Objects, far from being treated objectively, are personified. Nature, in an odd throwback to Schelling, the quintessential philosophical idealist, seems to have unconscious Spirit. For example, when Voshchev leaves the factory at the start: "The air was empty, the motionless trees *carefully held* the heat in their leaves, and the dust lay tediously on the unpeopled road— such was the situation in nature" (*K*, 108; emphasis added). As Voshchev wanders, he watches it grow dark: "The unpeopled night came on; in the distance only water and wind *populated* this gloom and nature, and only the birds could sing of the sadness of this great matter [*veshchestvo*] because they flew up above and they had an easier time of it" (*K*, 114; emphasis added). In contrast to the birds, inorganic nature is heavy and empty.

For the engineer Prushevsky, the dead body becomes a metaphor for material nature. Although Prushevsky is, by conviction, a materialist, he is starting to question the limits of materialist knowledge. He views nature as being easily manipulated and therefore dead: "He imagined the whole world as a dead body—he judged it by the parts that he had already turned into building structures: the world yielded in everything to his attentive and imagining mind, itself limited only by the consciousness of the inertness of nature; material [*material*] always yielded to precision and patience, which meant that it was dead and uninhabited" (*K,* 118). Prushevsky implicitly believes that there could be no god—or, more generally, no basis for philosophical dualism—since nature is dead, inert, and malleable. It is "material" (*material*), not "stuff" or "matter" (*veshchestvo*). Thus he agrees with textbook dialectical materialism that nature, the material world, is objectively, fully knowable to the senses and the scientific mind.

Platonov uses three different terms in speaking of matter and materialism: *veshchestvo, material,* and *materiia.* Of these, *veshchestvo* and *material* appear the most frequently and have the greatest meaning. The Russian-root word *veshchestvo*—matter, stuff, substance—is the key to Platonov's own belief in materialism. It is used by the narrator, the workers (*K,* 115: "You don't work, you don't experience the stuff [*veshchestvo*] of existence"), Voshchev (*K,* 116: "Now I, too, want to work on the stuff [*veshchestvo*] of existence"), and even Prushevsky (*K,* 118: "people alone were alive and worthy amid all the gloomy matter [*veshchestvo*]")—all of whom implicitly want to believe that there is something special, secret, and powerful about this "substance of existence." Later, *veshchestvo* is used to describe people as special stuff to be molded and shaped with a new, more powerful consciousness. The activist at the new collective farm views his public quite arrogantly as such "matter." He asks them: " 'Well, how are we to be, citizens?'—pronounced the activist to the stuff [*veshchestvo*] of the people that was located in front of him. 'What are you, going to sow capitalism again or have you remembered yourselves?' " (*K,* 168). Here, interestingly, *veshchestvo* is the narrator's word, not the activist's. *Veshchestvo,* as a concept, appears to imply to its users a metaphorical meaning that is more profound than simply concrete dead objects and the everyday. The activist, by contrast, wants only to control the people, not to respect the spontaneous "stuff" in them, which has organic, living potential.

The more common, concrete word *"material"*—physical items such as building materials—is used by a few people, but particularly by those who are involved in engineering or building. The labor organizer, Safronov, uses the concept *"material"* as a measuring stick to assess people's worth. He remarks to Voshchev, "people have become valuable nowadays, just as valuable as material" (*K,* 116). Prushevsky uses *material* when he thinks of nature as building material for socialist dreams. It is dead and easily manipulated: "material always yielded to precision and patience, which meant that it was dead and empty" (*K,* 118). At the end of *The Foundation Pit* Misha, the blacksmith-bear who has impressed everyone with his proletarian zeal for work, is, ironically, found beating some iron into a pulp so that it will be useless. The collective farmers plead with him not to "torment the material

[*material*]" (*K*, 186), but in a frenzy, almost like a windup toy, he keeps beating the "material" absurdly, as if beating it to death. This scene embodies the general, ideological overemphasis on material and matter that has ended in death, both spiritual and physical, and has rendered even the basic building blocks of matter meaningless and useless for human or any other consumption. Matter, which had seemed to Prushevsky so easily manipulated, has turned out to be easily wasted by being overly manipulated.

"Consciousness," compared to matter, is quite complex. In accordance with dialectical materialist theory, Platonov appears to view consciousness as the quality of being aware, a characteristic only of highly organized matter, that is, of people and animals. Thus nature is imbued with certain feelings and moods; animals can react; and only people can think, reflect, and make sense of, or change, their lives. As with the concept of "matter," Platonov uses many words to create a field of meaning around the concept of "consciousness." The word *soznanie* generally has two meanings. It can mean "class consciousness," an awareness of the role of one's class in history that merges easily into politically correct thinking as directed by the Communist Party. The adjective *nesoznatel'nyi* means politically incorrect, that is, socially irresponsible and lacking awareness of one's predetermined social and historical role. Thus, at the very start, the factory committee that relieves Voshchev of his original job claims that he is "irresponsible" because he is "unconscious": "We can't stand up for you, you lack consciousness [*nesoznatel'nyi*], and we don't want to end up in the rear guard of the masses" (*K*, 109). When Voshchev first joins the work gang at the foundation pit, the other workers echo the sentiment: "He's irresponsible [*nesoznatel'nyi*]. Never mind, capitalism made fools of our kind, and this one is just another holdover from that gloom" (*K*, 115). By contrast, a "*soznatel'nik*" or "*soznatel'nitsa*" is a politically and socially aware person, one who has gained the "correct" political consciousness (*K*, 136). For example, the little girl Nastia and her "bourgeois" mother accept that their class is dying out, and the mother, in compliance, physically dies.

"*Soznanie*," in its more important sense, for Platonov, denotes personal self-consciousness or self-awareness. What most interests him is the nature of self-consciousness and what makes some people self-conscious. Indeed, an awareness of oneself, of not quite fitting in, makes one question one's existence and the point of one's actions. A person with self-awareness is more than just a mindless body or boring matter. One becomes self-conscious when one feels hopelessly outside the general order of life, when things or people either resists one's will or when one cannot submit to the common will. From this condition comes the fear of isolation or overwhelming isolation itself. Voshchev, of course, the central figure in Platonov's existentialist allegory, is consumed by anxiety: he cannot eat, sleep, or work for he is con-

tinually worrying about his purpose in life, about life in general. The first
night after being fired, he tries to coax himself to sleep: "Voshchev slid
down into a ravine and lay on his stomach in order to fall asleep and take
leave of himself. But sleep required peace of mind, forgiveness of past mis-
fortune, and Voshchev lay there in the dry tension of awareness, not knowing whether he was of any use to the world or whether everything would go
on just fine without him" (*K,* 109). Except for a few brief moments when
he thinks he has found the meaning of life, Voshchev always feels as if he
were "living at a distance," "isolated in the narrowness of his own sorrow"
(*K,* 113).

Self-consciousness conflicts with inert matter and leads one to wonder
what else there is in life, what the meaning of existence might be. Now self-
consciousness truly reaches beyond matter. It makes a person behave in a
way that does not exist in nature: it makes one posit negative concepts. If
"A" designates material nature, the self-conscious mind wonders what "–A"
or "not A" might be. As in Dostoevsky's *Notes from Underground,* in *The
Foundation Pit* the image of a wall becomes a metaphor for the existential
condition in which one becomes self-conscious and questions the meaning
of existence. More characters in this story than one might expect actually
inquire into what (according to a class-based analysis of consciousness) used
to be the domain of metaphysics, the area one could not know rationally
and into which, according to Kant, one had to take a "leap of faith." The
first to come up against this wall is the thoughtful engineer Prushevsky,
who, like Voshchev, continually worries about his place in the world:

> At the age of twenty-five the engineer Prushevsky had felt the narrowness of
> his consciousness and the end to further comprehension of life, as if a dark
> wall stood right in front of his perceiving mind. Since that time, he has been
> tormented, moving about near his wall, comforted that, essentially, the most
> average, true structure of matter [*veshchestvo*], from which people and the
> world were assembled, was accessible to him—all everyday [*nasushchnaia*]
> science was arranged before the wall of his consciousness, and behind the
> wall was only some boring place where one need not go. But all the same it
> would be interesting to know whether someone had gotten ahead of the wall
> and beyond it. (*K,* 123)

In Prushevsky we find a newly forming Kantian consciousness. Voshchev's
kindly comrade, the foreman Chiklin, realizes the metaphor when he is dig-
ging and comes up against hard rock: "Right away Chiklin started to think,
because his life had no place to go once its exodus into the earth was cut
short; he leaned his sweaty back against the slope of the excavation pit,
looked into the distance, and imagined a memory—he was incapable of
further thought" (*K,* 125). Literally one starts to think and be conscious of

oneself and the conditions of one's existence when one is frustrated by limits. As Shestov had repeated so often, one starts to philosophize when one has no recourse to physical action, when one is in despair.

The question now arises as to how dialectical materialism undertakes to combat this "bad" kind of self-consciousness that resists matter and casts doubt on the meaning of existence inside the wall. What is the new consciousness that will relieve questions and anxiety? What is the "meaning" of this new life? All the debates of the late 1920s and early 1930s provide no answers, and we must turn to an older, far more inspiring proletarian myth. The frequently recurring words *schast'e* (happiness) and *entuziazm* (enthusiasm) give clues as to the hoped-for result of all the physical labor. For a new, satisfying sense of life, Platonov's laborers and organizers alike draw on a myth that has its roots in the prerevolutionary God-building movement of Gorky, Lunacharsky, and Bogdanov.[29] The basic rift between the conscious self and the collective other was to be overcome through consciousness-altering, physical labor. The result would be the fusion of individual selves into a new collective "we," a transformed, monumentally creative, larger-than-life mass of selves that would be joined together as a collective super-consciousness. This fusion would be accompanied by a new and vital sense of life, which Lunacharsky called "enthusiasm," the feeling of ecstasy at becoming a vigorous, new whole with the power to transfigure life itself.

In *The Foundation Pit* this new collective lends meaning to hard labor and raises backbreaking drudgery to the level of a ritual during which one is initiated into a vital, life-affirming consciousness. One is revitalized, now functioning as a joyful part of the mighty proletariat. Now "right feeling" replaces "meaning." Body and matter become the sites of the true *feeling* that is *meaning,* as mind and self-consciousness fade into insignificance. The first hint of this theme comes at the start when the factory committee firing Voshchev proclaims that "happiness comes from materialism . . . not from meaning" (*K,* 109). Voshchev's first encounter with the workers at the foundation pit repeats the contest between the consciousness of the self-conscious individual and the consciousness of the newly converted proletariat. When Voshchev claims that he cannot live without truth, this answer comes back: "What is your truth! . . . You don't work, you don't experience the stuff of existence, so where can you remember thought from!" (*K,* 115). Labor is now turning into a religious ritual during which one comes into contact with the "real thing," the "stuff of existence." Although Voshchev notes that these people do not look ecstatic—in fact, just the opposite, they

29. See Raimund Sesterhenn, *Das Bogostroitel'stvo bei Gor'kij und Lunacharskij, bis 1909* (Munich: Otto Sagner, 1982); and Clowes, *The Revolution of Moral Consciousness,* 200–223.

look dour and live in silence—he decides that they must know something that he does not, and so he decides to join them.

Chiklin's dream of the new proletarian home provides the next stage of higher existence that this ritual is meant to produce, that is, whole unalienated, collective thought. He imagines the new house that will be built on the foundation now being dug to provide the proletariat and their children a happy life, secure against the elements. Under these conditions, he believes, "joy will turn into thought" (*K*, 118). In other words, the enthusiasm of collective unity will lead to more productive kinds of thought in which body and spirit, self and other, are well integrated.

Chiklin's almost mystical dream expresses the workers' spontaneous surge of hope for the future. Soon, however, we hear the voices of the political organizers—that is, we may assume, of the Party—on the subject of collective enthusiasm. Whatever spontaneity one might have felt in the words of the workers is now lost, because enthusiasm imposed from above is no enthusiasm at all. A new fault line has been created between the inside and the outside—the bottom and the top—of the social structure, and with this split come doubts, alienation. Now, in his implicit attack on the idea of "*partiinost'*," Platonov is most critical and lays bare his substantial differences with official dialectical materialism. The party organizer at the foundation pit, Safronov, is the character that delivers the loudest lectures on enthusiasm and does so in increasingly harsh terms. The first instance comes at the end of the workday. Although Prushevsky informs the workers that they have completed their allotted hours, Chiklin and Safronov want to keep working. As Safronov says, "It's a long while until evening, why should we waste our lives, we're better off making something. After all, we are not animals, we can live for the sake of enthusiasm" (*K*, 120). The desire to feel enthusiastic becomes a way to keep tired workers at their shovels.

The next conversation about enthusiasm occurs when Voshchev again raises the frequently heard objection that he needs truth in order to work more productively. Safronov answers: "The proletariat lives for the enthusiasm of labor, Comrade Voshchev! It is high time you accepted this trend. The body of each and every member of the labor union should burn from this slogan" (*K*, 139). Now the enforced "should" of moralizing and preaching takes the place of spontaneous belief and feeling. Everything is expressed in the third person: Safronov does not feel this truth himself but imposes it as a rule on others.

With time, in the fall, the workers' dormitory is equipped with a radio. Personal speech is now fully replaced with political dogma, which the anarchistic invalid, Zhachev, calls, appropriately, the "noise of consciousness" (*K*, 142). When the radio malfunctions and falls silent, Safronov waxes eloquent in defense of the radio rhetoric. Afraid to "forget the duty of joy" (*K,* 142–143), he assumes the tone of Stalin and continues in the latter's style: "Whoever has a party membership in his pants must continually be sure that his body has enthusiasm for labor. I challenge you, Comrade Voshchev, to compete for a mood of the highest happiness!" (*K,* 143). He then embroiders on the origins of enthusiasm in Stalinist myth: "Let us ask the question: where did the Russian people originate! And we answer: in bourgeois triviality! It would have been born somewhere else but there wasn't any more room. And therefore we must throw each person into the soup [*rassol*] of socialism so that the skin of capitalism peels off and the heart pays attention to the heat of life around the camp fire of class struggle, and enthusiasm would come to life!" (*K,* 143). In this awful brew of mixed metaphors and odd logic the human, spontaneous element of enthusiasm has been lost. In this dogmatic way of thinking people are nothing but bits of sausage and meat in a briny broth. Though in theory they are "highly organized matter," to repeat Mitin's encyclopedia article, people in this Stalinist world are treated as *merely* matter.

Platonov's final commentary about the terrible effect of political control on the original vivifying idea of enthusiasm and communal consciousness comes in his depiction of the nameless activist at the communal farm who loves to study directives and manipulate matters in such a way as to create a good future for himself. The activist, who is quite a bureaucrat, sits awake at nights studying the new directives handed down to him: "Every night he read a new directive with the curiosity of future enjoyment, as if he were taking a peek into the passionate secrets of the adults in the center. It was a rare night when a directive did not appear, and before morning the activist would study it, by dawn accumulating the enthusiasm for unconquerable action" (*K,* 155). The activist's only motivation is to please the people at the "center"—that is, Stalin and his operatives in Moscow—never to serve the people on the farm. His bureaucratic self-interest has replaced even the stultifying dogmatic belief we find in Safronov. Whereas Safronov had dampened the original, semi-mystical enthusiasm of actual workers, the activist finally and fully perverts the concept. Thus the whole chain of development from feeling to dogma has been unfolded. "Enthusiasm" has become just a word that organizers and bureaucrats use to drive people to hard, senseless labor. Even this dialectical materialist "consciousness" has been killed.

Meanwhile, Voshchev's question about the meaning of life remains: Does dialectical materialism give us a sense of the significance of our lives? Just as in his unpublished article, "On Love," and in the novella, "The Innermost Man," Platonov, now more insistently, repeats the thought that, having destroyed religion, the new Soviet government must replace it with something more powerful. Although the God-building idea of "enthusiasm" may once

have inspired someone, in its vulgar, dogmatic form, it does not answer a religious need. Early on the factory committee had answered his query, as we
saw above, with the words: "Happiness will come from materialism . . . not
from meaning." When Voshchev asks his question of the activist, he receives
a similar answer: "The proletariat gets movement, . . . and whatever comes
his way, everything is his: whether it is truth or a kulak's sweater stolen with
lots of other things—everything goes into the organizational cauldron, and
you won't recognize anything" (K, 158). What is clear at the beginning, the
middle, and at the end of *The Foundation Pit* is that those in charge care
nothing for even trying to define what truth might indeed be. As Stalin had
suggested in his newspaper polemics in 1906, now, too, the "truth" can shift
and, by implication, be manipulated. Platonov has ferreted out this cynicism
at the heart of dialectical materialism from his own particular and increasingly independent "philosophical" standpoint.

The social implications of the dialectical materialist merging of self and
other into a united, enthusiastic proletarian whole means that there also
should be increasingly fewer differences between mental (for example, Prushevsky's) and physical (for example, Voshchev's) kinds of labor. Conse-
quently the tension between consciousness and matter should become less
palpable. Everyone will become conscious materialists, determined by the
same historical conditions and therefore conscious of the same thing. Everyone will believe that the proletarians are the rulers of the earth and that they
will open the way to a bright future, once they have cleared away the debris
of capitalism, its disjunctions and inequalities as well as its ideological
double standards. Theoretically only holdovers from an earlier, bourgeois
social order can sow the seeds of doubt. Someone like Prushevsky becomes
suspect, because he is educated and thus from the "middle class." Intellectually he is much more discerning than anyone else. In the proletariat there
is no room for doubt and alienation. Voshchev is scorned as a worker ruined
by bourgeois conditions, a holdover, someone who obviously has failed in
becoming reeducated. However, in fact, a great many "good workers" in the
story ask themselves questions and wonder about the meaning of the Soviet
project. It is not just Prushevsky and Voshchev but, much more secretly,
Chiklin, and even the political organizers Safronov and the collective farm
activist (K, 131, 155).

According to dialectical materialist theory, only people like Prushevsky
and a few holdovers, "worker-intellectuals" like Voshchev, should be *self*-
conscious. In theory, only the "bourgeoisie," that is, anyone with an education and engaged in "mental" labor, should question the limits of matter.
Proletarians are meant to be completely satisfied by the conditions of dialectical materialism and fully happy in their sense of belonging in the
world. Thus it is all the more pointed that not only Chiklin but the two po-

litical organizers, Safronov and the activist, also question their existence in their most secret thoughts. Gazing at his surroundings at the pit, Safronov looks at nature and starts to doubt whether their project to build a large home for the proletariat will work: "If one were to look along the bottom [of the pit], at the dry bits [*meloch'*] of soil and the grass that lived in the dregs, in poverty, then there was no hope in life; the common, universal ugliness and the uncultured gloominess of the people worried Safronov and jolted his ideological grounding. He even began to doubt the happiness of the future which he imagined to be something like blue summer lit by a motionless sun—day and night it was just too confused and futile around here" (*K*, 131). Safronov even trusts Chiklin enough to voice his worries: "But why is the field lying so boringly? Could it really be that inside the whole world is boredom and it is only we who have the five-year plan?" (*K*, 131). Similarly the activist spends his life at the communal farm, waiting happily for the next party directive. Nonetheless: "He occasionally froze for a moment at the thought of life's ennui—at such times he looked mournfully at any person who happened to be in front of him; now he felt the memory that he was a blockhead and a derelict—at least that was what he had sometimes been called in papers from the regional center" (*K*, 155). In both these instances, even for the party faithful, a gaping rift opens between "dialectical materialism," with its insistence on happiness and optimism, and the "reality" that many characters suspect actually exists.

The Foundation Pit concludes with a number of personal acts of revolt against dialectical materialism. Voshchev, who has been trying to satisfy his spiritual needs by surrendering himself to "ideology," decides that matter by itself contains no truth: "Voshchev also had grown so weak of body without ideology that he could not pick up an ax, and he lay down in the snow: all the same there was no truth in the world, or maybe it was to be found in some plant or heroic creature but a highway beggar came along and ate the plant or trampled the oppressed creature, and he himself died in an autumnal ravine, and the wind blew his body into nothing" (*K*, 171). The next sign of revolt can be seen in Voshchev's habit of collecting dead and forgotten things in his little kit bag. One sees this bag three times in the course of the novel, and each time it seems to carry a different meaning. The first time is at the start of the book, in late summer, when Voshchev puts a leaf into his bag (*K*, 111). The second is on his day of rest, when he collects "all kinds of unhappy junk of nature as documentation of the unplanned creation of the world, as facts of the melancholy of any living breath" (*K*, 138). Here the bag may be seen as proof against the idealists that there is no inherent, a priori order to the world. By the end of the novel, the bag contains many items that Voshchev has gathered from the collective farm. Now he registers his "possessions" in the bag with the activist at the collective farm, wanting to believe that everyone and everything will find its proper place in the sunny future of socialism: "Without actually realizing it, Voshchev accumulated in his bag, in a miserly way, the material remains of lost people who had lived like him without truth and who had died before the victorious end. Now he was presenting those liquidated laborers to the personage in power and in charge of the future in order by means of organization of eternal meaning for people to take revenge—for those who lay in the depths of the earth" (K, 182). Influenced by the activist and by his own dialectical materialist ideology, Voshchev, paradoxically, wants to believe in a final victory, an apocalypse, when everything will become meaningful. Such a victory is, of course, impossible if one is a true materialist and believes in the changing nature of the world and of values. (The activist makes an inventory of the items he uses for his own bureaucratic purposes, labeling them "census of the rich peasant [kulak], liquidated to death as a class, by the proletariat, in accordance with the escheated remains" [K, 182].) The bag of forgotten things perhaps gains its final significance in its third appearance as a bag of unusual toys for the little orphan Nastia. As toys, the items lose their significance as memories of meaningless lives, but they have gained new meaning as the building "material" for the imagination of a young person. They can now become part of some new whole.

The revolt that the bag of forgotten things represents is more subtle than the other forms of rejection of dialectical materialism. The bag functions as a metaphor for Voshchev's mental journey and, as such, emphasizes consciousness over pure matter. Perhaps in the spirit of Nikolai Fedorov's view of books as the living memory and personality of its author, each object is to be an "eternal memory of a forgotten person."[30] Memory and the constant consciousness that one needs to build meaning out of the past and in one's own present life far outweigh in importance actual things, tangible material being. Life is to be found in the synthetic power of memory and consciousness.

As the communal farm fails—it has used up everything confiscated from the kulaks and has no food of its own—Voshchev decides once again to take to the road. Here is his third rejection of "matter" as a philosophically deep and meaningful concept: "Voshchev opened the door of the Administration Building [Orgdom] out into space and recognized the desire to live into this fenced-off distance, where his heart could beat from more than the cold air, from the *true joy* [*istinnaia radost'*] of conquering the whole muddled *substance* [*smutnoe veshchestvo*] of the earth" (K, 193; emphasis added). Finally he feels real joy, and he has no doubts about it whatsoever. He does reappear

30. Michael Hagemeister, *Nikolaj Fedorov: Studien zu Leben, Werk und Wirkung* (Munich: Otto Sagner, 1989), 37.

to bring the bag of toys to Nastia and to give the dying girl one last hug and kiss. He has also brought along the peasants, who have begun to believe and want to help build the big house on the foundation pit. And then, after Nastia's death, he leaves once again, rejecting both dialectical materialism and communism (*K*, 196).

The Foundation Pit ends with a final rejection of two key ideas: the idea of matter as eternally shifting, changing substance and the opposing idea of happy, *unchanging*, collective, proletarian existence based on materialism. Here we are speaking of Nastia's burial in the foundation pit. Instead of promising a safe and happy communal existence, the foundation has become a grave for a little girl who had symbolized the promise of the future. Moreover, she is buried in such a way as to reject the notion of continual change in nature: "At noon Chiklin started to dig a special grave for Nastia. He dug for fifteen hours straight so that it would be deep and neither worm nor root nor warmth nor cold would dare to penetrate and so that the child would never be perturbed by the noise of life from the surface of the earth. The bed of the grave he hollowed out in eternal stone and prepared for it, as a kind of roof, a granite slab, so that the huge weight of the earth in the grave did not lie on the girl" (*K*, 197). Despite the materialist concept of continual change, what people really want is stability and security, both in life and in death.

It is time to ask, with Seifrid, whether *The Foundation Pit* is primarily political-philosophical satire or whether it makes a positive argument and assumes a position that could replace dialectical materialism.[31] Seifrid contends that Platonov, in his novel, approaches an existentialist worldview, which implies disagreement with dialectical materialism and its historical optimism, determinism, and dependence on a totalizing, centralized political order. Although no one in the novel articulates a debater's position against this pseudo-philosophy, there is certainly, as we have seen, a strong implicit argument against it. If there is a positive value defended in this darkly humorous book, then it is the value of continuing to ask questions and to worry about meaning. What has happened in *The Foundation Pit*, as in so many of Platonov's works, is that thinking, questioning, and doubting by ordinary people, carried on through conversation with oneself or with others, has gained new life. It can be said that at least the spirit of philosophy itself has been preserved—perhaps in its original, oral, most primitive sense, but nonetheless preserved.

If we can say that philosophy has been preserved, in what space and time does it exist? What authority does it have? Classical, idealist philosophy resides in a garden, private house, or some other place outside the ordinary,

---

31. Seifrid, "Writing against Matter," 371.

public locations of human affairs. If materialist thought resides within the bounds of chronological time, then idealist philosophy implies an eternity outside chronological time. "Philosophy"—understood here as the basic need to question, to think about "truth," and to make sense of one's existence, as the original "love of wisdom"—then Platonov's chronotope of philosophy suggests a time and place that is open and oriented in the present. As in Shestov's view, the road is perhaps the clearest image associated with the openness of philosophizing as questioning and questing. Voshchev, who is the most obvious and basic questioner, is associated with the road (*K*, 108–111, 193). The road contrasts with the construction site, where faith and hope reign, and with factories and farms, enclosed places where people live and dogmatism easily takes hold.

In conclusion, philosophical discourse with its interrogatives has been separated, in *The Foundation Pit,* from journalistic-political speech with its indicative and imperative forms. This fundamental discourse is oral, not bookish. It belongs to every human being, unlike Lev Karsavin's type of philosophy, which Platonov so firmly rejected in 1922. Rather like Shestov's thinking, it is interrogative in its syntax and antidogmatic in its orientation. Unlike dialectical materialism it gives equal weight to the two basic principles of consciousness and matter, and finds a complex and nuanced relationship between the two. Here dogma is the "matter" with philosophy in more than one way—dogmatic language ossifies the flow of the questioning consciousness as a "thing," almost as physical "matter," and thus dogma is what can go wrong with any abstract, conceptual thinking. Finally, this newly re-created openness and resistance to dogmatism is supported by the philosophical, questing chronotope of the road, which Shestov also preferred. A philosophical free will of sorts has been reasserted, in a much different style from that of Karsavin in his lecture of June 1921. And a new philosophizing voice arguing for principled subjectivity had the courage to be heard—no mean feat at the start of the Stalinist tyranny.

Chapter Ten

"Sheer Philosophy" and "Vegetative Thinking": Pasternak's Suspension and Preservation of Philosophy

Art never began. It was always there before it came into being. It is endless. And here at this moment behind me and in me, it is . . . as if it were bringing the moment up to take an oath.

Esthetics does not exist. It seems to me, its non-existence is a punishment for lying, simplifying, pandering, and condescending.

—Boris Pasternak, "A Number of Positions," 1918

Plato's thoughts about art are very close to me. . . . Tolstoy's intolerance, and even, as a type of quick temper, Pisarev's barbaric, iconoclastic gestures, as well. All this is close to me but in quite a different form. You should not think that art by itself is a source of greatness. By itself, it is a force of attraction that can be justified by the future alone.

—Letter from Boris Pasternak to V. Vs. Ivanov, July 1, 1958

"I don't like works that are devoted to philosophy alone. In my view, philosophy should be a spice used sparingly in art and in life. To make it the sole focus of one's efforts is just as strange as eating only horseradish."

—Boris Pasternak, *Doctor Zhivago*, 1957

AMONG SOVIET-ERA WRITERS Boris Pasternak (1890–1960) has given the best articulated and most complex definitions of, and "arguments" both for and against, his two great intellectual loves, poetry and philosophy. Pasternak was by far the most cultivated and educated of the philosophical writers, even more so than Losev. He was the only writer actually to have studied philosophy at a university and, as such, was a rare phenomenon in Russian cultural history. Critics have often argued that in Pasternak's literary work philosophy and poetry found a certain symbiosis.[1] In one sense they did enrich each other. Pasternak's poetry and prose is deeply philosophical, meditating on a number of issues relating to the nature of the self, perception, and creativity. Yet "philosophy"—for all Pasternak's love for the academic pursuit—was a problem that ran like a red thread throughout his life and work. His passion for philosophy put a certain stamp on his personal relationships, and he often had difficulty reconciling it with the expectations of the people closest to him, both friends and family. Most importantly, as I will argue here, it is philosophy as a *problem*—and not as a well-established language or intellectual practice that fuses easily with his poetic interests—that motivates his experiments with long prose narratives, his first autobiography, *Safe Passage* (*Okhrannaia gramota*, 1930), and *Doctor Zhivago* (1957).

Pasternak's memories of his childhood and student life leave a strong impression of philosophical culture in prerevolutionary Moscow. In *Safe Passage* he recalled the two key parts of this culture, philosophizing as artistic fashion and philosophy as an academic field, a form of knowledge. As an arbiter of intellectual fashion, the Symbolist-era composer Aleksandr Skriabin played a crucial role in Pasternak's adolescent years. Close to the Pasternak family, he was in some ways typical of Symbolist culture in that he enfolded his art in a patina of German philosophy.[2] Pasternak credited Skriabin with stimulating his interest in philosophy and directing him to study philosophy at Moscow University. The poet described the composer as he remembered him in 1904, before his prolonged sojourn in Italy: "He plays—which is beyond description—he takes supper with us, starts philosophizing, fools around and cracks jokes. I have the strong impression that he is terribly bored."[3] This kind of philosophizing, greatly inspired by Nietzsche, the most widely popular philosopher of the day, was part of a mystique, a persona.

Art and philosophy were discussed most substantially at meetings in the Symbolist publishing house Musaget.[4] Here Andrei Belyi and other Symbolists ran a regular "seminar" where philosophical ideas and approaches were discussed critically and in detail. Pasternak attended these meetings for

---

1. Lazar Fleishman, *Boris Pasternak: The Poet and His Politics* (Cambridge, Mass.: Harvard University Press, 1990), 38; Anna Han, "Poetika i filosofiia: Boris Pasternak i Gustav Shpet: vvedenie k teme," *Studia Slavica Academiae Scientiarum Hungaricae* 42, nos. 3–4 (1997): 301–316.

2. Ann M. Lane, "Bal'mont and Skriabin: The Artist as Superman," *Nietzsche in Russia*, ed. B. G. Rosenthal (Princeton, N.J.: Princeton University Press, 1986), 209–218.

3. Boris Pasternak, *Sobranie sochinenii*, 5 vols. (Moscow: Khudozhestvennaia literatura, 1989–1992), 4:152. Hereafter all citations in the text from Pasternak's works are given as *SS5* with the relevant volume and page numbers.

4. Magnus Ljunggren, *The Russian Mephisto: A Study in the Life and Work of Emilii Medtner* (Stockholm: Almquist and Wiksell, 1994), 38–44.

the first time in 1910 and then took part more seriously after his summer of philosophical study in Marburg. In 1913 he read his first paper, "Symbolism and Immortality," in this forum.[5]

The second aspect of philosophical culture that Pasternak described in his autobiography was the still poorly developed milieu of academic philosophical study at the university. At first the young student was dazzled by his classes and their daily revelations from Kant and Hegel. But eventually he realized that the academic study of philosophy was failing him where he needed it most (SS5, 4:159). He described his university courses as a "strange jumble of outlived metaphysics and uninspired enlightenment activity [neoperivsheesia prosveshchenstvo]. . . . The history of philosophy became dogmatic, and psychology degenerated into a lot of hot air and editorializing" (SS5, 4:165). Nonetheless, despite his misgivings about the intellectual qualifications of some of the older professors, Pasternak liked the younger faculty, particularly the Husserlian Gustav Shpet. He soon understood, however, that these few younger people were powerless to change the academic culture in which they worked.[6]

Pasternak makes an interesting and significant observation about the academic study of philosophy in these years: a great number of students were from relatively newly literate families and had often read very little. As a result the faculty was compelled to "teach in a popularizing way, spelling everything out," because so many of the students were inadequately prepared (SS5, 4:165), experiencing formal philosophy for the very first time. Pasternak's observation provides additional evidence that, in the first two decades of the twentieth century, philosophy was developing a truly broad appeal among an ever-growing body of students.

An intense café culture developed among small circles of Moscow University philosophy students. Pasternak remembered with great fondness and a measure of irony his philosopher friend, Dmitry Samarin, with whom he met frequently at the Café Grecque: "As soon as Samarin appeared and sat down at our table, he started to philosophize and, arming himself with a dry cookie, he would hold it out, like a conductor with his baton, and start to mark the logical rhythms of his speech. Throughout the pavilion there wafted a bit of Hegelian infinity, composed of alternating assertions and denials" (SS5, 4:166).

Not surprisingly Pasternak saw Russian philosophical culture as much less substantive than the German philosophy he experienced firsthand during his Marburg summer of 1912. Philosophy clearly occupied a prominent

---

5. Fleishman, Boris Pasternak, 46–54.
6. For information on Pasternak's relationship to Shpet, see, especially, Han, "Poetika i filosofiia."

place in German culture. The books by Marburg professors sold in ordinary bookshops and were obviously of interest to more than just a tiny circle of academics. Moreover, during the summer of 1912, Pasternak and his fellow students were excited about participating in a dramatic historical moment, the final year in the teaching career of the famous neo-Kantian philosopher Hermann Cohen.

Aside from Skriabin and a few student colleagues, Pasternak was quite isolated in his philosophical undertakings in Moscow. He had placed himself in an area of study that he truly enjoyed but one that was distant from the subjects he and his closest relatives loved most—art and music. In an early letter to the art historian P. D. Ettinger, from 1907, Pasternak wrote: "Papa has frequently criticized me for my philosophizing. . . . But what is art if not philosophy in a condition of ecstasy, if not the contemplation of cognition, passing into the realm of delight . . . or suffering."[7] Clearly Pasternak's father, and very likely this entire family of artists, viewed the arts as the highest form of human expression.

Judging from his early essays, Pasternak seemed to be trying to fit philosophy into this particular hierarchy. There is strong reason to believe that the young Pasternak had taken on the study of philosophy not as an end in itself but as an experience of ascetic cleansing in preparation for writing poetry.[8] By immersing himself in philosophy he was forcing himself away from the world of immediate sensory impressions. In *Safe Passage,* written much later, he remembered that during his university years he considered his attempts at poetry writing a weakness that he hid from all but his good friend, Sergei Durylin (*SS5,* 4:164). But in a fragment about the early nineteenth-century German writer Heinrich Kleist, written on the one hundredth anniversary of the writer's death in 1911—before the Marburg summer—Pasternak gave an account of Kleist's university study of philosophy that is more appropriate to his own particular evaluation of philosophical discourse.[9] At least at the initial stage Pasternak described Kleist holding philosophy and poetry in a close discursive relationship. In Pasternak's words: "When an artist joins a philosophical school, more than anyone he

7. Boris Pasternak, *Ob iskusstve* (Moscow: Iskusstvo, 1990), 295.

8. L. Fleishman, H.-B. Harder, and S. Dorzweiler, introduction to *Boris Pasternaks Lehrjahre: neopublikovannye filosofskie konspekty i zametki Borisa Pasternaka,* ed. L. Fleishman, H-B. Harder, and S. Dorzweiler, 2 vols. (Stanford: Stanford Slavic Studies, 1996), 2:1, 52. The editors of that volume see Pasternak's article on Kleist as an allegorical analysis of his own study of philosophy, emphasizing synthesis over system. In my view, the synthesis model ("symbiosis" [2:126], the "organic" life of philosophy in Pasternak's poetry [2:132]), operates to a degree for Pasternak, that is, at the early stages of the interaction between philosophy and poetry, but eventually it becomes strongly contested.

9. After a number of years in the army Kleist briefly studied philosophy, physics, mathematics, and government finance at the University of Frankfurt an der Oder.

turns out to be a philosopher at the first dialectical stage of development: his basic, inborn melody is a denial of the spontaneity of intuition" (*SS5*, 4:679).

Pasternak wrote in a speculative and personal vein about Kleist as an ascetic, performing "*podvigi,*" or acts of self-denial:

> I imagine Kleist almost insanely intense, a studious ascetic. I imagine him in his true philosophical moments, deeply into the unities that make up the fabric of nature and the systematic structure of its truth. He probably experienced these acts of self-cleansing-through-practicing-logic as a deep inward breath, full of tension, leading to a great, growing sigh. He probably also experienced these methodological unities as an intense leave-taking [from art], as straight as a shaft of light. Sensing in this voluntary exile of consciousness that he had abandoned the disorderly Heraclitan flow of the irrational, he sank into a creative-methodological slump and delayed his return [to art]. (*SS5*, 4:679–680)

We can elicit from this clumsy piece that the study of philosophy is appropriate for a person who knows he will eventually become a poet but has yet to mature inwardly. This person gains the critical skills to discern the "false forms around him, what is not eternal and not chaotic but merely familiar, and what is moral in a natural way, almost naturalist in the everyday, but not cultured in an ascetic way" (*SS5*, 4:680). The study of philosophy means an ascetic removal from sensory perception. It offers an artistic nature a measure of "alienation" (*SS5*, 4:680), a distance from the natural, sensory, and familiar that excites the artistic imagination.

This pattern of ascetic self-denial that Pasternak found in Kleist can also be seen directly in his own letters to his family during his summer in Marburg. His first letters to his parents conveyed a sense of guilt at enjoying himself so much: "Nature's lively enchantment . . . keeps me from studying despite my desire to study" (*SS5*, 5:27). He referred to this sensual appeal of nature as the "seducer," and he assured his parents, "I am pretending here that I don't understand the language of the seducer" (*SS5*, 5:27). He insisted: "I could quit everything and, of course, theory first and foremost, and be left with one thing: a sharp receptiveness and a kind of obedience to my impressions. That's precisely how art starts. . . . But I came here to study" (*SS5*, 5:27). Despite this attempt to deny himself the pleasures of Marburg culture and the bucolic surroundings, his letters are filled with intense descriptions of nature that border on ecstatic eroticism.

In his discussion of Kleist Pasternak formed an initial concept of philosophy that made this discourse an essential stage in the growth of an artist: through the lenses of logic an artist learns to see more than what is directly and randomly "out there." Philosophy provides the basic framework for "culture" and for creative activity, which Pasternak conceived as deeply as-cetic, in the sense that a person had to sublimate and rechannel basic human pleasures in order to perceive and produce art of lasting value. Phi-losophy provides a discipline through which erotic energy is sublimated as creative energy. However, beyond this initial stage, the languages of philos-ophy and poetry part ways and are no longer complementary. Here the symbiosis ends. Again referring to Kleist, Pasternak asserted: "When a philosopher develops to the level of system-making, or, following one branch of the system, becomes an academic, the artist takes his leave of him—his [the artist's] idealism is a game, not a system—a symbolic con-struct, but not reality" (*SS*5, 4:681). Already in 1911 Pasternak understood that his philosophizing would remain at the first level of a critical, ascetic act of distancing oneself from reality in order to perceive it more fully. De-spite his enjoyment of formal philosophy and the fact that his talent at-tracted the admiring attention of his professors both in Russia and Ger-many, he would choose not to philosophize at the level of rigorous, systematic thought. He undoubtedly respected academic philosophy, par-ticularly, as in the case of Shpet or Cohen (*SS*5, 5:30), when it was an intel-lectual passion and a life drama, but he was not inclined to follow it.

During the early part of the summer of 1912 Pasternak's letters home ex-pressed his suspicion that there was very little of the truly "philosophical" in him: "I have lost that simplicity which is the simplicity of good order and of a system in the making" (*SS*5, 5:28). Although he knew he could "do" sys-tematic, critical philosophy, he was not sure that philosophy was really vital to him: "I can find my way to it. But I am overcome with doubt: do I need this?" (*SS*5, 5:29). Although in the sketch of Kleist Pasternak had implied that philosophy is "truer" than art, somehow closer to reality, now, a year later, he was much more aware of the importance and potential truth of art. As he wrote to his family: "Local nature and Gothic architecture make the exceptional position of art so obvious" (*SS*5, 5:29).

At first implicitly and later more directly, Pasternak began to probe the ways in which art comes to dominate philosophy. His letter to his sister, Josephine, of May 17, 1912, first expressed what would be a lifelong concern with the truthfulness of perception, of "seeing," and of all writing. He ad-vised her: "Only write the truth, the truth. . . . Don't fake" (*SS*5, 5:32). Here Pasternak is already implicitly defying the age-old philosophical assertion, since Plato in *The Republic,* that art is removed from truth. This is a concern that clearly makes philosophical demands on art and challenges classical philosophy on its claim of its more reliable "truth."

In notes to a presentation entitled "Symbolism and Immortality" ("Simvolizm i bessmertnost'"), given at Musaget in February 1913, Pasternak explicitly probed the impact of verbal art on philosophy. He recounted

Socrates' dream from *Phaedo* in which the philosopher is called to compose music. Socrates assumes that he already was "composing music" by engaging in philosophy, which he calls the "noblest and best of music." Pasternak was sensitive to the classical argument between philosophy and poetry, and he emphasized the "envy" philosophy "feels" toward poetry. Although "poetry has always loved philosophy," Pasternak claimed, it is an "unequal" love, unrequited by philosophical discourse (*SS5*, 4:246). His attitude toward this relationship was succinct: "One of philosophy's outlived tasks is to take revenge on music." He continued: "Philosophy is jealous of poetry, it often imagines the insult that music brought to its deity. Revenge can be carried out on music" (*SS5*, 4:246). The problem philosophers traditionally find with lyric poetry—and here Pasternak anticipated by many decades a post-structuralist view of language—is the difference in the type of speech that distinguishes poetry from philosophy; it is the same old disparity of associative language versus representative language: "The music of the word is not a direct reference, the [poetic] word has no direct meaning. Such devices always reveal the lack of correspondence between the topic and the expression. The trope is witness either to the surplus of expression or its inadequacy, about pathos or about difficulty" (*SS5*, 4:247). An even clearer articulation of this thought is expressed in a letter, from July 1914, to his parents. Here he marked out the originality of poetic speech as that which "is capable at this moment of slipping away from a similarity with itself."[10]

Curiously, despite his attraction to poetry and poetic language, and his determination to abandon philosophy, Pasternak was still identifying himself as a "philosopher" as late as 1913 in his notes to "Symbolism and Immortality" (*SS5*, 4:247). Much has been written recently about the reasons for Pasternak's departure from the field of philosophy.[11] Surely it was not a foregone conclusion, despite the young writer's continual enchantment with the possibilities of poetry. Indeed, in *Safe Passage,* he wrote that he assumed he might eventually work in some way with philosophy (*SS5*, 4:165). And although he did not pursue an academic career in philosophy, the question of philosophy clearly remained at the center of his artistic consciousness.

A genuine problem in opting for philosophy as a career in Russia was the lack of a close professional philosophical community. Although certainly Pasternak had his group at the Café Grecque, he admired some of the philosophy faculty at Moscow University, and he had the seminars at the Musaget Publishing House, but these bits and pieces were not enough. There was no support for formal philosophy among his family, and particularly among his women friends and relatives whose opinion he valued

10. Pasternak, *Ob iskusstve,* 305.
11. See, especially, Fleishman, Harder, and Dorzweiler, Introduction, 1:11–138.

highly. As with the Bakunin sisters in the 1830s, philosophy seemingly held no interest for the young women relatives and friends closest to Pasternak. As early as the winter of 1910, his cousin, Olga Freidenberg, who would later become a leading classicist in Leningrad, wrote to invite him to St. Petersburg. Her explicit purpose was to dissuade her young cousin from a career in philosophy: "I want to tell you not to study philosophy, that is, not to make it a goal in itself. That would be a mistake you would live with the whole of your life."[12] Freidenberg's diary from that romantic summer of 1910 continues in a more personal vein: "He [Pasternak] sat at a distance and philosophized, trying to speak louder and more dryly than usual, and I was bored and felt disappointed."[13] Freidenberg hoped for romance, while Pasternak appeared to her simply to be holding forth on abstractions.

During the Marburg summer of 1912 Pasternak was filled with anxiety and excitement at the prospect of studying philosophy with one of the great names of the day. He thrilled at the heightened atmosphere around Hermann Cohen and loved the dramatic verve of the old man's lectures. He wavered between his perpetual feelings of inadequacy and his pride at being offered the possibility of making a career of philosophy in Germany. The actual turning point in his decision to leave philosophy as a career possibility came when his sister, Josephine (who later became a philosopher!), and the two Vysotskaia sisters, whom Pasternak admired, mocked him for his philosophical interests. At a birthday party in Kissingen for Ida Vysotskaia, in July 1912, Josephine, Ida, and her sister, Olga, apparently made terrible fun of Pasternak. A few days later Pasternak, in a dark mood, wrote to his good friend, A. L. Stikh: "I'm burying philosophy. . . . All the people I care most about have turned away from me, either openly or in secret" (*SS5*, 5:64). He went on to cite a series of responses from Josephine and the others:

> Olia: "God, how boring all your conclusions are!" Ida: "Try to live normally; your life style has led you astray; all these people who haven't had a square meal or a good sleep find in themselves all sorts of wild, fantastic ideas." Zhonia: "Tell me, Boria, have you gotten stupider? Have you gotten to be like everyone else? Your studies may be different from those of other people in the sense that you can't do anyone any good with it." (*SS5*, 5:64)[14]

12. E. V. Pasternak and E. B. Pasternak, *Perepiska Borisa Pasternaka* (Moscow: Khudozhestvennaia literatura, 1990), 21.

13. Ibid., 26.

14. Ironically a number of these young girls ended up, as adults, quite drawn to and active in philosophy. Josephine studied philosophy in Berlin in the 1920s, and in 1929 she received a Ph.D. in Munich for a thesis on the psychology of perception. It was she who ultimately published in philosophy. She died in 1993; an essay she wrote on cognition was published posthumously. See Josephine Pasternak, *Indefinability: An Essay in the Philosophy of Cognition* (Copenhagen: Museum Tusculanum Press, 1999). Olga Freidenberg also became involved in philosophy through her study of classical literature. See E. V. Pasternak and E. B. Pasternak, *Perepiska Borisa Pasternaka*, III, 137.

Pasternak's response to this barrage was to shun philosophy: "I have a horror of work that the feminine half [*zhenstvennost'*] neither acknowledges nor needs" (*SS5*, 5:66).

This lack of a close community, and particularly of a community in which women participated, would be decisive for the evaluation of philosophy as a discourse in Pasternak's two major prose works, *Safe Passage* and *Doctor Zhivago*. In these works philosophical and poetic speech each have a formative influence, although finally philosophical discourse is accorded second place. And, in both, Pasternak would see women playing a decisive role in this diminution of philosophy.

Pasternak's sensitivity to the judgments of the women around him may possibly have been crucial to the structure of *Safe Passage*. The German scholar and Pasternak's friend, Nikolai Vilmont, wrote in his memoirs that philosophy—indeed academic, formal philosophy—was to have played a much more central role in *Safe Passage* than it did. Through a kind of self-censorship, according to Vilmont, Pasternak decided to exclude three pages devoted to a supposedly original idea he had expressed in a conversation with the philosopher, Ernst Cassirer, in Marburg. The following is Vilmont's version of the conversation that allegedly took place during Cohen's jubilee in 1912:

> During the conversation Boris Leonidovich touched on the question of the "modality" of concepts, about their "principle non-identity," as he put it, in connection with their "includability" [*vkliuchaemost'*] in various spheres of scientific and cultural consciousness, in general. He especially asserted, that, for example, the concept of time as the "fourth dimension" in no way excluded other "modal" meanings along with the one it acquired in Einstein's theory—let us say, in the sphere of history, in the function of a "regulatory concept of the historical process." And, further, he expressed the thought that, according to his understanding, it is possible to approach the problem posed by the head of the Marburg School [Cohen]—the problem of the "integrity of human nature," and in the same way the concept of man—only from the standpoint of *Sprachphilosophie* . . . the *critical philosophical history of language formations* that rests on the analysis of "modality" of concepts that have taken shape in the course of centuries in language as all cultured humanity has used it—in its past, present and probable future.[15]

We find in this idea, as Vilmont reproduced it, a "linguistic turn," that is, a linguistic perspectivism that subtly challenges the notion of the absoluteness

---

15. Nikolai Vil'mont, *O Borise Pasternake* (Moscow: Sovetskii pisatel', 1989), 148; emphasis added. There is some doubt as to the validity of these memoirs, which have never been verified. In a phone conversation of December 1998 Pasternak's son, Evgenii Borisovich Pasternak, claimed that the three pages have never been found and that Vil'mont's memoirs, written many years after the fact, could clearly contain errors.

of concepts, long before it became fashionable to do so in the West. If Vilmont is correct, Pasternak was pointing to the historicity of word usage and its impact on the way that concepts are formed. It is entirely plausible that Vilmont was remembering accurately, since the entire passage about Venice in part 2 of *Safe Passage* is devoted to pointing out the mutability of concepts, but now narrated in the guise of the musings of a student-traveler.[16]

Vilmont recounted that, when Pasternak read the three pages to him concerning the conversation with Cassirer, he begged Pasternak to include them in *Safe Passage* since his was such an original idea. Sensitive to the historical impact of poetry on philosophy, Vilmont compared this idea to the "infamous youthful sketch of Hölderlin that supposedly lay at the foundation of the philosophical systems of his classmates, Schelling and Hegel, at Tübingen Theological Seminary—a sketch that was constantly discussed in all the most recent works on the history of German classical idealism."[17] Equally sensitive to the political position of philosophy, and particularly idealist philosophy, in the Soviet state, Pasternak declined to reinsert these philosophical pages. He was aware that the increasingly tight censorship might prevent such a discussion from seeing the light of day.

Still more intriguing is the other reason Pasternak allegedly gave for deleting this passage, as it corroborates the pattern of hypersensitivity to his female audience that develops in *Safe Passage* itself. As reported by Vilmont, Pasternak sensed that the passage in question would "turn many [readers] away from *Safe Passage* because it is sheer philosophy."[18] Of particular note, Pasternak named the two women in his life in 1930 whose opinions, at least as he imagined them to be, mattered a great deal: Zina Neigauz, who would soon become his second wife, and Irina Asmus, the wife of Pasternak's good friend, the historian of philosophy V. F. Asmus.

Despite his hesitations about formal philosophy Pasternak kept a warm personal interest in philosophy. In the 1920s Vilmont, according to his own memoirs, largely learned to read philosophy under Pasternak's influence. Pasternak was a signatory in 1924 to a letter sent to the Marburg neo-Kantian Paul Natorp, on his seventieth birthday. Later, in the 1930s, he was involved with a small circle of friends who were engrossed in philosophy. And

---

16. It is curious that Pasternak, in this instance, would seem to be in agreement with a philosopher with whom he never agreed, Nietzsche, who, in *The Gay Science* and *Beyond Good and Evil*, among other works, is sensitive to the ways that word use changes and the effect this has on particular concepts. Nietzsche's focus, of course, is on ethics and morality, whereas Pasternak's is on the cultural impact of concepts first introduced by those who assume political power. It is also true that this trend in Pasternak's thinking anticipated the emergence of discourse theory in its Foucaultian version, as we are using it here, in his concern with the "philosophical history of language formations."

17. Vil'mont, *O Borise Pasternake*, 149.

18. Ibid.

finally, as mentioned above, V. F. Asmus, one of the only reputable Soviet-era historians of philosophy, was Pasternak's close friend and spent many summers at his dacha in Peredelkino.[19]

Although Pasternak mistrusted "sheer philosophy" and worried about the reactions of both his official and female readers, still he placed a discussion about the value of philosophy at the center of *Safe Passage*. His intentions concerning discourse in *Safe Passage* were made clear in a letter from March 1931 to his English-language translator, George Reavey. The focus of this work, he wrote, was intentionally philosophical. He was constructing an "aesthetic," although it was meant to be the self-defined aesthetic of a free artist who was interested in asserting himself and his art as a force and power unto itself, not the handmaiden of a philosophical system or a political power. Pasternak described *Safe Passage*: "This is a series of recollections. By themselves they would not be of any interest, if they did not include honest and direct efforts to understand what culture and art are" (*SS*5, 4:811). In a letter from November 1932 he asserted even more clearly that his speech in *Safe Passage* is not meant to be poetic or associative but rather to be representative. In short, he was employing the language of discourse: "For me this is the most important of all my works so far. In this book I *do not depict* but think and converse. I try to be not so much interesting as *precise*" (*SS*5, 4:812; emphasis added). He further conveyed to Reavey that *Safe Passage* needed to be translated "precisely," as one would a "scientific" work.

In his book, *The Philosophical Disenfranchisement of Art* (1986), Arthur Danto argues convincingly that in the modernist period artists in all media fought back against the tendency of systematic philosophy to theorize art, thereby bracketing, controlling, and devaluing it.[20] Artists and writers have articulated their own aesthetics, thus contesting discursive territory traditionally accorded to philosophy. In these letters, as well as in *Safe Passage* itself, we hear the voice of a person intent on using representative language, the "exact" language of a scientific or formal philosophical discourse. In his effort to generate his own definitions and boundaries, to make critical thinking serve to defend his art, Pasternak is a supremely "modernist" artist.

The narrative form and general "plot" of *Safe Passage*, if indeed there is one, is a story of liberation from various claims on art and different attempts to subjugate it. Pasternak starts with an association of art with femi-

19. For more about Asmus's teaching in philosophy at Moscow Univeresity, see N. V. Motroshilova, "Pamiati Professora (Predislovie k publikatsii)," *Voprosy filosofii* 6 (1988): 67–70.

20. Arthur Danto, *The Philosophical Disenfranchisement of Art* (New York: Columbia University Press, 1986), 11–12.

ninity, unfree and in chains: "In the spring of 1901, in the zoo, there was an exhibition of a division of amazons from the [African] country of Dagomey. . . . [M]y first sense of woman was linked to the sensation of a naked body, suffering and enclosed in itself, a parade from the tropics to the beat of a drum. . . . [E]arlier than normal I became a slave to forms [*forma*] because I had seen on them [the amazons] the (uni)form [*forma*] of slaves" (*SS*5, 4:150). The book then ends with the suicide of the Futurist poet and enfant terrible of the literary world Vladimir Mayakovsky, which Pasternak ascribes to a concept of self enslaved to egotism and self-will.

In the course of *Safe Passage*, Pasternak defines and justifies verbal art, particularly poetry, in relation to other kinds of speech—historiography, music, philosophy, and political rhetoric. He proceeds by denying that he is a successful practitioner of any of these types of speech, but then he appropriates, amoeba-like, key aspects of the language relevant for the artistic domain. Like Aristotle, in *The Poetics*, Pasternak starts out by finding "history" most wanting in terms of its truth-value. Aristotle criticizes historiography because it describes only what has been and produces statements only about specific, "singular" issues, whereas poetry expresses the power of imagination and has the ability to articulate universal statements. Pasternak reproaches the kind of reader who "loves fables and horror stories, and who views history as a story with a never-ending continuation" (*SS*5, 4:151). This type of reader likes what is familiar and what has already been interpreted for him. In short, this reader does not want to think: "He drowns in forewords and introductions, whereas, for me, life opened up only where [this reader] is inclined to draw conclusions" (*SS*5, 4:151). Because historiography surveys and narrates the little dead parts and pieces of the past without understanding the whole, Pasternak associates it with death: "The inner structure of history is associated in my understanding with the image of inevitable death. I came fully to life only in those situations when the tedious boiling down of parts came to an end and, having dined on the whole, well-fed feeling broke free in all its breadth" (*SS*5, 4:151). It is worth noting that in his critique Pasternak makes use of poetic figures, particularly paronomasia, to underscore obliquely, by association, the weakness of "rational understanding" (*ponimaniiu*) and its link to "inevitable" (*neminuemoi*) death. "Rational understanding" and "inevitability" are concepts that Pasternak connects not logically but figuratively. Historical events give him the raw material that his imagination can then synthesize in new ways. At the end of *Safe Passage* Pasternak's reproach is tied to the final scene of the suicide of Mayakovsky, who "had been spoiled by the future," had rejected all history and always lived for the future, but whose life now, in 1930, ironically belonged wholly to the past (*SS*5, 4:239).

Another "language" in Pasternak's field of cultural languages is, as with Losev, music. But whereas Losev views music as a pre-discursive link to primal chaos and dark matter, Pasternak sees it as a "grammar," highly ordered and logical in its own way. He speaks, for example, of the "syntax" of his mother's piano playing, and refers to a certain number of measures in a piece as a "sentence" (SS5, 4:152). Recall that Pasternak was such a gifted pianist and composer that as a young man he gave serious thought to devoting his life to music. Looking back, he punishes himself with the memory that he lacked perfect pitch and was unfit to "speak" in the language of music, thus forcing himself to forfeit his dream (SS5, 4:154). He elevates his mentor, Skriabin, and praises his music as a medium that leads to new "knowledge," meant here as experience that can open up new realms. Pasternak described Skriabin's rehearsals of "Ecstasy" in 1909: "This was the first human settlement in worlds opened by Wagner for fantasies and mastodons" (SS5, 4:153).

Early on, Pasternak composed his own musical pieces, which he proudly showed to his idol, Skriabin. He was shocked and chagrined, however, when Skriabin, who had the perfect pitch that Pasternak coveted, hugely improved these compositions simply by changing the key. In Safe Passage, following this particular incident with Skriabin, music ceases to function as a language unto itself. Still, Pasternak reminds us that the question as to "what music is" will continually reemerge later "in relation to poetry" (SS5, 4:159). His point of departure is the art of the great Symbolists Aleksandr Blok and Andrei Belyi, in which music interlaces with poetry. He then moves beyond these mentors to relate verbal and musical art to the mundane detail of the everyday as the three ingredients of art that ultimately give meaning to "real" history and historical discourse. He writes: "We drag everyday life into prose for the sake of poetry. We drag prose into poetry for the sake of music. That was how I named art, in the broadest sense of the word, placed on the clock of the living human race, [regularly] striking its generations" (SS5, 4: 161). By inference, the image of humanity as a clock that strikes regularly during each generation suggests that music can convey a historical rhythm. Still later, it will be the language of music that makes philosophy less acceptable to Pasternak. Dmitry Samarin's rhythm, when he uses a cookie at the Café Grecque to beat out the rhythm of his latest idea, is at once comical and annoying (SS5, 4:166). Philosophy, by implication, lacks the genuine rhythm of the everyday.

At first glance, the role of philosophical discourse per se does not seem to be very significant in Safe Passage. We have seen how paranomasia and other uses of associative language overshadow the logical, direct, generalizing discourse of rigorous philosophizing. As we know, Pasternak studies philosophy to hide his efforts at writing poetry (*SS*5, 4:164). He abandons philosophy because he believes that his formal philosophizing is unoriginal and because his audience disapproves. Perhaps most important, however, is his sense that philosophy is leading him nowhere. He realizes that he is yielding to what he calls "vegetative thinking" (*SS*5, 4:184). For him, vegetative thinking is the tendency of an overzealous student writing a term paper not to focus on primary issues but to branch out, overemphasizing and overly researching minor points. The final result is "vegetative" in the sense that, although the term paper is decorated with an abundance of citations, like leaves on a tree, it is not "organic." There is no dynamic, aggressive growth toward genuine insight.

Despite this rejection of formal philosophy, philosophy is at least as important as the musical "grammar" of rhythm for the structure of *Safe Passage*. Part 1 is "about" philosophy as a problem in Pasternak's creative life. Philosophical discourse plays a palpable role in his efforts to "think" and "converse," to say something "precise" about art. Although in his descriptions of his philosophical studies in Marburg, as well as other experiences of that summer in 1912, he appropriates philosophical territory while parodying and sloughing off philosophical discourse itself, he also uses reasoned discourse to define, justify, and defend his art against historiographical, philosophical, and political encroachments. In doing so, he develops his own brand of living critical thought, with its claims to truth and authenticity, and he structures his own kind of aesthetic theory that, despite his disclaimers, emerges from within his art and is not imposed on art by other discourses.

The chief aspects of philosophizing that Pasternak appreciates are precisely its art, its passion, and its drama. In Marburg the lectures of Hermann Cohen—vibrant, passionate, original, and deep—revitalize Pasternak's enthusiasm for abstract thought. He now sees that philosophy is a serious part of the history of culture, available in ordinary bookstores, read by educated people, and followed and adored by crowds of students. Pasternak notes:

The Marburg movement captivated me in two ways. First, it was original; it razed everything to its foundations and built on bare ground. It did not share the lazy routine of all kinds of "isms" that always grasped onto a facile tenth-hand omniscience—always ignorant and always—for that as well as other reasons—fearful of scrutiny in the free air of the eons of culture. The Marburg school did not succumb to terminological inertia and always kept to the primary texts, to the original receipt slips of thought, left behind in the history of science. If popular philosophy talks about what this or that writer thinks, and popular psychology speaks of what an average person thinks, if formal logic teaches how to proceed in a bakery so you get the right change—then the Marburg school was interested in how science has thought throughout its uninterrupted authorship of twenty-five centuries, at the hot beginnings and sources of world-class discovery. In this situation, as if authorized by history itself, philosophy grew young again and became unrecognizably intelligent, turning from a problematic discipline into a true discipline about problems—which is what it should be. (SS5, 4:169)

Pasternak is also attracted by how well the Marburg philosophers know history and how much they value it—not as a "shrine" but "with Hegelian eyes, that is, ingeniously generalized but still within the exact borders of sound truthfulness" (SS5, 4:170). These philosophers "did not speak of the stages of the world but rather, for example, about the correspondence of the Bernouilli family, and at the same time they knew that any thought from however distant a time, caught red-handed at the scene and in the act, must completely withstand our logical analysis. That is, a very old philosophy can come alive again in our own day; otherwise it belongs to archaeology" (SS5, 4:170). The philosophers of the Marburg school insist that philosophical texts participate in current, living dialogue. These qualities of intellectual independence, energy, and rigor are precisely what attracts Pasternak to Cohen.

The second section of *Safe Passage* is devoted to establishing the authority of art. At the start of part 2, Pasternak claims for art a profound truthfulness, as if in answer to Plato's contention that art, as a mere image of an ideal form, is further from the true form itself than philosophy is. To Plato, art is deceptive. Pasternak agrees that art deals in images, for example, not with humanity itself but with the image of humanity, "*obraz cheloveka.*" Here the agreement with Plato ceases, because Pasternak insists that the image of the historically existing object is more than that object itself. Thus the image of humanity is "more than humanity" (SS5, 4:179). Pasternak maintains, moreover, that, however earnestly it may be held, truth is always relative. Even if one tells the truth all the time, each of the truths one tells is conditional. It passes from the context in which it was told into a new context and, at that point, can be deceptive (SS5, 4:179). Pasternak claims that only an *image* has the ability to remain true over time. He sees it as the difference between the Russian verbs *vrat'* (to fib) and *obmanyvat'* (to deceive): "In Russian *vrat'* means to embellish [*nesti lishnee*] rather than to deceive [*obmanyvat'*]. In this sense art lies as well. Its image embraces life, not looking for an audience. Its truths [*istiny*] are not decorative but capable of eternal development" (SS5, 4:179). In Pasternak's view, for example, art talks about love and sex but, in doing so, does much more than merely serve the needs of biological instinct. Art is neither a medical theory nor a guide to hygiene, nor is it a work of pornography meant to whet sexual appetites.

Although Pasternak agrees with Formalist analysis of literary art as device and technique (techne), he also insists that it is a language of mystery. It is true in that it is close to nature, but it also embellishes on nature. Even as it distances and estranges us from the familiar, it also has the power to name and thus to shape and focus reality. In the presence of art, Pasternak writes, "we cease to recognize reality. [Reality] appears before us as some new category. And this category seems to be the proper condition of [reality] and not to have been made by us. Apart from this condition, everything in the world has been named. It alone has no name and is new. We try to name it. Art is the result" (SS5, 4:186). Thus art is a kind of surplus that penetrates reality and lends it force.

A space for Pasternak's own aesthetic philosophizing is provided ironically through disclaimer and denial that he is indeed offering an aesthetic theory. For example, in defining what exactly Safe Passage is about, he speaks of his thinking in the subjunctive rather than the indicative mood. However, while seeming not to commit himself to a rigorous, "scientific" aesthetic, he takes scientific inquiry as his point of departure:

> If with my knowledge, capabilities, and spare time I were to decide now to write a creative aesthetic, I would base it on two concepts, the concepts of force [sila] and of symbol. I would show that, in contrast to science—which analyzes nature in the dichotomy of a shaft of light—art is interested in life as it is *penetrated* by a ray of force [luch silovogo]. I would understand my concept of force in its broadest sense—as theoretical physics does—with the only difference that I would not be talking directly about the principle of force but about its voice, its presence. I would explain that, in the framework of self-consciousness, force is called feeling. (SS5, 4:187)

Pasternak suggests that with his "creative aesthetic" he will do more than scientific thinking can accomplish. His writings will show art as a force that penetrates much deeper into the nature of reality than science with its empirical mode of inquiry and representative forms of language can do. He compares his project with "science," drawing on scientific imagery, basing his idea of force loosely on the concept of natural force in physics. His focus is not, however, to establish objective principles but to speak of subjective "voice" and "presence," to establish the artist's autonomy and authority. In the framework of artistic identity, "force" is the same as "feeling."

Pasternak proceeds to build an alliance of art and science, with their concepts of "force," against the claims of political rhetoric. He aligns literary "realism" with science in the sense that art "did not invent metaphor but found it in nature and reproduced it devoutly [sviato]" (SS5, 4:188). Art is driven by the same keen, or perhaps even more intense, powers of observation that are at the heart of science, the same capacity to describe things exactly as they are. Art goes beyond science, according to Pasternak, in that it is "realist as an activity but symbolic as a fact" (*SS5*, 4:188). Pasternak's concept of true art resembles Viacheslav Ivanov's symbolist concept of a "higher reality," one that surpasses mere sensory reality. Art borders on the religious and the mythical in its ability to synthesize meaning. Here Pasternak remarks cryptically:

> Art is symbolic in the figure of its attraction. Its only symbol is in the brightness of its images, free of dogma, which is true of all art. The mutual interchangeability [*vzaimozamenimost'*] of images is a sign of a situation in which the parts of reality are mutually indifferent. The mutual interchangeability of images—or art—is a symbol of force [*sila*].
>
> Properly speaking, only force requires a language of physical proof. The other aspects of consciousness do not require comment. For these [aspects] it is but a step to conceptual analogies for light: a number, a precise concept, an idea. But force, the fact of force, force lasting just the moment of its own appearance, has nothing beside the shifting language of images, that is, the language of signs that accompanies it.
>
> The direct speech of feeling is allegorical and irreplaceable. (*SS5*, 4:188)

And in his note to this last sentence Pasternak adds: "Individual words in art, like all concepts, come alive through cognitive processes. But the word of all art, [a word] that does not lend itself to citation, resides in the movement of allegory itself, and this word speaks symbolically of force [*sila*]" (*SS5*, 4:188 n. 1). Here Pasternak draws the chief distinction between scientific-philosophical discourse and poetic language that makes artistic language more powerful and more meaningful than scientific language alone. The artistic word can be "discourse," but it is also more than discourse because it is not interchangeable with other synonyms. It is equal only to itself because it has such a broad field of meanings and associations that scientific discourse lacks. And it is precisely this allusiveness that permits the artistic word to be the conduit for this mystical "force" that Pasternak intuits and that raises it above mere discourse. Pasternak's high valuation of instinctive, revelatory language bears a distant resemblance to Solovyov's (and perhaps Losev's) preferences. All three focus on images of light as the key to higher meaning. Indeed, for Pasternak, images of light contain the very essence of the concept of "force" [*sila*].

Pasternak's central concern in his discussion is to put art beyond the reach of political control. He raises the poetic image above the straightforward symbols of political power. He dwells, for example, on the *pianta leone,* the lion of St. Mark, a representation of medieval Venetian power, and the guillotine of revolutionary France—both of which decayed, respectively, into comic images of Pantaloon in the Commedia dell' Arte and the guillotine brooch in nineteenth-century France. By contrast, in Pasternak's view, images that carry "force," as biblical images do, continually come back to life and are filled with new meaning. He writes: "The Bible is less a book with a fixed text than the scrapbook of humanity, and that is true of everything that lasts through the ages. . . . it is alive not when it is dogmatic, but rather when it is receptive to all allegorical texts through which the ensuing centuries look back on it" (*SS5*, 4:208). Art that participates in this deep textual history possesses self-awareness and does not become a slave to political ideologies, to religious dogma, or to any sort of value imposed on it. Art, as Pasternak conceives it, withstands Nietzsche's criticism in *On the Genealogy of Morals* that art is merely the servant of power.

Let us now return to Pasternak's uses of philosophical discourse in *Safe Passage*. Although he bids farewell in part 1 to the study of formal philosophy, philosophical discourse and the vocabulary of concepts and ideas continue to reemerge in a reduced form that underscores the non-absolute quality of abstract thought, its changeability, its ultimate historicity. He remarks playfully, for example, that colors, in his dreams, "moved and drew conclusions" (*SS5*, 4:206). In his discussion of the shift from a symbol of power to a symbol of popular culture he notes the process of change in the meaning of "concepts" (*SS5*, 4:206).

In conclusion, Pasternak's chief goal in *Safe Passage* is to assert that verbal art has greater expressive power, force of truth, and longevity than both philosophy and science, on the one hand, and political symbol, on the other. And if Vilmont has indeed remembered correctly, Pasternak's point resounds even louder in that he actually "erased" overt philosophical discourse from this very important work as he did not dare to include his own original philosophical thought. At the same time, this alleged "erasure," if true, adds further testimony to the great importance the poet still attached to philosophical concerns. In any case, if Pasternak has "suspended" philosophy, he has also "preserved" it, at least in part, by upholding aesthetics as a critical area of thought. Now, however, it is no longer the domain of the philosopher but the realm of the autonomous, articulate artist. The key point is that Pasternak has established poetry as that area in which both critical thought and symbolic insight are synthesized, bringing to poetry the authority of both discourses.

When we turn to *Doctor Zhivago* we encounter a number of discursive problems. If Platonov preserves philosophical activity through play with the vocabulary of dialectical materialism, then Pasternak, in *Doctor Zhivago,* is overtly critical of all rationalized, formulaic thinking and the language that goes with it. Such discourse, he will show repeatedly, kills the organic possibilities of human language through its stiffness and "deafness." So far, only the tension between literary speech genres has been addressed in Pasternak criticism. *Doctor Zhivago* opens with the discourse of a philosopher, Nikolai Vedeniapin, who is an amalgamated image of the philosophical idealists of the Russian Renaissance. And it ends with Lara, the least philosophical of the major characters, philosophizing about the Russian Revolution while restricting philosophy itself to the role of a verbal "spice," never a dominant cultural language. Perhaps less obvious but essential to the novel is the use of philosophical discourse that both suspends and preserves the philosophical discourse of Russian philosophers at the turn of the twentieth century. In Pasternak's novel a philosophy of the principled subject is canonized as particularly "Russian" in the figure of beloved Uncle Nikolai. In a way that reminds us of another Nikolai, Nikolai Berdiaev, Uncle Nikolai's discourse combines the genres of social commentary and essay writing with an idiosyncratic, nondogmatic religious speech.[21] His ideas, of course, are pervasive, growing organically throughout the book.

Doctor Zhivago is by no means uniformly "literary" in any traditional sense. Even in broad Bakhtinian terms, *Doctor Zhivago* is not just a novel but is a meta-novel in which many different discourses are juxtaposed and subsumed to a thoroughly dominant poetic register. Poetry absorbs discursive qualities and argues for its own high authority as truth. Poetic and philosophical discourses interact in complex ways, once again undermining the familiar contention that they are well harmonized in Pasternak's work. Although the authority of one discourse does not automatically obscure that of another, those that destroy the suppleness of language are themselves condemned. In this attitude Pasternak and Platonov, as unlike as they were, have much in common.

Iury Zhivago's intellectual ideal, it would seem, is that of discursive harmony, the "eighteenth-century man," a Faustian figure who imparts scientific, philosophical, and poetic "knowledge" with equal ease. In his notebooks, written during the long winter of 1918–1919 in Iuriatin, Iury conveys his dream of achieving harmony. "Everyone," he writes, "is born a Faust to embrace everything, experience everything, express everything" (*SS*5, 3:282). Nevertheless, eventually Iury does draw clear discursive borders between cultural discourses. "In science," he points out, "a step forward is taken according to the principle of repulsion, starting with the overthrow of reigning delusions and false theories" (*SS*5, 3:282). Art, in contrast, is not discursive in this sense; Iury claims that it does not aim to clear space to assert its own authority. He argues (quite disingenuously) that "a step forward in art

---

21. For a discussion of the parallels between Berdiaev's three-tiered concept of history in *The Meaning of the Creative Act*, written, published, and discussed publically at just the time of the action of *Doctor Zhivago*, see Edith W. Clowes, "From beyond the Abyss: Nietzschean Myth in Zamiatin's *We* and Pasternak's *Doctor Zhivago*," in *Nietzsche and Soviet Culture: Ally and Adversary*, ed. B. G. Rosenthal (Cambridge: Cambridge University Press, 1994), 313–337. Similarly, *Doctor Zhivago* begins also with a bow to Solovyov and his theory of love. For a discussion of *The Meaning of Love* and *Doctor Zhivago*, see Jerome Spencer, " 'Soaked in *The Meaning of Love* and *The Kreutzer Sonata*': The Nature of Love in *Doctor Zhivago*," *Doctor Zhivago: A Critical Companion*, ed. E. W. Clowes (Evanston, Ill.: Northwestern University Press, 1995), 76–88.

is taken according to the principle of attraction, starting with imitation, following and honoring one's favorite precursors" (*SS5*, 3:282). It should be pointed out, however, that Iury's goal in his notebooks is precisely to celebrate the power of art. Although they deal with many subjects, they always return to a kind of artistic discourse in which the superior truth of art is repeatedly asserted.

Iury's aesthetic, even more so than the aesthetic Pasternak expresses in *Safe Passage*, is far from a traditional, structured "philosophical" one. It pursues the same transcendental aesthetic from *Safe Passage,* presenting art as the manifestation of a hidden force: "I have long thought that art is not the name for a category or an area that embraces an innumerable multitude of concepts and phenomena that branch out but rather something narrow and focused, a marking out of a beginning, that then becomes a part of the work of art, the name of a force [*sila*] or of a truth [*istina*] at work in it. Art never struck me as an object or an aspect of form, but rather a mysterious and hidden part of the content" (*SS5*, 3:279). Rather than being a discourse per se, founded on reasoned observation and argument, and built on communication within and between groups in society, poetic language takes as its object something beyond the senses and beyond reason to which it alone has access. It is the conduit through which revelation occurs. Thus poetry and all verbal art can never be subordinate to philosophy, science, or any other form of theory or dogma. Once again, and to a greater extent than in *Safe Passage,* we find in *Doctor Zhivago* that idiosyncratic, Pasternakian combination of artistic discourse that defends verbal art as something beyond discourse.

Continuing the conceptualization of verbal art as both discourse and not discourse, and, as such, superior to science and philosophy, Iury Zhivago appropriates the realm of "thought" from philosophy. He claims that art is "some sort of thought, some kind of assertion about life which, because of its all-embracing breadth, cannot be broken down, and when a tiny amount of this force becomes a part of some more complicated mix, the admixture of art outweighs the significance of all the rest and turns out to be the essence, soul, and foundation of what has been depicted" (*SS5*, 3:279). Iury claims, for example, that art most often captures the tempo of historical time in any given epoch. For instance, Pushkin's iambs and Nekrasov's ternary meters synthesize the beat of Russian life at different moments of the nineteenth century.

Iury Andreevich implicitly rejects philosophical argument in art as a measure of artistic depth or greatness. Art need not be philosophical to be true. Great art in itself, he claims, is much closer than science and philosophy are to the ordinary and the everyday, which are the real sources of vitality. Iury's favorite writers, Pushkin and Chekhov, are not among Russia's greatest literary-philosophical minds. He admires their "modest lack of concern with loud things like the final ends of humanity and their own [personal] salvation. They understood these things well, but why should they bother to indulge in such brashness. . . . Gogol, Tolstoy, and Dostoevsky prepared for death, they worried, they sought meaning, drew conclusions" (*SS5*, 3:283). Here Iury is certainly functioning discursively, as he claims "science" does, arguing with "false" art. Through openly devaluing the nineteenth-century Russian tradition of philosophical fiction, he can clear space for his own particular brand of philosophical art.

Throughout the novel we encounter many instances of false philosophizing and false learning that implicitly devalue systematic thinking. For example, although Uncle Nikolai's ideas are powerful, and spread and evolve in a rhyzomatic way among the next generation—Iury Andreevich, Misha Gordon, Sima Tuntseva, and finally Lara—the man and his concrete utterances become outmoded. As the year 1917 plays itself out, we are told that "events crowded [Vedeniapin] out" (*SS5*, 3:176). Although Uncle Nikolai tries hard to stay with the times, he leaves the impression of being a foreigner, too controlled, too reasoned, but ironically standing on the sidelines of history, cheering on "full-scale revolution." In the case of Uncle Nikolai, Pasternak conveys his view that a real person, even though he might be a seminal thinker, is bounded and ultimately obscured by the flow of time. A person ought never to become an icon. It is only ideas that live on, and only if they are transfigured and developed in the minds of others, not when they become fixed as dogma.

Cases of utterly false logic range from the grotesque, as in the case of the cocaine-sniffing, fatuous, but murderous leader of the partisans Liberius Mikulitsyn (whose Latin name "Liberius" resonates ironically with the notion of "liberation") to the horrific, as in the case of the partisan Pamfil Palykh, who murders his whole family with an ax in order to "save" them from the Whites. The most important example is that of Pasha Antipov-Strelnikov. We are told that Pasha has a mediocre mind that settles on an idée fixe that, in turn, prevents him from understanding living human experience. Lara feels that he loses sight of the notion of human selfhood (*lichnost'*), the whole, integral human person: "It was as if something abstract entered this shape [*oblik*] and drained away its color. A live human face [*litso*] became an embodiment [*olitsetvorenie*] . . . of an idea" (*SS5*, 3:396). Pasha's search for the grounds of universal justice blinds him to the feelings that motivate his search, his own personal passion for revenge on people who treated him and his loved ones unjustly. The result is a generalized hatred of whole classes of people that unleashes a bloodbath in which any idea of justice is lost.

Indeed, the popularized political theory that drives the Russian Revolution is shown to be an epidemic of false logic in which public discourse—

and language itself—goes awry and loses its anchor in genuine social inter-action. As she chronicles the revolution, Lara pays particular attention to the quality of discourse: "Formulaic speech [*frazy*] gained the upper hand" (*SS5*, 3:398–399). No one escaped the bad effect of this false theorizing: "a measure of foolish pontificating crept into our conversations as well; [it ex-pressed itself] as a kind of showy, forced wit in the usual conversations about solving the world's problems" (*SS5*, 3:399). We find it in the forced gaiety of Shura Slesinger, a friend of the Gromekos, who suddenly, after the February revolution, starts to see herself as an "old battle-ax" (*SS5*, 3:180). With her, the sense of freshness, of opening a new, "more genuine" reality becomes something of a formula (*SS5*, 3:179–180). In Iuriatin the intellectu-ally pretentious Mikulitsyns talk in trivial details, a kind of "Trivial Pursuit" of the day, to show their high level of education. What we find is that their "knowledge" has no grounding. It leads nowhere and would be silly if it were not so murderously anarchic. Their son, Liberius, the leader of the Forest Brotherhood, loves to "philosophize at night" while he sniffs cocaine (*SS5*, 3:341) and tells utter and even dangerously optimistic lies about the current progression of the civil war.

As with Herzen nearly a century earlier in *My Past and Thoughts*, Paster-nak points out in his novel the ill effect of abstraction and generalization on the Russian language. Now empty revolutionary rhetoric covers the work-place with a patina of falsity. Although the claim is made to welcome what is innovative and honest, what is really expected is the current form of po-litical correctness. As Lara puts it: "People take the appearance of thought for thought itself, a verbal garnish in praise of the revolution and those in power" (*SS5*, 3:401).

A final overt devaluation of philosophy comes as Lara meditates on the terrible events of the last few years. Given Pasternak's concern for what he thought was the antipathy of his women friends and relations to philoso-phy, it is consistent for a woman character to condemn overly abstracted ar-guments. Lara views philosophy only as a kind of "spice" to make the lan-guage of life and art more interesting. In no way should it be allowed to dominate: "I don't like writing that is wholly devoted to philosophy. In my view, philosophy should be a pinch of spice added to art and life. Just to de-vote oneself to it alone is as strange as eating horseradish by itself" (*SS5*, 3:401). Reason itself is weak, and without intuition it degenerates into dog-matism. Despite this relatively limited and limiting evaluation, it should be said that Lara does not reject philosophy. Indeed, philosophy is that very "spice" which allows us to taste, to discern, to differentiate, and to synthe-size meaning.

This last harnessing of philosophy carries great authority with Pasternak. It comes in the last chapter in which the results of the revolution are summarized and evaluated. Lara, the least philosophically trained of the novel's main characters, has the highest authority—perhaps even more than Vedeniapin, Zhivago, and Tuntseva. She chronicles and passes judgment on the course of turn-of-the-century Russian history. She stands both within and outside it, and, more than any other character, she is able to see its effect clearly. Along with the other main characters in *Doctor Zhivago,* she discredits "philosophy" per se—understood as systematic, abstract, generalizing ratiocination—while reappropriating critical discourse, now situated in a concrete historical context, in order to draw conclusions and reassert the basis of genuine critical thinking in intuition.

Where, in conclusion, does Pasternak "place" philosophy in the hierarchy of language uses? In an article on speech act theory, "Philosophical Discourses and Fictional Texts," Peter McCormick cites an example from one of Vedeniapin's philosophical speeches. McCormick asks whether philosophizing reproduced in art is really philosophizing.[22] His purpose is to show that all philosophy in itself is in some way "fictional" and that, although it incorporates fictional elements, it still can be seen to make serious truth claims. What I miss here is a consideration of the truth claims made in fiction about the very authority of fiction itself. McCormick writes: "What makes Pasternak's text fictional is the nature of certain linguistic and epistemic marks that ensure that the readers of the text, *Doctor Zhivago,* construe that text's supposed illocutions as representations and not as performances."[23] Here McCormick ignores the lively discursive use of this and other representations to dispute the very role of abstract, philosophical argument in the life of a society. Is *Doctor Zhivago,* then, just a reflection of philosophical argumentation, or is it an argument in and of itself?

Clearly the literary context puts thinking into a spatial and temporal framework in which thinking functions as a response to another person's utterance and, in turn, will draw a response. It no longer exists in and of itself but is "applied," dramatic, relevant to a given time and place, and open to immediate critique. In a very real way, although ideas become more exciting and stimulating through this kind of literary displacement, they lose the quality of cool, objective judgment. The process of philosophizing is defamiliarized and is laid open to criticism. While systematic philosophy tries to separate itself from art by putting itself *outside* of time and by empowering itself through theorization and generalization, art brackets philosophy by reimmersing it in its original drama, by putting it back into the flow of time.

Although Pasternak is by no means rejecting philosophy, he belongs to

22. Peter McCormick, *Literature and the Question of Philosophy,* ed. A. Cascardi (Baltimore, Md.: The Johns Hopkins University Press, 1987), 54–74.

23. Ibid., 60.

the Russian tradition in that he does not accord to philosophy alone the high truth-value that it traditionally has enjoyed in the Western canon. Only in the context of art does generalized truth become empowered. In a sense, Danto's complaint about the modern "disenfranchisement" of art by philosophy cannot really hold for Pasternak and, more generally, for Russian modernity. Pasternak clearly preserves some key themes from the subjectivist philosophies of principled *lichnost'* of the turn of the century, particularly of Solovyov and Berdiaev, but he does more than that. He appropriates philosophical discourse to devise and incorporate an idiosyncratic aesthetic theory in his artistic practice. He makes it his own on the territory of a fictional speech genre. At the same time that he appears to be reevaluating philosophical claims to truth, he can certainly be said to be "suspending" and "preserving" logical, critical thinking at the heart of philosophical discourse. Despite his own alleged self-censorship, he succeeds in reasserting philosophical discourse in a cultural-political context from which it had been decisively banned.

Conclusion

THROUGHOUT THE MODERN era philosophizing in Russia has been a language and a practice on the edge of the possible but also verging on nonacceptance and oblivion. It has been a dissident discourse. This language is psychologically, indeed at times mystically, oriented. Even such successful professional, systematizing philosophers as Solovyov and Losev embraced a figurative language with strong nondiscursive elements that reach beyond the borders of speech to a "higher" mystical realm. Russian philosophy is a philosophy of oxymoron, paradox, and apophasis in which rhetorical figure is alive with possibilities for interpretation and meaning. From Chaadaev to Losev, Russian philosophy focused less on objective authority, which was always denied it for religious and political reasons, than on authenticity of philosophical voice and persona. In these works we find speaking voices that are true above all to themselves and that dramatically, often convincingly, avow their right to an audience and their right to exist; in so doing, they speak to concerns that are vital to us all.

These were the major achievements of Russian philosophizing in the 140–year time span from the 1820s, when Pushkin called for a philosophical language and Odoevsky experimented with Russian words for German Idealist concepts, to the 1950s, when Pasternak, in *Doctor Zhivago,* reanimated the rich but fragile philosophical culture of the early twentieth century. What traces, if any, of this heritage remain in our own post-Soviet time? I see at least four significant outcomes, which, in some form, have endured even the ravages of Leninism and Stalinism. The first was the emergence of an educated readership ready and eager to read and engage in a kind of philosophizing. If this readership was not generally interested in formal academic argumentation or the history of philosophy (although there were notable exceptions that had some nonprofessional following, such as Sergei Trubetskoi's study of the ancient Greeks, *Metaphysics in Ancient Greece* [1890]), it was very much interested in the discussion of philosophical issues in other, more personal genres and contexts.

The second result was the emergence of a very productive and original philosophical-literary community, which fostered serious public dialogue and out of which came innovative philosophizing that, in turn, interacted outside Russian borders with contemporary European philosophy. If writers in the early nineteenth century associated with a small number of peers, and mostly in secret, in the early twentieth century large public associations often gathered hundreds of people together to hear lectures on philosophy. As we will see, this community continued to exist, albeit in a tattered form.

The third important outcome was what we might call a philosophical identity. For the first time in Russian history—with very few isolated exceptions—a number of prominent writers thought of themselves as "philosophers." This appellation had become not only acceptable but was associated with positive qualities of fearless critical thinking, bold dissent, and the defense of just and true positions that often ran counter to popular opinion or governmental policy. Thus some philosophers, such as Solovyov, Shestov, and Berdiaev, built around themselves a dramatic or heroic public persona of the philosopher as a courageous person with a deeply probing mind who stood apart from social institutions of the academy, the state, or public opinion and could tell the truth.

The final and certainly most significant result was the development of a taste for philosophy that experimented with language, that was personalist, disputatious, concretely linked to personal life experience, and typically opposed to modern European traditions of systematic, logical thought. In some of these points this Russian philosophy first anticipated European existentialism of the 1940s and 1950s and, in others, anticipated postmodern French and Italian philosophical tastes developed in the 1970s. I suggested, in the introduction to this book, that Russian philosophy could be called "weak" in the special meaning of "anti-absolute," "anti-authoritative," opposing traditional systematic thought. In this writing there is a new basis for legitimacy: here personal "authenticity" replaces the "authority" of formal logical rules; frankness and inner credibility replace syllogistic logic. After the death of Solovyov there emerged a number of philosophies aimed at experiencing, knowing, and creating rather than teaching and indoctrinating. The writings of Rozanov, Shestov, and Berdiaev "proved" nothing but could be nonetheless powerfully convincing.

A red thread running through the philosophical writing we have considered here is the attention to questions of language and discourse. Before any thought of a "linguistic turn," some Russian philosophers understood that the vocabulary, style, imagery, rhetoric, and genre that one chooses are central to the type of truth claim and the basis for authority that one might build. Speech, and not some preexisting receptacle of Truth, such as God or History or Mind, is the basis for whatever authority is to be had. Truth and authority are constructed in words. They do not exist a priori, to be discovered through philosophical logic. Nonetheless, there are major differences between this Russian tradition and the postmodernists. What distinguishes the philosophies of Solovyov, Losev, or even Rozanov, for example, from those of Vattimo, Derrida, or Lyotard is the desire somehow to do away with language altogether and to break through at some level to mystical insight, to an ultimate sphere in which one could "know" spontaneously, where one could experience wordless but "True" insight, as it were, the light revealed on Mt. Tabor.

Another common thread that characterizes the philosophical taste formed in much of the writing considered here is discursive dispute, the effort to enhance the legitimacy and truth of one's own philosophical voice by taking on all competing cultural languages. Most obvious is the sustained critique of all "strong" claims to truth made by empirical science or by philosophical metaphysics. For example, Shestov eviscerates both scientific and metaphysical claims to truth from a standpoint of metaphysical groundlessness. Seventy years later Jacques Derrida would replace "metaphysics" with "metaphorics," an exposure of the impoverished economy of metaphors (that seem to promise a "profit" of meaning but actually produce "loss") that provides the all-too-weak pillars of Western metaphysics.[1]

The other side of this coin of discursive dispute is the part-alliance and part-dispute of both Russian and postmodern philosophy with literary art, with its clear language games and richness of interpretive possibilities. For example, although he clearly identifies himself as a philosopher, Shestov openly sees in literary art a number of powerful speech genres that he appropriates for philosophizing. Dostoevsky and Rozanov criticize their contemporaries' standards of "literary art" in order to point out the assumptions underlying its structures and language, and then to appropriate for their writing the powerful poetic and rhetorical qualities traditionally associated with literature.

Yet another important aspect shared by both the modern Russian philosophical experience and the postmodern European one is the relationship of writers to philosophers. In both, literary art had announced and continued to defend its discursive independence from philosophy and science. In both situations art went beyond its basis in poetic, figurative language and developed a discourse, an implicit or explicit argument in defense of a certain kind of verbal art. Turgenev and Dostoevsky, and then, in the twentieth century, writers as different as Platonov and Pasternak, offer critiques of nonliterary discourses, bracketing them and implicitly asserting the more solid truth of literary art. Danto and Derrida, each in his own way, focus on

---

1. Jaques Derrida, "The White Mythology," in *The Margins of Philosophy*, trans. A. Bass (Chicago: University of Chicago Press, 1986), 219.

the assertions by literary modernists of independence from philosophy.[2] Famously or infamously, Derrida appropriates word play and "metaphorics" as the engine for his philosophizing. Nussbaum examines the dispute about the efficacy of formal philosophical ethics in *The Golden Bowl* by Henry James.[3] What is different, once again, in this Russian tradition is not the simple dispute or alliance between fiction and philosophy but the tendency in both philosophy and philosophical art to attack "Philosophy" as systematically argued and proven "truth," and to defend "philosophy" as true, authentic personal experience, as a process of "becoming who you are" through creative acts of insight and intellection.

Can we speak of a modern Russian philosophical culture with rules of the game that, while certainly related to, also show a disjunction or a disconnect with the Western tradition? The answer is certainly yes, in the sense that first writers and later philosophers did not accept and continually challenged Western scientific rules of the game, but they often combined what cannot be combined—mystery and physical observation, revelation and logical proof, and proof through overt poetic figure. Here Russian philosophy seems not fully "modern" in its projects of rereading and revalorizing mysticism in a modern setting, and yet, in part, for our contemporary taste, it seems even "postmodern" in its philosophers' bold confrontations with the underlying "grammar" of modern faith in science and its concepts of "true" and "authoritative" knowledge. Sometimes deeply conservative, as in the case of Rozanov, Russian Renaissance philosophers could also at times strike one as radical. They came to a view of language and an approach to the world that would only become thinkable in the West well after the colossal political failure of Marxist socialism in the 1970s. Using Roman Jakobson's scheme of six language functions, we can say that the modern Western tradition focuses on the "referential," or denotative, function. Russian philosophers focus on three other language functions—the "phatic," or reaching the reader; the "emotive," emphasizing the speaking voice; and the "poetic," highlighting the verbal medium as message.[4]

How does the picture of Russian writing culture that we have gained here through a focus on discourse differ from the one offered in traditional reception histories? Typically reception histories would agree with a some-

---

2. Arthur Danto, *The Philosophical Disenfranchisement of Art* (New York: Columbia University Press, 1986).

3. Martha Craven Nussbaum, "'Finely Aware and Richly Responsible': Literature and the Moral Imagination," *Literature and the Question of Philosophy* (Baltimore, Md.: The Johns Hopkins University Press, 1986), 167–191.

4. Roman Jakobson, "Linguistics and Poetics," *Language and Literature* (Cambridge, Mass.: Harvard University Press, 1987), 62–94.

what broader statement of the following assertion from the leading Russian journal of philosophy, *Voprosy filosofii*, from 1993: "In the passionate intensity ... of its philosophical arguments great Russian literature came of age—a literature that was, in the view of many critics, an idiosyncratic answer to German philosophy."[5] What has emerged from a discursive approach is a picture of a considerably more complex Russian writing culture, one not only oriented toward Western sources but to developments within the Russian literary language itself.

What, finally, is left of this lively philosophical activity that was effectively stamped out by a crass Stalinist ideology intolerant of any competing claims to authority and quite oblivious to concerns of authenticity? Incredibly, in the late 1940s and 1950s, a generation of young philosophers emerged at Moscow University. Among them are names familiar in philosophical circles outside their own countries—Aleksandr Zinoviev, Aleksandr Piatigorsky, Nelli Motroshilova, Valery Podoroga, Merab Mamardashvili. Although they were, as Mamardashvili put it, like "people absolutely robbed naked," they managed against all odds to piece together the most basic knowledge necessary for professional philosophical activity.[6] Vadim Sadovsky, who studied philosophy at Moscow University at that time, remembered that it took much more time and energy than it normally would to assemble that minimal knowledge and to learn genuine skills for thinking philosophically.[7] Still, books were available from unexpected sources. The artist Ernst Neizvestnyi—known, among other things, for creating the gravestone for Khrushchev's grave in Novodevichy Monastery—remembered that in the early 1950s at the Academy of Arts a small group of students understood that they could not receive a full education under the current conditions and undertook a bold, even foolhardy "self-education."[8] Knowing well what the consequences could be, they found *Vekhi*, Shestov, Berdiaev, Solovyov, and Lossky, among other authors, in private collections and in secondhand bookstores.[9] This generation of young professional philosophers, unable to read about developments outside the borders of the Soviet Union and not inclined to look to other discourses, launched a serious analysis and critique of the capstone work of the Marx-

5. "Ot Moskovskogo Filosofskogo Fonda," *Voprosy filosofii* 6 (1993): 187.
6. Cited in V. N. Sadovskii, "Filosofiia v Moskve v 50–e i 60–e gody: Nekotorye soobrazheniia o filosofii i filosofskom obrazovanii v pervye poslevoennye desiatiletiia," *Voprosy filosofii* 7 (1993): 148.
7. Ibid., 149.
8. Ernst Neizvestnyi, "Katakombnaia kul'tura i vlast'," *Voprosy filosofii* 10 (1991): 3.
9. See also Mamardashvili's memoirs: M. K., Mamardashvili, "Mysli pod zapretom," *Voprosy filosofii* 4 (1992): 70–78.

ist-Leninist tradition, Marx's *Capital*. Zinoviev was the first among them to shake up the School of Philosophy at Moscow State University with his rigorous, antidogmatic reading of *Capital*. He shocked his teachers, as well, with his humorously paradoxical attitude. He became infamous, and suffered the consequences, for such bons mots as this humorous paraphrase of Marx's critique of Feuerbach: "If philosophers only used to interpret the world, now they don't even do that"; and the thought that "material is objective reality given to us by God through our senses."[10]

In the 1960s and 1970s works of prerevolutionary Russian philosophy started to reappear in new editions through the efforts of *tamizdat*, or émigré, publishers, who reprinted the books outside the USSR and had them brought through the Iron Curtain in the suitcases of myriad travelers.[11] The Russian personalist tradition that focused on the aesthetically and morally integral *lichnost'*, or self, had given many people the courage to keep asking and thinking, and not to give into the terrifying twilight zone of the Stalinist years. For some, Solovyov became the underground "Virgil" who gave one hope and led the way through hell.[12] In *Doctor Zhivago* Pasternak had preserved the memory of Solovyov and Berdiaev, among many others, and showed how, through the rhyzomatic spread of ideas from generation to generation, a philosophical culture could survive. Platonov had recaptured the questing subject and the very "stuff" of language itself at the bottom and most despairing levels of human existence. And now they were becoming available. In these years a new generation of writers discovered the prerevolutionary heritage. Siniavsky-Terts and later Venedikt Erofeev sprang to life in their own literary responses to Rozanov. Solzhenitsyn took up the mantle of curator of philosophical memory. In *Cancer Ward* two characters mention Solovyov and also observe that one heard of him more "inside," in the camps, than elsewhere. They discuss the future of socialism and the proposition of a Christian socialism, somewhat in the mold of Berdiaev's thinking.[13] In the 1970s Solzhenitsyn revived the Vekhi tradition with a philosophical almanac, *From under the Rubble* (*Iz-pod glyb*). Of all the Soviet-era philosophical writers, Platonov alone has stimulated productive critical and philosophical thought in the 1990s.[14]

Although in the 1960s conditions for teaching philosophy changed con-

10. Sadovskii, "Filosofiia v Moskve," 155.

11. Lev Kopelev and Raisa Orlova, *My zhili v Moskve, 1956–1980* (Moscow: Kniga, 1990), 143.

12. A. Krasnov-Levitin, *Likhie gody, 1925–1941* (Paris: YMCA, 1977), 225.

13. Aleksandr Solzhenitsyn, *Cancer Ward* (New York: Bantam, 1972), 440–444.

14. See, for example, Valerii Podoroga, "The Eunuch of the Soul: Positions of Reading and the World of Platonov," in *Late Soviet Culture: From Perestroika to Novostroika* (Durham: Duke University Press, 1993), 187–232. See also Vladimir Malakhov, "Über 'russische postmoderne' Philoso-

siderably, Marxism-Leninism and dialectical materialism remained, of course, dominant. After 1985 everything changed. Since then, a lively and, at times, quite anxious debate about the existence of a Russian philosophical tradition and its place in world philosophy has formed the keynote of new philosophizing.[15] Prerevolutionary and émigré works have been republished in a veritable boom, with multiple editions and collections of the critical discussion around them. The institutional infrastructure for philosophical education has changed altogether. There are several excellent publishing houses and bookstores devoted to philosophy of all kinds, as well as good, though small, philosophical journals.[16] Also, for the first time in Russian history, academic philosophy can actually boast of a large group of serious, well-trained, high-quality professionals.[17] The basis for a vibrant philosophical culture—the living language, the disputes, the networks, new ideas, and major, leading philosophers—is still in the process of revitalization. The lively experimentation with philosophical language and form so familiar in Russian philosophizing has started to be felt.[18] The conditions for a philosophical culture now exist in Russia. If Russian philosophical culture is still problematic, then certainly it is a culture that has more than a past. It has a future.

---

phie," in *Russische Philosophie im 20. Jahrhundert*, ed. K-D. Eichler and U. J. Schneider (Leipzig: Leipziger Universitätsverlag, 1996), 61.

15. For a stimulating discussion of the current situation, see *Russische Philosophie im 20. Jahrhundert*, especially part 1.

16. Some notable philosophy journals are *Voprosy metodologii, Nachala, Targum, Stupeni, Logos* (one in St. Petersburg and one in Moscow), *Zdes' i teper', Paralleli, Silentium, Put'*, and *Ad marginem*. The major journal of philosophy, lasting from the Soviet era, *Voprosy filosofii*, publishes an occasional review of the philosophical journals. See, for example, V. N. Zhukov, "O novykh filosofskikh zhurnalakh," *Voprosy filosofii* 1 (1995): 184–188.

17. Sadovskii, "Filosofiia v Moskve," 148.

18. There are some notable attempts at experimentation. See, for example, various works on the border between fiction and philosophy: the novel by Viktor Pelevin, *Chapaev i Pustota* (first published 1996; Moscow: Vagrius, 2000); Boris Groys, *Dnevnik filosofa* (Paris: Sintaksis, 1989); and A. M. Piatigorskii, "Filosofiia odnogo pereulka," *Izbrannye trudy* (Moscow: Iazyki russkoi kul'tury, 1996), 407–498.

Appendix: The Generations and Networks of Russian Philosophy

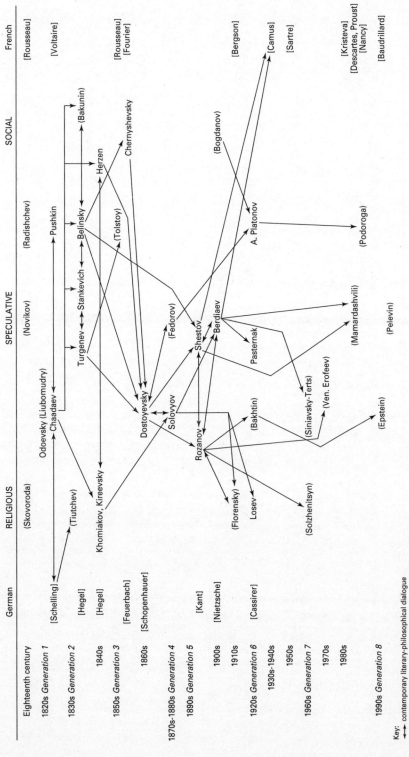

Key:

↕ contemporary literary-philosophical dialogue
↕ intergenerational interaction
[ ] non-Russian interactions
( ) Russian writers, critics, and philosophers who are mentioned but do not receive critical attention in the book

Index